HISTORICAL DICTIONARIES OF
INTERNATIONAL ORGANIZATIONS SERIES
Edited by Jon Woronoff

1. *European Community*, by Desmond Dinan. 1993
2. *International Monetary Fund*, by Norman K. Humphreys. 1993
3. *International Organizations in Sub-Saharan Africa*, by Mark W. DeLancey and Terry M. Mays. 1994
4. *European Organizations*, by Derek W. Urwin. 1994
5. *International Tribunals*, by Boleslaw Adam Boczek. 1994
6. *International Food Agencies: FAO, WFP, WFC, IFAD*, by Ross B. Talbot. 1994
7. *Refugee and Disaster Relief Organizations*, by Robert F. Gorman. 1994
8. *United Nations*, by A. LeRoy Bennett. 1995
9. *Multinational Peacekeeping*, by Terry Mays. 1996
10. *Aid and Development Organizations*, by Guy Arnold. 1996
11. *World Bank*, by Anne C. M. Salda. 1997
12. *Human Rights and Humanitarian Organizations*, by Robert F. Gorman and Edward S. Mihalkanin. 1997
13. *United Nations Educational, Scientific and Cultural Organization (UNESCO)*, by Seth Spaulding and Lin Lin. 1997
14. *Inter-American Organizations*, by Larman C. Wilson and David W. Dent. 1997
15. *World Health Organization*, by Kelley Lee. 1998

Historical Dictionary of the World Health Organization

Kelley Lee

Historical Dictionaries of
International Organizations, No. 15

The Scarecrow Press, Inc.
Lanham, Md., & London
1998

353.6
L47h

SCARECROW PRESS, INC.

Published in the United States of America
by Scarecrow Press, Inc.
4720 Boston Way
Lanham, Maryland 20706

British Library Cataloguing in Publication Information Available

Library of Congress Cataloging-in-Publication Data

Lee, Kelley, 1962–
    Historical dictionary of the World Health Organization / Kelley
Lee.
        p.   cm.—(Historical dictionaries of international
organizations ; no. 15)
    Includes bibliographical references.
    ISBN 0-8108-3371-9 (alk. paper)
    1. World Health Organization—History—Dictionaries.   2. World
Health Organization—History.   I. Title.   II. Series.
    RA8.L44   1998
    353.6'211—dc21   97-26820
                                                                            CIP
JK

ISBN 0-8108-3371-9 (cloth : alk. paper)

♾ ™ The paper used in this publication meets the minimum
requirements of American National Standard for Information
Sciences—Permanence of Paper for Printed Library Materials,
ANSI Z39.48-1984. Manufactured in the United States of America.

For my two sisters with love,
Janice and Jennifer

Contents

Contents

Editor's Foreword

The World Health Organization (WHO), celebrating its fiftieth anniversary in 1998, has long enjoyed an exceptional reputation among international organizations. This high regard has been earned through its unique contributions of scientific and technical expertise to international health cooperation. Most prominent among WHO's activities have been the disease-centered campaigns, including the achievement of the worldwide eradication of smallpox in 1979, and the advocacy of policies, such as those relating to primary health care and essential drugs, aimed at improving health in developing countries. However, WHO has not been entirely free from controversy. Criticism has sometimes been directed at the questionable effectiveness and appropriateness of particular activities. More recently, there has been considerable concern over its leadership, management and administration. Constrained by tight budgets, like the rest of the United Nations (UN) system, WHO has had to cut back and set priorities.

Despite such challenges, which have placed other international organizations under serious threat, there remains wide consensus that a world organization for health continues to be much needed. In an increasingly globalized world, ever more health challenges have emerged that demand cooperative action across national boundaries. For this reason, it is crucial to better understand the structure and functions of WHO as the UN specialized agency for health. WHO's constitutional mandate is to support the achievement "by all peoples of the highest possible level of health." With health defined broadly as "a state of complete physical, mental, and social well-being and not merely the absence of disease or infirmity," the work of WHO over the past fifty years has been remarkably wide ranging.

This book addresses WHO's constituent bodies, related organizations, and numerous programs launched in specific fields. There are also entries on significant persons and events. A chronology and introduction briefly summarize the history of WHO. Readers wanting to know more about the organization, its mandate, or its specific programs can consult the bibliography, which includes both publications by WHO and books and articles written by outside observers.

The author of this volume, Kelley Lee, has become familiar with both the health activities and institutional structures of WHO through her research and teaching at the London School of Hygiene and Tropical Medicine. Following detailed study of other aspects of the UN, including telecommunications and development assistance, Dr. Lee has focused in recent years on the UN organizations concerned with health (i.e., WHO, the UN Children's Fund, the UN Population Fund, the World Bank, and the UN Development Programme). This has included participation in major studies of extrabudgetary funds in WHO (1995) and WHO support to programs at the country level (1997). This dictionary is a welcome addition to our knowledge of a particularly important, but insufficiently studied, international organization.

Jon Woronoff

Preface and Acknowledgments

The purpose of this dictionary is to provide an introductory reference text detailing the main structures and functions of the World Health Organization (WHO). Given the long history and the complexity of the organization, and a broad and dynamic field such as health, it is inevitable that only selected aspects of WHO's 50-year history have been included. Yet, although this dictionary is not wholly comprehensive, it does provide an appreciation of the range and diversity of activities undertaken by the UN's specialized agency for health.

The entries of the dictionary span a period of five decades, with particular emphasis on recent history of the past ten years. It should also be noted that WHO is currently undergoing a process of substantial internal reform, which will result in further changes to many of the organization's divisions and programs. These reforms have been included as far as possible to the end of 1996; additional changes will be accommodated in future editions. In many cases, entries have been cross-referenced by key subject (e.g., AIDS, Global Programme on) to enable the reader to locate entries related to a single subject. Decisions on who should be included as significant individuals have been more difficult. In addition to directors-general and regional directors, I have included selected persons who were seminal to the creation of WHO or to major aspects of its work. This has, admittedly, been an imperfect process, and suggestions to rectify omissions in the future are encouraged.

The compilation of a reference text of this nature invariably draws on the detailed knowledge and experience of many people. First, I am thankful for the support of colleagues at the London School of Hygiene and Tropical Medicine. Malayah Harper, in particular, began this project by gathering basic materials and beginning to draft some of the dictionary's entries. Documentation and comments were provided by Virginia Berridge, Kent Buse, Sandy Cairncross, Susan Collinson, Renee Danziger, Susan Foster, Lucy Gilson, Laura Hawken, Barbara McPake, Anne Mills, Rudiger Pittrof, Anne-Marie Rafferty, Carolyn Stephens, Steve

Tollman, Patrick Vaughan, Gill Walt, and Anthony Zwi. In addition, Sir Donald Acheson provided insights into the workings of the Executive Board, the European Regional Office, and emergency health assistance. Adetokunbo Lucas provided comments on the draft, especially on the UNDP/World Bank/WHO Special Programme for Research and Training in Tropical Diseases. David Bradley provided comments on the history of the Intensified Malaria Eradication Programme. Vanessa Lavender and Lucy Paul kindly provided invaluable and efficient secretarial support.

Second, I would like to express my appreciation to current and former staff members of the World Health Organization who have given generously of their time and energies. At WHO headquarters in Geneva, my thanks to Ilona Kickbusch (director of the Division of Health Promotion, Education, and Communication), who organized the circulation of the draft manuscript to an editorial and review group within WHO. Carol Modis (WHO Library) gave invaluable advice on historical writings on WHO and biographical details of key individuals. Ann Kern reviewed the manuscript and supplied advice and further documentation on key aspects of WHO's work. I would also like to thank the following program staff, who kindly provided documentation: Alexander Kalache (AHE); F. Bassani, Jean-Paul Menu, and Lisa Chan (EHA); Carol Martin (EOS); Sue Lambert (FRH); A. Kochi, Paul Nunn, Klaus Klaudt, C. McMahon, Chris Elliot, and Susan Horsfall (GTB); J. W. Lee (GVI); H. Benaziza (HPR); Margaret Squadrini (HST); John Martin and Eugenio Villar (ICO); Melissa Starr (INA); D. N. Berg (ISM); Helena Mbele-Mbong (Nursing and Midwifery); Andrew Smith (PDH); Derek Yach (Policy Action Coordination Team); B. Mansourian (RPS); and Tore Godal (TDR).

I would like to thank the following people from the regional offices for providing a variety of materials: Ebrahim Samba, E. Lambo, and A. M. D'Almeida (AFRO); M. H. Khayat, Marthe Everard, and Adil Salahi (EMRO); Josep Figueras (EURO); George Alleyne, Irene Klinger, and Silvia Torresano (PAHO/AMRO); Than Sein, V. Fedenev, and B. R. Pande (SEARO); and N. V. K. Nair (WPRO). These documents allowed me to cite some of the substantial activities that take place at the regional and country levels. Further thanks go to the following individuals, who provided information on specific WHO activities and commented on the manuscript in whole or in part: Yves Beigbeder, Thomas Gilmore, Kathleen Kay, Sigrun Mogedal, Martin Jennings, James Jackson, and Paul Weindling. Despite the extensive assistance provided by all those mentioned above, however, the author remains solely responsible for any errors of interpretation or omission.

This project was undertaken as part of a broader program of research within the International Health Policy Programme, London School of Hygiene and Tropical Medicine. Funding of the program is provided in part by the Economic and Social Research Council (United Kingdom) and the Social Science and Humanities Research Council of Canada.

Abbreviations and Acronyms

The following is a list of the main bodies within WHO, including its key divisions and programs, and the regional offices. Relevant international organizations that are, or have, worked in the field of international public health are also included.

ABFC	Administration, Budget, and Finance Committee (Executive Board)
ACHR	Advisory Committee on Health Research
ADA	Prevention and Control of Alcohol and Drug Abuse
ADG	Assistant director-general
ADH	Adolescent Health and Development Programme
AFRO	African Regional Office
AFROPOC	African Regional Office Programme Operations Coordination System
AGFUND	Arab Gulf Programme for United Nations Development Organizations
AHE	Aging and Health
AIDS	Acquired immunodeficiency syndrome
AMPES	American Region Planning, Programming, Monitoring, and Evaluation System (PAHO)
AMRO	American Regional Office
ARI	Programme for the Control of Acute Respiratory Infections
ASD	Office of HIV/AIDS and Sexually Transmitted Diseases
BFI	Division of Budget and Finance
BI	Bamako Initiative
BMN	Basic Minimum Needs Approach
BVI	Programme on Bacterial, Viral Diseases and Immunology
CCEE	Countries of central and eastern Europe
CCO	United Nations Committee of Cosponsoring Organizations

CDC	United States Centers for Disease Control and Prevention
CDD	Programme for the Control of Diarrhoeal Diseases
CDR	Division of Diarrhoeal and Acute Respiratory Disease Control
CDS	Division of Communicable Diseases
CEH	Control of Environmental Health Hazards
CEHA	Center for Environmental Health Activities
CEHANET	Regional Environmental Health Information Network (EMRO)
CENDES	Center for Development Studies (EMRO)
CEPANZO	Pan American Zoonoses Center
CEPIALET	Pan American Center for Training and Research in Leprosy and Related Diseases
CEPIS	Pan American Center for Sanitary Engineering and Environmental Sciences
CFNI	Caribbean Food and Nutrition Institute
CGS	Division of Conference and General Services
CINDI	Countrywide Integrated Noncommunicable Disease Intervention
CIOMS	Council for International Organizations of Medical Sciences
CLAP	Pan American Center for Perinatology and Human Development
CTD	Division of Control of Tropical Diseases
CVI	Children's Vaccine Initiative
DALY	Disability adjusted life years
DAP	Drug Action Programme/Action Programme on Essential Drugs
DG	Director-general
DGP	Director-General's and Regional Directors' Development Programme
DHA	United Nations Department of Humanitarian Affairs
DIESA	United Nations Department of International Economic and Social Affairs
DMP	Division of Drug Management and Policies
DOTS	Directly Observed Treatment, Short-Course (Tuberculosis)
DPM	Drugs Policies and Management Unit
EB	Executive board
EBF	Extrabudgetary funds
ECEH	European Center on Environment and Health

ECH	Office of Global and Integrated Environmental Health
ECO	Pan American Center for Human Ecology and Health
ECOSOC	United Nations Economic and Social Council
EHA	Division of Emergency and Humanitarian Action
EHG	Office of Global and Integrated Environmental Health
EMC	Division of Emerging and Other Communicable Diseases
EMF	Electromagnetic fields
EMRO	Eastern Mediterranean Regional Office
EOS	Division of Operational Support in Environmental Health
EPI	Expanded Programme on Immunization
EPR	Emergency Preparedness and Response Programme
EPTA	Expanded Programme for Technical Assistance
ERO	Division of Emergency Relief Operations
EURO	European Regional Office
FAO	Food and Agriculture Organization
FHE	Division of Family Health
FHS	Family Health Services
FIELDLINCS	Field Links for Intervention and Control Studies
FNU	Division of Food and Nutrition
FRH	Family and Reproductive Health Programme
GATT	General Agreement on Tariffs and Trade
GCA	Global Commission on AIDS
GOBI-FFF	Growth Monitoring, Oral Rehydration, Breastfeeding, Immunization, Family Spacing, Food Supplements and Female Education
GPA	Global Programme on AIDS
GPC	Global Policy Council
GPV	Global Programme for Vaccines and Immunization
GTB	Global Tuberculosis Programme
HAI	Health Action International
HEE	Global Programme for Health of the Elderly
HELLIS	Health Literature, Library, and Information Services
HFA	Health for All
HMD	Health Manpower Development

HPR	Division of Health Promotion, Education, and Communication
HRH	Division of Development of Human Resources for Health
HRP	Special Programme of Research, Development, and Research Training in Human Reproduction; Expanded Programme of Research, Development, and Research Training in Human Reproduction
HST	Division of Health Situation and Trend Assessment
IAAG	Interagency Advisory Group on AIDS
IAO	Office of Internal Audit and Oversight
IARC	International Agency for Research on Cancer
IASC	United Nations Inter-Agency Standing Committee
IBFAN	International Baby Food Action Network
ICC	Interagency Coordinating Committee
ICDDR,B	International Center for Diarrhoeal Disease Research, Bangladesh
ICIDH	*International Classification of Impairments, Disabilities, and Handicaps*
ICIFI	International Council of Infant Food Industries
ICN	International Conference on Nutrition
ICO	Division of Intensified Cooperation with Countries
ICPD	International Conference on Population and Development
ICRC	International Committee of the Red Cross
IDD	Elimination of Iodine Deficiency Disorders
IFPMA	International Federation of Pharmaceutical Manufacturers Associations
IFRC	International Federation of Red Cross and Red Crescent Societies
IICC	Interagency Immunization Coordination Committee
ILO	International Labour Organization
INA	Division of Interagency Affairs
INCAP	Institute of Nutrition in Central America and Panama
INFACT	Infant Formula Action Coalition
INPPAZ	Pan American Institute for Food Protection and Zoonoses
IPCS	International Programme on Chemical Safety

IPHECA	International Programme on the Health Effects of the Chernobyl Accident
ISM	Division of Information System Management
IUATLD	International Union against Tuberculosis and Lung Disease
IWC	Intensified Cooperation with Least Developed Countries
JCB	Joint Coordinating Board
JCHP	Joint Committee on Health Policy (WHO/ UNICEF)
JNSP	Joint WHO/UNICEF Nutrition Support Programme
LACRIP	Latin American Cancer Research Information Project
LEG	Office of the Legal Counsel
LEP	Action Programme for the Elimination of Leprosy
MAC	Management Advisory Committee
MAG	Management Advisory Group
MAL	Malaria Control
MCH	Maternal and child health
MDC	Management Development Committee
MECACAR	Mediterranean, Caucasian, and Central Asian republics
MEP	Malaria Eradication Programme
MIP	Meeting of interested parties
MRC	Management Review Committee
MSA	Division of Mental Health and Prevention of Substance Abuse
MSM	Maternal Health and Safe Motherhood Programme
NAM	Nonaligned movement
NCD	Division of Noncommunicable Diseases
NGO	Nongovernmental organization
NID	National Immunization Day
NIPEH	National Integrated Programme on Environment and Health
NIS	Newly independent states
OAS	Organization of American States
OCP	Onchocerciasis Control Programme
OECD	Organization of Economic Cooperation and Development
OIHP	Office International d'Hygiène Publique

OPV	Oral polio vaccine
PAHO	Pan American Health Organization
PANAFTOSA	Pan American Food-and-Mouth Disease Center
PAPCHILD	Pan Arab Project for Child Development
PASB	Pan American Sanitary Bureau
PASO	Pan American Sanitary Organization
PBD	Programme on the Prevention of Blindness
PCB	Programme Coordination Board (Executive Board)
PCC	Policy and Coordination Committee
PCS	Programme for the Promotion of Chemical Safety
PDC	Programme Development Committee (Executive Board)
PDH	Prevention of Deafness and Hearing Impairment
PEH	Programme for the Promotion of Environmental Health
PER	Division of Personnel
PHA	Pharmaceuticals Unit
PHC	Primary health care
PHT	Programme on Health Technology
PLL	Division of Publishing, Language, and Library Services
PMC	Programme Management Committee
PSA	Programme on Substance Abuse
PVD	Programme for Vaccine Development
RBF	Regular budget funds
RDDF	Regional Directors' Development Fund
REDPANAIRE	Pan American Network for Normalized Sampling of Air Pollution
RHDAC	Regional Health Development Advisory Council
RHFA	Renewing the Health for All Strategy
RID	Division of Research and International Development
RPS	Office of Research Policy and Strategy Coordination
SAGE	Scientific Advisory Group of Experts
SAPEL	Special Action Projects towards the Elimination of Leprosy
SCH	Schistosomiasis Control
SCI	Sick Child Initiative

SCRC	Standing Committee of the Regional Committee
SEARO	South-East Asia Regional Office
SHS	Division of Strengthening of Health Services
SIREVA	Regional System for Vaccines (PAHO)
SMI	Safe Motherhood Initiative
STAC	Scientific and Technical Advisory Committee
STAG	Scientific and Technical Advisory Group
TAG	Technical Advisory Group
TCDC	Technical cooperation in developing countries
TCO	Division of Technical Cooperation
TDR	UNDP/World Bank/WHO Special Programme for Research and Training in Tropical Diseases
TNCs	Transnational corporations
TOH	Tobacco or Health
TPC	Technical Preparatory Committee
UNAIDS	Joint United Nations Programme on HIV/AIDS
UNCED	United Nations Conference on Environment and Development
UNDP	United Nations Development Program
UNESCO	United Nations Educational, Scientific, and Cultural Organization
UNFDAC	United Nations Fund for Drug Abuse Control
UNFPA	United Nations Population Fund
UNHCR	United Nations High Commissioner for Refugees
UNICEF	United Nations Children's Fund
UNIPAC	United Nations Children's Fund Packing and Assembly Centre
UNRRA	United Nations Relief and Rehabilitation Administration
USAID	United States Agency for International Development
VFHP	Voluntary Fund for Health Promotion
VPH	Veterinary Public Health Programme
WDR	World Development Report
WEOG	Western European and Other Group
WER	*Weekly Epidemiological Record*
WFP	World Food Programme
WHA	World Health Assembly
WHD	Women's Health
WHO	World Health Organization

WHOPES	World Health Organization Pesticide Evaluation Scheme
WPRO	Western Pacific Regional Office
WR	WHO representative
WTO	World Trade Organization

Chronology

Prior to 1946

1830s	Sanitary, Medicine, and Quarantine Board is founded in Alexandria, Egypt.
1838	Superior Council of Health is founded in Constantinople (Istanbul) with Ottoman and European representation.
1840	International Board of Health is created in Tangier, Algeria.
23 July 1851	First International Sanitary Conference is held in Paris. It fails to produce an International Sanitary Convention.
1856	European Commission of the Danube is established, which takes over certain powers on health issues.
1859	Second International Sanitary Conference is held in Paris.
1863–64	International meetings of Red Cross societies are held in Geneva, which eventually lead to the creation of the League of Red Cross Societies in 1919.
1866	Third International Sanitary Conference is held in Constantinople to discuss cholera.
1867	First International Medical Congress is held in Paris.
1 July 1874	Fourth International Sanitary Conference is held in Vienna.
1889	Congrès International d'Assistance is held in Paris.
1891	International Lists of Diseases and Causes of Death are introduced by the International Statistical Institute.
1892	First International Sanitary Convention is

	approved, proposing such international health measures as quarantine and hygiene practices.
1902	International Sanitary Bureau of the Americas is established in Washington, D.C., as the world's first permanent international health organization. The organization will later become the WHO Regional Office for the Americas.
	International Central Bureau for the Campaign against Tuberculosis is founded in Berlin.
1903	Eleventh International Sanitary Conference is held in Paris. The meeting agrees to consolidate and codify four existing International Sanitary Conventions, including those on cholera and plague.
1906	First International Agreement for the Unification of the Formulae of Potent Drugs is adopted.
9 December 1907	Office International d'Hygiène Publique (OIHP) is created in Paris by the Rome Agreement, signed by 12 European countries. The new organization includes a permanent secretariat and committee of senior public health officials.
1909	Rockefeller Sanitary Commission for the Eradication of Hookworm in the United States is initiated.
1913	Rockefeller Foundation is created, which includes the International Health Commission.
1915	International Health Commission of the Rockefeller Foundation adopts resolution to eradicate yellow fever in the Americas.
1918	Global campaign to eradicate yellow fever is launched by William Crawford Gorgas, with the support of the Rockefeller Foundation. It is the first concerted effort to eradicate a human disease.
1919	League of Red Cross Societies is established.

1920	Health Organization of the League of Nations is created in Geneva to assist in the prevention and control of disease.
1923	International Sanitary Bureau of the Americas is renamed the Pan American Sanitary Bureau (PASB).
1924	First Pan American Sanitary Code is adopted.
1926	International Sanitary Convention is revised to include provisions against smallpox and typhus.
1931	International Council of Scientific Unions, a nongovernmental organization, is created.
1938	Final International Sanitary Conference is held in Paris. Conseil Sanitaire, Maritime, et Quarantenaire (forerunner to the WHO Eastern Mediterranean Regional Office) in Alexandria is handed over to Egypt.
1940	Special Office for Europe (forerunner of European Regional Office) opens.
1943	United Nations Relief and Rehabilitation Administration (UNRRA) is created, with its operations to include meeting health needs in Europe and the Far East.
1945	UNRRA assumes responsibility for the Office International d'Hygiène Publique.
September 1945	United Nations Conference on International Organization, in San Francisco, unanimously approves a proposal by Brazil and China to establish a new international health organization at the International Health Conference, to be held in New York in 1946.

1946

15 February	United Nations Economic and Social Council (ECOSOC) adopts a resolution calling for an international health conference.
18 March–5 April	Technical Preparatory Committee for the

	International Health Conference meets to set the agenda for the forthcoming meeting and prepare a draft of the WHO constitution.
April	Final session of the Assembly of the League of Nations approves the transfer of functions of its Health Organization to the United Nations.
19 June–22 July	International Health Conference is held in New York, attended by 61 countries. It drafts and adopts the WHO constitution. Interim Commission is formed to prepare for the establishment of a permanent organization, perform statutory functions of existing health organizations, and continue emergency health work during the postwar period.
October	Responsibilities of the UNRRA are transferred to the Interim Commission.
1 December	UNRRA and its activities are formally terminated.

1948

7 April	WHO constitution officially enters into force following its ratification by the 26th of 61 member states. This date is inaugurated as the annual World Health Day. The OIHP is correspondingly dissolved.
24 June	First World Health Assembly (WHA) opens in Geneva and is attended by 53 member states.
June	Organization of American States (OAS) is created with the adoption of the OAS Charter. It immediately initiates negotiations with the PASB on the working relationship between the two organizations.
21 July	Dr. Brock Chisholm (Canada) is elected by member states as WHO's first director-general.
31 August	Interim Commission ceases to exist by

resolution of the First WHA and all its property, records, assets, liabilities, responsibilities, and obligations are transferred to WHO.

Joint Committee on Health Policy (JCHP) is created by WHO and United Nations Children's Fund (UNICEF) to coordinate the health acitivities of the two organizations.

WHO and UNICEF begin to provide support for mass treatment programs for syphilis and other treponematoses such as yaws.

4–5 October   First regional committee meeting for Southeast Asia is held in New Delhi.

1949

1 January   South-East Asia Regional Office (SEARO) is established in New Delhi, India.

A Special Office of WHO opens in Geneva to serve the health needs of the European region.

April   WHO and the Pan American Sanitary Organization (PASO) sign a formal agreement recognizing PASO as an "independent entity" that can carry out and finance its own programs in the Americas provided they are "compatible with the policy and programmes" of WHO.

USSR and other Socialist countries withdraw their membership from WHO in protest against insufficient technical assistance from WHO.

1 July   Eastern Mediterranean Region Office (EMRO) is established in Alexandria, Egypt.

Agreement between WHO and the PAHO comes into force, and the latter becomes the American Regional Office (AMRO) of WHO.

Second WHA is held in Rome, Italy.

1950

OAS and the Pan American Health Organization (PAHO) reach agreement that the latter is to act as the inter-American specialized organization for health.

Standing Committee on Nongovernmental Organizations (NGOs) is created, and the first NGOs enter into official relations with WHO.

The delegations of Denmark, Norway, and Sweden propose unsuccessfully that WHAs be held on alternate years for the purpose of financial economies.

Pan American Sanitary Conference commits PAHO to regional programs to eradicate yaws, malaria, and smallpox.

May   The government of the Republic of China (Taiwan) notifies the director-general of its withdrawal from WHO.

1951

The text of the new International Sanitary Regulations is adopted by the fourth World Health Assembly. The regulations replace the previous International Sanitary Conventions.

May   The creation of an African Regional Office (AFRO) is agreed to by the majority of member states in the region. Its first session is held in the autumn of the same year, and an office is eventually opened in Brazzaville, Congo.

Western Pacific Regional Office (WPRO) is established and holds its first meeting in Geneva.

Autumn   First meeting of the European Regional Office is held in Geneva.

Arab League states decide not to cooperate with Israel in the Eastern Mediterranean

region, leading to failure of regional
committee to hold its annual sessions
between 1951 and 1953.

1952

1 February
Special Office for Europe in Copenhagen,
Denmark, becomes the WHO European
Regional Office (EURO).
WHA adopts resolution stating that no
member state shall contribute more than
one-third of regular budget funds.

September
WPRO is transferred from a temporary
office in Hong Kong to Manila, Philippines.

1953

July
Dr. Marcelino Candau (Brazil) is appointed
as WHO's second director-general.

1954

20 May
The dispute within EMRO over
membership of Israel leads to the
establishment of two subcommittees.
Pan American Sanitary Conference resolves
to eradicate malaria in the Americas.

1955

Intensified Malaria Eradication Programme
is launched as the first and largest of
WHO's mass campaigns so far against
disease.

30 May
Eighth WHA opens in Mexico City, Mexico.

1956

U.S. President Eisenhower decides to give

substantial financial support for Intensified Malaria Eradication Programme, leading to a rapid expansion of operations.

1957

January
: The governments of Bulgaria, Albania, and Poland inform the director-general that they are resuming active membership in WHO.

April
: The government of the Soviet Union announces the renewal of its active membership in WHO.

: Tenth WHA is held in Minneapolis, United States.

23 May
: The government of Romania notifies the director-general of the renewal of its active membership in WHO.

June
: EURO moves from Geneva to Copenhagen, Denmark.

1958

January
: The government of Czechoslovakia resumes active membership in WHO.

: Eleventh WHA is held in Minneapolis, United States.

1959

May
: 12th WHA resolves to undertake the global eradication of smallpox following initiative by the Russian deputy minister of health, Viktor Zhdanov.

: Soviet Union submits unsuccessful request to participate in the South-East Asian region in addition to the European region.

: Advisory Committee on Health Research (ACHR) is created, followed by the creation of similar regional committees.

WHO publishes the first *World Health Situation Report*.

1960

Act of Bogota is signed by member states of the OAS.

Cholera Research Laboratory is established in Dhaka, Bangladesh, which later develops into the International Center for Diarrhoeal Disease Research, Bangladesh (ICDDR,B).

Voluntary Fund for Health Promotion is established.

1961

January   Executive Board is expanded from 18 to 24 members.

1 July–31 October   The first use of oral rehydration therapy (ORT) is documented by a WHO advisory team in Egypt.

1962

Adverse reactions to the drug thalidomide leads WHO to establish an international system to provide information on drug safety and efficacy.

Codex Alimentarius Commission is created by WHO and the Food and Agriculture Organization (FAO).

Immunology Research Programme is created.

1963

WHO sets up information scheme on adverse drug reactions.

1964

WHA recognizes family planning as an essential aspect of the basic health system.

Geneva Group of the 13 largest financial donors to the United Nations convenes its first meeting in Geneva.

WHA agrees to withdraw South Africa's voting rights in protest against the country's adoption of apartheid. The South African government withdraws its membership shortly afterward.

1965

International Agency for Research on Cancer (IARC) is created.

Small program for research on human reproduction and the medical aspects of fertility and infertility is created.

WHO puts forth the basic health services model.

1966

May   Inaugural ceremony is held to celebrate the completion of WHO's headquarters building in Geneva, Switzerland.

1967

January   WHO launches the Intensified Smallpox Eradication Programme. Delay in its creation was largely due to lack of extrabudgetary funding.

1969

The new International Sanitary Regulations

are renamed the International Health Regulations, excluding louse-borne typhus and relapsing fever and leaving only cholera, plague, smallpox, and yellow fever. Director-general submits report on problems of Intensified Malaria Eradication Programme with call for revised strategy. A certification scheme on "good practices in the manufacture and quality control of drugs" is adopted by WHA.

1971

Review by the UNICEF/WHO Joint Committee on Health Policy recommends that family planning be provided as a component of comprehensive health services.

1972

Expanded Programme on Research, Development, and Research Training in Human Reproduction (HRP) is created.

1973

January
A report from the Executive Board concludes there is widespread dissatisfaction with health services and the need for radical change.

May
26th WHA decides that WHO should collaborate with, rather than assist, its member states in developing guidelines for national health care systems.

21 July
Dr. Halfdan Mahler (Denmark) is elected as WHO's third director-general.

1974

May
WHA adopts Resolution WHA22.43 on breast-feeding and breast milk substitutes.

Expanded Programme on Immunization (EPI) is created to protect children against poliomyelitis, measles, diphtheria, whooping cough, tetanus, and tuberculosis.

Nestlé files lawsuit against the Swiss NGO Arbeitsgruppe Dritte Welt Bern.

Special Programme on Onchocerciasis is created.

1975

January
Executive board increases from 24 to 30 members.

May
Director-General Halfdan Mahler presents report on concept of essential drugs to WHA, which passes Resolution WHA28.66 in support of national drug policies.

1976

May
WHA adopts resolution calling on WHO to spend at least 60 percent of regular budget funds for technical cooperation and provision of services by the end of the 1970s.

UNDP/World Bank/WHO Special Programme for Research and Training in Tropical Diseases is created.

1977

May
30th WHA adopts Resolution WHA30.43 on Health for All by the Year 2000, which aims to achieve a basic level of health by the turn of the century that will enable all people to lead a socially and economically productive life.

WHA adopts Resolution WHA30.33 in support of the International Drinking Water and Sanitation Decade.

WHO publishes Model List of Essential Drugs.

Drug Policies and Management Unit created to implement the new WHO policy based on the essential drugs approach.

July   Infant Formula Action Coalition (INFACT) calls for boycott of Nestlé products in protest against marketing practices.

26 October   The last naturally occurring case of smallpox is detected in Somalia.

1978

September   A Joint WHO/UNICEF International Conference is held at Alma-Ata, USSR. The Alma-Ata Declaration on Primary Health Care is signed by 134 countries as the key strategy for attaining the goal of Health for All by the Year 2000.

EMRO adopts essential drugs concept.

1979

A global commission declares that the worldwide eradication of smallpox has been achieved, with the last known case occurring in Ethiopia in 1977.

Arab states boycott meetings of the EMRO held in Alexandria, Egypt, following the Camp David Accords between Egypt and Israel.

May   Proposals are set forth by Arab states at the 32nd WHA to transfer EMRO from Egypt to another regional member state.

WHA endorses the Alma-Ata Declaration on Primary Health Care as the key to the strategy of Health for All by the Year 2000.

October   WHO-UNICEF meeting on infant and

young child feeding, attended for first time by NGO delegates, initiates need for code on marketing of breast milk substitutes.

1980

Programme for the Control of Diarrhoeal Diseases (CDD) is established.

A policy is adopted of zero real growth in the regular budgets of United Nations specialized agencies, including WHO.

May   WHA adopts Resolution WHA33.3, declaring that the campaign to globally eradicate smallpox is successful.

Programme for the Promotion of Chemical Safety is created.

Programme for the Global Elimination of Dracunculiasis is created.

1981

February   Action Programme on Essential Drugs (DAP) is created and begins activities three years after being approved by the 31st WHA in 1978.

Global strategy for Health for All by the Year 2000 is adopted by WHO and endorsed by the United Nations General Assembly.

March   International Federation of Pharmaceutical Manufacturers Associations (IFPMA) launches voluntary code for the pharmaceutical industry on marketing of drugs in developing countries.

May   International Code on the Marketing of Breastmilk Substitutes is adopted by the WHA, amid protest from the U.S. government and transnational corporations.

Health Action International formed by 50 NGOs during WHA.

WHA adopts Resolution WHA34.82 on the global strategy for achieving Health for All.

Autumn   IFPMA launches a voluntary industry code for the marketing of pharmaceuticals. The announcement is in anticipation of a campaign for WHO to adopt a code similar to that for breast milk substitutes.

SEARO and WPRO adopt essential drugs concept.

1982

March   IFPMA issues supplementary statement to industry code on pharmaceuticals stressing the industry's commitment to adhering to its provisions.

Programme for Control of Acute Respiratory Infections is created.

UNICEF launches GOBI-FFF initiative in the midst of debates over selective versus comprehensive primary health care.

1983

DAP moves to the Office of the Director-General.

August   Regional meeting of scientists and public health workers is organized by PAHO, United States National Institutes of Health, and United States Centers for Disease Control to exchange information on AIDS.

October   Regional meeting is organized by EURO, Danish Cancer Society, and the European Organization for Cooperation in Cancer Prevention Studies on AIDS in Europe.

22–25 November   Consultative meeting on AIDS is held in Geneva by WHO to assess the international implications of the epidemic.

1984

Pharmaceuticals Unit moved to Office of the Director-General.

Task Force for Child Survival is formed and cosponsored by WHO, UNICEF, UNDP, World Bank, and Rockefeller Foundation.

1985

January

Executive Board increases from 31 to 32 members with additional member from the Western Pacific region.

April

First International Conference on AIDS is held in Atlanta, United States, organized by the U.S. Centers for Disease Control and cosponsored by WHO and U.S. Department of Health.

May

Resolutions on Palestine and Israel at 38th World Health Assembly leads to debates on politicization of WHO.

Israel transfers its membership from the Eastern Mediterranean to the European region.

PAHO adopts proposal for action for the eradication of poliomyelitis from the Americas by 1990.

Essential Drugs Monitor is established.

1986

29th WHA endorses efforts to eliminate dracunculiasis country by country in association with the International Water Supply and Sanitation Decade.

June

WHO Control Programme on AIDS is established within the Division of Communicable Diseases.

November

The first of a series of International Conferences on Health Promotion is held in

Ottawa, leading to the signing of the Ottawa Charter for Health Promotion.

November
African Regional Conference on AIDS held by WHO to discuss epidemiological information on extent of the epidemic in Africa.

1987

1 February
Special Programme on AIDS, later renamed the Global Programme on AIDS, is created.

May
30th WHA declares HIV/AIDS a worldwide emergency.

Safe Motherhood Initiative launched by WHO, UNFPA, and World Bank.

International Conference on Better Health is held.

UNICEF announces Bamako Initiative at meeting of the African Regional Committee.

20 October
United Nations General Assembly receives special briefing from WHO Global Programme on AIDS, which leads to the adoption of Resolution 42/8 confirming WHO's essential global directing and coordinating role in the global AIDS strategy.

1988

26–28 January
Summit on AIDS is held, jointly organized by WHO and the British government, leading to adoption of London Declaration on AIDS Prevention.

WHO/UNDP Alliance to Combat AIDS is formed.

May
WHO Tuberculosis Programme is created.

WHA agrees to goal of the global eradication of poliomyelitis by the year

2000, based on the Polio Eradication Initiative.

World No Tobacco Day is inaugurated as an annual event by the WHA.

HRP becomes cosponsored by the World Bank, the UNDP, and the UNFPA.

21 July — Dr. Hiroshi Nakajima (Japan) is elected as WHO's fourth director-general.

Action Programme on Essential Drugs (APED) and Pharmaceuticals Unit moved from Office of the Director-General to newly created Division of Drug Management and Policies.

1 December — World AIDS Day is inaugurated as an annual event.

1989

Restructuring of governing body of APED by director-general leads to the creation of the Management Advisory Committee.

An external evaluation of the APED is carried out.

Division of Intensified Cooperation with Countries is established.

1990

May — WHA agrees to goal of eliminating iodine deficiency diseases as a major public health problem in all countries by the year 2000.

Division of Diarrhoeal and Acute Respiratory Disease Control is created.

Division of Control of Tropical Diseases (CTD) is created.

Programme on Tobacco or Health is created.

World Summit for Children, organized by UNICEF, is held in New York, leading to the signing of the World Declaration on the

Survival, Protection, and Development of Children.

Children's Vaccine Initiative is launched by WHO, UNICEF, UNDP, the World Bank, and the Rockefeller Foundation.

European Center on Environment and Health is established.

Adolescent Health and Development Programme is established.

INTERHEALTH Programme is launched in Helsinki, Finland, to address diseases arising from unhealthy lifestyles.

Programme on Substance Abuse (PSA) is established.

1991

May

WHA agrees to goal of eradicating dracunculiasis by the end of 1995.

WHA requests that increased support be given to member states for the eradication of leprosy by the year 2000.

At 44th WHA, director-general calls for new paradigm to address intractable international health problems.

Committee on the Rights of the Child is formed, in the follow-up to the World Summit for Children, with WHO as a committee member.

A Strategy and Action Programme for the Elimination of Leprosy is adopted by the WHA.

September

Saitama Public Health Summit is held in Saitama, Japan, on issues of health transition.

1992

May

Director-General Nakajima initiates

	organizational reform under the WHO Response to Global Change.
July	Memorandum of Understanding for the Implementation of the WHO/UNDP Alliance to Combat AIDS is signed.
26 October	A new control strategy for malaria is launched at a meeting of health ministers held in Amsterdam, Holland.
	Integrated Management of the Sick Child approach is put forth by WHO and UNICEF.
	Division of Food and Nutrition is created in response to the World Declaration and Plan of Action for Nutrition adopted at the International Conference on Nutrition.

1993

	Riga Initiative is launched by WHO and the World Bank to provide assistance for prevention and control of HIV/AIDS in central and eastern Europe.
	Global Commission on Women's Health is established under the auspices of WHO.
23 April	WHO declares a global tuberculosis emergency at a news conference in London.
June	World Bank publishes the *World Development Report: Investing in Health*.
	ECOSOC Resolution 1993/51 is adopted asking the director-general to study the feasibility of creating a UN joint and cosponsored program on HIV/AIDS.
	Council on the Implementation of the Earth Summit's Action Program for Health and the Environment is established to follow the UNCED, based on WHO's Global Strategy for Health and Environment.
	Task Force on Health Economics is launched by the director-general.
	Task Force on Health in Development is created.

1994

Interagency Immunization Coordinating Committee is established.

Division of Emergency and Humanitarian Relief is created to replace the Division of Emergency Relief Operations.

April   Global Programme for Vaccines and Immunization (GPV) is created.

September   International Conference on Population and Development (ICPD) is held in Cairo, where WHO puts forth and has adopted its definition of reproductive health.

Task Force on Health in Development is set up as an advisory body to WHO.

1995

May   A process for Renewing the Health for All Strategy is launched.

June   WHO publishes its first *World Health Report*.

World Summit on Social Development is held in Copenhagen, Denmark, which puts forth 20/20 Initiative.

Programme on Aging and Health is established with the reorganization of the Global Programme for Health of the Elderly.

International Scientific and Technical Committee for the Control of Ebola Hemorrhagic Fever is created.

Division of Emerging and Other Communicable Diseases (EMC) is created to take over much of the Division of Communicable Diseases (CDS).

1996

1 January   A new UNAIDS program replaces the WHO Global Programme on AIDS. The

new program is cosponsored by five UN organizations: WHO, UNICEF, UNFPA, UNESCO, and the World Bank.

Executive Board establishes for a limited duration an ad hoc working group on health systems development for the future.

March   Center for Health Development is opened in Kobe, Japan.

24 March   World Tuberculosis Day is inaugurated as an annual event.

May   Division of Women's Health is created.

46th WHA declares the prevention of violence as a public health priority and sets up a Task Force on Violence and Health.

International Vaccine Institute is created in Seoul, Republic of Korea, under the umbrella of the Children's Vaccine Initiative.

1997

January   Executive Board reviews the role of WHO country offices and asks the director-general to accept recommended changes to their operations.

June   Development begins of a global health charter to achieve a renewal of the Health for All strategy.

1998

January   Dr. Gro Harlem Brundtland is elected as WHO's fifth director-general.

May   WHO celebrates its fiftieth anniversary.

Introduction: A Brief History of the World Health Organization

International Health Cooperation before 1945

The World Health Organization (WHO) came into formal existence in 1948 as the United Nations (UN) specialized agency for health. However, the newly created organization was to some extent an amalgamation of a number of existing organizations that together represented a long history of international health cooperation dating from as early as the 14th century. With the growth in international trade and commerce across continents came the increased threat of the spread of disease across national boundaries. In response, governments, scientists, and public health officials worked ever closer together to develop appropriate knowledge, policies, and procedures. By the 19th century and the Industrial Revolution, international health cooperation was becoming well developed in response to the exigencies of burgeoning international trade, migration, and warfare. Between 1851 and 1903, a series of 11 International Sanitary Conferences was held to facilitate international action largely to control the spread of diseases, such as plague, cholera, and yellow fever, from colonial territories into Europe. Informed by developments in medical science, the first International Sanitary Convention proposing measures for quarantine and hygiene practices was agreed to in 1892. A total of four conventions were eventually agreed upon, which were codified and consolidated at the 11th International Sanitary Conference in 1903. In addition, the meeting reached agreement on the creation of a permanent organization for maintaining and reporting epidemiological data and coordinating quarantine measures. Hence, the Office International d'Hygiène Publique (OIHP) was created by the Rome Agreement of 1907 with headquarters in Paris.[1] Another early international health body, the Health Organization of the League of Nations, was founded in 1920. The founders saw its role as going beyond that of the OIHP to include a more active role in dealing with the resurgence of diseases such as typhus and influenza following the First World War. However, the ability of the Health Organization to carry out this work proved problematic from its inception, due to the nonmembership of the United States government in the League of Nations. Also, rivalry between the OIHP and the Health Organization soon emerged, preventing the two organizations from working more closely together.[2]

A number of health-related nongovernmental organizations (NGOs) were also founded during this period of postwar internationalism. The League of Red Cross Societies, for example, later known as the International Federation of Red Cross and Red Crescent Societies, was established in 1919 "in view of a worldwide crusade to improve health, prevent sickness, and alleviate suffering."[3] Consolidating an initiative that had begun in the 1860s by Swiss citizens seeking to provide humanitarian assistance during times of war, the organization became a worldwide movement of national societies independent of governments. Similarly, the Save the Children Fund (SCF) was created in 1919 by the British woman Eglantyne Jebb in response to the humanitarian needs of people in Europe affected by the First World War. In 1920, the Save the Children International Union was formed in Geneva as an umbrella body for organizations in France, Germany, Ireland, Sweden, and the United Kingdom. SCF's work grew rapidly to involve famine relief and the provision of shelter, health, and education services for disadvantaged children throughout the world.[4] Charitable foundations, notably the Rockefeller Foundation, were also rapidly developing international health programs in cooperation with other organizations.

This period also saw the creation of regional intergovernmental organizations formed for similar purposes. Foremost among them was the International Sanitary Bureau of the Americas, formed in 1902 by governments in the Americas, as the world's first permanent international health organization. Renamed the Pan American Sanitary Bureau (PASB) in 1923, it was the forerunner of the Pan American Health Organization (PAHO), which became a regional office of WHO after the Second World War. Like the OIHP, the PASB played an important role in collecting epidemiological data and exchanging such information with other health organizations. Yet, unlike the European organization, the PASB also played an active operational role, for example, initiating a campaign to eradicate yellow fever from the Americas.[5] This balance between information-based and operational activities, as well as its unique independence and affiliation with the Organization of American States (OAS), would later set the organization apart from other WHO regional offices.

Other regional health organizations existed during this time, each with varying composition, functions, and efficacy. The Conseil Supérieur de Santé de Constantinople, dating from the Ottoman Empire in the late 1830s, was created to address the spread of plague through the adoption of quarantine measures. In 1840 the Conseil Sanitaire de Tanger was formed in Morocco to limit the spread of epidemic diseases, notably plague and cholera. In 1843 the Egyptian Quarantine Board was established in Alexandria to protect the country from imported epidemics; it later became the regional epidemiological bureau of the OIHP. In 1867 the Shah of Persia established the Conseil Sanitaire de l'Empire, which met irregularly to address public health matters. In Europe, the creation of the European Commission for the Danube in 1856 included a limited range of public health measures within its remit.[6]

Overall, the history of international health cooperation before the end of the Second World War was a rich one, with international, regional, and nongovernmental organizations working in response to the emerging health needs of a changing world. Admittedly, activities centered on the self-interests of dominant trading interests in Europe and elsewhere; yet by the 1930s these early initiatives had laid a firm foundation for expanding international cooperation to promote public health in general. With the outbreak of war in 1939, the demands on many of these organizations increased manifold. The war also signaled the imminent end of the Health Organization of the League of Nations, which would later be restructured according to postwar visions of world order.

The Technical Preparatory Committee and the International Health Conference of 1946: Toward Organizational Unification

As many parts of the world lay in ruin following the end of the Second World War, world leaders agreed to convene a conference to discuss the creation of a truly international health organization as part of the newly created United Nations. Interestingly, the idea for a UN specialized agency for health was not initially included in the charter agreed on at the United Nations Conference on International Organization held in San Francisco in 1945. It was only following strong support by the Brazilian and Chinese delegations, who argued that "medicine is one of the pillars of peace," that a declaration was issued at the conference recognizing health as a field with which the United Nations should concern itself. To this end, in February 1946 the UN Economic and Social Council agreed that an International Health Conference would be convened in New York in June of the same year "to consider the scope of, and the appropriate machinery for, international action in the field of public health and proposals for the establishment of a single international health organization of the United Nations."[7]

The important responsibility of preparing for this conference was given to the Technical Preparatory Committee, consisting of 16 "experts in the field of international health"[8] and chaired by Dr. Rene Sand, of Belgium. Almost all these experts were prominent in the medical field, serving as ministers of health or senior public health officials in their respective countries. The committee met in Paris during March–April 1946 to "prepare an annotated agenda and proposals for the consideration of the Conference," including a draft constitution and other accompanying resolutions. This work was assisted by detailed proposals submitted by individual delegates from France, the United Kingdom, and the United States, serving in a personal capacity, as well as statements from existing health organizations, on the constitution of the new organization. Working with these submissions, the committee drafted proposals on key aspects of the organization's governing structure, administration, financing, mandate, and even title. However, the committee decided to leave two questions for resolution by the conference itself: where to locate the headquarters and, a more complex issue, whether regional organizations would be associated or fully integrated with the new organization. The latter question, in particular, would prove a sticking point for many years to come.

The International Health Conference opened in June 1946 as the first international conference to be held under United Nations auspices. The conference was attended by all 51 member states of the United Nations as well as 13 nonmember states, the Allied Control Authorities for Germany, Japan, and Korea, and observers from relevant UN organizations. Significantly, existing international health organizations were also invited to attend in a consultative capacity. During the four and a half weeks of the conference, delegations agreed on the constitution of the new organization (see Appendix A), a protocol for the termination of the OIHP, and the setting up of an Interim Commission to assume its duties as well as those of the Health Organization of the

League of Nations and the temporary United Nations Relief and Rehabilitation Administration (UNRRA), until WHO was actually established.[9]

The Establishment of the World Health Organization

The World Health Organization formally came into existence in September 1948, following the receipt of the 26th signature by a member state ratifying the constitution. This lapse of over two years from the time of the International Health Conference had been unforeseen by those keen to quickly establish the new UN specialized agency. The main cause of the delay was the onset of the Cold War, which soon led to a decline in internationalism and to debates over the precise role of the United Nations. In the health field, amid rising East-West tensions, the United States government became wary of what it saw as socialized medicine. The assertion in WHO's constitution of health as "one of the fundamental rights of every human being" and the responsibility of governments "for the health of their peoples" was viewed with considerable suspicion by those who equated social equity with the Communist threat.

As a result of this delay, existing international and regional health organizations continued to play a crucial role during the immediate postwar period, providing much-needed assistance, in particular to war-torn areas. Among the most active were the International Committee of the Red Cross and UNRRA. The United Nations International Children's Emergency Fund (UNICEF) was created in 1946 as a temporary organization designed to meet the basic needs of war-affected children. Health soon became an important aspect of UNICEF's work, and when WHO finally came into being two years later, the Joint Committee on Health Policy (JCHP) was immediately formed to ensure harmonization of the two organizations' activities. When UNICEF became a permanent UN fund in 1953 and was renamed the United Nations Children's Fund, the JCHP was also continued to carry out this task.[10]

The basic composition and organizational structure of WHO have changed little since its establishment in 1948 (see Appendix D). WHO is open to all members of the United Nations, along with states invited to the International Health Conference and other states approved by a simple majority of the World Health Assembly (see below). In consideration of the number of colonial territories that still existed after the Second World War, associate membership was extended to "territories or groups of territories which are not responsible for the conduct of their international relations."[11] In 1948, WHO had 55 member states. This principle of universal membership reflected the belief that health concerns could not be confined within national boundaries but required cooperation across all countries.

Second, all member states of WHO are represented in its plenary and legislative body, the World Health Assembly (WHA). Delegations of member states consist of not more than three delegates most qualified by their technical competence in the field of health, preferably representing the national health administration of the member state. Representatives of other relevant international organizations and recognized nongovernmental organizations (see Appendix H) are permitted to attend as observers. The WHA meets annually, usually in May, to determine the overall policy direction of WHO's six-year General Programme of Work, review and approve reports and activities of the Executive Board, and review and approve the annual budget, among other things. In carrying out this work, the WHA is assisted by a number of committees with specified responsibilities (e.g., the Committee on Administration, Finance, and Legal Matters and the Committee on Programme and Budget). The WHA also has the authority to adopt regulations in such fields as sanitary and quarantine requirements; nomenclature for diseases, causes of death, and public health practices; and standards with respect to the safety, purity, and potency of biological, pharmaceutical, and similar products. These regulations are binding unless member states choose to opt out. Decisions are formally governed by the principle of "One state, one vote." In practice, the majority of WHA decisions are presented as recommendations (i.e., resolutions), and most decisions are made by consensus.[12]

The Executive Board (EB) is the executive body of WHO that oversees the implementation of decisions taken by the WHA. Importantly, while member states are elected by the WHA to propose EB members, individuals serving as EB members serve in a personal capacity as "technically qualified in the field of health" rather than as representatives of particular governments.[13] EB members serve for three-year terms, and each year one-third of EB members is retired. Initially, the EB consisted of 18 members. By 1996, in response to WHO's growing membership, this number had been increased to 32. The EB meets twice yearly, in January and after the WHA meeting in May. Among its main responsibilities are preparing the agenda for the WHA, giving effect to WHA decisions, submitting a draft General Programme of Work, reviewing the proposed program budget, advising on questions of constitutional and regulatory matters, submitting advice or proposals of its own initiative, taking emergency measures regarding WHO's finances and functions, and performing any other functions entrusted to it.[14] As with the WHA, there are committees to assist in this work. Member states may respond within a year to proposals put forth by the EB, in the form of a report to the WHA.

The Secretariat is the administrative and technical organ of the WHO, responsible for actually implementing the organization's activities. It consists of the headquarters in Geneva, six regional offices, and country offices in selected member states. After much discussion at the International Health Conference, the representatives agreed to locate the headquarters in Geneva, Switzerland, at the former site of the Health Organization of the League of Nations. The Secretariat is headed by the director-general, who is nominated by the EB and appointed by the WHA for a five-year term. Among the primary responsibilities of the director-general, as chief technical and administrative officer, are the appointment of Secretariat staff, the preparation of annual financial statements, and the drafting of the proposed program budget. A more detailed discussion of WHO financing is provided below. Since 1948, four directors-general have served long terms (see Appendix E), all medically qualified and having previous experience in other parts of the WHO or its predecessors. Medical professionals have also been strongly represented on the staff of the Secretariat, leading David Pitt to describe it as a "medical mafia."[15]

The Secretariat also includes six regional offices, which are unique within the UN system in terms of their independence and decision-making powers.[16] There were two main reasons for the creation of regional offices. The first was early recognition that effective international health cooperation requires both global and local action. An organizational structure encompassing headquarters, regional, and country-level activities was expected to enhance WHO's capacity to carry out its work. How to consequently balance the work of the three levels, however, has been the subject of ongoing debate. Some argue that "regionalization, so liberally interpreted, has been one of the factors which has contributed most to success—particularly in securing worldwide co-operation."[17] Others, supporting a strongly centralized WHO, have been concerned that an overly decentralized organization tips the balance inappropriately away from the WHA and the EB.[18] Indeed, WHO's regional structure received early criticism by the Technical Assistance Board (TAB) of the United Nations

Special Fund, the mechanism through which, until 1950, UN specialized agencies coordinated their plans and work. The TAB argued that WHO's work plan and regional structure impeded efforts to achieve an integrated development assistance program,[19] a criticism that continues to be raised in the present day.

The second, and more politically significant, reason for regional offices is the prior existence of well-established regional health organizations at the time of WHO's creation. While it was widely agreed that these organizations needed to be integrated into WHO's work, the process of negotiation was a highly sensitive and political one, given its implications for distribution of authority, membership, and financing. Supporters of the PASB, later the Pan American Health Organization, and the Egyptian Quarantine Board were especially committed to retaining the independence of the highly successful organizations. Further problems were posed by the criteria for delineating member states into regions. In the end, it was agreed that member states themselves would choose which region to join, a situation that has resulted in a number of geographic anomalies. Despite these difficulties, regional offices were established by 1951 in Africa (AFRO), the Americas (PAHO), the Eastern Mediterranean (EMRO), Europe (RURO), Southeast Asia (SEARO), and the Western Pacific (WPRO).

The regional office is the administrative organ of the regional committee, a plenary body of representatives (usually ministers of health) of the member states of the region. In PAHO, this body is known as the Directing Council. Each regional office is headed by a regional director (see Appendix E) who serves as the chief technical and administrative officer of the region. Regional directors are formally appointed by the Executive Board but are nominated by members of their respective regional committees. Regional committees meet annually to formulate policies with a regional dimension, review the regional program budget proposed by the regional director, and monitor WHO's collaborative activities for health development in that region. In principle, decisions are then formally approved by the WHA and the EB to ensure that they are appropriate to global policies. In practice, the agendas of these bodies have grown to such an extent that tight policy and budgetary control is not possible. This has given regional directors and committees considerable discretion over regional activities.

In addition to the global headquarters and regional offices, country offices are located in selected member states. The purpose of the country office is to work with the government, through the national ministry of health, to implement WHO policies and programs and, more generally, to support the development of the country's health system. While there is considerable regional variation in the size and activities of country-level offices, most are headed by a WHO representative (WR). The WR is appointed by and answerable to the relevant regional office. The work of the country office may also be supported by technical and support staff located at the country level. In 1996, there were 139 country offices in 189 member states.

The Formal Mandate of WHO: Normative versus Technical Cooperation Activities

The constitution of WHO states that its overall purpose is the promotion and pursuit of "the attainment by all people of the highest possible level of health."[20] Toward achieving this aim, the document lists 22 functions intended to guide specific activities. Foreseen by its founders as the UN organization for health, WHO's functions are wide ranging and broadly worded so that virtually all aspects of health are included within them. In this way, considerable flexibility is available to interpret WHO's formal mandate.

WHO's activities are frequently classified as either normative or technical cooperation activities. Normative activities, sometimes referred to as central technical activities, are generally defined as "the business of exhortation, asserting values, specifying goals, and proclaiming norms."[21] These information-oriented activities include such tasks as proposing and adopting conventions, agreements, and regulations to prevent ill health; promoting international standards and nomenclatures with respect to food, biological, pharmaceutical, and similar products; collecting health statistics and epidemiological information; promoting and conducting research and disseminating its findings; supporting the training of health workers; and promoting cooperation among scientific and professional groups concerned with health.[22] Outputs of this work include the compilation and dissemination of the International Lists of Causes of Death, the International Nomenclature of Diseases, and operation of the Epidermiological Intelligence Network.

Technical cooperation activities concern direct assistance to governments, notably in low- and middle-income countries, upon their request, to strengthen their health systems. This can be achieved through the transfer of skills and knowledge, initiation of practical projects, health manpower planning, and coordination of health programs.[23] Since the late 1970s, the term technical cooperation, rather than technical assistance, has been used to emphasize the partnership relationship WHO seeks to develop with member states. In contrast to a donor–recipient relationship, technical cooperation begins with the principle that each country has the sovereign right to develop its national health system and services in the way that it finds most rational and appropriate to its needs. WHO's contribution to such activities includes technical expertise to prevent, control, or treat disease; training materials for health professionals; and seed money to mobilize additional external resources.

While this classification of WHO activities may reflect the intentions of the organization's founders, from its earliest years debates arose over the appropriate balance between the two types of activities. For example, as part of its opposition to what was perceived as socialized medicine the United States government strongly supported normative, rather than technical, cooperation activities. From the late 1960s, there has been a shift toward increased technical cooperation activities as a result of the increased numbers of developing countries who have become member states. Since the 1980s, there has been criticism by large financial donors to the organization that the balance between the two types of activities has unduly shifted toward technical cooperation, which now accounts for at least 70 percent of WHO's regular budget. Others emphasize the need for WHO to return to its "comparative advantage," namely, its unique international role in collecting, coordinating, and disseminating scientific and technical information.

As well as debates over the balance of activities to be achieved,[24] there is the more difficult issue of the usefulness of the normative/technical cooperation typology to describe the actual work of the organization. While the terms are widely used, they are not entirely satisfactory. It is assumed, for example, that normative activities are those that take place at the global level for the benefit of all member states. In contrast, technical cooperation is seen to take place at the country level. Many argue that this is an oversimplification of how health cooperation occurs. Knowledge generated at the global level, for example, is often derived from the testing of knowledge through technical cooperation at the country level. Similarly, technical cooperation frequently depends on knowledge shared at the global level.[25] Thus, rather than viewing WHO's formal mandate as clearly set and static, with absolute definitions of appropriate and inappropriate activities, it is more useful to understand how the broad provisions of he constitution have been interpreted by·member states as membership, resources, knowledge, and the organization itself have changed over time.

The War against Disease: The Growth of Prevention, Control, and Eradication Programs

During its initial years, WHO focused on the demands of postwar reconstruction, including the rebuilding of health services in war-affected countries. It was agreed that WHO would assume the work of UNRRA, which, according to the latter's major financial donors, was intended to have a limited duration and mandate. This early focus of WHO's General Programme of Work became known as the Big Six target areas: malaria, tuberculosis, sexually transmitted diseases, maternal and child health, environmental sanitation, and nutrition. Action on these target areas centered on a project approach, by which health needs were identified with a government, an expert, or team of experts as recruited and briefed by WHO, and experts were sent to the country to work with the national health administration.[26] These projects, expressed in high-minded declarations "to vanquish disease in the wake of war,"[27] reflected a concern among the major postwar powers with both the immediate consequences of large-scale conflict on international health and the importance of health to "building a firmer foundation for permanent peace and security."[28] These ideals eventually led to the creation of such affiliated institutions as the International Center for Diarrhoeal Disease Research, Bangladesh (ICDDR,B) in 1960 and the International Agency for Research on Cancer (IARC) in 1965.

By the mid-1950s, this trouble-shooting approach to health development began to broaden for two reasons. First, efforts aimed at short-term interventions, rather than longer-term strategies, began to be seen as inconsistent with the constitution's broad definition of health as "a state of complete physical, mental, and social well-being."[29] Second, the creation of regional offices as an integral part of WHO led to a greater appreciation of the specific health needs in individual regions and member states. While projects continued to be an important part of WHO's assistance to member states, other ways of working were soon added to the organization's repertoire.

The most prominent of these, during the first 25 years of WHO's history, was the mass campaign for the prevention, control, and eradication of selected diseases. The first and largest of these was the Intensified Malaria Eradication Programme (MEP) initiated in 1955 and continuing until the early 1970s, when it reverted to a control program.[30] Malaria had long been recognized as one of the world's most prevalent and endemic diseases. Afflicting populations throughout the tropical regions of the world, malaria killed more people each year (an estimated 2.5 million in 1955) than any other disease.[31] By the 1950s, many were convinced that WHO should change its strategy goal from control of the disease to complete eradication.[32] One of the strongest supporters of disease eradication programs at this time was the director of the PASB, Dr. Fred Soper, who, during his public health career, initiated regional eradication programs for yellow fever, yaws, malaria, and smallpox. For malaria, the key to the proposed strategy was the discovery of the insecticide dichlorodiphenyltrichloroethane (DDT) during the Second World War. Trials of the insecticide seemed to enable a successful and relatively long-term attack on the disease's vector, the anopheline mosquito.

For these reasons the MEP became the first mass eradication program to be coordinated by an international health organization and, up to that point, the largest public health campaign in history. A Malaria Eradication Special Account was set up to receive extrabudgetary funds (EBFs) for the campaign, supplemented by regular budget funds. The program commenced worldwide, with the notable exceptions of sub-Saharan Africa, the Soviet Union, and China, with high hopes and much fanfare. Across the globe, spray crews armed with DDT dispersed to carry out house-to-house visits. Predictions abounded that the disease would be eradicated within a decade or less, and thoughts turned to other diseases that could be tackled with newly emerging technologies and the spirit of international health cooperation.

Although the program enjoyed apparent initial success, by the mid-1960s serious doubts as to the actual effectiveness of the strategy began to be voiced in both target countries and donor governments. In 1967, the director-general was asked to study how best to reexamine the global strategy, and his report in 1969 identified a range of operational, technical, planning, and budgetary problems. By then malaria eradication was proving far more problematic than anticipated. The main technical problems were the eventual resistance of mosquitoes to DDT and other insecticides, the behavioral characteristics of the vector, and the dangers of DDT to the human and natural environment. These problems highlighted other weaknesses, notably a total dependence on DDT and hence a failure to develop other control strategies, the high expense of the program given the limited resources of developing countries, and the lack of flexibility in the global strategy to respond to local needs. By the late 1960s, a revised strategy called for malaria control where eradication was not quickly achievable. Contributions of EBFs for the MEP gradually declined, and the program effectively ended in 1973 by reverting to the Malaria Action Programme.[33]

The important lessons learned from the MEP were applied to the Intensified Smallpox Eradication Programme launched in 1967. The issue of smallpox eradication was not new to WHO, having been the subject of discussion in the WHA from the late 1940s. It was not until 1959, a year after Professor Viktor Zhdanov, then deputy health minister of the Soviet Union, had presented a lengthy and detailed report to the WHA on how smallpox could be eradicated, that member states finally agreed that the task should be undertaken. In contrast to malaria, the global strategy to eradicate smallpox was favored by the nature of the disease and effective developments in medical technology, including vaccination against the disease. The disease could be readily detected, owing to the characteristic rash produced, and transmission occurred only through close contact with individuals having the rash. There was also a 10- to 15-day delay between each generation of the disease, which meant that control of its spread could be achieved through isolation of the patient and vaccination of close contacts. With the development of an effective, long-term, and easily administered vaccine against smallpox, the feasibility of the strategy became strongly established.

The long period between the decision to undertake smallpox eradication in May 1959 and the eventual launch of the intensified programme in 1967 was largely due to a shortage of resources. Indeed, the two eradication programs competed for the world's attention and contributions of EBFs into the early 1970s. Between 1959 and 1966, total expenditures for the MEP represented over 27 percent of all WHO funds. In comparison, less than 1 percent was spent on smallpox programs during the same period. Efforts to raise EBFs for control of smallpox were met with limited donations. Significant interest began to grow only in 1965, when the United States government agreed to commit resources to a regional strategy in west and central Africa. Encouraged by this shift in policy, the Soviet government requested that the director-general prepare a proposed budget for an intensified campaign for smallpox eradication, a program which was finally begun in January 1967.

Based on lessons from the malaria program, it was recognized that successful eradication depended on an appropriately designed and well-executed global strategy centered on cooperation among member states. National eradication programs were set up in country after country, all of which needed to be coordinated and supported at the local, regional, and global levels. Innovative means of detection, such as financial rewards to the public, were developed, which proved successful in ensuring accurate and comprehensive reporting mechanisms. There were also difficult challenges. The level of resources for the program remained an important limitation, with EBFs and donated vaccine in continually short supply until well into the campaign. The administrative structure of WHO, notably the independence of the regional offices, also needed to be overcome to ensure close cooperation across regions and countries. Finally, sustaining national and international commitment to the program, particularly in countries where smallpox was not a high priority, required ongoing effort.[34]

Despite these challenges, the Intensified Smallpox Eradication Programme proved to be the greatest achievement of WHO's history to date. On 26 October 1977, the last naturally occurring case of smallpox was detected and contained in southern Somalia. On 9 December 1979, the Global Commission for the Certification of Smallpox Eradication, set up in 1978 to assist in the verification of the disease's eradication, concluded that global eradication had been achieved. This remarkable feat was declared to the world at the 33rd WHA in May 1980.

Financing the World Health Organization:
Regular Budget and Extrabudgetary Funds

The constitution states that WHO is primarily financed by the assessed contributions of its member states, calculated biennially (every two years) according to the UN scale of ability to pay (based on GNP and population). These contributions are known as regular budget funds (RBFs). Assessed according to this system, a small number of industrialized countries soon provided most of these funds. In 1962, more than half of the regular budget was provided by the Soviet Union, the United Kingdom, and the United States and another quarter by Canada, China, France, Germany, India, Italy, and Japan.[35] To ensure that WHO would not be overly dependent on the financial contributions of a single member state, it was agreed that no country would pay more than one-third of the total regular budget. The largest contributor to the regular budget has remained the United States, at 25 percent.

In addition to regular budget funds, the WHO constitution states that the "Health Assembly or the [Executive] Board acting on behalf of the [World] Health Assembly may accept and administer gifts and bequests made to the Organization provided that the conditions attached to such gifts or bequests are acceptable and are consistent with the objectives and policies of the Organization."[36] These additional contributions, given voluntarily by other United Nations organizations, member states, private organizations, or individuals, are known as extrabudgetary funds (EBFs).

Until the mid-1950s, EBFs came primarily from the Expanded Programme for Technical assistance (EPTA) and the United Nations Special Fund (consolidated in 1962 as part of the United Nations Development Program [UNDP]). The former was created in 1949 for the purpose of promoting economic development through the transfer of technical skills of the United Nations and its specialized agencies. Working through a technical assistance board on which the director-general of WHO served, EPTA channeled EBFs through UN organizations for development activities. For WHO, funds received from EPTA were used to strengthen health administrations, control communicable diseases, and train professional and auxiliary staff.[37] The United Nations Special Fund was formed in the 1950s to mobilize greater resources for UN economic and social development activities.

The launch of the Intensified Malaria Eradication Programme in 1955 and the Intensified Smallpox Eradication Programme in 1967 led to a substantial rise in voluntary contributions to WHO. In 1956, United States President Dwight Eisenhower decided to provide substantial funds for malaria eradication on both humanitarian and foreign policy grounds.[38] Other major contributions followed from UNICEF. After a slow initial start, the Intensified Smallpox Eradication Programme eventually received most of its funding from EBFs, again following the American financial impetus in the mid-1960s.

While EBFs were vital to the disease control and eradication programs of the 1950s and 1960s, the period since the 1970s has seen the most significant growth of EBFs. With the creation of special programs (see below), EBFs were given for research in such areas as human reproduction and tropical diseases. This rapid expansion of EBFs led the Executive Board to initiate a major study in 1975 of the "increasingly important role which extrabudgetary resources have played and will continue to play in supplementing the regular program budget of WHO."[39] The study found EBFs to be a welcome source of funding, especially given the expansion of technical cooperation activities being undertaken by WHO from the mid-1970s. Within this context, it concluded that "if WHO is to pursue its constitutional mission it is evident that the upward trend in extrabudgetary resources must continue."

This generally positive reception toward EBFs set the scene for an even more rapid increase in voluntary contributions during the 1980s. In 1970, EBFs accounted for 20 percent of total WHO expenditures, with over half of these funds coming from other UN organizations. By the 1990–91 biennium, EBFs exceeded RBFs for the first time.[40] During this period, further disease-focused programs were established, including the Programme for the Control of Diarrhoeal Diseases in 1980, the Programme for the Control of Acute Respiratory Infections in 1982, and the Global Programme on AIDS in 1987 (see below). Substantial EBFs were also given for programs aimed at strengthening health research and systems such as the Action Programme on Essential Drugs established in 1981. As discussed in the following sections, the rapid expansion of WHO's activities during this period was largely funded by EBFs, with the result that WHO's total budget grew to become the largest among the UN specialized agencies.

A Shift in the Health Paradigm:
From Disease Programs to Primary Health Care

The period from 1948 to the late 1960s saw rapid growth in WHO's membership, programs, and budget. During the postwar period, WHO focused on reconstruction of health systems. By the early 1950s, attention turned to disease prevention, control, and eradication, an agenda that met with mixed success over the following decades. By the late 1960s, the conceptualization of the health needs of member states was changing once again. Foremost was the growing number of developing countries in Africa, Asia, and Latin America and the Caribbean that were looking to the United Nations for greater development assistance. In WHO, there were 24 such countries, representing 43 percent of member states in 1948. By 1970, this number had increased to 90 developing countries, or 70 percent of member states.[41]

The 1970s also brought greater instability in international relations which presented serious challenges to postwar internationalism. For the world economy, a crisis of capitalism followed the breakdown of the Bretton Woods monetary system, the oil crises of 1974–75 and 1979–80, economic recession, and growing inflation and unemployment. For world politics, the end of the Vietnam War and the strengthening of the Nonaligned Movement and the Group of 77 countries signaled a greater questioning of the American-led world order. For the United Nations, this period marked unprecedented controversy in many of the specialized agencies. For developing countries, this controversy centered on a growing and direct challenge to traditional development theories of the 1950s and 1960s.[42] Faced with deteriorating terms of trade, rising protectionism for markets in industrialized countries, mounting foreign debt, and limited development assistance, developing countries voiced their collective demand in the United Nations General Assembly for a new international economic order (NIEO). As part of a fundamental rethinking of the development agenda, the NIEO included a radical restructuring of global economic relations and the large-scale transfer of resources to the developing world.

As an extension of this movement, the demands made by member states of WHO began to change in the early 1970s. Developing countries expressed their dissatisfaction with the quality and quantity of development assistance offered. Much of this assistance was defined by the Western biomedical model of health care with its emphasis on urban hospitals, curative care, expensive technology, and highly trained health personnel. This model proved of limited relevance to the acute needs of developing countries with limited available resources. This situation found a sympathetic ear in Halfdan Mahler, who was elected director-general in 1973. He was concerned that "in many countries, the health services are not keeping pace either in quantity or quality with the changing populations, and many are even getting worse."[43] WHO's constitutional, as well as moral, responsibility was therefore to act as an international health conscience by drawing attention to, and leading the world in addressing, the needs of poorer countries. This was the purpose behind the adoption of Resolution WHA30.30 in 1976, upon the request of the director-general, stating that he would "reorient the working of the Organization with a view to ensuring that allocations of the regular program budget reach the level of at least 60 percent in real terms towards technical cooperation and provision of services by 1980." As Edgren and Moller write, this put WHO on the road to becoming "the specialized agency most heavily oriented towards the provision of technical co-operation."[44]

As part of this shift in emphasis, a new paradigm in thinking about health also began to emerge, centered on the principles of primary health care (PHC) and the related Health for All by the Year 2000 strategy. In previous decades, WHO had focused on technical approaches to health that targeted specific diseases (e.g., malaria, smallpox), transferal of expertise and know-how from the richer to poorer countries, the training of medical professionals, and the construction of hospitals, largely in urban areas. The main problem with this approach was that limited benefits trickled down to the poorer and rural communities. In contrast, the objectives of the PHC approach was to provide equitable access to basic health services for all people. Recalling WHO's definition of health as a fundamental human right, ways were sought to promote health within the limits of available resources, using appropriate technology and paramedical community health workers. To put this approach into operation, the WHA adopted Resolution WHA30.43 in 1976, calling on WHO and national governments to seek "the attainment by all the citizens of the world by the year 2000 of a level of health that will permit them to lead a socially and economically productive life." The key to achieving Health for All by the Year 2000 was primary health care, which would shift health resources from high-tech, vertical, urban, and hospital-based services to low-tech, holistic, locally appropriate, and community-based approaches. Inspired in part by the "barefoot doctors" of China, PHC principles led to the training of thousands of community health workers and the establishment of hundreds of rural health centers. Other programs were initiated to promote safe drinking water, basic sanitation, food supply and nutrition, essential drugs, and maternal and child health. Declaring their shared commitment to these goals, WHO and UNICEF issued a joint report on PHC and cosponsored the International Conference on Primary Health Care held in Alma-Ata, Kazakstan, in 1978. The conference was a landmark in international public health. Participants enthusiastically pledged their support in the Declaration of Alma-Ata, which urged governments to formulate national policies, strategies, and plans of action to launch and sustain primary health care.

Another important development in WHO activities during this period was its challenge of the commercial practices of transnational corporations (TNCs). As an extension of demands by developing countries for a NIEO and corresponding efforts to reduce their vulnerability to instabilities in the international political economy, it was argued that codes of conduct were needed to regulate the commercial and industrial activities of TNCs in the developing world. As part of this movement, TNCs in the pharmaceutical, food, and tobacco industries came under increased scrutiny by scholars, NGOs, activists, and policy makers. Beginning with the food industry, concerns began to be raised in the early 1970s that poverty, unsanitary conditions, and illiteracy were leading to misuse of breast-milk substitutes or infant formula products. Attention began to be drawn to the many children in developing countries who were becoming malnourished, and even dying, as a result of mothers using products that were marketed as superior to breast milk. The campaign was taken up in WHO in 1974 when the WHA passed Resolution WHA27.43, which urged "member countries to review sales promotion activites on baby foods and to introduce appropriate remedial measures, including advertisement codes and legislation where necessary." This was followed by many years of intense lobbying by NGOs for an international agreement, among them the Infant Formula Action Coalition and International Baby Food Action Network, on a scale unprecedented in WHO. In May 1981, the WHA adopted the International Code on the Marketing of Breastmilk Substitutes by a vote of 118:3:1 (the United States opposed). The voluntary code restricts companies from such marketing practices as distributing free samples to new mothers in hospitals, paying commissions to health workers for sales, and using uniforms for sales representatives similar to those of nursing staff.[45]

The political mobilization of NGOs and their increased activism in WHO extended to the marketing of pharmaceuticals during this period. Until the mid-1970s, WHO's role in drug policy was confined to important tasks concerning nomenclature, labeling, safety, and quality control. This was carried out through the Pharmaceuticals Unit. This limited remit began to change with growing evidence of bad practice in the promotion, prescribing, and use of drugs. Foremost were the problems of overprescribing, antibiotic resistance, reliance on expensive imports, and rapidly rising drug costs. Amid growing debates at the national and international levels over drug policies, WHO issued a Model List of Essential Drugs in 1977, to be used by national governments to guide the acquisition and use of drugs in such a way as to optimize limited resources. Access to safe, affordable, and effective drugs was recognized in the Declaration of Alma-Ata as one of the eight basic components of primary health care. A new unit, the Drugs Policies and Management Unit, was created to implement the new approach, which led to the creation of the Action Programme on Essential Drugs in 1981. A voluntary code on the marketing of drugs in the developing world was adopted soon thereafter by the pharmaceutical industry.[46]

The period that began in the early 1970s, with the increased role of WHO in advocating the right to health by all people, did not come without controversy. Indeed, the adoption of the International Code on the Marketing of Breastmilk Substitutes and the Model List of Essential Drugs brought unprecedented conflict to the organization. The initiatives represented a direct challenge to established paradigms of thinking in health and development and, equally important, to major interest groups linked to these paradigms. The debates that ensued abolished the earlier myth of health as apolitical.

The Growth in Special and Other Targeted Programs

While the 1970s proved a heady if often stormy time for WHO, a number of important and major programs were also created that avoided much of this controversy. Many were created jointly with other international organizations, such as the World Bank, UNICEF, the United Nations Population Fund (UNPF), and the UNDP, as well as NGOs such as the Rockefeller Foundation. Due largely to the success of the Intensified Smallpox Eradication Programme, strong support grew for other intensified initiatives to tackle specific health programs. Among the programs created were the Special Programme of Research, Development, and Research Training in Human Reproduction in 1972; the Expanded Programme of Immunization in 1974; the Special Programme for Research and Training in Tropical Diseases in 1974; the Programme for the Control of Diarrhoeal Diseases in 1980; and the Programme for Control of Acute Respiratory Infections in 1982. These were followed from the late 1980s by the Global Programme on AIDS, the Global Programme for Vaccines and Immunization, and the Global Tuberculosis Programme. For the most part, the initiative for these new programs came from within WHO, although, in several cases, other UN organizations, bilateral aid agencies, and private foundations (e.g., the Rockefeller Foundation) were vital as cosponsors and providers of large amounts of EBFs. Indeed, this was the start of unprecedented growth in WHO's budget, as well as a shift in resources from RBFs to EBFs. WHO's total budget grew from approximately U.S.$77.4 million in 1970 to U.S.$427.3 million in 1980.[47] The bulk of these additional resources went to the newly created programs, enabling WHO to expand its activities in response to improved knowledge about major health programs. These resources would also prove vitally important following the imposition of the policy of zero real growth in RBFs in many UN organizations by member states of the Geneva Group since 1980 (see below).

The creation of the Special Programme of Research, Development, and Research Training in Human Reproduction (HRP) was particularly notable in that it represented an expansion of WHO's work in the population field. The question of whether WHO should be involved in population activities first arose in the 1950s when the WHA and the EB decided against direct involvement because of political and religious sensitivities. Then, in the 1960s, amid changing attitudes and policies toward assistance in population control, WHO gradually accepted more involvement. The United States Agency for International Development and Scandinavian governments, in particular, began to provide significant amounts of population assistance, while many developing countries called for a greater role by the United Nations in this field. In response, the World Bank started lending for population programs, and the UNFPA was created in 1969.

By the mid-1960s, WHO was also reconsidering its limited population activities in recognition that "size and structure of the population have repercussions on health conditions."[48] From a biomedical perspective, population became defined within WHO in terms of human reproduction. It was acknowledged that "scientific knowledge with regard to the biology of human reproduction and the medical aspects of fertility control is insufficient" and that WHO could contribute significantly to this research. The results of such research, in turn, could be used to give member states, upon their request, technical advice "for the development of activities in family planning, as part of an organized health service."[49] By the late 1960s, family planning was accepted as "an important component of basic health services," and WHO's effective mandate was interpreted to firmly include assistance to address the "urgent nature of the health problems associated with changes in population dynamics" in some countries.[50] This opened the way for WHO to become even more actively involved in the population field during the 1970s, through the creation of the HRP in 1972. The purpose of the program was to serve as "the main instrument within the United Nations system for conducting, promoting, evaluating and coordinating international research on human reproduction, fertility regulation and family planning." This mandate changed little until 1988, when the World Bank, the UNDP and the UNFPA became cosponsors of the HRP, while WHO remained as executing agency. In addition, the scope of its formal mandate was expanded to include a global coordinating role in reproductive health research.[51]

The Health Paradigm Shifts Again: The Politics of Health Economics

Whereas the 1970s to the early 1980s can be described as a period when WHO focused on the principle of equity in health, as pursued through PHC and the Health for All strategy, by the mid-1980s the health paradigm began to shift again. This shift was due to changes in thinking and practice, both within the health sector and within the wider international development community. In the health sector, a critical debate emerged between advocates of comprehensive and selective PHC. Comprehensive PHC represented WHO's original approach and strategy to support holistic, basic, and appropriate health care. In contrast, the selective PHC approach argued that, given limited resources in most developing countries, only selected health interventions could be targeted and delivered at one time (e.g., immunization, vitamin A supplementation).[52] UNICEF was a strong advocate of this latter approach, which soon led to serious tensions between the two organizations.[53] This debate, between a "horizontal" and a "vertical" approach to health development, remains a key issue of contention to the present day.

Within the broader development community, changes in thinking were entwined with structural changes in the international political economy that directly shaped WHO's working environment. The 1980s brought further recession, a second oil crisis, escalating debt or deficit spending in many countries, and general instability due to rapidly globalizing forces in the world economy. These factors were accompanied, and exacerbated, by ideological shifts toward neoliberalism, which questioned the role of government and supported a strengthening of the private sector. As part of the subsequent downsizing of the public sector, governments worldwide began to pursue health sector reforms that sought to expand the role of the private sector in health financing and health service provision.

In this context, growing discontent was expressed by the major financial contributors to the United Nations over policies associated with achieving a NIEO. The most vocal of critics by far was the American government, particularly under successive Reagan administrations, which withdrew from the International Labour

Organization (ILO) between 1977 and 1980, from the International Atomic Energy Agency (IAEA) between 1982 and 1983, and from the United Nations Educational, Scientific, and Cultural Organization (UNESCO) after 1984 (joined by the United Kingdom and Singapore in 1985). This selective "retreat from multilateralism" was intended to pressure the United Nations to adopt reform measures that would reduce alleged politicization of its activities.

In WHO, similar questions were raised as to its appropriate role in international health cooperation. Although the organization did not experience the degree of acrimony that was directed toward other UN organizations, neither did it escape criticism. Among the charges made against WHO was inappropriate politicization of its technical role. While it was recognized that politics of a "certain kind," namely, questions of membership and representation (e.g., South Africa, Israel, China), had existed in WHO since its creation, politicization in more recent years was seen as part of a broader UN malaise. For some governments, WHO's advocacy of policies that championed the needs of developing countries was seen to be at the expense of its own interests. As well as criticizing certain programs, such as the Action Programme on Essential Drugs, difficult controversies arose in the WHA over Israeli membership in the Eastern Mediterranean Regional Office (EMRO), Egypt's recognition of Israel, and health conditions in the Palestinian territories during the middle to late 1980s. Overall, it was argued that WHO had inappropriately shifted away from normative activities to an overemphasis on technical cooperation activities.[54] As Dadzie writes, by the late 1980s approximately 60 percent of RBFs were being spent on technical cooperation in developing countries.[55] It was clear that there was no longer consensus on what the balance between the two types of activities should be.

While WHO received growing criticism, international health was becoming a far more crowded environment. Many other UN organizations were now active in the health sector, along with NGOs, bilateral agencies, and private foundations. The most prominent has been the World Bank, which rapidly became a key institutional player in the health sector during the 1980s. Until the 1970s, the World Bank largely regarded development in terms of building of infrastructure such as dams, roads, and bridges. Under the influence of WHO and other organizations, it came to recognize the value of investing in human capital and resources. From providing no loans specifically for health projects in 1980, by the early 1990s the World Bank had become the largest source of financing for health. Between 1981 and 1990 annual loan disbursements for health (excluding population and nutrition) grew from U.S.$33 million to U.S.$263 million. Disbursements are expected to exceed U.S.$1 billion by the year 2000. To provide such loans and credits, the World Bank steadily built up health expertise among its staff. This was accompanied by a more vocal role in the development of international health policy, marked by such key publications as *Financing Health Services in Developing Countries: An Agenda for Reform (1987)* and the *World Development Report: Investing in Health* (1993). The main feature of World Bank policies has been strong support for health sector reforms based on neoliberal economic principles and backed by financing unmatched by any other organization.[56]

For WHO, changes in its financing have also been an important consequence of this changing environment. First, the contribution of RBFs came under closer scrutiny and control, notably with the adoption of a policy of zero real growth of RBFs in 1980. Because of discontent with UN financial reform as well as domestic economic problems, RBFs have remained frozen ever since.[57] Second, the United States government withheld or made late payments of RBFs to pressure the organization. In 1985, at the height of American disaffection with the UN system, the Kaussebaum Amendment to the Senate Foreign Relations Act was adopted, which stipulated a 20 percent underpayment of United States contributions to selected organizations until budgetary reforms acceptable to the United States were implemented. This led to serious financial shortfalls in WHO of U.S.$35 million in 1987 and U.S.$50 million in 1988–89. In September 1989, WHO was owed about 38 percent of the current assessment from the United States, with total arrears amounting to over U.S.$65 million for 1990–91.[58] Third, the total budget shifted even more toward voluntary contributions, with EBFs (54 percent) exceeding RBFs (46 percent) by 1990. EBFs were seen as a way a donor government could overcome the principle of "one state, one vote" in the WHA, by which specific activities could be targeted for support through the earmarking of funds. Hence by the late 1980s, the main contributors of EBFs had changed from other UN organizations to a small number of member states. By 1992–93, ten countries contributed 89 percent of EBFs.[59]

An important exception to WHO's budgetary constraints was the Global Programme on AIDS (GPA) created in 1987. Following a series of regional WHO meetings in the mid-1980s and the first International Conference on AIDS held in 1985, a small Control Programme on AIDS was created within the Division of Communicable Diseases in June 1986. Headed by Jonathan Mann and initially funded by RBFs, the program was expanded into the Special Programme on AIDS and, shortly thereafter, the GPA. In addition, the United Nations General Assembly recognized HIV/AIDS as a "worldwide emergency" and called upon WHO to play the "essential directing and coordinating role" within the United Nations in fighting AIDS. National governments were encouraged to establish AIDS programs based on the Global Strategy for the Prevention and Control of AIDS, and "appropriate organizations of the UN system" were requested to work closely with WHO, including channeling technical and financial support. The expansion of staff, funding, and activities that followed during the late 1980s was unprecedented in global health cooperation. Between 1987 and 1990, GPA funding increased from U.S.$18 million to U.S.$100 million. Staff at headquarters grew from three to more than one hundred. By 1988 the GPA had established collaborative projects in 170 countries, with the urgent development of national AIDS strategies the focus of its work. Notably, the GPA went beyond WHO's traditional focus of providing technical expertise, becoming involved in a wide range of activities including mobilizing and channeling resources, training health workers, advocating policy change, and initiating and coordinating research.[60]

Multiple Pressures for Reform: A Renewed World Health Organization for the 21st Century

Despite widespread and strong support given to the GPA and other WHO programs, during the late 1980s to early 1990s criticism of its role in international health began to emerge. Since its creation in 1948, WHO's structure and functions have been the subject of periodic review in response to changes in its operating environment. In 1960, for example, the Secretariat was reorganized by amalgamating field and central services into functionally oriented divisions, thus giving the director-general greater control. Similarly, in 1980 Director-General Halfdan Mahler reported on "WHO's structure in the light of its functions."[61] More recent debates, however, have been spurred by a widespread belief that the organization, as constructed five decades ago, needed to change in order to be able to respond most effectively to the health needs of a different world. By the early 1990s, debates over reform grew as a result of a number of pressures on the organization. The first stemmed from continued discontent on the part of major financial contributors, as described above. Initially seeking to reassert greater influence within the organization, these member states soon initiated a broader discussion of WHO's leadership, decision-making processes, management and administration, and overall raison d'etre. Controversy over the reelection of Director-General Hiroshi Nakajima in 1993, linked to concerns about management style and personal disagreements with prominent members of staff, added further fuel to the debates.[62]

The second source of pressure for reform has come from increased numbers and types of actors in international health. As discussed above, other UN organizations—the World Bank, UNICEF, the UNFPA, the UNDP, the ILO, the Food and Agriculture Organization, the World Food Programme, and the United Nations High Commissioner for Refugees—along with regional organizations (e.g., the European Union), bilateral aid agencies, and NGOs are all contributing to health cooperation and development in the 1990s. Most agree that this increased recognition of the importance of health has been much welcomed. At the same time, this growth of actors has increased confusion over their respective mandates. Competition, rather than cooperation, has characterized the activities of many organizations in an era of insecure and declining funding. The challenge for WHO in this context has been to rethink and reassert its distinct contribution to world health.[63]

Third, many new health needs have emerged. In 1948, WHO had 55 member states, although it carried out activities in many nonmember territories. In the late-1990s this number had almost quadrupled, to 190 member states, following postwar decolonization and, more recently, changes in central and eastern Europe. The new member states do not necessarily have the same needs as those of developing countries in Asia, Africa, and Latin America.[64] In a new world order of newly industrializing countries (NICs), emerging markets, economies in transition, and "countries in greatest need," it is clear that the international community is struggling with conceptualizing and responding to the needs of a more diverse range of countries.

The health needs of member states are also more diverse. In coming decades, all countries will need to address demographic shifts, most notably the trend toward a "greying" world. The links between environmental degradation and health are only beginning to be understood. Environmental degradation is suspected to be behind one of the most worrying health challenges—newly emerging diseases. While the Ebola virus (hemorrhagic fever) has dominated media attention, many other unknown disease agents are regularly discovered. To these emerging diseases must be added new biotypes of existing diseases, such as cholera and tuberculosis, which have evolved, for instance, through multidrug resistance. Deaths from the acquired immunodeficiency syndrome (AIDS) are also expected to exceed eight million by the year 2000, with the fastest infection rates occurring in Asia.

The capacity to respond to more complex situations of conflict, within and between countries, and their consequences has also become a key issue. While the number of major armed conflicts has declined since the end of the Cold War, intermediate and minor armed conflicts have increased.[65] Furthermore, traditional definitions of conflict as taking place between sovereign states do not adequately describe the growing numbers of countries that are politically or economically unstable or are in crisis (e.g., Russia, Liberia). Within countries, there is widespread and growing conflict on a social scale as people struggle to cope with deteriorating life expectancy. Death from accidents, violence, and suicide is increasing in both rich and poor countries, with poverty in almost every category playing a significant role in increasing the likelihood of death or injury from such external causes (e.g., unsafe working conditions, social breakdown, inadequate housing).[66] The result has been a growing number of "complex emergencies," which combine armed conflict with human or natural disasters and social disintegration (e.g., Somalia). The health needs of such populations under stress require different ways of defining and providing health assistance.

Perhaps the biggest challenge for international public health is the growth of poverty worldwide since the late 1980s, resulting in wide disparities across countries and regions along basic health indicators such as life expectancy and infant mortality rate. Life expectancy worldwide ranges from 79 years in Japan to 42 years in Uganda. The health picture is very different in lower and higher income countries. Disease of the circulatory system is by far the biggest killer in the industrialized world, accounting for 47 percent of total deaths in 1993. In contrast, infectious and parasitic diseases remain the greatest threat to life in the developing world, causing 42 percent of all deaths. Among such diseases are malaria (2 million annual deaths worldwide and the cause of 90 percent of all deaths in Africa) and tuberculosis (1,000 new cases every hour and 3 million deaths each year), diseases that until recently were thought to be under control. The substantial re-emergence of tuberculosis, in particular, has been clearly linked to growing poverty and the AIDS pandemic. Almost all cases have occurred among people in the developing world or among poor people in the developed world. Thus, the challenge of providing basic health for all remains an elusive goal.

Fourth, and finally, there have been changing patterns of funding for health cooperation. The United Nations has long been underfunded for the breadth of activities that it has been given responsibility to fulfill. In the late 1990s, major financial contributors to the United Nations face renewed constraints on foreign aid budgets, and there are regular announcements of the United Nation's impending bankruptcy. Health is a sector that has suffered proportionately less from the financial constraints of recent years, given its recognition as a key sector in poverty alleviation and human security. What is changing is the form of financing (i.e., grants versus loans), the institutions through which funds are channeled (i.e., the World Bank, NGOs), and the purpose for which funds are being used (i.e., complex emergencies, health sector reform).

As a consequence of the above pressures, since the early 1990s substantial attention has been given to reforming WHO. In 1992 the EB created a Working Group on the WHO Response to Global Change to study the repercussions of "fundamental political, social, and economic changes taking place throughout the world" on the world health situation and health development work in countries. The working group was asked, in particular, to make recommendations on WHO's structure, leadership role, mission, and means of promoting international health; its coordinating role within the UN system; its priorities, targets, and measurable outcomes; and the technical quality of its work.[67] The report of the working group was discussed at length by the EB in January 1993. The recommendations presented in the report were wide-ranging, with discussion of the mission of WHO, its governing bodies, organizational levels, and country offices, coordination with other UN organizations, technical expertise, research, communications, and budgetary and financial arrangements. The latter included recommendations on the need for clear priority setting, an imput/output approach to budget preparation, and greater involvement of the EB in the management of EBFs. In May 1993 the WHA adopted this report and requested that the EB set priorities among its many recommendations, create mechanisms to monitor their implementation, and report back annually on the progress of reforms. A three-stage schedule for the implementation of recommendations, between 1994 and 1996, was then agreed on, based on six development teams. The responsibility of these teams, composed of multidisciplinary groups of global and regional-level WHO staff, was "to develop policy concepts and management tools to implement rapidly and effectively"[68] recommendations on policy and mission (to report in 1997); program development and management, including financial matters; management information system; information and public relations policy; the role of WHO country offices; and personnel policy.

In 1995, the director-general reported to the EB and WHA that many of the recommendations had already been implemented and that all the recommendations were expected to be implemented "within two to three years depending on the funding available."[69] He assured both groups that he was "carrying the spirit of global change even further than originally requested."[70] Among the key areas of change was the creation of a more "user-friendly" and strategic budget. An initiative for renewing the Health for All strategy was also begun, to reassert the importance of health development on the international agenda and to stimulate individual countries to address the serious health challenges of the coming decades. For this purpose, a new global health policy is being developed through a process of broad consultation with national decision makers, technical experts, politicians, NGOs, business and trade union leaders, religious leaders, and the general public. Over a five-year period, participants in the consultation are encouraged to "take stock of their health situation and expected trends in the next 25 years to identify the main health issues for the country."[71]

The response to efforts by WHO to reform itself has been varied. In general, members of the EB have "commended the progress made in the implementation of the recommendations on global change." At the 1995 meeting of the WHA, member states also approved the direction of change and requested that the director-general "accelerate and sustain the work of the development teams to carry forward the process of WHO reform."[72] The Japanese government, for example, stated that it was "pleased to see tangible achievements and progress, such as the establishment of committees to promote closer cooperation and a more effective relationship between WHO headquarters and its regional offices, financial reforms and efforts to develop a new health strategy for the twenty-first century."[73] However, other member states have been more reserved in their assessments. While there has been recognition that considerable efforts have been made by WHO staff, there remain concerns over the fundamental issues of WHO's mandate and the need to improve priority setting. As stated by the representative of Sweden, "A weakness in the reform process is that WHO's policy and mission have not been discussed. The results have not led to clear conclusions on either priorities or on how to restructure the work of the Organization. It is necessary to identify and then concentrate on strategic areas where WHO can make a difference in global health."[74] More fundamentally, there are concerns that the reform process had been too internally driven by the management (i.e., the Secretariat) rather than by the governing bodies (i.e., the WHA and the EB) themselves.

While WHO has busied itself with internal reforms, a number of initiatives have been presented by members states seeking to exert greater influence over the process. In 1994, the governments of Australia, Norway, and the United Kingdom sponsored a study of EBFs in WHO at the global level. This is being followed up in 1996–97, with the additional sponsorship of Canada, Italy, and Sweden, by a study of WHO support to country programs in 12 low- and middle-income member states. In February 1996, a separate initiative was launched at the Pocantico Retreat in New York, organized by the Rockefeller Foundation, the United States Social Science Research Council, and the Harvard School of Public Health, on enhancing the performance of international health institutions.[75] A further initiative was put forth by the Dag Hammarskjold Foundation, which in April 1996 held a Consultation on Global Health Cooperation in the 21st Century and the Role of the UN System. The initiative is seen as "a starting point for the global reform process leading up to WHO's 50th Anniversary and the World Health Assembly in 1998."

One of the most prominent reforms since the early 1990s has been the replacement of the Global Programme on AIDS (GPA) with the Joint United Nations Programme on HIV/AIDS (UNAIDS) in January 1996. As described above, the GPA was created in 1987 in response to growing concern about the rapidly developing pandemic. It was agreed that the new program would be part of WHO, despite being largely funded by EBFs, and that WHO would be the lead UN organization to direct and coordinate the global strategy to prevent and control the disease.[76] The evolution of United Nations AIDS activities since the late 1980s, however, did not lead to a coordinated effort. Other UN organizations active in the health sector, joined by bilateral donor agencies and NGOs, eventually developed their own HIV/AIDS programs, which came to operate separately from and even competitively with the GPA. Differences in approach emerged that served to distance organizations further. Some argued that WHO's appraoch to the disease remained too biomedically dominated and thus inadequate to provide a multisectoral response to the disease. It was agreed to change the GPA from exclusively a WHO program to UNAIDS, consisting of six cosponsoring UN organizations: WHO, UNESCO, UNICEF, the UNFPA, the UNDP, and the World Bank.[77] The replacement of the GPA with UNAIDS cannot, however, be separated from the high-level politics to reform WHO and the UN system as a whole.

Conclusion

As WHO reaches its fiftieth anniversary in 1998, it can look back proudly at a large number of important achievements. In disease prevention and control, the global eradication of smallpox remains most celebrated. Efforts to eradicate poliomyelitis, leprosy, and dracunculiasis are well under way, and WHO remains central to the prevention, control, and treatment of many other diseases, including malaria, cholera, onchocerciasis, schistosomiasis, measles, and HIV/AIDS. Less visible, perhaps, but equally vital to international health have been WHO's ongoing contributions to epidemiological surveillance, statistical collection and dissemination, nomenclature, technical guidelines, standards, quality control measures, and other knowledge-driven work. WHO remains the world's foremost source of scientific and technical knowledge in health, which it routinely shares with member states and other international organizations through meetings, publications, and technical cooperation. Furthermore, WHO remains the world's "health conscience," advocating the principle of equity through its Health for All strategy and related policies. It is for all of the above work that the world recognizes the need for WHO as a cornerstone of international relations.

In reaching its half century, however, WHO faces a number of fundamental challenges. Some stem from the broader, more globalized environment within which the organization operates. Others are of specific concern to WHO. The answer lies in building on the accomplishments of WHO's past history while responding to the health needs of the imminent future. As with many international organizations in the late 1990s, this begins with the rebuilding of consensus behind the institutions of global governance of which WHO is a central pillar.

Notes

1. N. Howard-Jones, *International Public Health between the Two World Wars: the Organizational Problems* (Geneva: WHO 1978); and WHO, *The First Ten Years of the World Health Organization* (Geneva, 1958), chap. 2.

2. M. D. Dubin, "The League of Nations Health Organisation," in *International Health Organisations and Movements, 1918–1939*, ed. P. Weindling (Cambridge: Cambridge University Press, 1995), 56–80.

3. International Red Cross and Red Crescent Movement, *Red Cross and Red Crescent: Portrait of an International Movement* (Geneva: ICRC, 1992), 15. See also B. Towers, "Red Cross Organisational Politics, 1918–1922: Relations of Dominance and Influence of the United States," in ed. Weindling, *International Health Organisations and Movements, 1918–1939*, 36–55.

4. A. Penrose and J. Seaman, "The Save the Children Fund and Nutrition for Refugees," in *'The Conscience of the World': The Influence of Non-Governmental Organisations in the UN System*, ed. P. Willetts (London: Hurst and Company, 1996), 241–69; and special issue of *Disasters* (1994), vol. 18.

5. WHO, *The First Ten Years of the World Health Organization*, 31–32.

6. WHO, *The First Ten Years of the World Health Organization*, 31–34; P. Weindling, "Constructing International Health between the Wars," in ed. Weindling, *International Health Organisations and Movements, 1918–1939*, 1–16.

7. *Official Records of the World Health Organization* (1948), 1: 39.

8. Ibid.

9. WHO, *The First Ten Years of the World Health Organization*, 44–45.

10. M. Black, *The Children and the Nations: The Story of UNICEF* (New York: UNICEF, 1986).

11. WHO (1948), "Rights and Obligations of Associate Members and Other Territories," *Official Records of the World Health Organization*, 13, 100, pp. 337. Also in WHO, *Basic Documents, 41st ed.* (Geneva, 1996).

12. H. K. Jacobson, "Medicine, Regionalism, and Managed Politics," in *The Anatomy of Influence, Decision Making in International Organization*, ed. R. Cox and H. K. Jacobson (New Haven: Yale University Press, 1974), 177.

13. Statement at the 16th meeting of the second session of the Executive Board, *Official Records of the World Health Organization*, November 9, 1948, 14, p. 46.

14. *Constitution of the World Health Organization*, chap. 6.

15. D. Pitt, "Power in the UN Bureaucracy: A New Byzantium," in *The Nature of UN Bureaucracies*, ed. D. Pitt and T. Weiss (London: Croom Helm, 1986), 29–30.

16. See, for example, E. Daes and A. Daoudy, *Decentralization of Orga-*

nizations within the United Nations System, Part III: The World Health Organization, UN Joint Inspection Unit, JIU/REP/93/2 (Pt. 3) (Geneva, 1993).

17. F. Brockington, *World Health* (London: Churchill Livingstone, 1975), 154.

18. C. Ascher, "Current Problems in the World Health Organization's Program," *International Organization* 6, no. 1 (1952): 39.

19. Ibid., 44.

20. *Constitution of the World Health Organization,* art. 1.

21. N. Sims, "The Roles of the United Nations," *Review of International Studies* 16, no. 1 (1990): 90.

22. For a detailed discussion of these activities, see S. Fluss and F. Gutteridge, *World Health Organization* (Boston: Kluwer Law and Taxation Publishers, 1993).

23. J. Forbes, "International Cooperation in Public Health and the World Health Organization," *The Theory and Structures of International Political Economy,* ed. T. Sandler (Boulder, Colo.: Westview, 1980), 119; and *Constitution of the World Health Organization,* chap. 2.

24. K. Forss, B. Stenson, and G. Sterky, "The Future of Global Health Cooperation: Designing a New World Health Organization," *Current Issues in Public Health* 2 (1996): 138–42.

25. J. P. Vaughan, S. Mogedal, S. E. Kruse, K. Lee, G. Walt, and K. de Wilde, *Cooperation in Health Development: Extrabudgetary Funds in the World Health Organization* (Oslo: Governments of Australia, Norway, and the United Kingdom, 1995), 7–9.

26. WHO, *The First Ten Years of the World Health Organization,* 150–52.

27. Ascher, "Current Problems in the World Health Organization's Program," 29–30.

28. *U.S. Department of State Bulletin* 37, no. 965 (December 23, 1957): 1003.

29. *Constitution of the World Health Organization,* preface.

30. For a historical discussion of the Intensified Malaria Eradication Programme, see J. Siddiqi, *World Health and World Politics: The World Health Organization and the U.N. System* (London: Hurst and Company, 1995), pt. 2.

31. E. Pampana and P. F. Russell, "Malaria: A World Problem," *WHO Chronicle* 9 (1955): 31.

32. Eradication is defined as the ending of transmission and the elimination of the reservoir of infective cases to such an extent that there is no resumption of transmission once the campaign ceases.

33. F. Fenner, D. A. Henderson, I. Arita, Z. Jezek, and I. D. Ladnyi, *Smallpox and Its Eradication* (Geneva: WHO, 1988), 379–86.

34. Ibid., 422–24.

35. UN, *Yearbook of the United Nations* (New York: United Nations, 1962).

36. *Constitution of the World Health Organization*, chap. XII, art. 57.

37. WHO, *The First Ten Years of the World Health Organization*, 136–39.

38. H. Cleaver, "Malaria and the Political Economy of Public Health," *International Journal of Health Services 7*, no. 4 (1977): 571.

39. WHO, *Organizational Study on the Planning for and Impact of Extra-budgetary Resources on WHO's Programmes and Policy*, Doc. EB57/25 (Geneva, 1975).

40. Vaughan et al., *Cooperation in Health Development*, 25–26.

41. UN, *Yearbook of the United Nations* (New York: United Nations, 1948); and UN, *Yearbook of the United Nations* (New York: United Nations, 1970).

42. W. Rostow, *The Stages of Economic Growth: A Non-Communist Manifesto* (Cambridge: Cambridge University Press, 1959).

43. H. Mahler, "An International Health Conscience," *WHO Chronicle* 28 (1974): 207–11.

44. G. Edgren and B. Moller, "The Agencies at a Crossroads: The Role of the United Nations Specialized Agencies," in *The United Nations Issues and Options*, by the Nordic UN Project (Stockholm: Almqvist and Wiksell International, 1991), 132.

45. K. Sikkink, "Codes of Conduct for Transnational Corporations: The Case of the WHO/UNICEF Code," *International Organization* 40, no. 4 (1986): 815–40.

46. N. Kanji, A. Hardon, J. W. Harnmeijer, M. Mamdani, and G. Walt, *Drugs Policy in Developing Countries* (London: Zed Books, 1991); and Z. Chowdhury, *The Politics of Essential Drugs* (London: Zed Books, 1995).

47. Vaughan et al., *Cooperation in Health Development*, chap. 4.

48. World Health Assembly, Resolution WHA18.49, Geneva, May 1965.

49. World Health Assembly Resolution WHA19.43, Geneva, May 1966.

50. World Health Assembly Resolution WHA20.41, Geneva, May 1967; and Resolution WHA21.43, Geneva, May 1968.

51. UNDP/UNFPA/WHO/World Bank Special Programme of Research, Development and Research Training in Human Reproduction, *Challenges in Reproductive Health Research: Biennial Report, 1992–1993* (Geneva: WHO, 1994).

52. J. Walsh and K. Warren, "Selective Primary Health Care: An Interim Strategy for Disease Control in Developing Countries," *New England Journal of Medicine* 301 (1979): 967–74; and J. Walsh and K. Warren, *Strategies for Primary Health Care* (Chicago: University of Chicago Press, 1986).

53. G. Walt, "WHO under Stress: Implications for Health Policy," *Health Policy* 24 (1994): 125–44.

54. L. Altman, "W.H.O. to Cut Staff in Shift of Goals," *New York Times*, January 30, 1977.

55. K. Dadzie, "The United Nations and the Problems of Economic Development," in *United Nations, Divided World*, ed. A. Roberts and B. Kingsbury (Oxford: Clarendon Press, 1988), 154.

56. K. Buse, "Spotlight on International Organisations: The World Bank," *Health Policy and Planning* 9, no. 1 (1994): 444–47.

57. L. Howard, "Where Is the Money to Come From," *World Health* (1986): 9–10; and WHO Doc. EB81/42/Annex, November 13, 1987, 3.

58. P. Taylor, "The United Nations System under Stress: Financial Pressures and Their Consequences," *Review of International Studies* 17, no. 4 (1991): 365–87.

59. Vaughan et al., *Cooperation in Health Development*, 31.

60. J. Mann and K. Kay, "Confronting the Pandemic: The World Health Organization's Global Programme on Aids, 1986–1989," *AIDS*, Supplement 2 (1991): 221–29.

61. WHO, "Study of WHO's Structures in the Light of Its Functions: WHO's Processes, Structures and Working Relationships," Report by the Director-General, World Health Assembly, Doc. A33/2, March 13, 1980.

62. F. Godlee, "WHO in Crisis," *British Medical Journal* 309 (November 26, 1994): 1424–28; F. Godlee, "Interview with the Director General," *British Medical Journal* 310 (March 4, 1995): 583–86; and B. Stenson and G. Sterky, "What Future WHO?" *Health Policy* 28 (1994): 235–56.

63. K. Lee, S. Collinson, G. Walt, and L. Gilson, "A Confusion of Mandates in International Health: Who Should Be Doing What in the United Nations?", *British Medical Journal* 312 (February 3, 1996): 302–7.

64. See, for example, M. Field, "The Health Crisis in the Former Soviet Union: A Report from the Post War Zone," *Social Science and Medicine* 41, no. 11 (1994): 1469–78.

65. Major conflicts are defined as those conflicts resulting in more than 1,000 deaths per year. Intermediate conflicts are defined as causing more than 1,000 deaths over the course of the conflict but fewer than 1,000 deaths per year. Minor conflicts are defined as causing fewer than 1000 deaths. See, for example, J. Macrae, "Conflict: An Aid Policy Issue?" *ODI Briefing Note* (1997).

66. WHO, *World Health Report: Bridging the Gaps* (Geneva: WHO 1995), 35.

67. WHO Resolution EB89(19), Geneva, January 1989.

68. WHO Executive Board, *Working Group of the Executive Board on the WHO Response to Global Change*, Doc. EB89(19), Geneva, January 28, 1992), and *Report of the Preparatory Group*, Working Group on the WHO Response to Global Change, Doc. EB90/4, Geneva, May 18, 1992; and WHO Doc. A48/23, March 22, 1995, p. 4.

69. World Health Assembly, Doc. A47/16, March 29, 1994, p. 3.

70. World Health Assembly, Doc. A48/23, March 22, 1995, p. 3. For a discussion of recent WHO reforms, see K. Lee and K. Buse, "The Reform of the World Health Organisation: What Progress So Far?" *UN and Health Briefing Note* 6 (1998): 1–6.

71. WHO, *Renewing the Health-for-All Strategy: Elaboration of a Policy for Equity, Solidarity, and Health* (Geneva: WHO, 1995).

72. World Health Assembly, Resolution WHA48.15, "WHO Response to Global Change," May 12, 1995.

73. Statement by the Representative of Japan, World Health Assembly, Doc. A48/VR/4, May 2, 1995, p. 13.

74. Statement by the Representative of Sweden, World Health Assembly, Doc. A48/VR/4, May 2, 1995, p. 10; and Sweden, *Statement by the Observer for Sweden to the Ninety-Ninth Session of the Executive Board of WHO*, Geneva, January 17, 1995.

75. *Pocantico Retreat: Enhancing the Performance of International Health Institutions, February 1–3, 1996* (New York: Rockefeller Foundation/Social Science Research Council/Harvard School of Public Health, 1996).

76. UN General Assembly, Resolution 42/8, October 1987. For a detailed discussion of the emergence of international cooperation on AIDS, see L. Gordenker, R. Coate, C. Jonsson, and P. Soderholm, *International Cooperation in Response to AIDS* (London: Pinter, 1995).

77. S. Collinson and K. Lee, "What the UN Does on HIV/AIDS: From the Global Programme on AIDS to UNAIDS," *UN and Health Briefing Note* 5 (September 1996): 1–6; and A. McGregor, "Renewed UN Drive against AIDS," *Lancet* 344 (December 17, 1994): 1693–94.

The Dictionary

A

ACCRA FORUM/INITIATIVE. An international forum held in Accra, Ghana, in December 1991, organized by WHO in collaboration with the government of Ghana, entitled "Health: A Conditionality for Economic Development—Breaking the Cycle of Poverty and Inequity." Attended by heads of state, government ministers, nongovernmental organizations (q.v.), and bilateral and multilateral donor agencies, the meeting addressed ways of integrating the promotion of health into economic policies and development strategies. The forum presented the concept of health conditionality, which states that, in development strategies, the objectives of protection and improvement of health status and quality of life should be defined alongside macroeconomic objectives. The forum adopted the Accra Initiative, in the form of a Declaration and Agenda for Action, which declares, among other things, that health must be given an equal place among other criteria in assessing the quality of development strategies. The initiative proposes that a special international fund be set up for this purpose and that global concern for health be embodied in a global health charter. In the 1992 follow-up to the forum, the World Health Assembly adopted Resolution 45.24, requesting that the director-general (qq.v.) establish a multidisciplinary task force, disseminate the results of the forum to other relevant international organizations, ensure that all WHO programs identify highly vulnerable economic groups, and provide a means of evaluating and improving their health status.

ACTION-ORIENTED SCHOOL HEALTH CURRICULUM. A project initiated by WHO and the United Nations Children's Fund (q.v) in 1985 following an International Consultation on Health Education for School-Age Children (q.v.). The purpose of this project is to access and educate children of school age about health, with emphasis on encouraging students to promote health within their families and communities. *See also* Global School Health Initiative.

ACTION PROGRAMME FOR THE ELIMINATION OF LEPROSY (LEP). A strategy and program adopted by the World Health Assembly (q.v.) in 1991 to eliminate leprosy (Mycobacterium leprae) as a public health problem by the year 2000. Elimination is defined as prevalence of less than one case per 10,000 population. The main strategy for this purpose is multiple drug therapy (q.v.), which was largely developed through research by the UNDP/World Bank/WHO Special Programme for Research and Training in Tropical Diseases (q.v.) and launched in 1985 as the main tool for leprosy control. In 1996 leprosy remained a problem in 60 countries or areas, with 16 countries containing 90 percent of all cases worldwide. Measures taken under this strategy include reaching patients in areas difficult to access, promoting diagnosis and treatment in communities, and setting and achieving targets toward elimination. WHO reports that active cases have declined by 90 percent (from 12 million cases). *See also* Pan American Center for Training and Research in Leprosy and Related Diseases; Special Action Projects towards the Elimination of Leprosy.

ACTION PROGRAMME ON ESSENTIAL DRUGS (APED). *See* Drug Action Programme/Action Programme on Essential Drugs.

ACT OF BOGOTA. An agreement signed in 1960 by member states of the Organization of American States (q.v.) to cooperate in promoting accelerated economic and social development in the Americas region. The agreement included a regional health policy aimed at improving living conditions. *See also* Charter of Punta del Este; Declaration of the Presidents of the Americas.

ACUÑA, HÉCTOR R. (1921–). Dr. Héctor Acuña, of Mexico, served as the director of the Pan American Health Organization (PAHO) (q.v.) from 1975 until 1983. He obtained his medical degree in 1947 and master of public health from Yale University in 1951. Early in his career, he came into contact with international health problems as an epidemiologist and later medical director of the Office for Inter-American Cooperation in Public Health, an agency of the Mexican Ministry of Health and Welfare. He joined the Pan American Sanitary Bureau (q.v.) in 1954 and served as chief medical adviser for eight years in the Dominican Republic, El Salvador, and Guatemala. From 1962 to 1964 he served as the WHO representative and chief medical adviser in Pakistan for the Eastern Mediterranean Regional Office (q.v.) before returning to Mexico to hold various public and private posts, including director for international affairs in the Ministry of Health and Welfare. During his tenure as director, he sought to make PAHO technical assistance to member states more dynamic and effective and to make optimal use of resources in light of political and economic changes taking place in the region.

ACUTE RESPIRATORY INFECTIONS, INTERAGENCY COORDINATING COMMITTEE FOR THE CONTROL OF. *See* International Consultation Meeting on the Control of Acute Respiratory Infections.

ACUTE RESPIRATORY INFECTIONS, INTERNATIONAL CONSULTATION MEETING ON THE CONTROL OF. *See* International Consultation Meeting on the Control of Acute Respiratory Infections.

ACUTE RESPIRATORY INFECTIONS, PROGRAMME FOR THE CONTROL OF. *See* Programme for the Control of Acute Respiratory Infections.

ADMINISTERING AGENCY. A term used to describe an organization responsible for the administration of a program that is jointly owned by more than one United Nations organization. For example, WHO is the administering agency of the Joint United Nations Programme on HIV/AIDS (q.v.). *See also* Executing Agency.

ADMINISTRATION AND STAFF SUPPORT SERVICES (SAS). *See* Division of Personnel.

ADMINISTRATION, BUDGET, AND FINANCE COMMITTEE (ABFC). A committee created in 1994, as part of the Executive Board Working Group on the WHO Response to Global Change (q.v.) reform process, to review the administrative, budgetary, and financial parameters of WHO programs. These responsibilities are of particular importance, given concerns among many member states (q.v.) over the need to simplify and clarify WHO's budgeting process, reduce the lead time for its preparation, and improve the organization's capacity to plan strategically. The seven-member ABFC is composed of the chair or vice chair of the Executive Board (EB) (q.v.) plus one EB member from each region. A member's term of office should not exceed two years. The committee selects a chair from among its members and meets annually in January to work in tandem with the Programme Development Committee (q.v.).

ADMINISTRATIVE DOCUMENT. A document for administrative purposes, including information circulars or forms. At headquarters (q.v.), such documents are prepared by the Secretariat's (q.v.) administrative staff in English and French and translated into other working languages of the organization. *See also* Governing Body Document; Technical Document.

ADOLESCENT HEALTH AND DEVELOPMENT PROGRAMME (ADH). A program created in 1990 to address reproductive and other health needs of adolescents, especially in developing countries. Health risks addressed include alcohol and drug abuse, unsafe abortion, tobacco use, HIV/AIDS, injury, and unhealthy lifestyles. Among its activities have been surveys of health needs, development of training and education materials, and support for regional plans of action. The program also contributes to the Global School Health Initiative, led by the Health Education and Health Promotion Unit within the Division of Health Promotion, Education, and Communication (qq.v.), which seeks to increase the capacity of schools to promote good health. The program was reorganized in 1996 within the Family and Reproductive Health Programme (q.v.). The ADH also works with the United Nations Population Fund and United Nations Children's Fund (qq.v.) in providing information on effective programs and a common agenda for cooperative work among different organizations. *See also* Division of Child Health and Development; Division of Reproductive Health (Technical Support); Special Programme of Research, Development, and Research Training in Human Reproduction; Women's Health.

ADVISORY COMMITTEE ON HEALTH RESEARCH (ACHR). A committee created in 1959, as the Advisory Committee on Medical Research, to advise, guide, and support the work of WHO in the area of medical and health research at the national and international levels. Members of the committee are senior scientists appointed by the director-general (q.v.) to serve for a four-year period. Over time the scope of the committee's work has been expanded. In 1974–75 the World Health Assembly (WHA) (q.v.) endorsed proposals for greater involvement by developing countries and regional offices (q.v.) through, among other things, the creation of regional advisory committees on health research. Regional advisory committees on health research work through each of the six regional offices. The global ACHR has the complex task of coordinating their activities. In 1977 the WHA called for greater collaboration with medical research councils and other institutions within member states (q.v.). With the adoption of the global strategy of Health for All by the Year 2000 the scope of research functions and activities was further broadened to address research issues in policy, organization, and management aspects of health care delivery at the primary level. To this end, WHO expanded its relationship with scientific institutions beyond the existing formal and informal program-related networks and now relies on tens of thousands of scientists worldwide to provide research and training facilities. In 1986 the committee was renamed the Advisory Committee on Health Research to reflect an added emphasis on health promotion and protection. *See also* Expert Advisory Panel; Expert Committee; Health for All; PAHO Advisory Committee on Health Research; WHO Collaborating Center.

AFRICAN GROUP. An informal caucus of African WHO member states (q.v.) whose representatives to the United Nations in Geneva meet periodically to share views and policies and to discuss and plan their positions on a range of global health issues arising in WHO. *See also* Asian Group; Geneva Group; Oslo Group; Western European and Other Group.

AFRICAN PROGRAMME FOR ONCHOCERCIASIS CONTROL (APOC). A program created in 1996 by the World Bank (q.v.) to intensify efforts to control onchocerciasis in the 16 remaining disease-endemic countries in Africa. Based in Ouagadougou, Burkina Faso, jointly with the WHO Onchocerciasis Control Programme (q.v.), the main strategy of APOC is to develop sustainable distribution programs, linked to primary health care (q.v.), for the drug ivermectin. This work is facilitated by the Nongovernmental Development Organizations Coordination Group for Ivermectin Distribution (q.v.) through its partnerships with ministries of health and development of national plans for APOC funding.

AFRICAN REGIONAL OFFICE (AFRO). One of six regional offices (q.v.) of WHO, AFRO was established in Brazzaville, the Congo, in 1951 to serve the health needs of member states (q.v.) in sub-Saharan Africa. The regional office is responsible for planning and executing WHO's work in the region in consultation with member states of the region, who are represented at annual meetings of the regional committee (q.v.). Initially, AFRO's activities were organized into four geographical areas: central, eastern, western, and southern. However, long-term political instability in the Congo caused disruption to AFRO's work and eventually led to the creation of three decentralized operational teams in Cameroon, Mali, and Zimbabwe. Since the 1980s, activities have been governed by the Charter for the Health Development of the African Region by the Year 2000 as part of the Health for All (q.v.) strategy. In recent years, AFRO has focused on organizational reforms under Regional Director Ebrahim Samba, including restructuring of the regional office, mobilization of extrabudgetary funds (qq.v.), and changes to personnel policies. For the period 1996–2000, AFRO's priority areas include the eradication of poliomyelitis and dracunculiasis; prevention and control of HIV/AIDS; malaria control; and implementation of the Renewal of the Health for All Strategy (q.v.). AFRO is also working with the World Bank (q.v.); WHO and the World Bank have been designated the lead agencies for implementing the health component of the United Nations Special Initiative on Africa (q.v.).

AFRICAN REGIONAL OFFICE PROGRAMME OPERATIONS COORDINATION SYSTEM (AFROPOC). A management system used by the African Regional Office (q.v.) for technical cooperation with its member states (qq.v.). The system was introduced in the early 1990s to address problems of decision making, transparency, and efficiency in resource utilization. This management tool, based on the principle of management by objectives, seeks to initiate, certify, and coordinate planning, programming, budgeting, monitoring, and evaluation functions involved in technical cooperation.

AGENDA 21. See United Nations Conference on Environment and Development.

AGING, VIENNA INTERNATIONAL PLAN OF ACTION ON. *See* Global Programme for Health of the Elderly.

AGING, WORLD ASSEMBLY ON. *See* Global Programme for Health of the Elderly.

AGREEMENT ON THE APPLICATION OF SANITARY AND PHYTOSANITARY MEASURES. *See* Codex Alimentarius Commission.

AIDS, ADVISORY COUNCIL ON HIV AND. *See* Global Commission on AIDS.

AIDS AND SEXUALLY TRANSMITTED DISEASES, OFFICE OF HIV/AIDS. *See* Office of HIV/AIDS and Sexually Transmitted Diseases.

AIDS, CONTROL PROGRAMME ON. *See* Control Programme on AIDS.

AIDS DAY, WORLD. *See* World AIDS Day.

AIDS, GLOBAL COMMISSION ON. *See* Global Commission on AIDS.

AIDS, GLOBAL PROGRAMME ON. *See* Global Programme on AIDS.

AIDS, GLOBAL STRATEGY FOR THE PREVENTION AND CONTROL OF. *See* Global Programme on AIDS.

AIDS MANAGEMENT COMMITTEE, GLOBAL PROGRAMME ON. *See* Global Programme on AIDS.

AIDS PREVENTION, LONDON DECLARATION ON. *See* Summit on the Global Impact of AIDS.

AIDS, SPECIAL PROGRAMME ON. *See* Global Programme on AIDS.

AIDS, STANDING COMMITTEE ON. *See* Steering Committee on AIDS.

ALLEYNE, GEORGE A. O. (1932–). Sir George Alleyne, of Barbados, has served as director of the Pan American Health Organization (PAHO), also known as the regional director of the American Regional Office (qq.v.), since 1995. He is a graduate in medicine of the University of the West Indies, Jamaica, where he was later appointed professor and chairman of the Department of Medicine. He also completed postgraduate training in the United Kingdom and the United States. His work with WHO began in 1970, when he became a member of the WHO Nutrition Advisory Panel. In 1972, he was appointed a PAHO consultant on postgraduate fellowship training in South America, and in 1974, an adviser to the Latin American Center for the Biological Sciences and chairman of the PAHO Advisory Committee on Medical Research (q.v.). He joined the staff of PAHO in 1981 as chief of the Unit of Research Promotion and Coordination, in 1983 as director of the Area of Health Programs, and in 1990 as assistant director in charge of supervising PAHO's 28 field offices and technical cooperation (q.v.) with member states (q.v.). He was also responsible for supervising the Emergency Preparedness and Disaster Relief Coordination Program (q.v.) and the Program on Women, Health, and Development. During his tenure as director, Sir George Alleyne has strengthened the responsiveness of PAHO to the technical cooperation needs of member states. He has also developed a strong reputation for efficient and effective management of the organization.

ALMA-ATA CONFERENCE. *See* International Conference on Primary Health Care.

AMERICAN REGIONAL OFFICE (AMRO). *See* Pan American Health Organization.

AMERICAN REGION PLANNING, PROGRAMMING, MONITORING, AND EVALUATION SYSTEM (AMPES). An administrative body created in 1978 by the Pan American Health Organization (PAHO) (q.v.) to formulate, execute, monitor, and evaluate its technical cooperation (q.v.) program. AMPES facilitates dialogue between PAHO and member states (q.v.) of the region regarding health programs and goals, allocation of resources, and PAHO's support to governments. During the 1990s, this internal management system has continued to be developed through the promotion of appropriate planning methods that can be applied to any context, such as the "logical approach" for executing and evaluating projects. This approach has been applied to the refinement of technical cooperation projects within the annual programming of projects, financed with both regular budget and extrabudgetary funds (qq.v.), to reflect more clearly activities aimed at attaining specific objectives and results. In addition, a standardized PAHO/WHO format for the presentation of profiles and projects has been developed, and training activities have been conducted with PAHO/WHO representatives (q.v.) and staff members responsible for projects within the framework of the Central American Health Initiative.

ANTITUBERCULOSIS DRUG RESISTANCE SURVEILLANCE. A special-purpose surveillance system set up in the mid-1990s by WHO and the International Union against Tuberculosis and Lung Disease to tackle the emergence of strains of *Mycobacterium tuberculosis* resistant to antimycobacterial agents. The surveillance system was established in response to significant outbreaks of the disease since the early 1990s caused by the chronic neglect of tuberculosis control. This has resulted in delayed diagnoses, inadequate treatment regimens, high mortality, and nosocomial transmission. The objectives of the global surveillance system are (a) to collect data on the extent and severity of antituberculosis drug resistance in a standardized manner at the country level worldwide; (b) to monitor drug resistance levels in countries identified by WHO as priority for assistance or in countries where knowledge of drug resistance levels may be important for global policy decisions; and (c) to help countries in developing a surveillance system that provides representative data and to improve the diagnostic capacity of laboratories. *See also* Global Tuberculosis Programme.

ARAB GULF PROGRAMME FOR UNITED NATIONS DEVELOPMENT ORGANIZATIONS (AGFUND). A program established in 1981 by Saudi Arabia and consisting of seven member states (q.v.): Bahrain, Iraq, Kuwait, Oman, Qatar, Saudi Arabia, and the United Arab Emirates. The purpose of AGFUND is to support development projects in developing countries and to organize and coordinate aid from the Arab Gulf states to support United Nations development projects that benefit underprivileged populations. While AGFUND has no specific health policy, it supports projects for maternal and child health, disabled people, and provision water and sanitation to rural areas. Between 1981 and 1991, it provided approximately U.S.$24 million to WHO for activities in 87 countries.

AREA OFFICE. An administrative division of the Pan American Health Organization (PAHO) (q.v.) created in the 1970s to replace the zone office (q.v.). The creation of area offices followed an evaluation of PAHO's structure in light of its functions, which led to efforts to strengthen country-level operations and decentralize authority. In 1984 the area office was replaced by the country office (q.v.) as part of a further delegation of authority and administration.

ASIAN BUREAU. See Health Organization of the League of Nations.

ASIAN GROUP. An informal caucus of Asian member states (q.v.) (including Australia, Japan, and New Zealand) established in 1996 whose representatives to the United Nations in Geneva meet periodically to share views and policies and to discuss and plan their positions on a range of global health issues arising in WHO. See also African Group; Geneva Group; Oslo Group; Western European and Other Group.

ASSESSED CONTRIBUTION. See Regular Budget Funds.

ASSESSMENT OF RISK AND METHODOLOGIES (ARM). See Programme for the Promotion of Chemical Safety.

ASSISTANT DIRECTOR-GENERAL (ADG). A senior official of WHO appointed by and directly answerable to the director-general (q.v.) to oversee responsibility for a major area of WHO's work. This may be policy-based, administrative, or an information area. Traditionally, ADGs in WHO are appointed from countries that are permanent members of the United Nations Security Council. This post is not subject to the United Nations scale of professional grades. In 1996 there were seven assistant directors-general in WHO. See also Executive Administrator; Executive Director.

ASSOCIATE MEMBER. A territory or group of territories that do not have responsibility for the conduct of their international relations, who are admitted by the World Health Assembly (WHA) (q.v.) upon application made on behalf of such territories by the member state (q.v.) or other authority having responsibility for them. Representatives of associate members should be chosen from the local population. Associate members have the right, among others, to participate without vote in the

WHA, its main committees, and selected subcommittees; to propose items for inclusion in the provisional agenda; to receive equally all notices, documents, reports, and records; and to participate equally in special sessions. Associate members may also submit items to the Executive Board (q.v.) but may not be members of it.

ASVALL, JO EIRIK (1931–). Dr. Jo Asvall, of Norway, has served as regional director of the European Regional Office (qq.v.) since 1985. After completing medical studies in Norway and the United States, he trained as a WHO malariologist in Jamaica, Mexico, and Ecuador and soon after became head of the WHO Malaria Team for Togo and Dahomey (Benin) in West Africa in 1959. In 1963, he returned to Norway to work as a clinician in a cancer hospital. He subsequently joined the Public Health Service in the Ministry of Social Affairs, where he served in a number of senior positions.

AUDIT AND OVERSIGHT, OFFICE OF INTERNAL. *See* Office of Internal Audit and Oversight.

AUDITED ACCOUNTS AND FINANCIAL STATEMENTS. An annual report of actual income and expenditure submitted by the Division of Budget and Finance to the World Health Assembly (qq.v.). *See also* Proposed Programme Budget.

AUDIT, OFFICE OF INTERNAL. *See* Office of Internal Audit and Oversight.

AUDITOR, EXTERNAL. *See* External Auditor.

B

BABYFOOD CODE. *See* International Code on the Marketing of Breastmilk Substitutes.

BABY-FRIENDLY HOSPITAL INITIATIVE. An initiative jointly organized by WHO and the United Nations Children's Fund (q.v.) that focuses on the role of health services in the promotion of safe motherhood, child survival, and primary health care (q.v.). The initiative puts forth a number of criteria that hospitals need to meet to obtain "baby-friendly" status. Among the criteria is nondistribution of free or low-cost supplies of breast milk substitutes. By 1995 more than 14,000 hospitals in some 160 countries had achieved "baby-friendly" status. *See also* International Code on the Marketing of Breastmilk Substitutes; Mother-Baby Package.

BAMAKO INITIATIVE (BI). An initiative first presented in 1987 by the executive director of the United Nations Children's Fund (UNICEF) (q.v.), James Grant, at the meeting of the regional committee of the African Regional Office (qq.v.) held in Bamako, Mali. The initiative, which was adopted at the meeting and subsequently jointly sponsored by WHO and UNICEF, seeks to establish a financing scheme for essential drugs in developing countries through community health revolving funds. The initiative proposed that UNICEF would provide essential drugs for use in maternal and child health clinics at the primary level and that the drugs would be sold to patients. The proceeds from this method of cost recovery would be spent on health workers' salaries and improving the quality of primary health care (q.v.) services. Mechanisms for community representation and participation in decision making were also proposed. The initiative was met by early concerns over the ethics and feasibility of user charges in developing countries and, in particular, its impact on access to health care. In WHO there were concerns that the initiative could even undermine the essential drugs policy. Despite these concerns, UNICEF set up the Bamako Initiative Management Unit (BIMU) to implement the policy in several African countries, supported by the African Regional Office (q.v.), as well as a joint committee with WHO to discuss policy development. By 1995 the BI had been implemented in 22 (out of 46) member states (q.v.) in the African region. In 1995 the BIMU was restructured, but the initiative continues to be supported in designated countries. *See also* Drug Action Programme/Action Programme on Essential Drugs.

BASIC HEALTH SERVICES MODEL. A model suggested by WHO in 1965 in an effort to rationalize the use of scarce health resources in developing countries. The proposed scheme resembled a planetary system, with a hospital in the center surrounded by three to four health centers, each with a group of health posts as their satellites. All would be organized under the national ministry of health. The health posts and centers would be responsible for basic curative and preventive care, health education, and maternal and child health services, while the hospital would provide maternity care and more specialized treatment for serious illnesses and accidents. To promote this model, WHO dispatched public health experts throughout the developing world to set up pilot projects that were intended to be replicated on national scales. In collaboration with WHO, the United Nations Children's Fund (q.v.) provided medical supplies, basic drugs, vaccines, laboratory equipment, refrigerators, and vehicles. Despite some initial successes at reducing infant mortality rates in some countries, by the late 1960s the pilot projects were deemed to be failing. The projects were not integrated with existing national health structures, were too dependent on highly trained staff, and were technologically inappropriate for the developing world. The failure of this model led, in the 1970s, to a rethinking of approaches to health care in the developing world. *See also* Health for All; Primary Health Care.

BASIC RADIOLOGICAL SYSTEM (BRS). A system supported by WHO from the mid-1970s to address the lack of access to modern radiology technology by most of the world's population. The BRS was developed using a simplified type of equipment capable of dealing with 80–90 percent of cases requiring radiological examination in a primary health care (q.v.) context. A series of meetings on the new system was held at the regional and headquarters level, including meetings with equipment manufacturers, during the 1970s and 1980s. However, acceptance and dissemination of the technology have remained limited by considerations of cost, maintenance, and energy supplies, harsh climatic conditions, and the need for qualified operators.

BEGG, NORMAN D. (1906–1956). Dr. Norman Begg, of the United Kingdom, served as regional director of the European Regional Office (EURO) (qq.v.) from 1952 to 1956. Born in China, he received his medical degree (1929) and doctorate in medicine (1933) from the University of Aberdeen, and his diploma in public health from the University of London (1932). He joined the United Nations Relief and Rehabilitation Administration (q.v.) in 1946 to work in Poland, first as an epidemiologist and then as chief of the health division. He became a staff member of the Interim Commission (q.v.) in 1947 and in 1949 was transferred to Geneva, where he was put in charge of the Special Office for Europe. With the steady expansion of WHO's work in Europe, EURO was created, and in 1951 Dr. Begg was elected its first regional director.

BERNARD, LEON (1872–1934). Dr. Leon Bernard, of France, served as regional director (q.v.) of the Special Office for Europe, the forerunner of the European Regional Office (q.v.), from 1940 to 1952. After completing training in medicine in 1900, he taught histology in the faculty of medicine at the University of Paris. He was appointed professor of hygiene in 1919 and, as such, placed great emphasis on social medicine and the problems of poor social conditions as a factor in the control of epidemics. His main specialty was tuberculosis, particularly in infants, on which he wrote extensively. Based on this work, he served on numerous public health commissions, including the Health Commission of the League of Nations. He is widely seen as one of the founders of the Health Organization of the League of Nations (q.v.). His subsequent career in international health included service as head of the Temporary Health Committee of the League of Nations, a long-standing member of the Health Committee of the League of Nations, professor of clinical tuberculosis, president of the Conseil Superieur d'Hygiène Publique (in the late 1920s), and secretary-general of the International Union against Tuberculosis. In this last capacity, he favored the creation of the Health Organization of the League of Nations, with the Office International d'Hygiène Publique (q.v.) obtaining representation in an advisory capacity. Since 1950, WHO has awarded a prize in his name for outstanding service to social medicine. See Leo Bernard Prize and Medal.

BIENNIAL BUDGET. See Proposed Programme Budget.

BIG SIX. A set of priorities for international health work, which was recommended by the Interim Commission to the first World Health Assembly (qq.v.) in 1948. These priorities were malaria, tuberculosis, venereal diseases, maternal and child health, nutrition, and environmental sanitation. The Big Six came to serve as a framework for the global and regional health activities of WHO until the early 1950s.

BLINDNESS, GLOBAL DATABASE ON. See Prevention of Blindness.

BLINDNESS, PREVENTION OF. *See* Prevention of Blindness.

BLUE BOOKS. *See* Proposed Programme Budget.

BLUE, RUPERT. Dr. Rupert Blue, of the United States, served as chairman of the Pan American Sanitary Bureau, the forerunner of the Pan American Health Organization (qq.v.), from 1911 to 1920.

BOARD OF TRUSTEES. *See* International Center for Diarrhoeal Disease Research, Bangladesh.

BRUNDTLAND, GRO HARLEM (1939–). Dr. Gro Harlem Brundtland of Norway has served as director-general (q.v.) since January 1998. Medically trained and educated in Oslo and Harvard University, she then held various posts in the government medical services. She became minister of the environment in 1974 and prime minister of Norway in 1979. Reelected three times, as prime minister she chaired the World Commission on Environment and Development, which led to the Rio Conference (q.v.). She also played a prominent role at the International Conference on Population and Development (q.v.) held in Cairo in 1994. Dr. Brundtland has expressed strong support for helping developing countries and reforming WHO internally.

BUDGET AND FINANCE, DIVISION OF. *See* Division of Budget and Finance.

BUDGET, PROPOSED PROGRAMME. *See* Proposed Programme Budget.

BUDGET SURPLUS. A financial term used in WHO to refer to the difference between the effective working budget (q.v.) and the total obligations actually incurred for the financial period concerned, after taking into account the net effects of the operation of the exchange rate facility (q.v.).

C

CAIRO AGENDA. The Agenda for Action on Relaunching Africa's Economic and Social Development, adopted in 1995 by African heads of state and government at a meeting held in Addis Ababa, Ethiopia. The agenda reaffirms that Africa's development is the responsibility of African governments and people and that priority must be given to (a) governance, peace, stability, and development; (b) food security; (c) human resources development and capacity building; (d) resource mobilization; and (e) regional economic cooperation and development. The Eastern Mediterranean Regional Office and African Regional Office (qq.v.) are contributing to efforts to translate these commitments into action. *See also* Working Group on Continental Africa.

CAMBOURNAC, FRANCISCO JOSE CARRASQUEIRO 1903–   ). Dr. Francisco Cambournac, of Portugal, served as regional director of the African Regional Office (qq.v.) from 1954 until 1964. After receiving his medical degree in 1929, he specialized in tropical medicine, hygiene, and malaria. From 1934 to 1943 he worked with the Rockefeller Foundation (q.v.) on malaria and other research. During the 1940s he served on several missions to study health conditions in Portuguese colonies. In 1946 he became professor of hygiene at the Tropical Medicine Institute, Lisbon, and served as an observer for the Portuguese government at the International Health Conference (q.v.).

CANCER COMMISSION. *See* Health Organization of the League of Nations.

CANCER INFORMATION DISSEMINATION SERVICE, SELECTIVE. *See* Latin American Cancer Research Information Project.

CANCER, INTERNATIONAL AGENCY FOR RESEARCH ON. *See* International Agency for Research on Cancer.

CANCER REGISTRIES, INTERNATIONAL ASSOCIATION OF. *See* International Association of Cancer Registries.

CANCER RESEARCH INFORMATION PROJECT, LATIN AMERICAN. *See* Latin American Cancer Research Information Project.

CANDAU, MARCELINO GOMEZ (1911–1983). Dr. Marcelino Candau, of Brazil, served as WHO's second director-general (q.v.) from 1953 to 1973. A trained malariologist who qualified in medicine and public health, he participated in the malaria eradication campaign undertaken by the Brazilian government in 1939 in cooperation with the Rockefeller Foundation (q.v.). Between 1943 and 1950, he was director of division, assistant superintendent, and superintendent of the Public Health Special Service in Brazil. Dr. Candau joined WHO in 1950 as director of the Division of Organization of Health Services, assistant director-general (q.v.) in charge of advisory services (1951), and assistant director of the Pan American Sanitary Bureau (1953) (q.v.). As director-general, he strongly believed in the need for centralized control at headquarters (q.v.). His period of office saw a significant expansion of WHO's activities, including the initiation of major programs to eradicate malaria and smallpox and the expansion of the environmental health program. The costs and difficulties of the Intensified Malaria Eradication Programme (q.v.), in particular, occupied much of his efforts.

CARIBBEAN FOOD AND NUTRITION INSTITUTE (CFNI). An institute founded in Kingston, Jamaica, in 1967 through an agreement signed by the Pan American Health Organization (q.v.), the Food and Agriculture Organization, the University of the West Indies, and the governments of Jamaica and Trinidad and Tobago. The purpose of the institute is to promote food and nutrition policies aimed at feeding the region's population through the provision of technical cooperation (q.v.) in human and material resource mobilization, personnel training, technical aid, information dissemination, and the promotion of norms, policies, and strategies relating to food and nutrition. As a result of the work of the institute, protein-calorie malnutrition is no longer a major problem in most Caribbean countries. *See also* Institute of Nutrition in Central America and Panama; International Conference on Nutrition; Joint WHO/ UNICEF Nutrition Support Programme.

CENTER FOR ENVIRONMENTAL HEALTH ACTIVITIES (CEHA). A center of the Eastern Mediterranean Regional Office (q.v.) created in 1985 in Amman, Jordan, as the technical arm and information exchange unit of the region's environmental health program. Its activities include the Regional Environmental Health Information Network (CEHANET) launched in 1988 to provide information services to member states (q.v.) of the region. CEHA also maintains a collaborative program with specialized regional and international organizations in various fields of environmental health.

CENTER FOR HEALTH DEVELOPMENT. A WHO center opened in March 1996 in Kobe, Japan, to undertake multisectoral research in support of policy decisions by studying health development and the interrelationships among its determinants (i.e., social, cultural, economic, demographic, epidemiologic, and environmental). The center seeks to bring together health and public health researchers and practitioners, as well as urban planners, economists, environmental scientists, social demographers, epidemiologists, and computer and health information specialists. Headed by a director (q.v.), the center forms part of a worldwide network of health research centers and institutions in both industrialized and developing countries. Research results are shared within the international community using modern communication technologies. The work of the center is financed by the Kobe city authorities and private enterprises, which have committed U.S.$6 million annually for its first ten years.

CENTERS FOR DISEASE CONTROL AND PREVENTION (CDC). An agency of the United States Department of Health and Human Services whose mission is to promote health and the quality of life by preventing and controlling disease, injury, and disability. With its headquarters in Atlanta, Georgia, the CDC includes 11 centers, institutions, and offices, including the National Center for Infectious Diseases, the National Center for Injury Prevention and Control, the National Immunization Program, the National Center for HIV, STD, and Tuberculosis Prevention, and the International Health Program Office. Staff total 6,900, based throughout the United States and overseas. The CDC frequently works with WHO to respond to sudden outbreaks of diseases in countries around the world. For example, the CDC was closely involved in responding to the outbreak of the Ebola virus in Zaire in 1995. *See also* Division of Emerging and Other Communicable Diseases.

CENTRAL EMERGENCY REVOLVING FUND. A fund of extrabudgetary funds (q.v.) set up in 1992 by the United Nations General Assembly to finance activities in response to natural and man-made disasters that lead to human problems. In 1992 the fund reached its target of U.S.$50 million in contributions from 25 member states (q.v.). Advances to United Nations organizations for emergency relief work included U.S.$5.5 million to WHO for its humanitarian programs in Somalia and the former Yugoslavia. *See also* Division of Emergency and Humanitarian Action.

CERTIFICATION SCHEME ON THE QUALITY OF PHARMACEUTICAL PRODUCTS MOVING IN INTERNATIONAL COMMERCE. A certification scheme adopted in 1969, and based in the Pharmaceuticals Unit (q.v.), to deter the export, import, and smuggling of falsely labeled, spurious, counterfeited, or substandard products, particularly in developing countries. The scheme is based on the principles that the concept of quality must be built into the product and that primary responsibility resides with the manufacturer. The resulting scheme is based on reliable national systems of licensing, independent analysis of finished products, and inspection to verify that all manufacturing operations are carried out in conformity with accepted norms referred to as "good manufacturing practices" (GMP). The principles stipulated by the scheme are periodically revised to take into account changes in manufacturing technology, and the development of new pharmaceuticals and their markets.

Following an evaluation in 1984, which concluded that the scheme had proven value, it was extended by the World Health Assembly (q.v.) in 1988 to also cover certification of (a) veterinary products administered to food-producing animals; (b) starting materials for use in dosage forms when they are subject to control by legislation in the exporting and importing member states (q.v.); and (c) information on safety and efficacy. In 1992, administrative guidelines were adopted by the WHA to promote and facilitate use of the scheme. The guidelines require that each participating member state attest to the competent authority of another member state whether (a) a specific product is authorized to be placed on the market within its jurisdiction or, if not, why that authorization has not been granted; (b) the plant in which it is produced is subject to inspection at suitable intervals to establish that the manufacturer conforms to GMP as recommended by WHO; and (c) all submitted product information, including labeling, is currently authorized in the certifying country. In 1993, 135 of 186 member states had agreed to participate in the scheme.

CHARTER OF PUNTA DEL ESTE. A charter agreed to at the Extraordinary Meeting of the Inter-American Economic and Social Council held in Uruguay in 1961, which emphasized the importance of planning in addressing social and economic development problems. The charter presented two objectives: (a) to increase life expectancy by a minimum of five years; and (b) to enhance the capacity of people to learn and produce by improving individual and collective health. It was recommended that each country prepare a national plan for the 1960s as a long-range measure to ensure well-planned health development. The charter was also accompanied by a Ten-Year Public Health Program, which served as a framework for national development policies that closely linked health objectives with overall social and economic development goals. The role of the Pan American Health Organization (PAHO) (q.v.) was to undertake programming and steering efforts to address the region's health problems, leading to the creation of an office at headquarters (q.v.) for planning purposes. With the adoption of the charter, PAHO convened a Task Force on Health at the Ministerial Level (q.v.) in 1963 to promote the health development goals of the charter and the program. An Alliance for Progress was also formed among regional governments to accelerate development and improve living conditions. *See also* Act of Bogota; Declaration of the Presidents of the Americas.

CHEMICAL SAFETY, INTERNATIONAL PROGRAMME ON. *See* International Programme on Chemical Safety.

CHEMICAL SAFETY, PROGRAMME FOR THE PROMOTION OF. *See* Programme for the Promotion of Chemical Safety.

CHEMICAL SAFETY, STEERING COMMITTEE ON. *See* International Programme on Chemical Safety.

CHERNOBYL. *See* International Programme on the Health Effects of the Chernobyl Accident (IPHECA).

CHIANG MAI DECLARATION. A declaration issued at the International Consultation on the Conservation of Medicinal Plants held in Chiang Mai, Thailand, in 1988 to prevent the extinction or severe genetic loss of such plants. The declaration affirms the importance of medicinal plants in health care, particularly in the use of traditional medicine in developing countries, and calls on the United Nations, other international organizations, and governments to take action on their conservation and sustainable use.

CHILD CONGRESS, PAN AMERICAN. *See* Pan American Child Congress.

CHILD GROWTH, WHO GLOBAL DATABASE ON. *See* WHO Global Database on Child Growth.

CHILD HEALTH AND DEVELOPMENT, DIVISION OF. *See* Division of Child Health and Development.

CHILD HEALTH FOUNDATION PRIZE AND FELLOWSHIP. A prize and fellowship given by the Child Health Foundation, which was created in 1980 with a contribution by Dr. Ihsan Dogramaci, then a member of the Executive Board (q.v.). The prize, consisting of a bronze medal and sum of money, is given biennially to a person having accomplished outstanding service in the field of child health. The fellowship is given every four years for research in social pediatrics.

CHILD HEALTH PHASE II. A five-year (1991–96) program to accelerate immunization in the Americas region, launched by the Pan American Health Organization (q.v.) and the United States Agency for International Development with additional support from Rotary International, the Canadian Public Health Association, and the Inter-American Development Bank. The purpose of the program is to provide additional financial resources to complete the campaigns to eradicate polio, measles, and neonatal tetanus as well as reduce the occurrence of all vaccine-preventable diseases. *See also* Children's Vaccine Initiative; Expanded Programme on Immunization; Global Programme for Vaccines and Immunization.

CHILDREN'S VACCINE INITIATIVE (CVI). An initiative launched in 1990 by WHO, the United Nations Children's Fund (UNICEF), the United Nations Development Program (UNDP), the World Bank, and the Rockefeller Foundation (qq.v.) to develop a "supervaccine" that would protect children against all major childhood diseases with a single vaccine. As such, the initiative can be seen as a Manhattan Project for vaccines, intended to provide a new infusion of technology into immunization. Initiated by UNICEF in the early to middle 1980s, following a decision by its executive director (q.v.), James Grant, to allocate 5 percent of the organization's budget to applied and operations research, the idea gradually gained support from other organizations. This support was expressed in the Declaration of New York presented at a meeting of interested groups and individuals concerned with immunization in September 1990. The declaration called on the world to use "current science to make new and better vaccines." The proposed vaccine would be given in one or two doses, early in life, combined in unusual ways so as to reduce the number of injections; it would be more heat stable and could be used against a wide variety of diseases; and it would be affordable. The declaration called on WHO to take the lead role. The CVI secretariat (q.v.) is located within the Global Programme for Vaccines and Immunization (GPV) (q.v.), whose director is also CVI's executive secretary, and its functions carried out by the GPV staff. Annual meetings of a consultative group review the current status of vaccines, immunization, and the control of infectious diseases worldwide. The budget for the initiative was U.S.$5.2 million in 1994. *See also* International Vaccine Institute; Task Force for Child Survival; World Summit for Children.

CHILDREN, WORLD SUMMIT FOR. *See* World Summit for Children.

CHILD SURVIVAL, TASK FORCE FOR. *See* Task Force for Child Survival.

CHISHOLM, GEORGE BROCK (1896–1971). Dr. Brock Chisholm, of Canada, served as the first director-general (q.v.) of WHO from 1948 to 1953, and is widely recognized as one of the principal architects and builders of WHO. A psychiatrist by training, he previously worked as the director-general of Medical Services in the National Department of Defence (1942–44) and deputy minister of National Health and Welfare (1944–46). In 1946 he became a member of the Technical Preparatory Committee (q.v.), for which he is credited with contributing to the broad definition of health achieved in the constitution (q.v.). He then served as executive secretary of the Interim Commission (q.v.) from 1946 to 1948 before being elected as director-general in 1948. During his tenure, he oversaw the establishment of WHO and the negotiation and setting up of the regional offices (q.v.). In his last year in office, Dr. Chisholm proposed to the World Health Assembly (q.v.) that a program of global smallpox eradication should be undertaken by WHO. The initiative was rejected by delegates at the time as too vast and complicated an endeavor, and the subject was not reconsidered until 1958.

CHOLERA RESEARCH LABORATORY (CRL). *See* International Center for Diarrhoeal Disease Research, Bangladesh.

CINDI (COUNTRYWIDE INTEGRATED NONCOMMUNICA-BLE DISEASE INTERVENTION) PROGRAM. A program launched in 1982 by the European Regional Office (q.v.) to support an integrated approach to noncommunicable diseases (i.e., cardiovascular disease, cancer, respiratory diseases, and cirrhosis) focused on risk factors, individual lifestyles, and environmental and social conditions. The program seeks to link partners in the health and nonhealth sectors for the purpose of action aimed at preventing disease and promoting health. Activities include demonstration programs to show how people within a community have understood and responded to health promotion messages and national activities to show policy makers how disease prevention is possible.

CODEX ALIMENTARIUS COMMISSION. An intergovernmental body created by WHO and the Food and Agriculture Organization (FAO) in 1962 to implement the Joint FAO/WHO Food Standards Programme. The program was created to ensure that internationally agreed-on food standards, guidelines, and recommendations are consistent with health protection. The commission draws on international scientific and technical knowledge to ensure that its guidelines and recommendations on food additives, contaminants, pesticide residues, hygiene, nutrition, and technological practices have a scientific basis. In 1993 membership in the commission totaled 145 countries. Since its creation, the Codex Alimentarius has served as a reference source for the General Agreement on Tariffs and Trade (GATT) with respect to technical barriers to trade. This status has increased with the agreement of the Final Act of the GATT Uruguay Round in 1994, the creation of the World Trade Organization, the entry into force of the Agreement on the Application of Sanitary and Phytosanitary Measures concerning the application of food safety, and animal and plant health regulations. *See also* Division of Food and Nutrition.

COMMISSION ON HEALTH AND ENVIRONMENT. *See* United Nations Conference on Environment and Development.

COMMISSION ON HEALTH RESEARCH FOR DEVELOPMENT (COHRED). A commission formed in 1987, as an independent international initiative, for the purpose of improving the health of people in developing countries by strengthening health research. The sponsors of the commission were a group of 16 donors from Europe, North America, Asia, and Latin America, with no funder providing more than 12 percent of the budget. The multidisciplinary commission consisted of 12 members actively involved with biomedical, social, or epidemiological research, with eight members from developing countries. The commission met eight times over two years and commissioned case studies of health research activities, research capacity, and support for research in ten developing countries (i.e., Bangladesh, Brazil, Egypt, Ethiopia, India, Mali, Mexico, the Philippines, Thailand, and Zimbabwe). The 1996 report of the commission, Health Research: Essential Link to Equity in Development, identifies the major research challenges, including persistent diseases, emerging threats, and changing patterns of illness, and presents the structure and needs of an emerging research system to deal with them. See also Essential National Health Research.

COMMISSION ON SUSTAINABLE DEVELOPMENT. See United Nations Conference on Environment and Development.

COMMITTEE A. A main committee of the World Health Assembly (WHA) (q.v.) primarily responsible for program and budgetary matters. Each delegation is permitted representation on the committee, with the chair elected by the WHA upon recommendation by the Committee of Nominations (q.v.). See also Committee B; Committee on Credentials; General Committee.

COMMITTEE B. A main committee of the World Health Assembly (WHA) (q.v.) primarily responsible for administrative, financial, and legal matters. Each delegation is permitted representation on the committee, with the chair elected by the WHA upon recommendation by the Committee of Nominations (q.v.). See also Committee A; Committee on Credentials; General Committee.

COMMITTEE OF COSPONSORING ORGANIZATIONS. See Joint United Nations Programme on HIV/AIDS.

COMMITTEE ON CREDENTIALS. A committee of the World Health Assembly (WHA) (q.v.) consisting of 12 delegates from as many member states (q.v.) appointed at the beginning of each session on the recommendation of the president. The purpose of the committee is to examine the credentials of delegates of members and associate members and to report to the WHA on their validity. Meetings of the committee are held in private.

See also Committee A; Committee B; Committee on Nominations; General Committee.

COMMITTEE ON NOMINATIONS. A committee of the World Health Assembly (WHA) (q.v.) consisting of 25 delegates from as many member states (q.v.) who are appointed at the beginning of each regular session by the president with due regard to geographical distribution, experience, and personal competence. The committee is responsible for proposing nominations for the offices of (a) president and five vice presidents of the WHA; (b) chairs, two vice chairs, and rapporteur for each of the main committees; and (c) members of the General Committee (q.v.). The meetings of the committee are held in private. *See also* Committee A; Committee B; Committee on Credentials; General Committee.

COMMITTEE ON THE RIGHTS OF THE CHILD. A committee created in 1991, as stipulated in the Convention on the Rights of the Child signed in 1989 at the World Summit for Children (q.v.) held by the United Nations Children's Fund (q.v.), to follow up on progress toward the achievement of agreed goals. As a member of the committee, WHO has carried out activities arising from the articles of the convention concerned with health. This includes an action plan covering advocacy, monitoring at the country level, and program development for child health programs.

COMMUNICABLE DISEASES, DIVISION OF. *See* Division of Communicable Diseases.

COMMUNICATIONS AND PUBLIC RELATIONS POLICY. A policy adopted in 1995 by the World Health Assembly (q.v.) to create greater awareness of the objectives and programs of WHO, foster involvement in its work, and advocate the Health for All (q.v.) strategy. The policy was adopted as part of the Executive Board Working Group on the WHO Response to Global Change (q.v.) reform process, as well as in response to unprecedented criticism of the organization.

COMMUNICATIONS SUPPORT UNIT. *See* Office of Health Communications and Public Relations.

COMMUNITY PARTICIPATION. A concept put forth by WHO and emphasized in the Declaration of Alma-Ata as an essential component of primary health care (q.v.). It is broadly defined as the involvement of local people and communities in decisions concerning their health and health care. However, given that the concept has been variably defined in practice, this has led to many different interpretations of its operationalization.

COMPREHENSIVE PRIMARY HEALTH CARE. *See* Primary Health Care.

CONFERENCE AND GENERAL SERVICES, DIVISION OF. *See* Division of Conference and General Services.

CONFERENCE OF EXPERTS ON THE RATIONAL USE OF DRUGS. *See* Revised Drug Strategy.

CONSEIL SANITAIRE, MARITIME, ET QUARANTENAIRE. *See* Egyptian Sanitary, Maritime, and Quarantine Board.

CONSTITUTION. The formal charter of WHO, which establishes the organization and sets out its purpose, objectives, membership, governing and administrative structure, rules and procedures, and financing. Adopted at the International Health Conference (q.v.), the constitution was signed by 61 countries on 22 July 1946. However, it did not come into force until 7 April 1948, when the formal ratification of the constitution by 26 governments was achieved. Amendments to the constitution have been made through resolutions (q.v.) adopted by the World Health Assembly (WHA) (q.v.) following a two-thirds majority vote.

As part of the Executive Board Working Group on the WHO Response to Global Change (q.v.) reform process, in 1995 the WHA requested that the Executive Board (EB) (q.v.) examine whether the constitution needed to be revised and, if so, how best the revision should proceed. The WHA noted that WHO was approaching its fiftieth anniversary and that there had been significant changes in the international system and the organization itself. It also noted that the constitution had not been thoroughly reviewed since its adoption in 1948. In response, the EB established a special group of six EB members late in 1995 to undertake an examination of the constitution and report back to the EB in 1997. The report of this special group, which met in May and October 1996, presented their deliberations in relation to WHO's mission and functions and advice on any provisions of the constitution that may need further examination. The five recommendations of the report included the need to coordinate constitutional reform with the Renewing the Health for All Strategy (q.v.), to improve coordination of mandates and operations of relevant United Nations organizations, and to review the evolutionary development of WHO since 1948 in terms of its achievements and weaknesses. *See* Appendix A.

CONSULTATIVE COMMITTEE ON PROGRAMME DEVELOPMENT. *See* South-East Asia Regional Office.

CONTROL PROGRAMME ON AIDS. A short-lived program created in 1986 by WHO in response to discussions held at the first International Conference on AIDS (q.v.) in 1985 on the need for a global response to the disease. Located in the Division of Communicable Diseases (q.v.), its activities were wholly funded by regular budget funds (q.v.). The program was then expanded as the Special Programme on AIDS in 1987, which became the Global Programme on AIDS (q.v.) soon after. *See also* Joint United Nations Programme on HIV/AIDS.

COORDINATING COMMITTEE ON NURSING AND MIDWIFERY. A committee established in 1992 at headquarters (q.v.) to ensure that nursing and midwifery are taken into account in policy making and program planning within WHO. The purpose of the committee is to support the efforts of the Nursing Unit, now known as Nursing and Midwifery, to gain recognition of the role of nurses and midwives in the work of many divisions and units of WHO at headquarters and at regional and country levels. *See also* Nursing and Midwifery.

COORDINATION, ADVISORY, AND REVIEW GROUP. *See* Global Tuberculosis Programme.

COSPONSORED PROGRAM. A program that is jointly initiated, owned, managed, and financed by two or more organizations, both from within and outside the United Nations system. Where such a program is based in WHO, WHO can serve as the executing or administering agency (qq.v.). For example, the Joint United Nations Programme on HIV/AIDS (q.v.) is cosponsored by WHO, UNESCO, the United Nations Population Fund, the United Nations Children's Fund, the United Nations Development Program, and the World Bank (qq.v.). *See also* Special Programme on Research, Development, and Research

Training in Human Reproduction; UNDP/World Bank/WHO Special Programme for Research and Training in Tropical Diseases.

COUNCIL ON THE IMPLEMENTATION OF THE EARTH SUMMIT'S ACTION PROGRAMME FOR HEALTH AND THE ENVIRONMENT. A council set up by WHO in 1993 following the United Nations Conference on Environment and Development (q.v.) of 1992. The purpose of the council, composed of senior representatives from selected member states (q.v.), is to advise on the implementation of WHO's strategy on health and the environment, which was developed in response to the conference. The WHO strategy covers issues such as primary health care (q.v.), disease prevention and control, safe water supply, pollution and chemical safety, climate change, and ozone depletion.

COUNTRY OFFICE. An office located within a member state (q.v.) of WHO, often based in the national ministry of health, from where the WHO representative (q.v.) operates. In addition to the WHO representative, the office may consist of other professional staff, temporary technical advisers and consultants, and support staff. However, there is currently significant variation in the size of country offices, with the largest located in the Americas region. The main purpose of the country office is to work with the national ministry of health to implement WHO programs and policies. There are currently about 139 country offices, of which 44 are in Africa. In 1984, the country office replaced the area office in the Pan American Health Organization (q.v.) as part of a further delegation of authority and administration to the country level. As part of the Executive Board Working Group on the WHO Response to Global Change (q.v.) reform process, a review of the role of the country office was initiated in 1995. Among the key concerns, in a report presented to the Executive Board (EB) (q.v.) in 1996, was the need to develop criteria for establishing a country office, guidelines for relations between WHO and the ministry of health, and procedures for the recruitment and appointment of WHO representatives. The director-general (q.v.) will report on the implementation of these recommendations to the EB in 1997. While welcoming this reform initiative, a number of member states, known as the Oslo Group (q.v.), were dissatisfied with the scope of change proposed. This led to the 1996 commissioning of a study of WHO support to programs at the country level. *See also* Area Office; Zone Office.

COUNTRY PROGRAMME ADVISER. *See* Joint United Nations Programme on HIV/AIDS.

COUNTRY STRATEGY NOTE (CSN). A strategy adopted by the United Nations General Assembly in 1989, and introduced in 1992, as part of wider reforms initiated by the Joint Consultative Group on Policies to harmonize and adapt program cycles, common premises, human development programs, and so on among United Nations organizations in the economic and social development fields. To give greater coherence to UN development activities at the country level, the CSN is a "document containing the integrated operational response of the UN system." It is intended to highlight the development needs identified in the national development plans of recipient countries and to outline the inputs of different UN organizations, including WHO, in response to these needs. Formulated by national governments, generally with the assistance of the United Nations Development Program (q.v.) through the resident coordinator system (q.v.), CSNs are submitted to the government bodies of relevant UN organizations to guide and encourage their country activities to be more responsive, relevant, and coordinated. By 1995, 84 countries were in the process of preparing CSNs.

COUNTRY THEME GROUP. *See* Joint United Nations Programme on HIV/AIDS.

CUMMING, HUGH SMITH (1869–1948). Dr. Hugh Cumming, of the United States, served as the director of the Pan American Sanitary Bureau (PASB), the forerunner of the Pan American Health Organization (qq.v.), from 1920 to 1946. During his tenure with the PASB, he also served as assistant United States surgeon general, a position facilitated by the close relationship between the PASB and the United States Public Health Service. In these roles, he represented the United States at many meetings of the Office International d'Hygiene Publique (OIHP) (q.v.) and was a long-standing member of the Health Committee of the League of Nations. In this capacity, he favored integration of the OIHP with the Health Organization of the League of Nations (q.v.). During the latter part of his tenure, Dr. Cumming strongly defended the continued independence of regional health organizations against the creation of a single international health organization.

D

DARLING FOUNDATION MEDAL AND PRIZE. A prize awarded by the Darling Foundation since the 1930s to honor the memory of Dr. S. T. Darling, who was accidentally killed during a study mission of the Malaria Commission of the League of Nations. Established by private funds, the foundation periodically grants a medal and prize to a malariologist for outstanding contributions in the field of epidemiology, therapy, and control of malaria. With the disestablishment of the Health Organization of the League of Nations (q.v.), WHO assumed responsibility for administering the prize in 1948. The Darling Foundation Committee recommends to the Executive Board (q.v.) the recipient of the prize, and the award is then presented at the World Health Assembly (q.v.).

DAUBENTON, FRANÇOIS. Dr. François Daubenton, of South Africa, served as regional director of the African Regional Office (qq.v.) from 1952 to 1954.

DEAFNESS AND HEARING IMPAIRMENT, PREVENTION OF. See Prevention of Deafness and Hearing Impairment.

DECLARATION OF CARACAS. See Pan American Child Congress.

DECLARATION OF NEW YORK. See Children's Vaccine Initiative.

DECLARATION OF THE PRESIDENTS OF THE AMERICAS. A declaration and program of action signed in Punta del Este, Uruguay, by governments of the Americas region in 1967 that addressed the need for regional economic and social development. The declaration recognized health as a fundamental factor in development and stipulated that health considerations be taken into account in all development projects. See also Act of Bogota; Charter of Punta del Este.

DEPUTY DIRECTOR-GENERAL. The senior official of WHO who is second in command to, and appointed by, the director-general (q.v.) to carry out all delegated responsibilities. This post is not subject to the United Nations scale of professional grades.

DIARRHOEAL AND ACUTE RESPIRATORY DISEASE CONTROL, DIVISION OF. *See* Division of Diarrhoeal and Acute Respiratory Disease Control.

DIARRHOEAL DISEASE RESEARCH, BANGLADESH; INTERNATIONAL CENTER FOR. *See* International Center for Diarrhoeal Disease Research, Bangladesh.

DIARRHOEAL DISEASES, PROGRAMME FOR THE CONTROL OF. See Programme for the Control of Diarrhoeal Diseases.

DIRECTING COUNCIL. The governing body of the Pan American Health Organization (PAHO) (q.v.), which performs functions delegated to it by the Pan American Sanitary Conference (q.v.), acts on its behalf between meetings of the conference, and carries out its decisions and policies. The council is composed of one representative from each member state (q.v.) of the region. The representatives are designated from among specialists in public health, preferably officials of national public health services. Each representative may be accompanied by one or more alternates and advisers. Each member state officially represented has the right to one vote. The director (q.v.) of PAHO also participates in the council *ex officio* without the right to vote. The functions of the council include electing member states to serve on the executive committee (q.v.), reviewing annual reports of the chairman of the executive committee and the director, reviewing and approving biennial programs and budgets, electing an interim director when necessary, and approving the establishment of branch offices.

DIRECTION, COORDINATION, AND MANAGEMENT. One of four broad and interlinked categories of WHO programs for 1990–95. The work in this category of programs is concerned primarily with formulation of WHO policy and its promotion among member states (q.v.) and in international political, social, and economic forums. *See also* Health Science and Technology; Health Systems Infrastructure; Program Support.

DIRECTLY OBSERVED TREATMENT, SHORT-COURSE (DOTS). A strategy for the treatment of tuberculosis promoted by WHO since the late 1980s as the key to halting the current global epidemic. The promotion of this strategy has included the production of guidelines for national programs, training materials, and workshops for health professionals. *See also* Global Tuberculosis Programme.

DIRECTOR. A senior staff member at headquarters (q.v.) who is responsible for a division within WHO. *See also* Assistant Director-General; Director-General; Executive Administrator; Executive Director.

DIRECTOR-GENERAL. The executive head of WHO, who serves as chief technical and administrative officer. He is elected by the World Health Assembly (WHA) (q.v.) every four years, following nomination by Executive Board (EB) (q.v.) members. His primary responsibilities include the appointment of Secretariat (q.v.) staff, the preparation of annual financial statements and budget estimates, and the representation of WHO in high-level United Nations meetings. Since 1948 there have been five long-serving and medically qualified directors-general (q.v.): Brock Chisholm (1948–53), Marcelino Candau (1953–73), Halfdan Mahler (1973–88), Hiroshi Nakajima (1988–1998) and Gro Harlem Brundtland (1998–present) (qq.v.). In January 1996, following controversy over the process of electing and reelecting the director-general, the EB adopted amendments to the constitution (q.v.) that set out criteria a candidate for the post must fulfill. These include a strong technical and public health background, competency in organizational management, sensitivity to cultural, social, and political differences, and sufficient skill in at least one of the official and working languages of the EB and WHA. In addition, nominations for the post may henceforth be submitted by any member state (q.v.) and not by EB members only. Selected candidates are then interviewed by the EB, which nominates one candidate on the shortlist by secret ballot. Finally, the maximum number of terms of office was set at two terms, with the then-current incumbent exempt from this stipulation.

DIRECTOR-GENERAL, ASSISTANT. *See* Assistant Director-General.

DIRECTOR-GENERAL, DEPUTY. *See* Deputy Director-General.

DIRECTOR-GENERAL'S AND REGIONAL DIRECTORS' DEVELOPMENT PROGRAMME (DGP). One of three functional components of WHO's management process known as program review (q.v.). As decided by the director-general and regional directors (qq.v.), this component provides support and seed money for innovative and high-priority technical cooperation (q.v.) activities that cannot be specifically determined during preparation of the Proposed Programme Budget (q.v.). The function of the program is to provide a flexible method for financing the initiation or strengthening of priority activities, generally on a one-time basis, thereby often attracting complementary funding. For example, funding may be used to meet emergency situations created by natural disasters or epidemics. *See also* Executive Management; Managerial Process for WHO's Programme Development; Regional Directors' Development Fund.

DIRECTOR OF PROGRAMME MANAGEMENT. A senior staff member in each regional office (q.v.) who is responsible for technical programs in the region. Reporting directly to the regional director (q.v.), responsibilities of the post include coordinating all activities that involve technical cooperation (q.v.) with member states (q.v.). The purpose of the post is to improve the planning, programming, monitoring, and evaluation of technical cooperation activities in the regions.

DIRECTOR PAN AMERICAN HEALTH ORGANIZATION. The executive head of the Pan American Health Organization (q.v.). This post also serves as regional director of the American Regional Office (qq.v.) of WHO.

DISABILITY ADJUSTED LIFE YEARS (DALY). *See* Global Burden of Disease.

DIVISION OF ANALYSIS, RESEARCH, AND ASSESSMENT (ARA). A division created in 1996, as part of the Health Systems Development Programme, with the restructuring of the Division of Strengthening of Health Services (qq.v.). The purpose of the division is to provide technical expertise for capacity building in member states (q.v.), to achieve the goal of Health for All (q.v.), and to increase quality, cost-effectiveness and equity (q.v.) in health care. *See also* Division of Organization and Management of Health Systems; Division of Strategic Support to Countries in Greatest Need.

DIVISION OF BUDGET AND FINANCE (BFI). A division created in 1948 to provide effective, efficient, and flexible budgetary and financial support and services at all organizational levels, under all sources of funds, in accordance with applicable regulations, rules, and resolutions. This is achieved through regular biennial meetings of headquarters (q.v.) and regional staff, who evaluate activities and review outstanding matters. All activities at the global level are subject to systematic internal management reviews. In addition, the work of the staff is regularly audited by both internal and external audit. *See also* Administration, Budget, and Finance Committee; External Auditor; Office of Internal Audit and Oversight.

DIVISION OF CHILD HEALTH AND DEVELOPMENT (CHD). A division created in 1996, within the Family and Reproductive Health Programme, to replace the Division of Diarrhoeal and Acute Respiratory Disease Control (qq.v.). The primary objective of the division is to significantly reduce mortality and morbidity associated with the major illnesses of childhood in the developing world. The division is responsible for promoting the Integrated Management of the Sick Child (q.v.) and, in collaboration with the United Nations Children's Fund, supporting the Baby-Friendly Hospital Initiative (qq.v.). The CHD also provides technical support to member states (q.v.) in planning, implementing, and evaluating national efforts to improve child health, including the provision of guidelines and training materials. *See also* Adolescent Health and Development Programme; Division of Reproductive Health (Technical Support); International Code on the Marketing of Breastmilk Substitutes; Special Programme of Research, Development, and Research Training in Human Reproduction; Women's Health.

DIVISION OF COMMUNICABLE DISEASES (CDS). A division created in 1948, as the Division of Communicable Disease Services, to carry out epidemiological surveillance in relation to communicable diseases, training in epidemiology, and maintenance of the International Health Regulations (q.v.). During the 1950s, this work focused on four main categories: venereal diseases and treponematoses; edemo-epidemic diseases; veterinary public health; and tuberculosis. By the 1960s, the emergence and reemergence of other diseases led to an increase in scope and size of the division, renamed the Division of Communicable Diseases, to include units for bacterial diseases, epidemiological surveillance, international quarantine, leprosy, parasitic diseases, smallpox eradication, and virus diseases. In October 1995 the division was disestablished, and many of its functions were assumed by a newly created Division of Emerging and Other Communicable Diseases (q.v.).

DIVISION OF COMMUNICABLE DISEASE SERVICES. *See* Division of Communicable Diseases.

DIVISION OF CONFERENCE AND GENERAL SERVICES (CGS). A division created in 1968, when WHO moved to its current headquarters (q.v.), to provide support services to programs and activities at headquarters and regional offices (q.v.) as required. Prior to this, WHO was located within the main United Nations site, and such services were provided by the United Nations. The division is divided into three units. Building and Office Services is responsible for maintaining all buildings, grounds, and technical installations at headquarters; producing all types of printed materials; and managing office accommodation and storage. Communications, Records, and Conference Services receives, distributes, and dispatches all communications; maintains files, archives, and related record systems; and coordinates arrangements for constitutional and other meetings. Supply Services procures supplies such as drugs, hospital and teaching equipment, and laboratory supplies; arranges for the transport of supplies and equipment, procures supplies for member states (q.v.) and other parties on a reimbursable basis; and organizes inventory control at headquarters.

DIVISION OF CONTROL OF TROPICAL DISEASES (CTD). A division created in 1990 to provide technical advice and assistance to all countries affected by tropical diseases. These are defined as diseases that occur in the tropical regions or areas located between the Tropic of Cancer and the Tropic of Capricorn, including malaria, leprosy, dracunculiasis, schistosomiasis, onchocerciasis, leishmaniasis, and Chagas disease. Together, these diseases affect one-tenth of the world's population. The objectives of the CTD are (a) to develop global strategies for integrated control of major tropical diseases; (b) to provide active support for planning and implementation of control programs at regional, subregional, and national levels; (c) to take part in mobilizing resources for disease control where needed and to coordinate national and international participation; (d) to promote research and training that is directly relevant to control needs; and (e) to propagate standards and indicators for epidemiological assessment of the effectiveness of control measures and to maintain information systems for global epidemiological data.

The CTD functions through regional offices, WHO representatives (qq.v.), and ministries of health and collaborates with other health-related organizations. It also participates in other WHO activities, such as the Programme for the Evaluation of Pesticides, the Panel of Experts on Environmental Management for Vector Control, and the Interdivisional Group on Vector Control. Disease control objectives and activities are reviewed by expert committees, study groups (qq.v.), regional and interregional meetings, and meetings of interested parties. The CTD had a total staff of 56 in 1994–95 and a budget of U.S.$13.2 million in regular budget funds (q.v.) and U.S.$8.8 million in extrabudgetary funds (q.v.). *See also* Intensified Malaria Eradication Programme; Onchocerciasis Control Program; UNDP/World Bank/WHO Special Programme for Research and Training in Tropical Diseases.

DIVISION OF DIARRHOEAL AND ACUTE RESPIRATORY DISEASE CONTROL (CDR). A division formed in 1990 with responsibility for the Programme for the Control of Diarrhoeal Diseases, the Programme for the Control of Acute Respiratory Infections (qq.v.), and the Sick Child Initiative. The division is concerned with important causes of childhood morbidity and mortality and emphasizes improved case management rather than disease prevention. The external monitoring of the division is carried out by a Management Review Committee consisting of representatives of WHO, the United Nations Children's Fund (UNICEF), the United Nations Development Program (UNDP), and the World Bank (qq.v.). The committee meets annually and is concerned with overall policy, donor coordination, and division management. In addition, each program within the division has a technical advisory group of scientific and technical experts and a meeting of interested parties composed of donor governments, other member states (q.v.), and participating organizations. Over 80 percent of contributions to the division, which reached U.S.$13 million for the 1994–95 biennium, comes from extrabudgetary funds (EBFs) (q.v.). The main contributors of EBFs have been Australia, Canada, Denmark, Finland, France, Italy, Japan, the Netherlands, Norway, Sweden, the United Kingdom, and the United States, with additional funds provided by UNICEF, the UNDP, and the International Development and Research Center (Canada). About two-thirds of funding is allocated for health services, and one-third for research. In 1996 the division was replaced by the Division of Child Health and Development (q.v.).

DIVISION OF DRUG MANAGEMENT AND POLICIES (DMP). A division created in 1988 to develop, harmonize, and promote national and international standards for monitoring and maintaining the quality, safety, efficacy, and rational use of pharmaceutical and biological products. The division consists of three main programs: the Biologicals Standardization Programme; the Drug Safety Programme; and the Quality Assurance Programme. In addition, the division supports national regulatory authorities through registration, legislation, and training. Overall development of guidelines and standards is carried out in consultation with member states, nongovernmental organizations (qq.v.), the pharmaceutical industry, regional offices (q.v.), and other WHO technical programs. In addition, three expert committees (q.v.) are regularly convened to make recommendations: the Expert Committee on Biological Standardization; the Expert Committee on Specifications for Pharmaceutical Preparations; and the Expert Committee on the Use of Essential Drugs. Finally, the work of the division is supported by the biennial meetings of the International Conference of Drug Regulatory Authorities (q.v.). *See also* Drugs Policies and Management Unit.

DIVISION OF EMERGENCY AND HUMANITARIAN ACTION (EHA). A division created in 1994 to replace the Division of Emergency Relief Operations (q.v.) as a result of recommendations by the Task Force on Emergency and Humanitarian Action (q.v.). The new division has responsibility for coordinating international responses to emergencies and natural disasters in the health field. The EHA works in partnership with other member organizations of the United Nations Inter-Agency Standing Committee (IASC) (q.v.) and within the framework set out by the United Nations Department of Humanitarian Affairs. In comparison with its predecessor, the EHA has a stronger and more extensive mandate in the area of humanitarian assistance in emergencies. Located within the director-general's (q.v.) office, the EHA operates in three main areas: emergency relief and rehabilitation, emergency preparedness, and safety promotion and injury control. The overall aim of the EHA is to strengthen the national capacity of member states (q.v.), notably disaster-prone countries, to reduce adverse health consequences of natural and man-made disasters. Activities are funded almost exclusively from extrabudgetary funds (q.v.), which totaled U.S.$32.3 million in 1994, raised through appeals launched independently or with other relief organizations. *See also* Central Emergency Revolving Fund; Division of Emergency Relief Operations; International Programme on the Health Effects of the Chernobyl Accident; Panafrican Emergency Training Centre.

DIVISION OF EMERGENCY RELIEF OPERATIONS (ERO). An expanded division created in 1989, incorporating the former Emergency Preparedness and Response Programme and newly created Emergency Relief Programme, to consolidate and strengthen WHO's ability to respond to health-related emergencies. WHO formally established an emergency unit in the 1970s to coordinate the technical support of various divisions at headquarters with regional offices (qq.v.) for emergency preparedness activities at the country level. In the 1980s, when natural and man-made disasters and complex emergencies increased in number and importance, member states (q.v.) called on WHO to tackle disaster relief as well.

WHO's involvement in emergency preparedness was boosted by the United Nations General Assembly's initiation of the International Decade for Natural Disaster Reduction in 1989 (Resolution 44/236). An interagency working group was subsequently set up to promote the activities of the decade, with WHO as a member. WHO, in turn, created the ERO to support health work in this area. Initially, the division focused on relief and reconstruction in Afghanistan, Namibia, and the occupied Arab territories. It quickly expanded this work, however, to other countries, including Angola, Cambodia, Iraq, Liberia, and the former Soviet Union and Yugoslavia. In 1991 the General Assembly adopted Resolution 46/182 on strengthening coordination of United Nations humanitarian emergency assistance. This led to the creation of the Department of Humanitarian Affairs (DHA) in 1992. In response to these efforts, WHO became a member of the DHA's Interagency Standing Committee and restructured its own emergency division once again in 1992. Relief units with a clear geographical focus were created, and an emergency information unit added. In 1994, the ERO was replaced by the Division of Emergency and Humanitarian Action (q.v.) after a comprehensive review by the Task Force on Emergency and Humanitarian Action (q.v.) of its global operations for humanitarian relief in a rapidly changing field. *See also* International Programme on the Health Effects of the Chernobyl Accident.

DIVISION OF EMERGING AND OTHER COMMUNICABLE DISEASES (EMC). A division created in 1995 to strengthen national and international capacity in the surveillance, prevention, and control of communicable diseases, including those that are new, emerging, and reemerging public health problems. The new division takes over a large part of the staff and activities of the Division of Communicable Diseases (q.v.) and is strengthened by program activities and staff from the Epidemiological Surveillance and Statistical Services unit and the Division of Diarrhoeal and Acute Respiratory Disease Control (q.v.). Following an assessment at headquarters (q.v.) of the organization's performance on recent epidemics (e.g., plague in India, Ebola in Zaire, and yellow fever in Kenya), it was recommended that WHO strengthen its capacity for epidemic response and, in particular, its ability to anticipate needs. To achieve this, the new division promotes the development of national and international infrastructure to recognize, monitor, prevent and control communicable diseases and emerging health problems and supports applied research on their diagnosis, epidemiology, prevention, and control. With an emphasis on rapid deployment, the EMC is intended to intervene more effectively in sudden and rapid outbreaks of disease. Within WHO, the division coordinates its technical support and expertise with the role of the Division of Emergency and Humanitarian Action (q.v.) in resource mobilization and operational support.

DIVISION OF FAMILY HEALTH (FHE). A division created in 1970 to undertake activities concerned with the crucial health factors in the life of the family and individual and to bring about more informed participation by the family in measures to improve its health and that of the community. Initially the division focused on four areas: maternal and child health, human reproduction, health education, and nutrition. Activities included provision of services and advice, training of personnel, operational research into better methods of organization and administration, and coordination with other organizations with related interests. With the creation and restructuring of other divisions, by the late 1980s the FHE was solely responsible for only nutrition and maternal and child health. Debates over potential overlap, or the need for improved integration of activities, with other parts of the organization, such as the Special Programme of Research, Development, and Research Training in Human Reproduction (q.v.), led to a review of family health-related activities in 1994. In 1996 the division was reorganized within a broader Family and Reproductive Health Programme (q.v.).

DIVISION OF FOOD AND NUTRITION (FNU). A division created in 1992 in response to the World Declaration and Plan of Action for Nutrition adopted at the International Conference on Nutrition (qq.v.). The division, accompanied by a strategy for implementing the conference's plan of action, is composed of three previously separate units: the Food Aid Programmes (FAP), Food Safety (FOS), and Nutrition (NUT). The role of the FAP, which is entirely financed by the World Food Programme (WFP), is to ensure that the health implications of food aid projects are properly identified by advising on the design and evaluation of projects in agriculture, rural development, and education. The activities of the FOS center on ensuring conditions and measures to prevent noninfectious health hazards in the animal food chain and to ensure that all food remains fit for human consumption after harvesting and during storage, processing, distribution, and preparation.

The NUT is responsible for supporting countries in five priority areas: assessment, prevention, and management of protein-energy malnutrition; overcoming micronutrient malnutrition; improvements in infant and young child nutrition; preparedness and caring for nutritional emergencies; and prevention of diet-related noncommunicable diseases. In 1994–95 the budget for food and nutrition activities in WHO totaled U.S.$15 million from regular budget funds (q.v.) and U.S.$13 million from extrabudgetary funds (q.v.). Harmonization of WHO's activities with other international organizations, such as the WFP, is carried out by the Global Nutrition Task Force and its working groups. *See also* Codex Alimentarius Commission; Institute of Nutrition in Central America and Panama; Joint WHO/UNICEF Nutrition Support Programme.

DIVISION OF HEALTH PROMOTION, EDUCATION, AND COMMUNICATION (HPR). A division created in the 1980s to implement the priority assigned to health promotion in WHO's ninth general Programme of Work through the integrated approach outlined in the Ottawa Charter for Health Promotion (qq.v.). The special focus of the division is to design and promote policies and programs that (a) maximize the health outcomes of community settings (e.g., schools, workplaces); (b) ensure the appropriate community health response to population aging and increasing chronicity and disability; (c) encourage healthy lifestyles and self-care throughout the lifespan; and (d) secure advocacy for health through media relations and communications support. These objectives are achieved through a communications strategy for WHO and its programs; technical cooperation (q.v.) to strengthen advice and support to member states; and innovation and research to analyze major lifestyle and health trends. To carry out these activities, the division is organized into five components: the Office of Health Communications and Public Relations; the Health Education and Health Promotion Unit; the Occupational Health Unit (OCH); the Rehabilitation Unit (RHB); and the Programme on Aging and Health (AHE) (qq.v.). The division gives priority to alliance building with partners from the public and private sectors and is building a global network for health promotion and communications. *See also* International Conference on Health Promotion.

DIVISION OF HEALTH SITUATION AND TREND ASSESSMENT (HST). A division created in 1996, with the reorganization of the Division of Epidemiological Surveillance and Health Situation and Trend Assessment, to maintain epidemiological and health statistics and to assess, publish, and disseminate validated information for use by member states (q.v.). This information can be used to develop and strengthen national information systems and support national health planning, management, and evaluation. The objectives of the program are (a) to analyze the global health situation and trends, make projects, monitor and evaluate the implementation of the Health for All (q.v.) strategy, and disseminate information related to health and health services; and (b) to cooperate with regional offices (q.v.) and, through them, member states in the development and strengthening of country health information.

The HST is organized into three main sections. The Office of the Director supervises and directs the program; coordinates and cooperates with related programs, regional offices, and relevant international organizations; and provides support for the use of information related to the program. The Health Situation Analysis and Projection (HSP) unit collects, validates, and maintains statistical databases and disseminates information; monitors and evaluates global health policy and strategy; analyzes future global health trends and projects; coordinates and cooperates in international statistical activities; and produces statistical and epidemiological publications. The Strengthening Country Health Information unit (SCI) works with member states to enhance health information systems, procedures, and networks; develop health futures methodology to support policy and planning; strengthen statistical capabilities; and enhance the use of computers for health and data management.

The HST disseminates information through a variety of means, including the WHO Statistical Information System and such publications as the International Classification of Diseases and Related Health Problems and World Health Statistics Annual and Quarterly (qq.v.). The main users of HST data are WHO senior management and technical programs, government institutions of member states, research and educational institutions, industry and commercial enterprises, international and nongovernmental organizations (q.v.), mass media, and the general public.

DIVISION OF INFORMATION SYSTEM MANAGEMENT (ISM). A division created in the 1990s to develop, manage, and maintain the information needs of WHO through computer and other telecommunications technologies. The division is organized into three units. The Management Information System Support (MIS) is responsible for managing, coordinating, and directing the development, maintenance, and implementation of the WHO Worldwide Management Information System (WHO/MIS) currently being phased in; promoting and coordinating the introduction of the WHO/MIS components in programs at headquarters, regional offices, and country offices (qq.v.); and establishing and managing data and database administrative services. Technological Services (TES) is responsible for managing the computer and related communications infrastructure supporting network-based services at headquarters. User Support and Training (USP) is responsible for managing the development, operation, and evolution of the electronic desktop environment of information technology hardware and software tools at headquarters and providing support to users of the facilities.

DIVISION OF INTENSIFIED COOPERATION WITH COUNTRIES (ICO). A division created in 1989 to promote and coordinate the Intensified Cooperation with Least Developed Countries (q.v.) initiative. Initially located within the Office of the Director-General (q.v.), in 1993 it was reorganized as a separate division headed by an assistant director-general (q.v.). The division was unique within WHO in that it focused not on particular diseases or health risks but rather on whole health systems. Its aim was to encourage and enable WHO to respond in a more coherent and coordinated fashion to the needs of developing countries. For this purpose, its work centers on policy formulation and development, with a strong focus on the country level. Financing of the division's work is strongly dependent on extrabudgetary funds (q.v.), of which Japan and France are the largest donors. In 1996 the division was disestablished, as part of the Executive Board Working Group on the WHO Response to Global Change (q.v.) reform process, and its staff merged with the Division of Strengthening of Health Services (q.v.).

DIVISION OF INTERAGENCY AFFAIRS (INA). A division created in 1988 to fulfill the following objectives: to serve as a focal point for ensuring the coordination of WHO's activities with external partners; and to maintain high-level contacts with member states (q.v.), organizations, and bodies of the United Nations system and other partners, including nongovernmental organizations (NGOs) (q.v.) in order to foster maximum collaboration, relevance, and effectiveness of action and full execution of WHO's mandate and policies. For NGOs, the INA serves as the secretariat (q.v.) of the Standing Committee on NGOs (q.v.), coordinates applications by NGOs for official relations, and establishes liaison with NGOs as a bridge for providing information on WHO policy making and operational activities and facilitating contacts with headquarters, regional offices, and country offices (qq.v.). In 1994, the INA sought to initiate closer working partnerships with health-related international organizations, which led to the first WHO/World Bank (q.v.) review meeting.

DIVISION OF MENTAL HEALTH AND PREVENTION OF SUBSTANCE ABUSE (MSA). A division created in 1996 by integrating a broad spectrum of WHO activities related to mental health and neurological disorders, human behavior, and substance abuse. The main areas of work of the division include mental health promotion; prevention of specific mental, behavioral, neurological, and substance abuse disorders; early diagnosis and treatment of people affected by those disorders; psychosocial rehabilitation; and legal, ethical, and human rights aspects of the work in these areas. *See also* Programme on Mental Health; Programme on Substance Abuse.

DIVISION OF NONCOMMUNICABLE DISEASES (NCD). A division created in the 1960s, as the Division of Health Protection and Promotion, to carry out epidemiological studies, develop guidelines, and support training in the area of noncommunicable diseases. Prior to this period, WHO carried out various programs and comparative studies on cancer and cardiovascular disease. From the late 1960s, the division focused on seven major areas: cancer, cardiovascular diseases, dental health, mental health, nutrition, occupational health, and radiation health. These areas, with the exception of nutrition, which has been moved to the Division on Food and Nutrition (q.v.), have remained key areas of work. In addition, the division carries out activities on chronic rheumatic disease and asthma, diabetes mellitus, human genetics, and methods, management, and coordination. In 1996, Cancer and Palliative Care was moved to the International Agency for Research on Cancer (q.v.). The division's work is supported by regional advisers who are based in regional offices (q.v.). *See also* Victoria Declaration on Heart Health.

DIVISION OF OPERATIONAL SUPPORT IN ENVIRONMENTAL HEALTH (EOS). A division created in 1994, within the Programme for the Promotion of Environmental Health (q.v.), to address the problems of environment and health in urban and rural settings. The Urban Environmental Health (UEH) unit focuses on enabling member states (q.v.) and municipalities to deal with their urban health environment and development situations in a more forward-looking, comprehensive, and integrated manner and promoting the incorporation of health and environment considerations into national and municipal policies and programs governing urban development and growth. In part, this is carried out through the Healthy Cities Initiative (q.v.). In terms of technical support for the solution of environmental health problems, WHO undertakes specific projects relating to air and water pollution, drinking water, waste disposal, sanitation, housing, vector control, and noise. The Rural Environmental Health (REH) unit focuses on the environmental health problems of rural populations, which constitute 50 percent of the world's population. The most serious problems are lack of safe water and basic sanitation, vector-borne diseases, use and misuse of agricultural chemicals, and poor indoor air quality. The aim of the unit is to provide member states with the rationale, tools, and support to improve environmental health services for rural populations and to encourage and enable people to manage their immediate environments to protect their health. *See also* Global Strategy for Health and Environment.

DIVISION OF ORGANIZATION AND MANAGEMENT OF HEALTH SYSTEMS (OHS). One of three divisions created in 1996 as part of the Health Systems Development Programme (q.v.). The purpose of the division is to provide technical expertise for capacity building to member states (q.v.). *See also* Division of Analysis, Research, and Assessment; Division of Strategic Support to Countries in Greatest Need.

DIVISION OF PERSONNEL (PER). A division created in 1948 to carry out the responsibilities of personnel adminstration and human resources management, including the formulation of personnel policies, coordination of the personnel operation, and maintenance of uniform standards and practices at headquarters, regional offices and country offices (qq.v.). The division is composed of four components. The Office of the Director is responsible for WHO's program of personnel management. The Joint Medical Service (JMS) provides medical examinations, emergency treatment, health counseling, and environmental hygiene information; administers sick leave; and maintains medical records of the staff of United Nations organizations based in Geneva and their field staff. Policies and Recruitment Services (SPR) is responsible for the formulation and evaluation of personnel policies; represents WHO at interagency bodies dealing with personnel matters; and supervises post classification and salary administration. Administration and Staff Support Service (SAS) deals with relations between the administration and staff including settling of disputes, staff appraisal and staff relations.

DIVISION OF PUBLISHING, LANGUAGE, AND LIBRARY SERVICES (PLL). A division of WHO responsible for responding to the need for up-to-date, validated, and authoritative information on health matters. Through expertise in scientific publishing, communication, and information sciences, the division acts as WHO's instrument for the transfer of health information to health workers, planners, and administrators in countries. The division has three main components: publishing, language, and library services. When WHO was created in 1948 it assumed the publishing functions of existing international health organizations. To promote wider dissemination of materials, a fund, known since 1959 as the Revolving Sales Fund (q.v.), was set up in 1948 to finance reprints.

Today, WHO's publications policy is guided by the Global Publications Policy Study (1986) and the Publications Committee, created in 1987. In 1993 turnover from publication sales was U.S.$3.6 million, more than double that in 1985. WHO publishes a wide range of materials in six official languages, including periodicals; international norms, standards, and classifications; and books. Low-cost or free distribution to health workers in developing countries enables wider access to WHO publications. Language services translate WHO's official, administrative, and technical documents (qq.v.) and sales publications into six working languages: Arabic, Chinese, English, French, Russian, and Spanish. The Office of Library and Health Literature Services supports people dealing with health issues in their efforts to obtain timely and appropriate information at minimum cost. It operates an information service for WHO and member states (q.v.) in setting up national infrastructures for health information services. *See also* Health Literature, Library, and Information Services.

DIVISION OF REPRODUCTIVE HEALTH (TECHNICAL SUPPORT) (RHT). A division created in 1996 within the Family and Reproductive Health Programme (q.v.). The division is intended to lead WHO's initiatives in reproductive health following the International Conference on Population and Development (q.v.). Units within the division include Family Planning and Population (FPP), Maternal and Newborn Health/Safe Motherhood (MSM), and Reproductive Tract Infections (RTI) (qq.v.). The division's main activities are (a) development and promotion of norms and standards regarding reproductive health services and technologies; (b) providing technical cooperation (q.v.) in the planning, implementation, and evaluation of reproductive health programs; (c) advocating the concept of reproductive health and the inclusion of family planning with maternal and child health programs (e.g., Mother-Baby Package [q.v.]); (d) supporting and carrying out research on technologies that support reproductive health care; and (e) developing training curricula and materials for all health workers concerned with reproductive health. The RHT maintains staff at the headquarters (q.v.) and regional level and has a budget for 1996–97 of U.S. $15.5 million. *See also* Adolescent Health and Development Programme; Division of Child Health and Development; International Conference on Population and Development; Mother-Baby Package; Special Programme of Research, Development, and Research Training in Human Reproduction; Women's Health.

DIVISION OF STRATEGIC SUPPORT TO COUNTRIES IN GREATEST NEED (SSC). One of three divisions created in 1996 as part of the Health Systems Development Programme (q.v.). The purpose of the division is to facilitate coordination of support for countries in greatest need for capacity building at the country level. Crosscutting themes, such as nursing and midwifery and human resources development, serve to integrate the work of the three divisions of the program. *See also* Division of Analysis, Research, and Assessment; Division of Organization and Management of Health Systems.

DIVISION OF STRENGTHENING OF HEALTH SERVICES (SHS). A division created in 1948, initially known as the Division of Organization of Public Health Services, to carry out responsibility for programs on organization of health systems based on primary health care (q.v.) and health systems research and development. In the 1960s the division was renamed the Division of Strengthening of Health Services. The division had the technical mandate to translate and develop the broad global health policies, such as Health for All (q.v.), into country-level operational policies, systems, and strategies. The division consisted of Health Systems Research and Development (HSR), District Health Systems (DHS), and National Health Systems and Policies (NHP). Some argue that its mandate partially overlapped with that of the Division of Intensified Cooperation with Countries (q.v.), creating ambiguities in function. In 1996, following an Informal Consultation on Health Systems Development, the division was restructured within the Health Systems Development Programme and renamed the Division of Analysis, Research, and Assessment (qq.v.). *See also* Division of Strategic Support to Countries in Greatest Need.

DRACUNCULIASIS ERADICATION, INTERNATIONAL COMMISSION FOR THE CERTIFICATION OF. *See* International Commission for the Certification of Dracunculiasis Eradication.

DR. A. T. SHOUSHA FOUNDATION PRIZE. A prize given annually by WHO since 1966 in memory of Dr. Aly Tewfik Shousha, who served as regional director of the Eastern Mediterranean Region (EMRO) (qq.v.) from 1949 to 1957. The prize, consisting of a bronze medal and a sum of money, is given to an individual who has made a significant contribution to any health problem in the region. The recipient of the prize is selected by the Dr. A. T. Shousha Foundation Committee, composed of the chairman, vice chairman, and two members of the Executive Board, with at least one member coming from a member state (q.v.) of EMRO.

DR. COMLAN A. A. QUENUM PRIZE. A prize established in 1987, upon the recommendation of the Regional Committee for Africa, in memory of Dr. Conlan A. A. Quenum, who served as regional director of the African Regional Office (qq.v.) from 1965 to 1984. The prize is given to an individual who has made an outstanding contribution to public health in Africa.

DRUG ABUSE CONTROL, UNITED NATIONS FUND FOR. *See* United Nations Fund for Drug Abuse Control.

DRUG ACTION PROGRAMME/ACTION PROGRAMME ON ESSENTIAL DRUGS (DAP). A program launched in 1981, replacing the Drugs Policies and Management Unit (q.v.), to provide leadership in mobilizing and coordinating global efforts to formulate and implement national drug programs in developing countries. Working in cooperation with member states, nongovernmental organizations (NGOs) (qq.v.), and multilateral and bilateral organizations, DAP's initial focus was to promote essential drugs as a key component of primary health care (q.v.). The concept of essential drugs was first put forth in a report by then director-general Halfdan Mahler to the World Health Assembly (qq.v.) in 1975 documenting the difficulties experienced by many developing countries in acquiring safe, effective, and affordable drugs. By 1977, the Expert Committee (q.v.) on the Selection of Essential Drugs had drawn up a Model List of Essential Drugs (q.v.) for the use of member states in developing similar national lists. While consumer associations and NGOs welcomed the essential drugs concept, large pharmaceutical companies argued that the policy was likely to result in substandard, rather than improved, medical care. They were also concerned that the adoption of essential drug lists would inhibit export markets to the developing world. Active lobbying of WHO from both sides ensued from the late 1970s, leading to unprecedented controversy and debate over the appropriate mandate of WHO.

Following its creation in 1981, there was initial indecision about whether WHO's role was general coordination or more operational. There were also limited resources to implement DAP at the country level, given restrictions on regular budget funds (q.v.) and the small amounts of extrabudgetary funds (EBFs) (q.v.) forthcoming. In 1983, DAP was given strong support from the director-general, who relocated the program to his office. DAP also began to concentrate more on demonstrating how essential drugs were being supported at the country level. Consequently, EBFs grew rapidly, from U.S.$400,000 in 1983 to U.S.$20 million by 1988–89. In 1988, the election of Director-General Hiroshi Nakajima (q.v.) was shortly followed by an attempted move to a newly created Division of Drug Management and Policies (q.v.), accompanied by managerial and administrative changes. This included the creation of a Management Advisory Committee in 1989 by the director-general as a governing body. The committee is composed of representatives of interested parties, namely donor governments, NGOs and other United Nations organizations. The role of the interested parties was formalized, and members were assigned the task of advising the director-general on various aspects of DAP's work. This restructuring was also intended to allow the committee to more closely monitor program activities and administration. Overall, the director-general emphasized that the organizational changes to DAP were ones of administration rather than policy. However, internal resistance led to DAP remaining a separate program, with its own director (q.v.).

Since the early 1990s, there has continued to be debate over whether WHO has, and should, come to play less of an advocacy role for essential drugs and to put greater emphasis on normative activities (q.v.). In the 1990s, activities have been guided by a framework for action known as "4 + 4 + 4", consisting of four underlying principles, four areas of work, and four technical areas of intervention. In 1994 DAP had a total staff at headquarters (q.v.) of 23 and a budget for 1994–95 of U.S.$19.8 million, with less than 10 percent from regular budget funds (q.v.). *See also* Essential Drugs Programme; International Federation of Pharmaceutical Manufacturers Associations.

DRUG DONATIONS, GUIDELINES FOR. *See* Guidelines for Drug Donations.

DRUG MANAGEMENT AND POLICIES, DIVISION OF. *See* Division of Drug Management and Policies.

DRUG MONITORING PROGRAMME, INTERNATIONAL. *See* International Drug Monitoring Programme.

DRUG QUALITY CONTROL LABORATORIES, LATIN AMERICAN NETWORK OF OFFICIAL. *See* Latin American Network of Official Drug Quality Control Laboratories.

DRUG REGULATORY AUTHORITIES, INTERNATIONAL CONFERENCE OF. *See* International Conference of Drug Regulatory Authorities.

DRUGS, ACTION PROGRAMME ON ESSENTIAL. *See* Drug Action Programme/Action Programme on Essential Drugs.

DRUGS AND VACCINES PROGRAMME, ESSENTIAL (EDV). *See* Essential Drugs Programme.

DRUGS, INTERNATIONAL NETWORK FOR THE RATIONAL USE OF. *See* International Network for the Rational Use of Drugs.

DRUGS POLICIES AND MANAGEMENT UNIT (DPM). A unit created in 1977 to implement a new WHO approach to drugs policy based on the concept of essential drugs. Located within the Division of Diagnostic, Prophylactic, and Therapeutic Substance, its staff and activities grew rapidly during the late 1970s. The first director of the unit, Hiroshi Nakajima (q.v.), was later elected as director-general (q.v.) in 1988. The unit was replaced by the Drug Action Programme (q.v.) in 1981.

DRUGS PROGRAMME, ESSENTIAL. *See* Essential Drugs Programme.

DRUGS, SINGLE CONVENTION ON NARCOTIC. *See* Single Convention on Narcotic Drugs.

DRUG STRATEGY, REVISED. *See* Revised Drug Strategy.

DY, FRANCISCO J. (1912–   ). Dr. Francisco Dy, of the Philippines, served as regional director of the Western Pacific Regional Office (WPRO) (qq.v.) from 1966 to 1979. He received his medical degree in 1937 and practiced medicine in the Philippines between 1937 and 1941. After receiving a master of public health degree from Johns Hopkins University in 1942, he joined the United States Army as a commissioned officer, where he served as a malariologist in the Far East. In 1944 he became deputy chief public health officer of the General Headquarters of the United States Army in the Pacific. After the Second World War, Dr. Dy worked as a senior surgeon with the United States Public Health Service before joining WHO in 1950 as deputy chief of the Malaria Section, later the Division of Malaria Eradication. He was transferred to the WPRO in 1951 as regional adviser on malaria and was appointed director of health services in 1958. In 1965, Dr. Dy was elected regional director.

E

EASTERN MEDITERRANEAN REGIONAL OFFICE (EMRO). One of six regional offices of WHO established in Alexandria, Egypt, on 1 July 1949 with 11 member states (qq.v.). Its predecessor, the Egyptian Health, Medicine, and Quarantine Board, later known as the Egyptian Quarantine Board, was created in the 1830s. This organization remained operational in the region until its offices were replaced by EMRO. The first session of the regional committee (q.v.) of EMRO was held earlier, in February 1949. From its early history, EMRO has been subject to periodic political disputes, notably over the recognition of Israel at regional meetings. Because of this dispute, no sessions of the regional committee were held between 1951 and 1953. This situation was addressed at the World Health Assembly (WHA) (q.v.) in 1952 and 1953, leading to a resolution in 1954 that "the Regional Committee for the Eastern Mediterranean should provisionally carry out its duties through being divided into two Sub-Committees." Subcommittee A, composed of ten Arab countries as well as the United Kingdom, France, and Italy by virtue of their dependent territories in the region, held annual meetings in Alexandria between 1954 and 1984 (no sessions were held in 1981 and 1982). Subcommittee B, composed of Israel, France, Italy, and the United Kingdom, held sessions in Geneva between 1958 and 1967. It was intended that the respective reports of each subcommittee would then be consolidated into a single report. This arrangement continued until 1978, when Arab governments severed diplomatic ties with Egypt following the Camp David Accord (1978) agreed to by Egypt, Israel, and the United States. In EMRO, this led to a boycott of Subcommittee A meetings and calls for the regional office to be moved to Jordan. Instead, Subcommittee A meetings were transferred to Tunis, while debate over transferring EMRO continued within the WHA until 1985, when Israel agreed to transfer its regional membership to the European Regional Office (q.v.). The EMRO subcommittees were disbanded soon thereafter, and annual regional committee meetings of remaining member states were resumed. Currently, EMRO consists of 22 member states, with Palestine as a participating member. Priority programs for 1998–99 include eradication of communicable diseases such as dracunculiasis, poliomyelitis, and leprosy; revitalization of the malaria control program; promotion of family and reproductive health; and improved responses to the health problems of natural and man-made disasters.

EBOLA HEMORRHAGIC FEVER, INTERNATIONAL SCIENTIFIC AND TECHNICAL COMMITTEE FOR THE CONTROL OF. *See* International Scientific and Technical Committee for the Control of Ebola Hemorrhagic Fever.

EFFECTIVE WORKING BUDGET. A financial term used in WHO budgeting, referring to those sections of the appropriation resolution (q.v.) against which the director-general (q.v.) is authorized to incur obligations for program activities.

EGYPTIAN QUARANTINE BOARD. *See* Egyptian Sanitary, Maritime, and Quarantine Board.

EGYPTIAN SANITARY, MARITIME, AND QUARANTINE BOARD (CONSEIL SANITAIRE, MARITIME, ET QUARANTENAIRE). An organization created in the 1830s, based in Alexandria, Egypt, to address the public health needs of people who went on pilgrimage to Mecca. The board had been attended by foreign delegations from the 1880s and was represented on the League of Nations Health Committee from 1924. In 1938 the board was renamed the Egyptian Quarantine Board. In 1949 its activities were subsumed under WHO, and the board was expanded to become the Eastern Mediterranean Regional Office (q.v.) of WHO.

ELIMINATION OF IODINE DEFICIENCY DISORDERS (IDD). *See* International Conference on Nutrition.

EMERGENCY AND HUMANITARIAN ACTION, DIVISION OF. *See* Division of Emergency and Humanitarian Action.

EMERGENCY AND HUMANITARIAN ACTION, TASK FORCE ON. *See* Task Force on Emergency and Humanitarian Action.

EMERGENCY PREPAREDNESS AND DISASTER RELIEF CO-ORDINATION PROGRAM. A program of the Pan American Health Organization (PAHO) (q.v.) created in 1987, following the Meeting on International Health Relief Assistance held in San Jose, Costa Rica, in 1986, to facilitate intercountry and intersectoral cooperation and to ensure emergency logistics and communications during emergency health situations. The meeting concluded that there was a need for all donor countries to consult with health authorities affected by natural and man-made disasters before sending relief assistance. Coordination of assistance would be carried out by member states (q.v.) notifying PAHO of their health needs following a disaster, and PAHO would work to strengthen technical cooperation (q.v.) for the development of health emergency preparedness programs and needs assessment. *See also* Division of Emergency and Humanitarian Action.

EMERGENCY RELIEF OPERATIONS, DIVISION OF. *See* Division of Emergency Relief Operations.

EMERGENCY TRAINING CENTRE, PANAFRICAN. *See* Panafrican Emergency Training Centre.

EMERGING AND OTHER COMMUNICABLE DISEASES, DIVISION OF. *See* Division of Emerging and Other Communicable Diseases.

ENVIRONMENTAL EPIDEMIOLOGY NETWORK, GLOBAL. *See* Global Environmental Epidemiology Network.

ENVIRONMENTAL HEALTH ACTIVITIES, CENTER FOR. *See* Center for Environmental Health Activities.

ENVIRONMENTAL HEALTH, DIVISION OF OPERATIONAL SUPPORT IN. *See* Division of Operational Support in Environmental Health.

ENVIRONMENTAL HEALTH INFORMATION MANAGE-
MENT (EHI). *See* Office of Global and Integrated Environmental Health.

ENVIRONMENTAL HEALTH, OFFICE OF GLOBAL AND IN-
TEGRATED. *See* Office of Global and Integrated Environmental
Health.

ENVIRONMENTAL HEALTH PLANNING METHODS AND
HUMAN RESOURCES DEVELOPMENT (EHP). *See* Office of
Global and Integrated Environmental Health.

ENVIRONMENTAL HEALTH, PROGRAMME FOR THE PRO-
MOTION OF. *See* Programme for the Promotion of Environmental Health.

ENVIRONMENTAL HEALTH RESEARCH, GLOBAL HAZ-
ARDS ASSESSMENT, AND RADIATION PROTECTION
(EHR). *See* Office of Global and Integrated Environmental
Health.

ENVIRONMENTAL HEALTH, RURAL. *See* Division of Operational Support in Environmental Health.

ENVIRONMENTAL HEALTH, URBAN. *See* Division of Operational Support in Environmental Health.

ENVIRONMENT AND DEVELOPMENT, UNITED NATIONS
CONFERENCE ON. *See* United Nations Conference on Environment and Development.

ENVIRONMENT AND HEALTH COMMITTEE, EUROPEAN.
See European Conference on Environment and Health.

ENVIRONMENT AND HEALTH, EUROPEAN CENTER ON.
See European Center on Environment and Health.

ENVIRONMENT AND HEALTH, EUROPEAN CHARTER ON.
See European Charter on Environment and Health.

ENVIRONMENT AND HEALTH, EUROPEAN CONFERENCE
ON. *See* European Conference on Environment and Health.

ENVIRONMENT AND HEALTH, NATIONAL INTEGRATED PROGRAMMES ON. *See* National Integrated Programmes on Environment and Health.

ENVIRONMENT AND HEALTH, PAHO REGIONAL PLAN FOR INVESTMENT IN THE. *See* PAHO Regional Plan for Investment in the Environment and Health.

ENVIRONMENT AND SUSTAINABLE DEVELOPMENT, TASK FORCE ON. *See* United Nations Conference on Environment and Development.

ENVIRONMENT, GLOBAL STRATEGY FOR HEALTH AND. *See* Global Strategy for Health and Environment.

ENVIRONMENT, LIBRARY MODULES, HEALTH AND. *See* Health and Environment Library Modules.

ENVIRONMENT LIBRARY NETWORK, GLOBAL HEALTH AND. *See* Global Health and Environment Library Network.

EPIDEMIOLOGICAL INTELLIGENCE SERVICE. *See* Health Organization of the League of Nations.

EQUITY. A principle long advocated by WHO as the basis for providing access to health and health care and, therefore, for guiding the organization's policies and activities. Equity, in relation to health, can be defined as the ability of all people to access health care according to their health needs, regardless of such factors as race, nationality, religion, gender, and wealth. This principle was recognized in the constitution (q.v.), which states that health is "one of the fundamental rights of every human being." During the 1970s, equity became a key policy issue in WHO, in response to evidence of significant disparities in health status and access to basic health care among and within member states (q.v.). This led to the adoption of such policies as Health for All, primary health care (qq.v.), and essential drugs, with Director-General Halfdan Mahler (q.v.) declaring WHO to be the "health conscience" of the world. In the 1980s, WHO expressed concerns over the impact on equity of the Bamako Initiative (q.v.) put forth by the United Nations Children's Fund (q.v.), and the concept of the global burden of disease (q.v.) put forth by the World Bank (q.v.). Since the mid-1990s, WHO has reemphasized the importance of equity and health through Renewing the Health for All Strategy (q.v.) and the publication of the World Health Report (1995) (q.v.).

ESSENTIAL DRUGS LIST. *See* Model List of Essential Drugs.

ESSENTIAL DRUGS PROGRAMME (EDP). A program created in 1977 to encourage governments to develop national drug policies based on the essential drugs concept. Initially known as the Essential Drugs and Vaccines Programme (EDV), it was later renamed the Essential Drugs Programme to reflect the fact that vaccines were handled by the Expanded Programme of Immunization (q.v.). The strategy behind the essential drugs concept derived from the primary health care (q.v.) approach, which required the integration of EDP into other health programs. WHO argued that, by implementing essential drugs programs in geographically designated areas, the supply and cost of essential drugs would be improved. *See also* Drug Action Programme/Action Programme on Essential Drugs; International Federation of Pharmaceutical Manufacturers Associations; Model List of Essential Drugs; Revised Drug Strategy.

ESSENTIAL NATIONAL HEALTH RESEARCH (ENHR). An initiative recommendation of the Commission on Health Research for Development (COHRED) (q.v.) that presents three key ideas. First, every country should develop the capacity to define its health problems and monitor and evaluate its efforts to address them (i.e., country-specific health research). In addition, each country should decide for itself what its contribution should be in addressing global health priorities. Second, undertaking the above depends on functioning partnerships between three key stakeholders: health providers, including health managers and policymakers, researchers, and communities. Third, the concept of health research encompasses the measurement, management and organizational, social and behavioral, and biomedical sciences. Global ENHR initiatives are coordinated through COHRED, which has a small secretariat based in the Geneva offices of the United Nations Development Program (q.v.).

EURO AD HOC COMMITTEE ON THE FUTURE ORIENTATIONS. *See* EURO Standing Committee of the Regional Committee.

EUROCARE PROJECT. A project established by the European Regional Office (q.v.) in 1992 to serve as a forum for high-level decision makers and advisers to discuss health care reform in Europe. The project works through a network that draws on experts in the fields of financing, management, training, and health services and brings together this expertise to discuss and debate key issues. The project also maintains a monitoring system to track health care reforms taking place in the region and to issue "health in transition" profiles and reform overviews on individual countries.

EUROHEALTH. A program initiated by the European Regional Office (EURO) (q.v.) in 1991 to provide a cooperative framework for addressing the health needs of member states (q.v.) of central and eastern Europe and newly independent states. The program has created WHO country liaison offices in target countries, set up a "clearinghouse" information system, and given assistance to governments in preparing frameworks for international collaboration under the Health for All (q.v.) strategy. A 1994 external evaluation of EUROHEALTH found that the program was successfully supporting countries most in need in the region and that there was a continued need for a comprehensive and coherent framework for international collaboration in health. By 1994 support by EURO to EURO-HEALTH represented 90 percent of country program activities in the region.

EUROPEAN CENTER ON ENVIRONMENT AND HEALTH. A center created in 1990 by the European Regional Office (q.v.), in the follow-up to the European Conference on Environment and Health (q.v.) held in 1989. The purpose of the center is to strengthen collaboration on the health aspects of environmental protection and improve understanding of the relation between environmental conditions, human health, and well-being. Coordinated from Copenhagen, Denmark, with additional offices in France, Italy, and the Netherlands, one of the main tasks of the center is to gather data on the nature and extent of environmental health problems in the region. See also European Charter on Environment and Health.

EUROPEAN CHARTER ON ENVIRONMENT AND HEALTH. A charter adopted at the European Conference on Environment and Health (q.v.) in 1989 to serve as the basis for action by central, provincial, and local government, and nongovernmental organizations (q.v.) to improve environmental conditions and human health. *See also* European Center on Environment and Health.

EUROPEAN CONFERENCE ON ENVIRONMENT AND HEALTH. A series of two European regional conferences of ministers of health and the environment to address the links between the environment and health. The first conference, held in 1989, led to the creation of the European Center on Environment and Health (q.v.). Following the second conference, held in Helsinki, Finland, in 1994, which issued the Helsinki Declaration, the European Environment and Health Committee was created by the European Regional Office (EURO) (q.v.) to serve as a permanent mechanism for cooperation among all major organizations dealing with the environment and health in Europe and to support the development of joint environment and health projects in Europe. This mechanism, in the form of a committee with EURO as the secretariat, is composed of representatives of health and environment ministers, EURO, the European Union, the Council of Europe, organizations of the United Nations system, and major development banks with projects in central and eastern Europe. The European Center on Environment and Health (q.v.) provides the main technical arm for the committee.

EUROPEAN ENVIRONMENT AND HEALTH COMMITTEE. *See* European Conference on Environment and Health.

EUROPEAN REGIONAL OFFICE (EURO). One of six regional offices (q.v.) of WHO created in 1952 and based in Copenhagen, Denmark. Its predecessor, the Special Office for Europe, was opened in 1940. The postwar reconstruction of health services was the initial focus for EURO's work, giving way to national health planning and comparative analysis of health services during the 1950s and 1960s. In addition, three long-term programs were established during the 1960s, focusing on the control of cardiovascular diseases, the control of environmental pollution, and mental health. During the 1980s, EURO focused on the approval and development of a European policy based on the principles of Health for All (q.v.). A joint strategy and common European health policy was adopted in 1984, which detailed 38 European targets, along with a system of indicators for monitoring and evaluation.

During the 1990s, EURO's emphasis has shifted to the health needs of countries in central and eastern Europe (CCEE) following the end of the Cold War. Between 1990 and 1995, the number of member states (q.v.) in the region increased from 30 to 50. In addition, Israel joined EURO in 1985, from the Eastern Mediterranean Regional Office (q.v.). The main causes of ill health in the EURO region in recent years have been cardiovascular diseases, injury, cancer, respiratory diseases, infectious and parasitic diseases, and war. However, as a consequence of social, political, and economic changes in the region, there have been greater pressures for EURO to address the resurgence of communicable diseases in countries in transition. In response to the widening health gap between the eastern and western parts of Europe, EURO adopted the EUROHEALTH (q.v.) program in 1991 committed to directing two-thirds of EURO activities to CCEE. To enable financing of increased activities for a growing number of member states in the region, EURO unsuccessfully requested additional regular budget funds (RBFs) (q.v.). While member states of EURO contributed 50 percent of RBFs, the region received only 6 percent of RBF expenditures. The total budget for the region is currently about U.S.$25 million in RBFs and U.S.$30 million in extrabudgetary funds (q.v.).

EUROPE, SPECIAL OFFICE FOR. *See* European Regional Office.

EURO STANDING COMMITTEE OF THE REGIONAL COMMITTEE. A committee set up in 1991, as the Ad Hoc Committee on the Future Orientations, as part of the Executive Board Working Group of the WHO Response to Global Change (q.v.) reform process in 1989. The committee was formally institutionalized in 1993 as a kind of regional Executive Board (q.v.) to create a closer link between the regional office and its member states (qq.v.) and to provide an impetus for change and priority setting for health care development in the European region.

EVANG, KARL (1902–1981). Dr. Karl Evang, of Norway, served as an active member of the Technical Preparatory Committee (q.v.) in 1946 and played a key role in the drafting of the WHO constitution (q.v.). After completing his medical training in 1929, he actively represented Norway in many international health conferences, including the Nutrition Council (1937), the United Nations Relief and Rehabilitation Administration (q.v.) conference (1944), and the San Francisco Conference (1945). As the delegate for Norway to the International Health Conference (q.v.), he is noted for taking joint action with Dr. Szeming Sze (q.v.), of China, and Dr. Geraldo de Paula Souza, of Brazil, to rectify the omission of health from the Charter of the United Nations drawn up in 1945. His support for the creation of a single international health organization led to agreement on a proposal, formally issued by China, to convene the International Health Conference in 1946.

EXCHANGE RATE FACILITY. A financial mechanism used in the budgeting process of WHO under which a charge may be generated against available casual income to finance the net additional costs to the regular budget (q.v.) resulting from differences between the WHO budgetary rates of exchange and the United Nations/WHO accounting rates of exchange prevailing during the financial period. Similarly, any net savings from more favorable rates of exchange are transferred to casual income. *See also* Budget Surplus.

EXECUTING AGENCY. An agency that oversees the implementation of a project funded by another organization. For example, WHO is one of five main executing agencies for projects financed by the United Nations Development Program (UNDP) (q.v.) as governed by the Standard Basic Executing Agency Agreement signed in October 1992. In 1992, the "support cost successor arrangements" were also introduced, resulting in major changes to UNDP's methods of determining how projects would be executed and implemented. In particular, an increase in national execution of UNDP-funded projects reduced the volume of projects for execution and implementation by other UN organizations and thus the level of support costs reimbursed to them. The effect on WHO is believed to be less severe than on other organizations, due to the limited amount of UNDP country-program funds for which WHO is responsible. *See also* Administering Agency.

EXECUTIVE ADMINISTRATOR. A senior official appointed by, and directly answerable to, the director-general (q.v.) to oversee responsibility for a major area of WHO's work. This post is not subject to the United Nations scale of professional grades. In 1996 there was one executive administrator in WHO responsible for health policy in development. *See also* Assistant Director-General; Executive Director.

EXECUTIVE BOARD (EB). A governing body of WHO, the Executive Board (EB) is responsible for giving effect to the decisions and policies of the World Health Assembly (WHA) (q.v.), including preparing budgets and agendas for the WHA, drawing up the six-yearly General Programme of Work (q.v.), advising on questions of a constitutional and regulatory nature, submitting advice or proposals, and taking emergency measures when necessary. The EB meets twice annually, usually in January and then in May following the annual meeting of the WHA. Countries from which EB members are chosen are initially nominated by the six regional committees (q.v.), according to an agreed-on regional allocation, and then appointed by the WHA on a three-year basis. Each year there is a rotating turnover of one-third of EB membership. It is customary that at least three of the five permanent members of the United Nations Security Council (i.e., China, France, Russia, the United Kingdom, and the United States) serve on the EB at any given time. The elected countries, in turn, choose individuals who are technically qualified health specialists and who are expected to act in the interests of international health rather than their national affiliation. A chair is chosen among EB members to serve for a one-year term. The first EB was appointed in 1948 and originally consisted of 18 members. This number was increased to 32 in 1996 to reflect the growth in member states (q.v.).

EXECUTIVE BOARD CHAIR. An official elected from among the membership at the Executive Board (EB) (q.v.) annual meeting in May/June. The functions of the chair include opening and closing each meeting of the EB, directing discussions, according the right to speak, putting questions and announcing decisions, and ensuring the application of rules of procedure. The chair may be assisted in these duties, when necessary, by two vice chairs. An individual who has served as chair is not eligible for reelection until two years have elapsed since he or she ceases to hold office.

EXECUTIVE BOARD SPECIAL FUND. A fund created by the World Health Assembly (q.v.) in 1955 to meet financial emergencies and unforeseen contingencies that may arise. Any amounts so used are replaced by making specific provision in the following budget unless recovered from other sources. *See also* Real Estate Fund; Revolving Sales Fund; Tax Equalization Fund; Working Capital Fund.

EXECUTIVE BOARD WORKING GROUP ON THE WHO RESPONSE TO GLOBAL CHANGE. A working group convened by the Executive Board (q.v.) in 1992 to study the repercussions of "fundamental political, social, and economic changes taking place throughout the world" on the world health situation and health development work in countries. The working group was asked to make recommendations on wide-ranging aspects of the organization: (a) its structure, leadership role, mission, and means of promoting international health; (b) its coordinating role within the United Nations system; (c) its priorities, targets, and measurable outcomes; and (d) the technical quality of its work. The internal consultation process that followed included the formation of regional development teams to prepare regional contributions to the reform process. The final report of the working group, adopted by the World Health Assembly (q.v.) in May 1993, made 47 recommendations for implementation between 1993 and 1998. A detailed schedule for the implementation of these recommendations was then agreed on and organized into six major groups: (a) policy and mission; (b) program development and management; (c) management information system; (d) information and public relations policy; (e) the role of country offices; and (f) personnel policy. *See also* Oslo Group; Rockefeller Foundation.

EXECUTIVE COMMITTEE. A governing body of the Pan American Health Organization (q.v.), equivalent to a regional Executive Board, composed of nine member states (q.v.) of the region elected by the Pan American Sanitary Conference or Directing Council (q.v.) for overlapping periods of three years. Each elected member state is entitled to designate one representative to the committee, accompanied by one or more alternates and advisers. A member state is not eligible for reelection until one year has elapsed since the expiration of its term of office. The executive committee meets two times each year. Its functions are to authorize the director (q.v.) to convene meetings of the council; to approve the provisional agenda of meetings of the conference and council; to consider and submit to the conference or council the proposed program and budget prepared by the director with any recommendations deemed necessary; to advise on matters referred to it; and to discharge any other functions assigned to it by the conference or council.

EXECUTIVE DIRECTOR. A senior official appointed by, and directly answerable to, the director-general (q.v.) to oversee responsibility for a major area of WHO's work. This work may be policy based, administrative, or in an information area. This post is not subject to the United Nations scale of professional grades. The functions of an executive director do not appear to differ significantly from those of an assistant director-general (q.v.). In 1996 there were two executive directors in WHO, broadly responsible for environmental health and family and reproductive health (q.v.). *See also* Executive Administrator.

EXECUTIVE MANAGEMENT. One of three functional components of WHO's management process known as program review (q.v.). Executive management comprises the offices of the director-general, regional directors, and assistant directors-general (qq.v.); internal committees established at the global and regional levels; and the Offices of the Legal Counsel, Internal Audit and Oversight (qq.v.), and Administrative Management. The functions of the executive management are "to manage the planning, programming, implementation, monitoring and evaluation of the Organization's activities in consonance with the policy directives of the governing bodies; to promote and defend the principles and functions set out in the Constitution and the legal interests of WHO; to ensure that WHO's activities are carried out in conformity with the policies and rules that form the basis for the implementation of programmes in accordance with the objective, role and function of WHO; and to review, by means of financial and management audits, the way in which activities are carried out at all organizational levels." *See also* Constitution; Director-General's and Regional Directors' Development Programme; Managerial Process for WHO's Programme Development.

EXPANDED PROGRAMME FOR TECHNICAL ASSISTANCE (EPTA). A program of technical assistance (q.v.) for economic development established by ECOSOC in 1949. Administered by the UN Technical Assistance Board, on which WHO was represented, the program sought to achieve economic development through the transfer of skills via United Nations organizations as executing agencies (q.v.). The programs in which WHO participated were primarily designed to strengthen health administrations, assist in the control of communicable diseases whose economic impact was especially serious, and train professional and auxiliary staff. EPTA continued to operate until 1966 when it, along with the United Nations Special Fund, became components of the newly created United Nations Development Program (UNDP) (q.v.). The two components were fully merged with the UNDP in 1972.

EXPANDED PROGRAMME OF IMMUNIZATION (EPI). A program created in 1974 by WHO and the United Nations Children's Fund (q.v.) to promote the delivery of immunization against six vaccine-preventable childhood diseases: measles, tetanus, pertussis, diphtheria, tuberculosis, and polio. When the program was established, fewer than 5 percent of infants in developing countries were fully protected against these diseases. The initial strategy of the program was to improve immunization coverage through better planning, procurement of potent vaccines, refrigerated storage in a "cold chain," and correct administration of vaccines to children in their first year of life. As disease incidence has declined, the EPI has placed greater emphasis on disease surveillance. The overall aim of the program is 90 percent immunization coverage of the world's children by the year 2000.

The oversight of the EPI's policies is carried out through an annual meeting of interested parties attended by representatives of financial contributors and governments of developing countries. A Global Advisory Group advises on the work of the EPI, assisted by additional consultants, subcommittees, and study panels for specific purposes as required. This body is composed of approximately 12 members appointed by the director-general (q.v.), with at least one from each WHO region as nominated by a regional office (q.v.). The remaining members are selected to provide geographical and technical balance. The program was subsumed under the Global Programme for Vaccines and Immunization (q.v.) in 1994. *See also* Children's Vaccine Initiative; Interagency Coordinating Committee; National Immunization Day.

EXPANDED PROGRAMME OF RESEARCH, DEVELOPMENT, AND RESEARCH TRAINING IN HUMAN REPRODUCTION (HRP). A program created in 1972 to promote, coordinate, support, conduct, and evaluate research in human reproduction, with particular emphasis on the needs of developing countries. The origins of the program can be traced back to a 1968 meeting of the Organization of Economic Cooperation and Development on human reproduction, which led to a Swedish proposal for an International Agency for Contraceptive Research and Development, to be based in Stockholm. The desire for such an organization stemmed from the perceived need by Scandinavian governments to balance United States dominance in research on fertility regulation during this period. Initially, the HRP did not undertake an advocacy role in the population field, as this was seen to be the realm of the United Nations Population Fund (q.v.). Instead, the program focused on research on improving or developing contraceptive methods, with activities funded mainly from extrabudgetary funds (q.v.). The HRP remained a part of the Division of Family Health until the former was established as the Special Programme of Research, Development, and Research Training in Human Reproduction (q.v.) in 1977.

EXPERT ADVISORY PANEL. A panel of experts from whom WHO may obtain technical guidance and support within a particular subject, either by correspondence or at meetings to which the experts may be invited (e.g., Expert Advisory Panel on Health Promotion and Education, Expert Advisory Panel on Information, Education, and Communication for Health). A member of such a panel is appointed by the director-general (q.v.), who undertakes to contribute by correspondence technical information on developments in his or her field and to offer advice as appropriate, spontaneously or upon request. A panel may be disestablished when its guidance and support are no longer required. Selected members of an expert advisory panel may be chosen to serve on an expert committee (q.v.). As of January 1996, there were 62 expert advisory panels and approximately 2,100 members of WHO expert advisory panels and expert committees.

EXPERT COMMITTEE. A committee composed of selected members of an expert advisory panel (q.v.), along with other individuals, who are appointed and convened by the director-general (q.v.) to review and make technical recommendations on a subject of interest to WHO (e.g., Expert Committee on Nursing Practice, Expert Committee on Malaria). Such committees may also be joint committees with other United Nations organizations (e.g., Joint FAO/WHO Expert Committee on Food Additives, Joint ILO/WHO Expert Committee on Occupational Health).

EXTERNAL AUDITOR. An individual appointed by the World Health Assembly (q.v.) to audit the financial accounts of WHO in accordance with agreed terms of reference and in conformity with generally accepted common auditing standards. The appointed person must be the auditor-general (or equivalent) of a member state (q.v.), must remain independent of the influence of any member state, and is solely responsible for the audit. The main responsibilities of the external auditor are to make observations on the compliance of financial transactions with prevailing rules and regulations, the adequacy of internal controls, and the verification of securities and moneys on deposit. Since 1948 there have been five external auditors. In 1995 the external auditor from the United Kingdom resigned on the grounds that he could not fulfill his duties because of unsatisfactory access to information within the organization. The external auditor for 1996–99 is from South Africa. *See also* Financial Audit in Policy and Programme Terms; Office of Internal Audit and Oversight.

EXTERNAL REVIEW COMMITTEE. *See* Global Programme on AIDS.

EXTRABUDGETARY FUNDS (EBFs). Funds defined by the United Nations as "all resources, other than those of the regular budget administered by the Organization." Such funds are voluntarily contributed by member states (q.v.), other multilateral organizations, nongovernmental organizations (q.v.), private foundations, and the private sector. EBFs are usually earmarked for specific purposes, programs, or activities and are given to support a wide range of WHO activities at the global, regional, and country levels. Early contributors of EBFs were the Expanded Programme for Technical Assistance (q.v.) and the United Nations Special Fund for specific projects. The establishment of the Intensified Malaria Eradication Programme and Intensified Smallpox Eradication Programme (qq.v.) from the late 1950s led to a steady increase in EBFs received by WHO. This increase in EBFs as a proportion of the total budget led to an organizational study on the planning for and impact of extrabudgetary resources on WHO's programmes and policies in 1976. The study's support for continued expansion of EBFs was followed by an even more rapid growth of funds, particularly for special programs. In 1995 a study sponsored by the Oslo Group (q.v.) found that EBFs represented about 56 percent of the total budget in the 1990s, with more that 80 percent of EBFs contributed by ten governments. *See also* Regular Budget Funds.

F

FAMILY AND REPRODUCTIVE HEALTH PROGRAMME (FRH). A program created in 1996, following the International

Conference on Population and Development (q.v.), to bring together related areas of work within WHO and to strengthen the organization's capacity to fulfill its activities related to reproductive health. This reorganization links more closely the Division of Reproductive Health (Technical Support) and the Special Programme of Research, Development, and Research Training in Human Reproduction (qq.v.). Other divisions within the FRH are the Division of Child Health and Development, the Adolescent Health and Development Programme, and Women's Health (qq.v.). The reorganization is also intended to strengthen the dissemination of research findings at the country level and to ensure that research responds to needs identified through technical support activities. Other activities include technical support in policy development and programming; provision of information about the health problems of women, children, young people, and families; guidelines consensus statements and technical reports on norms and standards; assistance in monitoring and evaluating programs; and linkages with women's health groups and other nongovernmental organizations (q.v.). Overall, the program's activities address the differing needs of family and reproductive health as they change throughout life and seek to strengthen the capacity of services to meet these needs through training, coordination, integration, and research.

FAMILY HEALTH, DIVISION OF. *See* Division of Family Health.

FAMILY PLANNING AND POPULATION UNIT. *See* Division of Reproductive Health (Technical Support).

FANG, I. C. Dr. I. C. Fang, of China, served as regional director of the Western Pacific Regional Office (qq.v.) from 1951 to 1966.

FAR EASTERN BUREAU. *See* Health Organization of the League of Nations.

FELLOWSHIP PROGRAMME. A program created in 1947 to fund the training of health professionals in developing countries through the awarding of individual fellowships. The aim of the program is to strengthen a country's national capacity and to reduce reliance on external skills and expertise. A fellowship is awarded in accordance with nationally approved health or health-related priorities, in the context of the Health for All (q.v.) strategy, and is consistent with national human resources policies and procedures. Candidates must be nominated by their government. Applications must have the written endorsement of the government and are submitted to the WHO representative (q.v.) by the ministry of health. WHO may also suggest candidates to governments. The duration of fellowships varies, with training taking place in an institutional setting or in the field, within or outside of the fellow's home country. In 1992–93, WHO funded more than 4,500 fellowships.

FIELD LINKS FOR INTERVENTION AND CONTROL STUDIES (FIELDLINCS). A program of the UNDP/World Bank/WHO Special Programme for Research and Training in Tropical Diseases (q.v.) set up in the late 1980s to bring together scientists from different disciplines, at different levels of experience, and from different cultural and scientific backgrounds. The program aims to work on problems related to the field application of new tools and provides training through practical hands-on experience in field research linked to disease control. The program also serves to channel information from the field to key research centers and its Secretariat at headquarters (q.v.) and to foster partnerships relevant to research goals and topics.

FINANCIAL AUDIT IN POLICY AND PROGRAMME TERMS. A type of evaluation introduced by the director-general (q.v.) in 1984 to assess the extent to which technical cooperation (q.v.) activities, expanded from the late 1970s, are in accordance with WHO's policy framework. The audit aims to identify how, by whom, and on the basis of what policy decisions on the utilization of resources are arrived at and implemented. It also aims to clarify when decisions are taken, that is, before or during the Proposed Programme Budget (q.v.) biennium, how they relate to the national, regional, and global strategies for Health for All (q.v.), and what has been achieved by joint government/WHO activities. Such audits are carried out at the regional and global level and do not replace other financial audit practices. *See also* External Auditor.

FINANCIAL STATEMENTS. *See* Audited Accounts and Financial Statements.

FLACHE, STANISLAS. Dr. Stanislas Flache, of France, served as assistant director-general (q.v.) from 1977 to 1988 and adviser to Director-General Hiroshi Nakajima (qq.v.) from 1988. After medical training in France and the United States, he worked as a medical officer for the United Nations Relief and Rehabilitation Adminstration (q.v.) after the Second World War. He joined WHO in 1961, when he was seconded as director of health to the United Nations Relief and Works Agency in Lebanon. He was then appointed WHO chief medical adviser to the United Nations Children's Fund (1964–70) (q.v.), director of health services in the Western Pacific Regional Office (1970–74) (q.v.), and special adviser to the director-general and director of the Division of Coordination (1974–77).

FORUM ON HEALTH SECTOR REFORM. A group established in 1995 by the Division of Strengthening of Health Services (q.v.) composed of senior technical experts from bilateral and multilateral institutions, regional development banks, ministries of health, and selected resource institutions. The group meets regularly, on the basis of a common interest in health policy and health sector reform, to share information, identify priority issues in health sector reform, review discussion papers, and discuss relevant country experiences and approaches to supporting reform in countries.

FRANCESCO POCCHIARI FELLOWSHIP. A fellowship created in 1991, with an endowment from the government of Italy, in memory of Professor Francesco Pocchiari, former director-general (q.v.) of the Istituto Superiore di Sanita in Rome. One or two fellowships are given biennially to enable researchers from developing countries to visit other countries in order to obtain new experience relevant to their research. The fellowships are awarded by a fellowship committee consisting of the director of the Istituto Superiore di Sanita and four members of the Advisory Committee on Health Research (q.v.) selected by its chairman.

FUND, GENERAL. *See* General Fund.

G

GAUTIER, RAYMOND (1885–1957). Dr. Raymond Gautier, of Switzerland, served as counsellor, and then director of the Geneva office of the Interim Commission (q.v.) between 1946 and 1948. This was followed by an appointment as one of the first of two assistant directors-general (q.v.) of WHO. He served in this capacity until retiring from WHO in 1950 to become the director of research at the International Children's Centre in Paris. Prior to joining WHO, his career in international public health included appointments as director of the Eastern Bureau of the Health Organization of the League of Nations (q.v.) and founder of the publication *Bulletin of the Health Organization*.

GEMS COLLABORATING CENTRE FOR FRESHWATER MONITORING AND ASSESSMENT. *See* Global Environment Monitoring System Water Programme.

GENERAL COMMITTEE. A committee of the World Health Assembly (WHA) (q.v.) responsible for facilitating the proceedings of the WHA and acting as its coordinating organ. It consists of 25 members, including the president, five vice presidents, chairs of the main committees, and elected delegates of the WHA. No one member state (q.v.) is permitted to have more than one member on the committee. The president of the WHA convenes and presides over the meetings of the committee. The duties of the committee include (a) deciding the time and place of all meetings of the WHA; (b) determining the order of business; (c) proposing to the WHA the initial allocation to committees of items of the agenda; (d) coordinating the work of all committees; and (e) fixing the date of adjournment of the WHA session. *See also* Committee A; Committee B; Committee on Credentials; Committee on Nominations.

GENERAL FUND. A fund established in 1948 to account for the income and expenditure of regular budget funds (q.v.). Contributions made by member states (q.v.), casual income, and any advances made from the Working Capital Fund (q.v.) to finance general expenditures are credited to this fund.

GENERAL PROGRAMME OF WORK. A report that outlines the major activities of WHO for a six-year period and serves as a broad general policy framework for orderly development of detailed yearly programs. The report is compiled by the regional office and headquarters (qq.v.), under the responsibility of the director-general (q.v.), and submitted as a proposed program of work to the Executive Board and the World Health Assembly (qq.v.) for consideration and approval. The report is also discussed by a committee on programs. The governing bodies may then put forth recommendations for revising the program of work. The ninth General Programme of Work covers the period 1996–2001.

GENEVA GROUP. An informal caucus, formed in the 1960s, of the 14 member states (q.v.) of the United Nations that provide the largest financial contributions to the UN system. The group consists of Australia, Belgium, Canada, France, Germany, Italy, Japan, the Netherlands, Russia, Spain, Sweden, Switzerland, the United Kingdom, and the United States. The group convened its first meeting in 1964 and has since met regularly in Geneva to discuss administrative and fiscal matters relating to the UN specialized agencies and policy coordination. *See also* African Group; Asian Group; Oslo Group; Western European and Other Group.

GEZAIRY, HUSSEIN ABDUL-RASSAQ (1934–   ). Dr. Hussein Gezairy, of Saudi Arabia, has served as regional director for the Eastern Mediterranean Regional Office (EMRO) (qq.v.) since 1982. After completing studies in medicine and general surgery at Cairo University, Egypt, he joined the staff of the University of Riyadh, Saudi Arabia. He undertook postgraduate studies in surgery in the United Kingdom, where he became a fellow of the Royal College of Surgeons (1965). He then became founding dean of the faculty of medicine at the University of Riyadh (1966), the first president of the Supreme Council of the Arab Board for Medical Specializations, and minister of health for Saudi Arabia (1975). In this latter capacity, he led his country's delegation to numerous sessions of the World Health Assembly and regional committee (qq.v.) before being elected as regional director of EMRO in 1982.

GLOBAL ADVISORY GROUP. *See* Expanded Programme on Immunization.

GLOBAL ADVISORY GROUP ON NURSING AND MIDWIFERY. A multidisciplinary group established in 1992 by the director-general (q.v.) to promote mechanisms for the coordination and integration of nursing and midwifery activities and to implement guidelines for national action plans. Through annual meetings, the group has developed specific recommendations for strengthening nursing and midwifery in support of Health for All (q.v.), as adopted in a resolution of the World Health Assembly (q.v.) in 1992, and has been instrumental in developing a country questionnaire to monitor progress toward this end. Members of the group play a role in fundraising and gaining support for nursing development at the country and the intercountry level. *See also* Nursing and Midwifery.

GLOBAL BURDEN OF DISEASE (GBD). A concept put forth by the World Bank (q.v.) in the *World Development Report: Investing in Health* (1993), which seeks to measure the impact in loss of healthy life from about 100 diseases and injuries. The GBD combines the loss of life from premature death with the loss of healthy life from disability. This is measured in units of disability-adjusted life years (DALYs). Disease and injury categories are based on the International Classification of Diseases (q.v.), and the criterion for selecting those studied was the expected magnitude of the burden within a specific age group. The selected diseases and injuries account for more than 90 percent of premature deaths and probably for a similar proportion of the burden attributable to disability.

Calculation of the disease burden is based on several assumptions, some of which involve decisions about ethical values or social preferences. The key factors are the potential years of life lost as a result of a death at a given age; the relative value of a year of healthy life lived at different ages; the discount rate, or extent of time preference for human life and health; and the disability weights used to convert life lived with a disability to a common measure with premature death. Since the publication of the 1993 World Development Report, the concept of the global burden of disease has been widely used to calculate the relative cost effectiveness of selected health interventions for many developing countries as a basis of policy reform. However, many have challenged the merits of the concept, particularly regarding its conflict with the principle of equity (q.v.).

GLOBAL COMMISSION FOR THE CERTIFICATION OF SMALLPOX ERADICATION. A commission appointed by the director-general (q.v.) in 1978 to assist and provide authoritative verification of the global eradication of smallpox. Members of the commission were senior staff of the WHO Smallpox Eradication Unit (q.v.) and high-level public health officials from all affected areas of the world. During the Intensified Smallpox Eradication Programme (q.v.), all affected countries were reviewed by international commissions for the presence of smallpox according to strict and standardized guidelines. Certification was given to countries assessed to be free of the disease. The commission met 11 times during 1978–79 to review and facilitate this process in specific geographical areas. A final report of the commission was submitted to the World Health Assembly (WHA) (q.v.) in 1980, which documented the reasons the WHA declared the global eradication of smallpox.

GLOBAL COMMISSION ON AIDS (GCA). A group of 25–30 scientists formed in 1989 to provide recommendations on the policy direction of the Global Programme on AIDS (GPA) (q.v.). Members of the commission included biomedical and social scientists, as well as specialists in primary health care, law, economics, communications, and technical and aid management, who were appointed by the director-general (q.v.) to carry out the following functions: (a) to review and interpret global trends and developments related to HIV and other human retroviral infections; (b) to provide a continuous review and evaluation, from a scientific and technical viewpoint, of the content and scope of global AIDS prevention and control activities; (c) to advise on the establishment of scientific working groups and on the GPA's research agenda and scientific priorities; and (d) to make any related proposals or recommendations to the director-general. The overall purpose of the commission was to provide the GPA Management Committee with a more direct link to the scientific community. In practice, however, it is generally believed that it did not play a prominent role, given its size, broad agenda, and annual meetings. In 1992, upon the recommendation of the GPA Management Committee and the External Review Committee, the commission was renamed the Advisory Council on HIV and AIDS, and its terms of reference were revised to better reflect its role of technical, scientific, and policy guidance.

GLOBAL COMMISSION ON WOMEN'S HEALTH. A commission established in 1993, under the auspices of WHO, as a high-level body to provide advocacy and advice on women's health issues and strategies for addressing them. The objective of the commission is to accelerate global action to improve the health of women as a fundamental right and to redress existing inequities in the health status of men and women. The commission is composed of scientists, politicians, women's health advocates, and international development specialists working in governmental and nongovernmental organizations (q.v.) around the world. The secretariat (q.v.) of the commission is located in the WHO Office of Health and Development Policies.

At its first meeting in April 1994, the commission agreed to focus on six areas considered to reveal many of the risk factors for morbidity and mortality in women: nutrition; reproductive health, including sexually transmitted diseases and HIV/AIDS; health consequences of violence; aging; lifestyle-related health conditions; and the work environment.

A global strategy and action plan for improving the health of women in these six areas was adopted in October 1994. In preparation for the fourth World Conference on Women held in Beijing, China, in September 1995, commission members attended each regional preparatory committee and lobbied for the inclusion of women's health in regional and global "platforms of action." In 1996 the commission adopted "Health Security for Women throughout the Lifespan" as its platform for future advocacy efforts, a concept that stresses health education, reduction in maternal mortality and morbidity, and women's freedom from violence as fundamental rights. *See also* Task Force on Health in Development; Women's Health.

GLOBAL DATABASE ON BLINDNESS. *See* Prevention of Blindness.

GLOBAL ENVIRONMENTAL EPIDEMIOLOGY NETWORK (GEENET). A network established in 1987 as part of the WHO initiative to create networks of professionals working on the health effects of environmental hazards and human exposure, pollution control technology, and environmental management and planning. GEENET aims to increase the national capacity of developing countries to secure environmental health by strengthening education, training, and applied research in environmental epidemiology. *See also* Global Health and Environment Library Network.

GLOBAL ENVIRONMENT MONITORING SYSTEM WATER PROGRAMME (GEMS/WATER). A program created in 1976, as a collaboration between the United Nations Environment Program, WHO, and UNESCO, to increase understanding of freshwater quality issues throughout the world. Operated from the GEMS Collaborating Centre for Freshwater Monitoring and Assessment based in Burlington, Ontario, Canada, the activities of the program include monitoring comparative assessment of water quality and assisting countries in their capacity to monitor local freshwaters. Implementation of GEMS/WATER is through several United Nations organizations, including WHO, which contribute technical information and collaborate in joint monitoring projects. *See also* Interagency Steering Committee on Water Supply and Sanitation; International Drinking Water and Sanitation Decade; Programme for the Global Elimination of Dracunculiasis.

GLOBAL HEALTH AND ENVIRONMENT LIBRARY NETWORK (GELNET). A network created in 1987 to support the development of documentation centers and reference libraries in member states (q.v.) at local, regional, and national levels so that scientific and technical information on health and environment becomes more widely and readily available. Within the framework of WHO's Global Strategy for Health and Environment (q.v.), and in collaboration with the United Nations Environment Program, the network aims to facilitate effective and systematic provision of scientific or technical health and environment information to policy makers, teachers, researchers, and so on. The underlying premise of GELNET is to take advantage of WHO's provision of publications free of charge to at least one library in most of its member states. The objectives of GELNET are (a) to encourage these libraries to make information they hold readily available; (b) to inform interested persons where and how to find information on health and environment in their country; and (c) to link these libraries to encourage the exchange of information and possibly documents. *See also* Division of Publishing, Language, and Library Services; Health and Environment Library Modules.

GLOBAL HEALTH POLICY. *See* Renewing the Health for All Strategy.

GLOBAL POLICY COUNCIL. A council created in 1993, composed of selected members of the Executive Board (q.v.), as part of the Executive Board Working Group on the WHO Response to Global Change (q.v.) reform process "to orient the long-term vision, policy direction and program priorities for the health sector and WHO." This entails such functions as restating WHO's mission in the light of global change, implementing the Renewing the Health for All Strategy (q.v.), ensuring that program implementation at global, regional, and country levels follows global policy and respects national priorities, and adjusting WHO's managerial structure in accordance with reforms emanating from WHO's Response to Global Change. For this purpose, the council created a series of multidisciplinary groups of the WHO Secretariat (q.v.) staff who examined specific reform issues and developed means of implementing the recommendations presented within the reform process. *See also* Administration, Budget, and Finance Committee; Programme Development Committee.

GLOBAL PROGRAMME FOR HEALTH OF THE ELDERLY (HEE). A program created in 1979 "to promote health and well-being throughout the entire lifespan and to assist Member States [q.v.] in developing strategies to ensure the availability and provision of comprehensive and holistic health care to elderly populations." The involvement of WHO in the health care of the elderly dates from the mid-1950s, but it was not until 1974 that an expert committee (q.v.) report on the subject was published. In 1979 the World Health Assembly (q.v.) adopted its first resolution to target the health needs of elderly populations, which led to the creation of the program. In 1982 the World Assembly on Aging was convened by the United Nations, which presented the Vienna International Plan of Action on Aging. The policy paper prepared by WHO for this meeting formed the basis of the program's goals from 1982 to 1987: to develop demographic and health profiles; to formulate programs for community-based health care for aging individuals; and to advocate issues related to health of the elderly within scientific and professional organizations. Other activities included organization of scientific studies on age-related issues and establishment of international research on the determinants of healthy aging, osteoporosis, age-associated dementia, and age-related changes in immune function. A Scientific Steering Committee appraised and approved such international research at its inception. This was complemented by supporting activities at the regional level. In 1995, the program was replaced by the Programme on Aging and Health (q.v.).

GLOBAL PROGRAMME FOR VACCINES AND IMMUNIZATION (GPV). A program created in 1994 with the merging of three bodies within WHO that are concerned with vaccines: the Expanded Programme of Immunization (EPI), the Programme for Vaccine Development (qq.v.), and parts of the Biologicals Unit. As restructured, the program has three operational units: the EPI, Vaccine Research and Development (VRD), and Vaccine Supply and Quality (VSQ). In addition, the program provides the secretariat for the Children's Vaccine Initiative (q.v.). The main objectives of the program are to support countries to become self-sufficient in their immunization programs; to support the control or eradication of vaccine-preventable diseases; and to stimulate and guide work in new and improved vaccine development, manufacture, and use. In addition, the program seeks to ensure that vaccine research is directly related to the needs of lower-income countries and that national managers plan for the integration of new vaccines into their programs as they are developed.

The broad policy of the program is reviewed by an annual meeting of interested parties (MIP) attended by representatives of financial contributors, governments of lower-income countries, nongovernmental organizations, the United Nations Children's Fund (UNICEF), the United Nations Development Program, and WHO regional offices (qq.v.). Activities are evaluated on an annual basis by a scientific advisory group of experts (SAGE) composed of scientists from outside of WHO recognized for their expertise, who review the program's activities, immunization strategies, vaccine supply policies, and research priorities. In addition, an interagency global consultative group for research on cholera vaccines was set up in 1994 to facilitate and coordinate cholera vaccine development.

Priority activities during 1996–2000 include eradication of poliomyelitis by 2000, promotion of vaccine research, and immunization of at least 90 percent of children under one year of age against childhood target diseases. In 1996 the GPV, in collaboration with UNICEF, first published its report, State of the World's Vaccines and Immunization. Funding for the program, which totaled U.S.$18.4 million in 1994, is from both regular budget funds and extrabudgetary funds (qq.v.). The leading financial contributors have been Japan, the Netherlands, and the United States. See also PAHO Regional System for Vaccines; Plan of Action for Vaccine Self-sufficiency; Programme for Vaccine Development.

GLOBAL PROGRAMME ON AIDS (GPA). A program created in February 1987, initially named the Special Programme on AIDS, to replace the Control Programme on AIDS (q.v.) and enable WHO to respond on a larger scale to the pandemic. Beginning with only two staff, including its first director, Jonathan Mann (q.v.), and a budet of U.S.$18 million, the GPA grew rapidly to become WHO's largest health program. By 1990 there were more than one hundred staff at headquarters (q.v.), and the total budget was U.S.$100 million, primarily from extrabudgetary funds (q.v.). The 1987 World Health Assembly

(WHA) (q.v.) adopted Resolution WHA40.26, which declared AIDS as a "worldwide emergency" requiring "urgent and vigorous globally directed action." Later the same year, the United Nations General Assembly confirmed WHO's "essential global directing and coordinating role" and directed all United Nations organizations to support the organization in its efforts to combat the disease.

One of the immediate tasks of the GPA was to articulate a global policy framework for action. The Global Strategy for the Prevention and Control of AIDS proposed three objectives: to prevent HIV transmission, to reduce the personal and social impact of the pandemic, and to unify national and international efforts to prevent, control, and treat the disease. The GPA's main operational tasks were to support and strengthen national AIDS programs and to provide global leadership to ensure international collaboration. For the development of national AIDS programs, this entailed the provision of technical guidance, field staff, and financial support. The program also played a vocal international advocacy role, particularly with respect to human rights. Within this remit, the scale and scope of the GPA's work expanded quickly under charismatic and dynamic leadership. By 1990, the GPA had assisted some 123 countries to put their HIV/AIDS national strategies into operation.

The GPA was officially governed by the WHA and the Executive Board (q.v.), with additional support from two advisory groups, the GPA Management Committee (GMC) and the Global Commission on AIDS (q.v.). The former consisted of representatives of the largest bilateral donors to the program, five UN organizations working cooperatively with WHO, nominees from the regional offices (q.v.), and other intergovernmental bodies (e.g., the European Community). The GMC provided overall guidance on managerial, organizational, and technical issues. Of the two advisory groups, the GMC played the more prominent role in monitoring and influencing the program. In addition, steering committees on aspects of HIV/AIDS (e.g., the Steering Committee on Diagnostics) provided advice on research.

In March 1990, Dr. Mann resigned from WHO as a result of differences with Director-General Hiroshi Nakajima (q.v.) over program strategy. Mann believed that the GPA should maintain a prominent advocacy role on human rights for people with HIV/AIDS and work closely with nongovernmental organizations (NGOs) (q.v.). Dr. Nakajima supported a more technical and biomedical focus for WHO, with less need for advocacy than in initial years. Under a new director, Dr. Michael Merson (q.v.), significant changes were made to staff and activities, drawing on WHO's traditionally strong biomedical expertise. In 1992 an updated and expanded global AIDS strategy was agreed upon, with increased emphases on care, better treatment of sexually transmitted diseases, prevention of HIV infection through improved women's health, education, and status, and attention to the public health dangers of stigmatization and discrimination.

By the early to middle 1990s, however, there were concerns that a rethinking of AIDS activities within the United Nations was needed. An external review committee, funded by major bilateral donors, reported in 1992 that the development of AIDS activities by other UN organizations, notably the United Nations Development Program, the United Nations Children's Fund, the United Nations Population Fund, and the World Bank (qq.v.), as well as bilateral agencies and NGOs, had been accompanied by poor coordination. Others argued that a biomedical approach was too narrow and that a more intersectoral approach to the disease was needed. Pressure for change also resulted from high-level politics over the reelection of Dr. Nakajima as director-general and overall reform of the UN system. These pressures led to the adoption in 1993 of Resolution WHA46.37, calling for a study of the feasibility of setting up a new AIDS program. A complex two-year consultation and planning process commenced shortly thereafter, with long and often difficult negotiations. During this period, the GPA experienced growing financial difficulties, with the budget for 1994–95 being reduced from U.S.$174 million to U.S.$134 million due to shortfalls in contributions. In June 1995, the United Nations Economic and Social Council endorsed a new program, and a memorandum of understanding was signed by six cosponsoring (q.v.) UN organizations. In January 1996, the GPA was formally replaced by the Joint United Nations Programme on HIV/AIDS (q.v.).

GLOBAL PUBLICATIONS POLICY STUDY. *See* Division of Publishing, Language, and Library Services.

GLOBAL REFORM PROCESS. *See* Executive Board Working Group on the WHO Response to Global Change.

GLOBAL SCHOOL HEALTH INITIATIVE. An initiative developed in 1996 to facilitate the common program for action on

the health needs of children of school age. The world's population of school-age children is over one billion, of whom almost
700 million are children of primary-school age (6–11 years).
The particular health issues of this age group include infectious
diseases, tobacco and illicit drug use, abortion, homelessness,
and sexually transmitted diseases. Based on research confirming the strong links between health, school attendance, and educational attainment, the aim of the initiative is to promote the
acquisition of health-related knowledge, values, skills, and
practices among children so that they are better able to pursue
a healthy life and to act as agents of change for the health of
their communities. The initiative works through the Expert
Committee (q.v.) on Comprehensive School Health Education
and Promotion. *See also* Action-Oriented School Health Curriculum.

GLOBAL STRATEGY FOR HEALTH AND ENVIRONMENT. A
strategy presented in 1992, and approved by the World Health
Assembly in 1993, following the United Nations Conference on
the Environment and Development (qq.v.). The conference
agreement, known as Agenda 21, designates WHO as task
manager for health, in that it has primary international responsibility for implementing six of 118 programs and subordinate
roles in 19 others. This global strategy is a framework for fulfilling these roles through collaboration with member states
(q.v.) in the area of health and the environment. The strategy
has been followed by the development of regional strategies
identifying priority areas for each WHO region.

GLOBAL STRATEGY FOR THE PREVENTION AND CONTROL
OF AIDS. *See* Global Programme on AIDS.

GLOBAL TUBERCULOSIS PROGRAMME (GTB). A program established in 1995, replacing the Tuberculosis Programme (q.v.),
to advise national governments on how to improve treatment
and prevention of tuberculosis, with emphasis on the directly
observed treatment, short-course (q.v.) strategy. The program
provides technical support to governments and other external
donors and supports basic and operational research on diagnosis and treatment. It also conducts research on the link between
tuberculosis and HIV/AIDS.
    Since 1988, the Global Tuberculosis Programme has grown
from a one-person program at headquarters (q.v.) to a 40-per-
son team, with increased staff in regional offices and country

offices (qq.v.). The program is managed by the Coordination, Advisory, and Review Group, composed of rotating representatives from tuberculosis-endemic countries, financial contributors, nongovernmental organizations (NGOs) (q.v.), and permanent members from the United Nations Development Program, the World Bank (qq.v.), and WHO. A technical and research advisory committee of individuals serving in a personal capacity reviews and advises the program on scientific and technical matters. In 1993, WHO declared tuberculosis to be a global emergency and sought to build a broad coalition of partners (i.e., NGOs, private industry, community groups, activists) to support the campaign against the disease. The GTB is funded by both regular budget funds and extrabudgetary funds (qq.v.). *See also* Tuberculosis Research Office.

GOODMAN, NEVILLE MARRIOTT (1898–1980). Dr. Neville Goodman, of the United Kingdom, served as one of the first of two assistant directors-general (q.v.) of WHO from 1948 to 1949, following his role as director of field services of the Interim Commission (q.v.). During his career in international public health, he was appointed as a British delegate to the Office International d'Hygiène Publique (q.v.), a member of the Health Committee of the League of Nations, and director of the health division of the European Regional Office of the United Nations Relief and Rehabilitation Administration (qq.v.). He left WHO in 1949 to join the Ministry of Health, where he served as deputy chief medical officer until retiring in 1963. During this period, he also served as the chairman of the United Kingdom Committee for WHO. In 1952 he published *International Health Organizations and Their Work*, which remains one of the key texts on the history of international public health work.

GOVERNING BODY DOCUMENT. A document prepared for the Executive Board (EB), the World Health Assembly (WHA), regional committees (qq.v.), or their subsidiary bodies before, during, or after their sessions. In addition to the main documents written to provide background for agenda items, the term refers to summary and verbatim records of meetings, conference and working papers, information and miscellaneous documents, and resolutions. Documents for WHO-governing bodies originate from technical and administrative programs. They bear the symbols identifying the body (i.e., A for World Health Assembly, EB for Executive Board), the session number, the type of document, and its place in the series. Governing body documents are distributed to WHA delegates and EB members, to intergovernmental and nongovernmental organizations (q.v.), and to WHO offices in accordance with an established pattern. At headquarters (q.v.), almost all governing body documents are produced in English and French, with selected others in the working languages of Arabic, Chinese, Russian, and Spanish. *See also* Administrative Document; Technical Document.

GOVERNING COUNCIL. *See* International Agency for Research on Cancer.

GUERRA DE MACEDO, CARLYLE (1937–). Dr. Carlyle Guerra de Macedo, of Brazil, served as regional director of the American Regional Office and director of the Pan American Health Organization (qq.v.) from 1983 to 1994. After training in medicine and public health, he specialized in family planning, population, and social and economic development. During his career in public health, he was professor in the National School of Public Health in Rio de Janiero and chief of the health division for the Northeast Brazilian Development Agency (SUDENE). He joined WHO in the 1970s as chief of training in Chile and was coordinator of a technical cooperation (q.v.) program in Brazil in 1976.

GUIDELINES FOR DRUG DONATIONS. A set of international guidelines issued by WHO in 1996 to improve the quality of drug donations in acute emergencies and development aid programs. The guidelines were developed by WHO, following efforts to standardize drug donations by such organizations as the International Committee of the Red Cross and the Christian Medical Commission of the World Council of Churches. The guidelines are also supported by major international agencies active in humanitarian emergency relief. By urging the adoption of common standards, WHO aims to better align drug donations with the needs of recipients and to reduce wastage in time and resources. The 12 articles of the guidelines are based on four core principles: (a) a drug donation should benefit the recipient to the maximum extent possible; (b) a donation should be given with full respect for the wishes and authority of the recipient and should support existing government policies and administrative arrangements; (c) there should be no double standards in quality between the donor and recipient countries; and (d) there should be effective communication between the donor and recipient.

GUINEA-WORM INFECTION. *See* Programme for the Global Elimination of Dracunculiasis.

GUNARATNE, VICTOR THOMAS HERAT (1912–1987). Dr. Victor Gunaratne, of Sri Lanka, served as regional director for the South-East Asia Regional Office (SEARO) (qq.v.) from 1968 to 1981. After studying medicine and public health in Sri Lanka (then known as Ceylon) and the United Kingdom, he returned home to pursue a long career in public health. He was serving as director of Health Services of Ceylon when he was elected president of the World Health Assembly (qq.v.) in 1967 and then regional director of SEARO in 1968.

H

HAN, SANG TAE (1928–   ). Dr. Sang Han, of the Republic of Korea, has served as the regional director of the Western Pacific Regional Office (WPRO) (qq.v.) since 1989. After completing medical training in Korea and the United States, he occupied senior positions in the Ministry of Health and Social Affairs, including director, Division of Preventive Medicine, and director-general (q.v.), Bureau of Public Health. He joined WHO in 1967 as medical officer on the National Health Services Development Project in Western Samoa (1967–70), regional adviser in Community Health Services (1970–73), director of Health Manpower Development (q.v.) and Family Health (1973–79), and director of Programme Management (1979–88) (q.v.). Between 1988 and 1989, he acted as a special representative of the director-general (q.v.) at the WPRO before being elected regional director.

HEADQUARTERS. The main offices of the Secretariat (q.v.) established in Geneva, Switzerland, in 1948. Initially the former site of the Health Organization of the League of Nations (q.v.), which in fact influenced the decision by founding member states (q.v.) to locate the new health organization in Switzerland, WHO moved to its current purpose-built premises in 1968. The buildings of the headquarters include office accommodation, a WHO library, facilities for publishing and distributing WHO documents, and conference facilities for holding meetings of the World Health Assembly, the Executive Board, and other bodies such as expert committees and study groups (qq.v.).

The structure of the headquarters consists of the office of the director-general (q.v.) and the organization's main management, administration, and legal offices. The remainder of the headquarters is structured according to divisions or major programs, each representing major areas of work (e.g., Division of Control of Tropical Diseases, Division of Drug Management and Policies (qq.v.). An assistant director-general (q.v.) is responsible for around three to six divisions or programs. Over time the subject areas and names of divisions and programs have been changed and reorganized regularly. In 1996 there were nine assistant directors-general (or the equivalent). There are about 1,500 staff presently located at headquarters, consisting of professional and general staff, representing about one-third of total WHO staff. *See also* Country Office; Regional Office.

HEALTH. The WHO constitution (q.v.) defines health as "a state of complete physical, mental and social well-being and not merely the absence of disease or infirmity."

HEALTH AND DEVELOPMENT POLICIES, OFFICE OF. *See* Task Force on Health in Development.

HEALTH AND ENVIRONMENT LIBRARY MODULES (HELM). A collection of key scientific and technical information on health and environmental issues developed by the Office of Global and Integrated Environmental Health (q.v.), in liaison with the Office of Library and Health Literature Services, the Distribution and Sales Office, and regional offices (q.v.), to support the dissemination of information to member states (q.v.). The collection of documentation modules includes the following subjects: air quality, chemical safety, environmental epidemiology, food safety, occupational health, solid and hazardous waste management, and vector control. The complete collection of HELM modules is deemed the standard minimum collection on health and environment that should be available to all members' libraries of the Global Health and Environment Library Network (q.v.).

HEALTH AND THE ENVIRONMENT, COUNCIL ON THE IMPLEMENTATION OF THE EARTH SUMMIT'S ACTION PRO-

GRAMME FOR. *See* Council on the Implementation of the Earth Summit's Action Programme for Health and Environment.

HEALTH COMMISSION. *See* Rockefeller Foundation.

HEALTH COMMUNICATIONS AND PUBLIC RELATIONS, OFFICE OF. *See* Office of Health Communications and Public Relations.

HEALTH ECONOMICS, TASK FORCE ON. *See* Task Force on Health Economics.

HEALTH EDUCATION AND HEALTH PROMOTION UNIT (HEP). A unit created in the 1980s, within the Division of Health Promotion, Education, and Communication (q.v.), to carry out the following objectives for health promotion and education: (a) to provide international direction and coordination; (b) to provide technical cooperation (q.v.) with countries, in collaboration with regional offices (q.v.), in strengthening national capacity and infrastructure; (c) to serve as an information source for regional offices; (d) to assist with developing and implementing the health promotion and education component of other WHO programs; (e) to promote and support training, research, and education activities; and (f) to establish an alliance and network of institutions, including United Nations organizations, nongovernmental organizations, WHO collaborating centers (qq.v.), and donor agencies. The three strategies to achieve these objectives are advocacy to generate political commitment for health supportive policies; capacity building to equip individuals and groups with knowledge, values, and skills that encourage effective action for health; and social support for developing alliances, partnerships, and social support systems that legitimize and encourage health-related action. *See also* Occupational Health Unit; Office of Health Communications and Public Relations; Programme on Aging and Health; Rehabilitation Unit.

HEALTH FOR ALL. Originally known as Health for All by the Year 2000. A historic resolution and declaration, Health for All was adopted by the World Health Assembly (WHA) (q.v.) in 1977, to achieve the goal of "the attainment by all citizens of the world by the year 2000 of a level of health that will permit them to lead a socially and economically productive life." The vehicle to achieve Health for All was designated as the primary health care (q.v.) approach, which was confirmed at the International Conference on Primary Health Care (q.v.) in 1978. Since the late 1970s, Health for All, and its basic principle of equity (q.v.), have been widely accepted as the underlying principle driving the work of WHO. To monitor and evaluate progress toward the achievement of Health for All, a global strategy was adopted by the WHA in 1981–82 consisting of a shortlist of indicators and a plan of action, including a schedule for regular monitoring and evaluating of progress in implementing regional strategies and the global strategy.

The first monitoring strategy was carried out in 1983, with subsequent exercises carried out in 1985–87 and 1991–93. The most recent monitoring exercise began in 1993, using a common framework for collecting, analyzing, and presenting quantitative information on 89 indicators or subindicators for each member state (q.v.). The framework also presented a list of indicators, jointly agreed upon by WHO and the United Nations Children's Fund (q.v.) and formulated by the World Summit for Children (q.v.), and invited countries to provide information on these whenever possible. The report on the results of the monitoring exercise provides a comparative analysis of the progress member states have achieved toward the goals of Health for All. In the 1990s, in light of the expected failure to achieve its goals by the millenium, the declaration is now known as Health for All. *See also* Renewing the Health for All Strategy.

HEALTH FOR ALL LEADERSHIP DEVELOPMENT. An initiative launched by the director-general (q.v.) in 1985 to familiarize senior policymakers, both within and outside the health sector, with the principles of primary health care and Health for All (qq.v.) strategy. The initiative is based on the premise that implementation of the strategy can be improved if individuals in leadership positions understand more fully the process involved in developing and implementing it, pursue its values, and develop within themselves the qualities and abilities required to lead the process in member states (q.v.). Through support for meetings, training, and promotion of staff within WHO, the aim of the initiative is to create or mobilize a critical mass of national leaders strategically located within health systems, research institutions, health professions, political organizations, nongovernmental organizations (q.v.), and the community.

HEALTH FOR ALL STRATEGY, RENEWING THE. *See* Renewing the Health for All Strategy.

HEALTH IN DEVELOPMENT, TASK FORCE ON. *See* Task Force on Health in Development.

HEALTH LEGISLATION UNIT. A unit created in 1948 to disseminate information on developments in health legislation in member states (q.v.). This is primarily achieved through the publication of the *International Digest of Health Legislation*, a journal published quarterly on changes in health legislation in member states (q.v.). The journal is used as a reference text by policymakers and legislators in the making and implementing of health law.

HEALTH LITERATURE, LIBRARY, AND INFORMATION SERVICES (HELLIS). A resource-sharing information network of the South-East Asia Regional Office (SEARO) (q.v.) created in the late 1970s to make better use of existing resources in the region. The HELLIS network was organized into national networks with national focal points coordinating activities at the national level and a regional network (served by SEARO) linking the national, regional, and international focal points and establishing liaison with other international organizations. To strengthen medical libraries, regional training programs for health science librarians were carried out. Following an evaluation of the network in 1984, it was agreed that further strengthening of its activities was needed, including links to other developing networks in the region. *See also* Division of Publishing, Language, and Library Services.

HEALTH MANPOWER DEVELOPMENT (HMD). An approach introduced in 1976 by WHO to address the problem of providing appropriately trained personnel for health services. The approach involves three interrelated components, which, in turn, are integrated with the overall development of health services: (a) health personnel planning; (b) health personnel production; and (c) health personnel management. The approach led to situational analysis of health personnel at the regional and country levels and the adoption of programs for health manpower development with periodic review of progress.

HEALTH OF THE ELDERLY, GLOBAL PROGRAMME FOR. *See* Global Programme for Health of the Elderly.

HEALTH ORGANIZATION OF THE LEAGUE OF NATIONS. An organization created in 1923, with headquarters in Geneva, Switzerland, to carry out the health activities of the League of Nations. Initially, member states (q.v.) intended that the new organization would assume the responsibilities of the Office International d'Hygiène Publique (OIHP) (q.v.) following a change of title, modification of statutes, and its placement under the authority of the League. It was believed that there was a need for a "central organism through which international activities of every sort can be co-ordinated," particularly for response to outbreaks of diseases (e.g., typhus, cholera, influenza). In addition, Article 24 of the Covenant of the League stated that "there shall be placed under the direction of the League all International Bureaux already established by the general treaties if the parties to such treaties consent."

Following the International Health Conference held in London in April 1920, convened at the request of the Council of the League of Nations, it was recommended that a permanent international health organization be created. While member states of the OIHP considered whether to agree to the proposed organization, a Provisional Health Committee operated during 1921–22. By August 1922, the word "provisional" was no longer used, and the organization became known as the Health Committee of the League of Nations. In a further effort to combine the work of the Health Committee and the OIHP, a Special Mixed Committee, with equal representation from both bodies, was formed in May 1923. The report of this committee led to the acceptance by the Assembly of the League of Nations of a complicated and unwieldy structure that remained in place until 1936. Notable was the agreement for the OIHP to remain autonomous and without modification to its constitution or functions. The result was two separate and autonomous international health organizations existing side by side until the creation of the United Nations in 1945.

The early work of the Health Organization was directed toward emergency situations created by epidemics and breaking new ground in epidemiological intelligence, with the creation and operation of the Malaria Commission (1923), the Cancer Commission (1928–30), the Anthrax Commission (1925–29), and other technical commissions. The Far Eastern Bureau was created in 1925, with the financial support of the Rockefeller Foundation (q.v.), to carry out epidemiological surveillance in East Asia. The Health Organization also made great strides in the field of nutrition from the mid-1930s and, in the years leading up to the Second World War, focused increasingly on social diseases such as malnutrition. By 1933 the organization had a staff of 53. The outbreak of war in 1939 brought this work to a virtual standstill. Staff continued to publish key publications, such as the *Weekly Epidemiological Record* (q.v.), and to deal with requests for information as resources permitted. In May 1944, epidemiological staff were transferred to the United States to form a research unit, which later became the Epidemiological Intelligence Service in the Health Division of the United Nations Relief and Rehabilitation Administration (UNRRA) (q.v.). With the formal dissolution of the League of Nations in 1945, all responsibilities of the Health Organization were assumed by UNRRA, the Interim Commission (q.v.), and eventually WHO.

HEALTH PROMOTION, EDUCATION, AND COMMUNICATION, DIVISION OF. *See* Division of Health Promotion, Education, and Communication.

HEALTH PROMOTION, INTERNATIONAL CONFERENCE ON. *See* International Conference on Health Promotion.

HEALTH RESEARCH, PAHO ADVISORY COMMITTEE ON. *See* PAHO Advisory Committee on Health Research.

HEALTH SCIENCE AND TECHNOLOGY. One of four broad and interlinked categories of WHO programs for 1990–95. The work of this category of programs is the application of methods and techniques that constitute the content of health systems. *See also* Direction, Coordination, and Management; Health Systems Infrastructure; Program Support.

HEALTH SECTOR REFORM, FORUM ON. *See* Forum on Health Sector Reform.

HEALTH SITUATION AND TREND ASSESSMENT, DIVISION OF. *See* Division of Health Situation and Trend Assessment.

HEALTH SYSTEMS DEVELOPMENT PROGRAMME (HSD). A program established in 1996 with the restructuring and combining of four former divisions: the Division of Development of Human Resources for Development, the Division of Intensified Cooperation with Countries (q.v.), the Division of Strengthening of Health Services (q.v.), and the Division of Informatics.

The purpose of the new program is to enable WHO to respond in a more coherent and integrated manner to the needs of member states (q.v.) at the country level. Its mission is to collaborate with countries in greatest need in developing and strengthening their capacity to achieve the goal of Health for All (q.v.) and to increase quality, cost-effectiveness, and equity (q.v.) in health care. The program is organized into three divisions: the Division of Strategic Support to Countries in Greatest Need, the Division of Organization and Management of Health Systems, and the Division of Analysis, Research, and Assessment (qq.v.). Theme groups and task forces crosscut the three divisions to design and implement new approaches in collaboration with national counterparts, regional offices, country offices (qq.v.), and other technical programs.

HEALTH SYSTEMS, DIVISION OF ORGANIZATION AND MANAGEMENT OF. *See* Division of Organization and Management of Health Systems.

HEALTH SYSTEMS INFRASTRUCTURE. One of four broad and interlinked categories of programs of WHO for 1990–95. The aim of this category of program work is to establish comprehensive health systems based on primary health care (q.v.). *See also* Direction, Coordination, and Management; Health Science and Technology; Program Support.

HEALTHY CITIES INITIATIVE/PROGRAMME/PROJECT. A project launched by the European Regional Office (q.v.) in Lisbon, Portugal, in 1986 at a meeting of representatives from 21 European cities. The participants agreed to collaborate in developing approaches to improving urban health based on the principles of Health for All (q.v.). Beginning with four to six European cities, the aim of the project was to bring together a partnership of public, private, and voluntary sectors to focus on urban health and to tackle health-related problems. However, the project has since grown into a worldwide network of more than 1,000 cities involved in a collaborative and intersectoral effort to put health on social and political agendas. In some regions, such as the Eastern Mediterranean Regional Office (q.v.), the initiative is being extended to include the concept of "healthy villages."

HELSINKI DECLARATION. *See* European Conference on Environment and Health.

HENDERSON, DONALD AINSLIE (1928–   ). Dr. Donald Henderson, of the United States, served as chief of the Smallpox Eradication Unit and Intensified Smallpox Eradication Programme (q.v.) between 1966 and 1977. After training in medicine and public health, he worked in various posts at the Communicable Diseases Center of the Department of Health, Education, and Welfare (1955–66). During this period he was also assistant professor of preventive medicine and community health at Emory University (1960–66). He joined WHO in 1966 as chief medical officer, where he led the historic campaign for the global eradication of smallpox. After leaving WHO, he became dean and professor of epidemiology and international health at the Johns Hopkins University School of Hygiene and Public Health (1977–90); associate director, Office of Science and Technology Policy, Executive Office of the President (1991–93); and deputy assistant secretary and senior scientific adviser, Department of Health and Human Services (since 1993).

HORWITZ, ABRAHAM. Dr. Abraham Horwitz, of Chile, served as director of the Pan American Health Organization (PAHO) (qq.v.) from 1958 to 1975. After receiving his medical degree in 1936, he specialized in public health and communicable diseases through a fellowship from the Rockefeller Foundation (q.v.) and further training in the United States. He then returned to Chile, where he became director of the School of Public Health and pursued an active teaching career. From 1950 to 1953 he served in various capacities in the Pan American Sanitary Bureau (q.v.), the forerunner of PAHO, until he was recalled to Chile to organize the country's National Health Service. In 1958 he was elected by the member states (q.v.) of the region as director of PAHO for the first of four consecutive four-year terms. During his tenure, PAHO experienced a period of growth in its programs focused on the promotion of the integration of health, as a social service, with economic development objectives. This led to large capital investments by the Inter-American Development Bank and other donor agencies for health programs in the region and to the formulation of a Ten-Year Health Plan for the Americas. Upon his retirement in 1975, PAHO created the Abraham Horwitz Award for Inter-American Health, which is given each year to an individual or group of individuals for scientific or pedagogic achievement in any field of health.

HUMAN REPRODUCTION, SPECIAL PROGRAMME OF RESEARCH, DEVELOPMENT, AND RESEARCH TRAINING IN.

See Special Programme of Research, Development, and Research Training in Human Reproduction.

HUMAN RESOURCES FOR HEALTH, PROGRAMME FOR DEVELOPMENT OF. *See* Programme for Development of Human Resources for Health.

I

IMMUNIZATION DAY. *See* National Immunization Day.

IMMUNIZATION, EXPANDED PROGRAMME OF. *See* Expanded Programme of Immunization.

INFANT FORMULA ACTION COALITION (INFACT). A United States-based nongovernmental organization (NGO) (q.v.) that actively campaigned for the boycott of the Swiss food company, Nestlé, in opposition to the latter's marketing of breast milk substitutes in developing countries. INFACT was among the participants in a meeting held by WHO and the United Nations Children's Fund (q.v.) in 1979 to discuss the feeding of infants and young children, the first such meeting where NGOs were represented as full delegates. The work of INFACT and other NGOs helped raise awareness within the World Health Assembly (q.v.) and worldwide of the marketing practices of large transnational corporations in the developing world. This attention eventually led to the adoption of the International Code on the Marketing of Breastmilk Substitutes (q.v.). *See also* Baby-Friendly Hospital Initiative; International Baby Food Action Network; International Council of Infant Food Industries; Mother-Baby Package.

INFLUENZA PROGRAMME. A program, originating in 1947, established to organize and support the rapid isolation and characterization of new influenza virus strains. The program also provides up-to-date information on the world epidemiological situation, including information on where and when epidemics occur and their subsequent spread. Two WHO collaborating centers (q.v.) for influenza (in Atlanta, Georgia, United States, and London, United Kingdom) and 110 national institutes in 79 countries carry out influenza surveillance activities. *See also* Division of Communicable Diseases.

INFORMATION SYSTEM MANAGEMENT, DIVISION OF. *See* Division of Information System Management.

INNOCENTI DECLARATION. *See* International Code on the Marketing of Breastmilk Substitutes.

INSTITUTE OF NUTRITION IN CENTRAL AMERICA AND PANAMA (INCAP). An institute founded in Guatemala City, Guatemala, in 1946, by agreement among six governments and the Pan American Health Organization (q.v.), to foster the development of nutrition science in Central America. INCAP's work has focused on developing practical solutions to nutrition-related problems through the use of local produce, improvements in traditional diets, and education. During the 1950s, efforts to reduce high infant mortality associated with malnutrition led to the development of a low-cost high-protein vegetable mixture known as INCAPARINA, which continues to be used today to feed children. The institute is also recognized as an important source of information, technical guidance, and expertise on nutrition matters. *See also* Division of Food and Nutrition; International Conference on Nutrition; Pan American Center.

INTEGRATED MANAGEMENT OF THE SICK CHILD. An approach proposed in 1992 in response to the need for more integrated diagnosis and treatment of the sick child as a whole rather than a focus on single diseases. Beginning as an initiative endorsed by WHO and the United Nations Children's Fund (q.v.) in 1992, when an integrated "package" approach to the management of sick children was defined, the approach received approval by the Executive Board (q.v.) in 1995 to seek extrabudgetary funds (q.v.) for its activities. Activities focus on the symptomatic identification of illnesses in outpatient settings; more appropriate and, where possible, combined treatment of all the major illnesses; and more rapid referral of severely ill children. The approach is coordinated by the Division of Diarrhoeal and Acute Respiratory Disease Control (q.v.) and involves a wide range of WHO programs, including the Division of Emerging and Other Communicable Diseases, the Division of Control of Tropical Diseases, the Action Programme on Essential Drugs, the Joint United Nations Programme on HIV/AIDS, the Global Programme for Vaccines and Immunization, Prevention of Blindness, Prevention of

Deafness and Hearing Impairment (qq.v.), Maternal and Child Health, and Family Planning, Nutrition, and Oral Health.

INTENSIFIED COOPERATION WITH COUNTRIES, DIVISION OF. *See* Division of Intensified Cooperation with Countries.

INTENSIFIED COOPERATION WITH LEAST DEVELOPED COUNTRIES (IWC). An initiative launched in 1989 to address the specific health needs of countries in greatest need. Coordinated and promoted through the Division of Intensified Cooperation with Countries (q.v.), the purpose of the initiative was to improve and expand WHO technical cooperation (q.v.) for developing countries. This was to be achieved by redressing imbalances between central, regional, and country-level activities and increasing the relevance of assistance to country-specific needs. For this purpose, the initiative had three operational objectives: (a) to build national capacity for integrated health development; (b) to strengthen internal WHO coordination and utilization of available resources; and (c) to improve external coordination among international organizations involved in health cooperation. This was carried out in relation to policy development, health reform, health finance, and the building of national capacity and capability. The initiative saw slow but steady expansion of support to countries. In 1995, 27 (out of 47) developing countries participated in the initiative. In 1996, the initiative was discontinued in the above form as part of the reorganization of the Division of Intensified Cooperation with Countries into the Division of Strategic Support to Countries in Greatest Need (q.v.).

INTENSIFIED MALARIA ERADICATION PROGRAMME (MEP). A program established in 1955 as the first and largest, in terms of countries involved and resources deployed, of WHO's mass campaigns to prevent, control or eradicate disease. Malaria was, and remains, one of the most serious health problems in tropical countries. Efforts prior to the 1950s to control the disease (i.e., drug therapy and environmental management) were costly. The development of the insecticide dichlorodiphenyltrichloroethane (DDT) during the Second World War provided a cheaper, and many believed highly effective, method of controlling the key vector of the disease, the anopheline mosquito. The argument for eradicating malaria was led by Dr. E. J. Pampana (q.v.), who proposed, as early as 1948, that a global campaign should be undertaken. He later became the first director (q.v.) of the Division of Malaria Eradication. Prior to the initiation of the global program, the Pan American Sanitary Conference began its own campaign in the early 1950s, encouraged by Dr. Fred Soper (q.v.), an ardent advocate of disease eradication programs.

In May 1955, the World Health Assembly (q.v.) endorsed global eradication of malaria as a worldwide policy goal, and the program was established soon thereafter within a newly created Division of Malaria Eradication. Using a standard strategy of spraying with DDT and treating with chloroquine, the program enjoyed initial success in reducing the incidence of malaria. Significant extrabudgetary funds (EBFs) (q.v.) were received for the campaign, which led to national malaria eradication programs being established in almost all affected countries. By the mid-1960s, however, the limitations of the strategy and its technical difficulties were becoming apparent. Difficulties included resistance to DDT by the mosquitoes, the high cost of the program in developing countries, and unforeseen human and environmental side effects to spraying. In 1969, the director-general (q.v.) reported that a new malaria strategy was needed that addressed these problems. This led in effect to a return to a control, rather than eradication, strategy by the early 1970s. Principal financial donors, such as the United Nations Children's Fund (q.v.) and the United States Agency for International Development, also phased out their EBF support by this time. *See also* Malaria Control.

INTENSIFIED SMALLPOX ERADICATION PROGRAMME. A program created in 1967 to achieve the global eradication of smallpox. The disease had been frequently discussed in the World Health Assembly (WHA) (q.v.) since 1950, but no agreement had been reached on the feasibility of eradication. A commitment to eradicate smallpox in the Americas region was made by the Pan American Sanitary Organization as early as 1950, which met with some success. However, it was not until 1959 that the WHA agreed to undertake a global eradication campaign following the submission of a report by Dr. Viktor Zhdanov (q.v.), of the Soviet Union, on its feasibility. This was followed by further delay due to a focus of energy and resources on the eradication of malaria.

In 1966 the WHA agreed on the need to intensify efforts to eradicate smallpox despite reservations arising from problems with the Intensified Malaria Eradication Programme (q.v.). In 1967 it was estimated that smallpox was endemic in 37 countries (total population of over one billion) and that ten to 15 million people were stricken with the disease, leading to two million deaths. The program initiated a two-pronged strategy of mass vaccination campaigns and the development of a surveillance system for the detection and investigation of cases and the containment of outbreaks. The former was made possible by the availability of a freeze-dried vaccine that was easy to administer and provided long-term protection with a single application. The latter was possible because the symptoms of the disease were readily identifiable, enabling the mobilization of public health officials and the public to assist in the detection of the disease. The program was also guided by three important principles: (a) all countries needed to participate, requiring global, regional, and national coordination; (b) flexibility and adaptability were required in the implementation of national programs; and (c) ongoing research, both in the field and in the laboratory, was needed to evaluate progress and define alternative directions and methods.

The program was primarily financed by extrabudgetary funds (q.v.) and cost an estimated U.S.$4.3 billion over 13 years, with regular budget funds (q.v.) rarely exceeding U.S.$2.4 million annually. In May 1980 the WHA declared that the global eradication of smallpox had been successfully achieved, with the last naturally occurring case of the disease found in Somalia on 26 October 1977. At the 97th session of the Executive Board (q.v.) in 1996, a resolution was adopted to destroy the remaining stocks of the smallpox (variola) virus currently being held in Russia and the United States in 1999 in order to minimize risk to populations.

INTERAGENCY ADVISORY GROUP ON AIDS (IAAG). An advisory group established in 1988 by WHO, the United Nations Children's Fund, the United Nations Development Program, the United Nations Population Fund, the World Bank (qq.v.), and the United Nations Educational, Scientific and Cultural Organisation to facilitate the coordination of AIDS activities among United Nations (UN) organizations. The activities of the group included the exchange of information and program experience. Until 1992 the group met annually and was chaired by WHO's Global Programme on AIDS (q.v.), which also served as its secretariat. A report by the Secretariat with input from all members on their HIV/AIDS activities was submitted to the United Nations Economic and Social Council and the United Nations General Assembly. In 1992 the group agreed that the IAAG needed to be strengthened as the primary coordinating body in the UN system. For this purpose, it was agreed that meetings would be held semiannually, the chair would rotate annually among all members, and accountability for the activities of the group would be improved through regular reporting and sharing of work plans. *See also* Task Force on HIV/ AIDS Coordination.

INTERAGENCY AFFAIRS, DIVISION OF. *See* Division of Interagency Affairs.

INTERAGENCY COORDINATING COMMITTEE (ICC). A committee created in 1985 to coordinate financial support for the Polio Eradication Programme (q.v.) in the Americas region. The eradication campaign is part of the work of the Expanded Programme on Immunization (q.v.), which was launched in the region in 1977. The members of the committee are the Pan American Health Organization, the United Nations Children's Fund (qq.v.), USAID, the Inter-American Development Bank, the Canadian Public Health Association, and Rotary International. To assist in resource mobilization, national committees chaired by a government representative were also set up in each country in the region. *See also* Polio Eradication Initiative.

INTERAGENCY IMMUNIZATION COORDINATING COMMITTEE (IICC). A committee established by the Kyoto Declaration of 1994 to strengthen national immunization programs, take immediate action on current and potential outbreaks of disease, and achieve vaccine self-sufficiency. The IICC is composed of the governments of Canada, Japan, Norway, Turkey, the United States, member states (q.v.) of the European Union, the International Federation of Red Cross and Red Crescent Societies (IFRC), the United Nations Children's Fund (q.v.), and WHO. WHO serves as the IICC's secretariat. *See also* Children's Vaccine Initiative; Expanded Programme of Immunization; Global Programme for Vaccines and Immunization.

INTERAGENCY STANDING COMMITTEE. *See* Division of Emergency Relief Operations.

INTERAGENCY STEERING COMMITTEE ON WATER SUPPLY AND SANITATION. A committee set up in 1989 to monitor the drinking water supply and sanitation component of Agenda 21 agreed on at the United Nations Conference on Environment and Development (q.v.). The committee is composed of United Nations organizations with activities related to water and sanitation, including the United Nations Environment Program, the United Nations Children's Fund, the World Bank (qq.v.), and WHO. WHO supports the work of the committee by providing information on the health implications of safe drinking water and sanitation. *See also* International Drinking Water and Sanitation Decade; Programme for the Global Elimination of Dracunculiasis.

INTERAGENCY TASK FORCE FOR CHILD SURVIVAL. *See* Task Force for Child Survival.

INTERHEALTH PROGRAMME. A program launched in January 1990 at a meeting held by WHO in Helsinki, Finland, to deal with diseases arising from unhealthy lifestyles. The meeting discussed evidence linking behavioral and environmental risk factors (e.g., tobacco, hypertension, obesity) to so-called diseases of affluence, which result from contemporary lifestyles. The purpose of the program is to encourage governments, scientists, and nongovernmental organizations (q.v.) to promote healthier lifestyles to prevent such risk factors. *See also* Division of Health Promotion, Education, and Communication.

INTERIM COMMISSION. A commission created in 1946, by an arrangement made at the International Health Conference (q.v.), to carry out responsibilities assigned to WHO until the latter organization could be formally established. It was initially believed that the commission would function for only a few months. However, because of delays in obtaining the required 26 signatures by member states ratifying the constitution (qq.v.), the commission operated for two years (1946–48). The commission consisted of 18 technically qualified experts in the field of health from nominated countries. Its main functions were to (a) prepare for the establishment of the permanent international health organization; (b) carry on the statutory functions of existing organizations; and (c) continue emergency international health activities. Its work was largely carried out through five internal committees: Administration and Finance, Relations, Technical Questions, Priorities, and Headquarters. During its existence, the commission held five sessions. Upon the formal creation of WHO in 1948, the commission was disestablished.

INTERNATIONAL AGENCY FOR RESEARCH ON CANCER (IARC). An agency established by WHO in 1965 to promote international collaboration in cancer research. Based in Lyon, France, the agency serves as a means through which participating member states (q.v.) and WHO, in liaison with the International Union against Cancer and other interested international organizations, may cooperate in the stimulation and support of all phases of cancer research. The agency is composed of (a) the Governing Council, comprising one representative of each participating member state and the director-general (q.v.); (b) the Scientific Council, comprising a maximum of 20 highly qualified scientists appointed by the Governing Council to discuss the annual report of the IARC and review and evaluate selected programs; and (c) the Secretariat, which serves as the agency's administrative and technical organ. The IARC is funded by annual contributions from each participating member state at levels determined by the Governing Council. *See also* Latin American Cancer Research Information Project.

INTERNATIONAL ASSOCIATION OF CANCER REGISTRIES (IACR). An association founded in 1966 to encourage the development and application of cancer registration and morbidity techniques to studies of defined population groups and to increase awareness of the importance of producing accurate and comparable morbidity and mortality data for cancer control as a means of improving services to the cancer patient. The membership of the association consists of institutions and individuals in 78 countries. Its activities include scientific meetings, publications, development of standard methods and techniques for registration practices, and epidemiological studies on aspects of cancer. The IACR is governed by an Executive Board (q.v.), composed of the president, general secretary, and deputy secretary, and regional representatives from Africa, Asia and the Pacific, South America, Europe and the Near East, and North America. The International Agency for Research on Cancer provides the secretariat (q.v.). The IACR was admitted into official relations with WHO as a nongovernmental organization (q.v.) in 1979. WHO, through the Division of Health Situation and Trend Assessment (q.v.), and the association also cooperate in the production of publications using data on cancer incidence worldwide.

INTERNATIONAL BABY FOOD ACTION NETWORK (IBFAN). An international coalition of nongovernmental organizations (q.v.) formed in 1979 to campaign against the marketing practices of manufacturers of breast milk substitutes, especially in developing countries. The organization successfully lobbied for the adoption of the International Code on the Marketing of Breastmilk Substitutes (q.v.) in 1981 and remained active in monitoring companies' adherence to the code. *See also* Baby-Friendly Hospital Initiative; Infant Formula Action Coalition; International Council of Infant Food Industries.

INTERNATIONAL BUREAU OF THE AMERICAN REPUBLICS. *See* Organization of American States.

INTERNATIONAL CENTER FOR DIARRHOEAL DISEASE RESEARCH, BANGLADESH (ICDDR,B). A center established in 1960 by WHO as the Cholera Research Laboratory to study the epidemiology, treatment, and prevention of cholera. Over the years, additional facilities and activities have been added, including the Matlab field station (1963), the Demographic Surveillance System (1966), the Urban Volunteer Programme (1981), the Matlab Health and Research Centre (1992), and the Sasakawa International Training Centre (1992). In 1978 the center became known as the International Center for Diarrhoeal Disease Research, Bangladesh. Today, the center is an independent, international, and nonprofit organization for research, education, training, and clinical service. Located in Dhaka, Bangladesh, it is the only truly independent health research institution based in a developing country. The mission of the center is broadly defined as "to develop and disseminate solutions to major health and population problems facing the world, with emphasis on simple and cost-effective methods of prevention and management," and today it is known as the ICDDR,B Center for Health and Population Research.

The results of research have provided guidelines for policy makers, implementing agencies, and health professionals in Bangladesh and worldwide. Its achievements include the development of oral rehydration solution in 1968 and advances in diarrhoeal disease control, maternal and child health, and nutrition and population sciences.

The ICDDR,B is governed by a 17-member international board of trustees comprised of researchers, educators, public health administrators, and representatives of the government of Bangladesh, WHO, and the United Nations Children's Fund (q.v.), who are responsible for providing general direction to the activities and interests of the center. The board appoints a director and four division directors to head scientific divisions (Clinical Sciences; Community Health; Laboratory Sciences; Population and Family Planning) and a Division of Finance, Administration, and Personnel. The board also appoints a 53-member Programme Coordination Committee to coordinate research with national health institutions, strengthen research capabilities, and promote collaborative research. A Research Review Committee reviews all research proposals with regard to scientific merit, relevance to objectives and priorities, and financial resources. A Training Coordination Bureau coordinates efforts to provide a broad training program for the development of human resources in child survival and population activities. The center currently has a total staff of 1,200, including approximately 200 researchers and medical staff from ten countries. It is funded by extrabudgetary funds (q.v.) by governments, foundations, and individuals; in 1995 the center's funding amounted to approximately U.S.$12.4 million.

INTERNATIONAL CENTER FOR TRAINING AND RESEARCH IN LEPROSY AND RELATED DISEASES. *See* Pan American Center for Training and Research in Leprosy and Related Diseases.

INTERNATIONAL CLASSIFICATION OF DISEASES AND RELATED HEALTH PROBLEMS. A reference text of all ailments known to medical science, published and regularly revised by WHO to promote international uniformity in the recording by statistical bureaus of mortality and morbidity data, as well as in the compilation of hospital records. *See also International Classification of Impairments, Disabilities, and Handicaps.*

INTERNATIONAL CLASSIFICATION OF IMPAIRMENTS, DISABILITIES, AND HANDICAPS (ICIDH). A multivolume reference text that lists all known impairments, disabilities, and handicaps according to internationally standardized classifications. *See also* International Classification of Diseases and Related Health Problems; International Statistical Classification of Diseases, Injuries, and Causes of Death.

INTERNATIONAL CODE ON THE MARKETING OF BREAST-MILK SUBSTITUTES. A code, in the form of nonbinding recommendations, adopted by the World Health Assemby (WHA) and the United Nations Children's Fund (qq.v.) in 1981 as a guideline on the marketing of breast-milk substitutes (infant formula) by food manufacturers. The adoption of the code followed an active campaign, beginning in the early 1970s, led by nongovernmental organizations (NGOs) (q.v.) against selected marketing practices aimed at new mothers in developing countries. The campaign presented evidence that the marketing practices were leading to harmful feeding practices. This led the WHA to adopt a resolution in 1974 urging member states (q.v.) to review the marketing of breast-milk substitutes in their countries. Despite protests from the food industry, the code was adopted by a vote of 118:3:1, with the United States opposed. Among the code's stipulations are that manufacturers not use health care facilities or health visitors to promote infant formulas, should not distribute free samples to new mothers, and should acknowledge the superiority of breast-feeding on product labels.

As a result of the code and the continual lobbing of NGOs, the Swiss company Nestlé signed an unprecedented agreement in January 1984 to adhere to the code. Since the mid-1980s, WHO has continued to develop activities to promote infant and young-child nutrition, including technical support to national governments for implementing the code. For this purpose, the Innocenti Declaration was adopted, which set operational targets for the code's implementation within member states. *See also* Baby-Friendly Hospital Initiative; Infant Formula Action Coalition; International Baby Food Action Network; International Council of Infant Food Industries; Mother-Baby Package.

INTERNATIONAL COMMISSION FOR THE CERTIFICATION OF DRACUNCULIASIS ERADICATION. An international body created in 1996 to deliberate on the conditions for certifying that individual countries have eradicated dracunculiasis (guinea-worm disease). Global eradication, defined as the absence of all clinical manifestations of the disease worldwide for three years, is expected to be certified by the end of the century. The campaign against the disease began in 1980 within the context of the International Drinking Water and Sanitation Decade (q.v.). Since 1986 global prevalence of the disease has been reduced by 97 percent. A lack of political support and resources led to the failure to achieve the interruption of guinea-worm transmission in all countries affected by 1995. This has led to an intensified effort through the Programme for the Global Elimination of Dracunculiasis (q.v.).

INTERNATIONAL CONFERENCE OF DRUG REGULATORY AUTHORITIES (ICDRA). A meeting created in 1979 under the aegis of WHO, and cosponsored (q.v.) by the United States Food and Drug Administration, to promote collaboration between national authorities on the regulation of drugs, to forge consensus on matters of mutual interest, and to discuss contemporaneous issues of international relevance. The meeting was first held in Annapolis, Maryland, United States, and is currently held biennially in Geneva, attended by officials of national regulatory authorities from ministries of health or drug administration agencies. The objectives of the meetings are to build consensus on matters of mutual interest, facilitate timely and adequate exchange of technical information, and discuss contemporary issues of international relevance to drug regulation. *See also* Division of Drug Management and Policies; International Conference on Harmonization of Technical Requirements for Registration of Pharmaceuticals for Human Use.

INTERNATIONAL CONFERENCE ON AIDS. A conference held annually since 1985, cosponsored by WHO, to bring together leading researchers and existing knowledge on HIV/AIDS. With AIDS seen initially as a biomedical problem, delegates to early conferences were largely from the biomedical sciences. By the time of the third conference, however, the balance had begun to shift toward a greater recognition of the need also to study the wider (e.g., social, economic) dimensions of AIDS. As such, the conference has grown rapidly, from an ad hoc meeting to one attended by thousands of delegates including researchers, medical professionals, and representatives of governments, nongovernmental organizations (q.v.), and private companies. WHO maintains a policy of nonsponsorship of international AIDS conferences in countries that place short-term travel restrictions on HIV-infected people and people with AIDS, a policy that was approved for application throughout the United Nations system in 1993. Accordingly, WHO and other UN organizations will not sponsor, cosponsor, or financially support international conferences or meetings on AIDS in countries whose entry requirements discriminate solely on the basis of a person's HIV status. To date, conferences have been held in Atlanta (1985), Paris (1986), Washington (1987), Stockholm (1988), Montreal (1989), San Francisco (1990), Florence (1991), Amsterdam (1992), Japan (1994), Vancouver (1996), and Geneva (1998).

INTERNATIONAL CONFERENCE ON HARMONIZATION OF TECHNICAL REQUIREMENTS FOR REGISTRATION OF PHARMACEUTICALS FOR HUMAN USE (ICH). A meeting instituted in 1991 as a forum for discussion between representatives of regulatory authorities of member states (q.v.) of the European Union, Japan, and the United States and experts from the pharmaceutical industry within these countries. WHO consults with the ICH to determine the global applicability of its proposals to the broader constituency of other member states. *See also* International Conference of Drug Regulatory Authorities.

INTERNATIONAL CONFERENCE ON HEALTH PROMOTION. A series of conferences organized by WHO to discuss the role of health promotion in international public health and to identify strategies and actions to be taken to contribute to the Health for All (q.v.) strategy. At the first conference, held in Ottawa, Canada, in 1986, the philosophy of health promotion and orientation for action and evaluation were expressed as principles in the Ottawa Charter for Health Promotion. The charter pledges WHO to "move into the arena of healthy public policy, and to advocate a clear political commitment to health and equity in all sectors; reorient health services and their disciplines, and, most importantly, with people themselves." It states that health promotion should go beyond prevention, protection, and education to include participation by people in taking control of their own health through methods of mediation, enablement, and advocacy. For this purpose a strategy of five action areas was suggested: (a) building healthy public policy; (c) creating supportive environments; (c) strengthening community action; (d) developing personal skills; and (e) reorienting health services. The second conference, held in Adelaide, Australia, in 1988, concentrated on healthy public policy as an arm of health promotion. The third conference, held in Sundsvall, Sweden, in 1991, focused on the creation of healthy environments and the adoption of the Sundsvall Declaration on Health Promotion.

INTERNATIONAL CONFERENCE ON NUTRITION (ICN). A conference convened in Rome, Italy, in December 1992 by the Food and Agriculture Organization and WHO to consider the problems of hunger, malnutrition, and the increasing incidence of diet-related diseases and how they can most effectively be addressed. The conference issued a World Declaration and

Plan of Action for Nutrition, which sought to reinforce commitment to action by countries and the international community. Since the conference, WHO has defined indicators for monitoring progress in countries toward the goals of the conference based on a two-fold strategy: (a) to encourage countries to reduce malnutrition and promote good nutrition through national plans of action; and (b) to provide normative guidance and information on scientific issues relating to the prevention, management, and monitoring of malnutrition. Of particular emphasis has been an initiative on the Elimination of Iodine Deficiency Disorders (q.v.) by the year 2000, for which efforts had been accelerated since the mid-1980s. Working with the United Nations Children's Fund (q.v.) and the International Council for the Control of Iodine Deficiency Disorders, WHO has provided technical guidance and program support to member states (q.v.) and the international community. *See also* Codex Alimentarius Commission; Division of Food and Nutrition; Vitamin A.

INTERNATIONAL CONFERENCE ON POPULATION AND DEVELOPMENT (ICPD). A conference held in Cairo, Egypt, in September 1994 to discuss population issues, bearing in mind the overall aims of sustained economic growth and development. It was the third United Nations conference on population to be held, with previous conferences held in Bucharest (1974) and Mexico City (1984). The conference was attended by more than 10,000 participants from 179 countries and included a large forum of nongovernmental organizations (NGOs) (q.v.). Convened with the cooperation of the United Nations Population Fund (q.v.) and the United Nations Population Commission, the conference adopted a program of action as a means of mobilizing renewed political support and resources in the population field. A prominent feature of the program of action was the shift in strategy, from a focus on population control toward an approach that emphasizes an individual's quality of life with respect to reproductive health.

WHO's participation in the ICPD began with contributions to meetings of the preparatory committee, expert group meetings, regional conferences, and roundtable meetings. It was during these preliminary meetings that WHO provided a working definition of the concept of reproductive health, based on the organization's definition of health overall, as "a state of complete physical, mental and social well-being and not merely the absence of disease or infirmity, in all matters relating to the reproductive system and to its functions and processes." This definition was later adopted in the ICPD program of action. Following the conference, WHO reviewed its role and responsibilities in carrying out the new global strategy on reproductive health. This was identified as comprising the following areas: (a) international and national advocacy for the concept of reproductive health and for the policies and programs promoted by WHO; (b) research aimed at assessing needs, at adapting and applying existing knowledge, and at developing new approaches and interventions, together with coordination of global efforts in these areas; (c) normative activities (q.v.) including the development of policies, strategic approaches, norms, standards, and guidelines; and (d) technical support to member states (q.v.) and others in formulating, implementing, and evaluating comprehensive national reproductive health policies and programs. To carry out these activities in light of the ICPD, WHO activities related to reproductive health were reorganized in 1996 with the creation of a new Family and Reproductive Health Programme (q.v.). *See also* Division of Reproductive Health (Technical Support); Special Programme of Research, Development, and Research Training in Human Reproduction.

INTERNATIONAL CONFERENCE ON PRIMARY HEALTH CARE. Also known as the Alma-Ata Conference. A historic public health conference co-convened by WHO and the United Nations Children's Fund (UNICEF) (q.v.) in 1978 in Alma-Ata, Kazakstan. The conference was held in response to international concern over the widespread inequities that existed in health and health care in both industrialized and developing countries. The origins of the conference began in 1974 when the World Health Assembly (WHA) (q.v.) drew attention to striking disparities in health and health services within and between countries and asked the director-general (q.v.) to explore the possibilities for more effective action. In 1975 the Executive Board (q.v.) and the WHA called for an international conference on the subject, which the former Soviet Union agreed to host. In 1977 the WHA adopted Health for All by the Year 2000, which specified that the main social target of governments and WHO in coming decades should be the attainment of all citizens of the world by the year 2000 of a level of health that would permit them to live a socially and economically productive life.

The conference was attended by 134 member states (q.v.)

and 67 United Nations organizations and nongovernmental organizations (q.v.). The main documentation for the conference was a joint report by the director-general of WHO and the executive director of UNICEF entitled "Primary Health Care," which was extensively discussed by participants. At the close of the conference, the participants unanimously issued the Alma-Ata Declaration, which set out the basic components of the primary health care (q.v.) approach as a framework and strategy for achieving Health for All (q.v.). The pronouncement of the Alma-Ata Declaration had an immediate effect on the global strategies of WHO and has dominated its policies and programs ever since. In 1988 WHO, UNICEF, and other interested parties held a meeting in Riga, Latvia, entitled From Alma-Ata to the Year 2000: A Midpoint Perspective, to review progress toward Health for All over the past decade. The participants reaffirmed commitment to the strategy of Health for All, and the WHA adopted a resolution to strengthen primary health care. *See also* Health for All; Renewing the Health for All Strategy; Appendix F.

INTERNATIONAL CONSULTATION MEETING ON THE CONTROL OF ACUTE RESPIRATORY INFECTIONS. A meeting held in Washington, D.C., in 1991 to analyze progress and declare commitment to the Programme for the Control of Acute Respiratory Infections (q.v.). Organized by WHO, the Pan American Health Organization (PAHO), the United Nations Children's Fund (UNICEF), and the United Nations Development Program (qq.v.), the meeting was attended by specialists and representatives of international organizations supporting the work of the program. The meeting was followed by the creation of an Interagency Coordinating Committee for the Control of Acute Respiratory Infections composed of PAHO, UNICEF, and the United States Agency for International Development.

INTERNATIONAL CONSULTATION ON HEALTH EDUCATION FOR SCHOOL-AGE CHILDREN. *See* Action-Oriented School Health Curriculum.

INTERNATIONAL COUNCIL OF INFANT FOOD INDUSTRIES (ICIFI). An organization created in 1975 to represent the interests of manufacturers of breast-milk substitutes (infant formula). The organization lobbied unsuccessfully during the 1970s against the adoption of the International Code on the

Marketing of Breastmilk Substitutes by WHO and the United Nations Children's Fund (qq.v.). *See also* Baby-Friendly Hospital Initiative; Infant Formula Action Coalition; International Baby Food Action Network.

INTERNATIONAL DECADE FOR NATURAL DISASTER REDUCTION. *See* Division of Emergency Relief Operations.

INTERNATIONAL DIGEST OF HEALTH LEGISLATION. *See* Health Legislation Unit.

INTERNATIONAL DRINKING WATER AND SANITATION DECADE. A ten-year campaign (1981–90) initiated by the United Nations in 1981 to promote awareness of the importance for health of safe drinking water and sanitation. Among the health implications of unsafe water supply and sanitation is the transmission of cholera and typhoid. WHO headquarters and regional offices (qq.v.) took part in the campaign by providing support for training, information dissemination, research, and promotion of appropriate technology. At the United Nations Conference on the Environment and Development (q.v.), WHO drew attention to the impact of deforestation and desertification on water supplies. Since the end of the decade, WHO has advocated continued efforts to ensure safe drinking water and sanitation following a decline in attention by international organizations. *See also* Global Environmental Monitoring System Water Programme; Interagency Steering Committee on Water Supply and Sanitation; Programme for the Global Elimination of Dracunculiasis.

INTERNATIONAL DRUG MONITORING PROGRAMME. A program and WHO collaborating center (q.v.) created in the 1960s, after the seriously adverse effects of the drug thalidomide on pregnant women became apparent, to provide an international system of monitoring and reporting on drug safety. The program was initially set up in Alexandria, Virginia, United States, and later moved to Uppsala, Sweden, in response to the Swedish government's funding of the program.

INTERNATIONAL EMF PROJECT. A project launched by WHO in 1996 to assess the health and environmental effects of exposure to electric magnetic fields (EMFs). Scheduled to last for five years and funded by extrabudgetary funds (q.v.), the project pools current knowledge and available resources of key international and national agencies and scientific institutions to arrive at scientifically sound recommendations for health risk assessments of exposure to static and time-varying EMFs. The project is intended to provide authoritative and independent peer review of the scientific literature and to identify and fill gaps in knowledge by establishing protocols for the conduct of research using compatible and comparable methodology.

INTERNATIONAL FEDERATION OF PHARMACEUTICAL MANUFACTURERS ASSOCIATIONS (IFPMA). An association that represents the interests of the pharmaceutical industry at the international level through lobbying of national governments and international organizations. With member associations in 47 countries, the IFPMA gained consultative status in WHO as a nongovernmental organization (q.v.) in 1971. It played a prominent role during the 1970s and 1980s when it opposed the Model List of Essential Drugs (q.v.). With the World Health Assembly's adoption of the International Code on the Marketing of Breastmilk Substitutes (qq.v.) in 1981, the IFPMA proposed its own voluntary code on the marketing of pharmaceuticals the same year. *See also* Drug Action Programme/Action Programme on Essential Drugs; Essential Drugs Programme.

INTERNATIONAL HEALTH CONFERENCE. A conference convened in New York by ECOSOC in June 1946 "to prepare a constitution or charter providing for the establishment of a World Health Organization." Those in attendance agreed to hold the conference following a resolution issued by the governments of Brazil and China to remedy the omission of health from the Charter of the United Nations signed in 1945. Preparations for the conference were carried out by a technical preparatory committee (q.v.) composed of ministers of health, or the equivalent, of United Nations member states (q.v.). A total of 51 delegates attended the conference, as well as observers from nonmember states, the Allied Control Authorities for Germany, Japan, and Korea, and relevant international organizations such as the United Nations Relief and Rehabilitation Administration (q.v.), the Pan American Sanitary Organization, and the League of Red Cross Societies. At the final session of the conference, four documents were signed: (a) the Final Act of the International Health Conference; (b) the WHO constitution; (c) an arrangement establishing the Interim Commission (qq.v.); and (d) a protocol on the disestablishment of the Office

International d'Hygiène Publique (q.v.) and the transfer of its functions to WHO upon the latter's creation.

INTERNATIONAL HEALTH DIVISION. *See* Rockefeller Foundation.

INTERNATIONAL HEALTH REGULATIONS. A set of regulations adopted by the World Health Assembly (WHA) (q.v.) in 1951, known as the International Sanitary Regulations, to govern the sanitary conditions required by all forms of transport (i.e., shipping, aircraft, trains, and automobiles) for preventing the international spread of disease. The regulations were adopted to consolidate and update the various International Sanitary Conventions that had been adopted and put into use since the nineteenth century. The new regulations replaced this multiplicity of conventions with a single code based on modern epidemiological principles and provided an international instrument that could be adapted to changing conditions with minimum delay. During 1946–48, preliminary studies were carried out by a series of expert groups jointly convened by WHO and the Office International d'Hygiène Publique (q.v.) to draft the regulations. In 1950 the draft regulations were submitted to the WHA for comment by member states (q.v.); the regulations were adopted in May 1951 and came into force in 1952.

The regulations include special provisions for diseases warranting quarantine, such as plague, cholera, louse-borne typhus, smallpox, and yellow fever, as well as conditions under which vaccination may be required as a condition for entering a country. Models of certificates of vaccination, deratting, and other health declarations were also provided. The regulations also stated that WHO be notified of the appearance of diseases warranting quarantine, information on which WHO depends for disseminating worldwide via the mass media and publication of the *Weekly Epidemiological Record* (q.v.). In 1995 an international consultation was held to consider the continuous evolution in the public health threat caused by infectious diseases, the likelihood that the increase in international travel will disseminate diseases more rapidly, and the need for and role of the International Health Regulations in the 21st century.

INTERNATIONAL LISTS OF CAUSES OF DEATH. *See* International Lists of Diseases and Causes of Death.

INTERNATIONAL LISTS OF DISEASES AND CAUSES OF DEATH. An internationally agreed-upon list introduced in

1891 by the International Statistical Institute to provide a single classification of medical nomenclature that can be uniformly used to determine and record all causes of disease and death. Initially known as the International Lists of Causes of Death, it was agreed in 1898 to revise the lists every ten years. This was carried out by an expert committee (q.v.), assisted by research by officially appointed bodies in member states (q.v.), in 1900, 1910, 1920, 1929, and 1938. One of the first activities of the Interim Commission (q.v.) was to set up an Expert Committee for the Preparation of the Sixth Decennial Revision of the International Lists of Diseases and Causes of Death and to hold a conference of this committee in Paris in 1948. The conference produced the International Statistical Classification of Diseases, Injuries, and Causes of Death (q.v.), together with Regulation No. 1, which was adopted by the World Health Assembly (q.v.) in July 1948.

INTERNATIONAL NETWORK FOR THE RATIONAL USE OF DRUGS (INRUD). A network established in 1989, by Asian and African countries with the support of a wide range of organizations, to promote the rational use of pharmaceuticals. INRUD consists of a network committee of representatives from ten African and Asian countries (Bangladesh, Ghana, Indonesia, Nepal, Nigeria, the Philippines, Tanzania, Thailand, Uganda, and Zimbabwe) and six support groups including WHO's Action Programme on Essential Drugs and Programme for the Control of Diarrhoeal Diseases (q.v.). INRUD's strategy includes (a) an interdisciplinary focus linking clinical and social sciences; (b) activities orginating from country-based core groups of individuals representing ministries of health, universities, nongovernmental organizations (q.v.), and private sector institutions; (c) belief in the importance of sharing relevant experience and technical cooperation (q.v.) among participating individuals; (d) emphasis on understanding behavioral aspects of drug use; (e) promotion of well-designed research studies to understand behavioral factors; and (e) development of useful tools for research, including standard research methodologies, simplified sampling and data collection strategies, and user-accessible computer software. *See also* Essential Drugs Programme; Model List of Essential Drugs.

INTERNATIONAL NOMENCLATURE OF DISEASES. A joint project of WHO and the Council for International Organizations of Medical Sciences to reduce confusion in medical nomenclature and facilitate information retrieval. For every known pathological entity, the nomenclature provides the following: (a) a single recommended name; (b) a comprehensive list of synonyms; and (c) a clear description or definition of the entity reflecting most-recent knowledge. The nomenclature is prepared with the guidance of an expert advisory panel (q.v.) and disseminated, through a series of publications, only when consensus is reached among its members.

INTERNATIONAL OBESITY TASK FORCE. A global initiative launched in 1996 to raise awareness of obesity as a serious medical condition and major health problem. Led by Dr. Philip James, director of the Rowett Research Institute in Aberdeen, Scotland, the initiative aims to challenge current management and prevention strategies, which are believed unable to address the rapidly rising incidence of obesity. The direct and indirect costs attributable to obesity represent nearly 10 percent of the total sick-care costs in Western countries. Severe obesity is associated with a 12-fold increase in mortality in 25- to 35-year-olds. *See also* Victoria Declaration on Heart Health.

INTERNATIONAL PHARMACOPOEIA. A reference text first published in 1953, and since periodically updated and expanded, to present norms for in-process control of biological preparations and for the testing of all finished products within national control laboratories. The specific objectives of the *International Pharmacopoeia* are (a) to provide specifications on the purity and potency of essential drug substances, widely used excipient materials, and related dosage forms; (b) to support such specifications with readily applicable methods of testing and analysis, with attention to the facilities available within control laboratories in developing countries; (c) to provide general methods of analysis that would be applicable not only to materials included in the pharmacopoeia but also to new products submitted for registration; (d) to accommodate, where appropriate, a measure of flexibility into methods and requirements that will facilitate the use of the International Pharmacopoeia on a global basis; and (e) to present all these elements in such a manner that the International Pharmacopoeia, or selected parts of it, can be officially adopted by any member state (q.v.). The text is prepared through the circulation of drafts for comment, prior to publication, by members of the Expert Advisory Panel (q.v.) on the International Pharmacopoeia and Pharmaceutical Preparations and regulatory authorities of member states. *See also* Pharmaceuticals Unit.

INTERNATIONAL PROGRAMME ON CHEMICAL SAFETY (IPCS). A cooperative program of WHO, the UN Environment Program (UNEP), and the International Labour Organization (ILO) created in 1980 to carry out cooperative activities on the public health, environmental, and occupational factors related to chemical safety. With WHO as executing agency (q.v.), the program's main activities are (a) to provide internationally evaluated scientific information to serve as a basis for chemical risk assessment, management, and safety measures by member states (q.v.); and (b) to strengthen national capabilities and capacities for chemical safety. For this purpose, the IPCS works through a network of about 75 institutions in 32 countries, which conduct basic research in assessing carcinogenic, mutagenic, and teratogenic effects of chemicals on health. This information, presented in the form of documents such as Environmental Health Criteria and Health and Safety Guides, is used by member states to develop national policies and measures to ensure the safe use of chemicals. The Steering Committee on Chemical Safety coordinates related activities within WHO. In 1992 the United Nations Conference on Environment and Development (q.v.) called on the program to strengthen its role in coordinating related activities of other international organizations and enhancing cooperation among them. Coordination between WHO, UNEP, and the ILO is carried out through regular meetings of an Inter-Secretariat Coordinating Committee. Policy advice to the executive heads of the three cosponsoring (q.v.) organizations is provided through meetings of a Programme Advisory Committee. All three United Nations organizations allocate regular budget funds (q.v.) to the IPCS, with extrabudgetary funds (q.v.) also received. The budget for the 1994–95 biennium was approximately U.S.$13 million.

INTERNATIONAL PROGRAMME ON THE HEALTH EFFECTS OF THE CHERNOBYL ACCIDENT (IPHECA). A program created in 1981 following the accident at the Chernobyl nuclear power station in the Ukraine. The objectives of the program are (a) to contribute to the alleviation of the health consequences of the accident by assisting the health authorities in Belarus, the Russian Federation, and Ukraine; (b) to consolidate the experience gained from treatment of overexposure to radiation and from other practical interventions so as to improve medical preparedness for the future; and (c) to acquire data in the fields of radiation epidemiology and disaster medicine. The program is envisaged as a flexible long-term effort whose duration will depend on need and available resources.

The program is guided by a management committee composed of representatives of the three affected states, countries that have donated resources to the program, and WHO. The primary tasks of the management committee are to review progress made in the implementation of the program, approve work plans, and consider matters of coordination, mobilization, and use of resources. The program is financed by extra-budgetary funds (q.v.) with the Czech and Slovak Republic, Finland, and Japan being the largest contributors. *See also* Division of Emergency and Humanitarian Action; Division of Emergency Relief Operations.

INTERNATIONAL SANITARY BUREAU. *See* Pan American Sanitary Bureau.

INTERNATIONAL SANITARY CONFERENCES (1851–1903). A series of 11 international conferences, beginning in Paris in 1851, to promote intergovernmental health cooperation. The conferences were initiated in response to the epidemics of cholera, plague, typhus, and influenza that periodically swept through Europe and other parts of the world. The conferences culminated with the agreement of International Sanitary Conventions and the establishment of the Office International d'Hygiène Publique (q.v.). *See also* International Health Regulations.

INTERNATIONAL SANITARY CONVENTION OF THE AMERICAN REPUBLICS. A series of intergovernmental conferences, beginning in 1902, to promote health cooperation in the Americas region. Delegates to the first convention agreed to the creation of the International Sanitary Bureau (later known as the Pan American Sanitary Bureau [q.v.]), the forerunner of the Pan American Health Organization (q.v.).

INTERNATIONAL SANITARY REGULATIONS. *See* International Health Regulations.

INTERNATIONAL SCIENTIFIC AND TECHNICAL COMMITTEE FOR THE CONTROL OF EBOLA HEMORRHAGIC

FEVER. An international committee of institutions created in 1995 to coordinate international efforts to control the outbreak of the Ebola hemorrhagic fever in Zaire. The committee consisted of staff of WHO from both the African Regional Office and headquarters (qq.v.), the United States Centers for Disease Control, the Institute Pasteur (France), the National Institute for Virology (South Africa), Medicins sans Frontieres (Belgium), and the Federation of Red Cross and Red Crescent Societies. Working on agreed-on aspects of the control program, the institutional members were able to contain the spread of the disease within two months. The outbreak resulted in 315 confirmed cases, of which 244 (77 percent) died. *See also* Division of Emerging and Other Communicable Diseases.

INTERNATIONAL STATISTICAL CLASSIFICATION OF DISEASES, INJURIES, AND CAUSES OF DEATH. A multivolume reference text created by the World Health Assembly (q.v.) in 1948 to provide an internationally standardized list of all known diseases, injuries, and causes of death. The classification is the successor to the International Lists of Diseases and Causes of Death dating from the nineteenth century. The classification is published in a manual and auxiliary publication, *Index Alphabeticus*, to assist countries using Latin medical terminology. In 1951, the WHO Centre for Classification of Diseases was established in London to deal with problems arising from the interpretation and application of the classification. The classification is revised every ten years under the guidance of an expert committee, working with the United Nations Statistical Office and International Labour Organization. The reference text is currently in its tenth revision and available in 30 languages. *See also International Classification of Impairments, Disabilities, and Handicaps.*

INTERNATIONAL VACCINE INSTITUTE (IVI). An institute created in 1996, under the umbrella of the Children's Vaccine Initiative (q.v.) and with the strong support of the United Nations Development Program (q.v.), to improve human health through research, development, and the strengthening of capabilities in vaccine sciences for developing countries. Based in Seoul, Republic of Korea, the institute was founded on the belief that the health of children in developing countries can be dramatically improved by the development, introduction, and use of new and improved vaccines. The institute is intended to be a center of vaccine research for public interest by catalyzing and facilitating research through in-house programs and collaboration with public and private sector institutions.

INTERORGANIZATIONAL COORDINATING COMMITTEE. *See* International Programme on Chemical Safety.

J

JACQUES PARISOT FOUNDATION FELLOWSHIP. A fellowship awarded periodically to an individual for his or her contribution to international public health. The fellowship was established in 1969 in memory of Jacques Parisot (q.v.), who served as president of the Health Committee of the League of Nations (q.v.) from 1937 to 1940. *See also* Child Health Foundation Prize and Fellowship; Fellowship Programme; Francesco Pocchiari Fellowship.

JOINT COMMITTEE ON HEALTH POLICY (JCHP). A committee created in 1948 as a forum for WHO and the United Nations Children's Fund (UNICEF) (q.v.) to consult and exchange information on their health activities. As the interagency committee of longest standing in the UN system, it consists of six members of the Executive Boards (q.v.) of each organization. The committee met every two years until 1990, since which it has met annually. It also holds liaison meetings twice each year. According to the principles laid down by the committee, WHO is "the directing and coordinating authority on international health work." While UNICEF's role is to contribute needed supplies and services. The meetings of the JCHP have led to a number of joint initiatives. For example, a joint program was initiated in 1981 following the establishment of the Action Programme on Essential Drugs. The JCHP also produces joint reports on tuberculosis, syphilis in pregnant women and children, malaria, training and fellowships, maternal and child health and nutrition, environmental sanitation, health education, and milk hygiene.

JOINT COORDINATING BOARD (JCB). *See* UNDP/World Bank/WHO Special Programme for Research and Training in Tropical Diseases.

JOINT GOVERNMENT/WHO POLICY REVIEW. A process of review initiated by the Eastern Mediterranean Regional Office (q.v.) in 1983 and carried out every two years. The purpose of the review exercise is to examine programs and relevant budget estimates for their contribution to national strategies for achieving Health for All (q.v.). This is undertaken jointly by member states (q.v.) of the region and includes, wherever possible, representation from other sectors concerned.

JOINT MEDICAL SERVICE. *See* Division of Personnel.

JOINT PROGRAMME REVIEW. A joint review of national health programs carried out by WHO and the government concerned to determine whether an activity would be an appropriate use of WHO resources. The reviews are carried out by joint program review missions consisting of staff from WHO and the national government.

JOINT UNITED NATIONS PROGRAMME ON HIV/AIDS (UN-AIDS). A program created in January 1996, replacing the Global Programme on AIDS (q.v.), to lead, strengthen, and support an expanded response for the prevention, control, and treatment of HIV/AIDS. It is a cosponsored program (q.v.) of six United Nations organizations: WHO, the United Nations Development Program (UNDP), the United Nations Children's Fund, the United Nations Population Fund, the World Bank (q.v.), and the United Nations Educational, Social, and Cultural Organization. While receiving administrative support from WHO in Geneva and support services at the country level from the UNDP, it is the first program of its kind in the UN system in its effort to achieve better global coordination of policies, multisectoral approaches, and funding.

A Committee of Cosponsoring Organizations (CCO), composed of the heads or a representative of the six cosponsors, was formed in 1994 to oversee the transition process from GPA to UNAIDS and later to facilitate the input of the cosponsors into the strategy, policies, and operations of the program. For this purpose, staff from each of the cosponsors formed a transition team to produce a comprehensive proposal specifying the new program's mission, terms and conditions of cosponsorship, organization, program, staffing, administration, and financing.

The four major functions of UNAIDS are (a) policy development and research; (b) technical support; (c) advocacy; and (d) coordination. At the global level, UNAIDS is the AIDS program of the six cosponsors. It carries out the roles of policy development and research, technical support, advocacy, and coordination. In turn, the cosponsors integrate HIV/AIDS-related issues and UNAIDS policies and strategies into their work. UNAIDS is headed by an executive director who is appointed by the UN secretary-general upon the recommendation of the cosponsors. The executive director reports directly to the governing body of UNAIDS, the Programme Coordination Board (PCB), which meets annually and consists of 22 representatives of member states (q.v.) (who hold voting powers) and representatives of the six cosponsors, nongovernmental organizations (NGOs) working in the HIV/AIDS field, and people living with AIDS (who do not hold voting powers). The term of office for a member state is three years, and seats are distributed regionally as follows: western European and others (q.v.) 7; Asia, 5; Africa, 5; Latin America and the Caribbean, 3; and Eastern European/Commonwealth of Independent States 2. It is notable that UNAIDS is the first UN program to have NGO representation on its governing body.

At the country level, UNAIDS works through country theme groups established by the UN resident coordinator (q.v.) to help integrate the UN with national activities. The theme group comprises representatives of some or all of the cosponsors, who meet regularly to jointly plan, program, and evaluate their AIDS-related activities. The chair of the group is chosen by the cosponsors. In selected countries, country programme advisers are posted to facilitate management and coordination of activities by the country theme group. UNAIDS is not a funding body but works through strategic alliances with cosponsors and other partners to mobilize resources. It maintains about 90 staff at headquarters (q.v.) and a further 74 professional staff in the field. It is financed from extrabudgetary funds (q.v.) from governments and the private sector. Cosponsors fund their own HIV/AIDS country-level programs and activities. For the 1996–97 biennium the total budget is U.S.$120 million, with 59 percent allocated to support country-level programs. *See also* Peter Piot.

JOINT WHO/FAO FOOD STANDARDS PROGRAMME. *See* Codex Alimentarius Commission.

JOINT WHO/UNICEF NUTRITION SUPPORT PROGRAMME (JNSP). A program created in 1982 to address malnutrition, especially among women of childbearing age and young children, under conditions of poverty. The work of the JNSP is based on the belief that nutrition can be immediately improved at reasonable cost by acting simultaneously on the manifold causes of malnutrition, such as breast feeding for too short a period, inadequate control of diarrhoeal disease and vaccine-preventable illnesses, and insufficient education and income among mothers. To address these causes, the JNSP has produced learning packages for the purpose of training community health workers in nutrition. See also Division of Food and Nutrition; Institute of Nutrition in Central America and Panama; International Conference on Nutrition.

K

KAPRIO, LEO A. (1918–). Dr. Leo Kaprio, of Finland, served as regional director emeritus of the European Regional Office (qq.v.) from 1967 to 1985. Under his directorship long-term programs for the control of cardiovascular diseases, control of environmental pollution, and mental health were established.

KAUSSEBAUM AMENDMENT. An amendment to the United States Senate Foreign Relations Act submitted by Senator Nancy Kaussebaum and adopted in 1985. The amendment stated that the United States government would withhold 20 percent of its contributions of regular budget funds (RBFs) (q.v.) to selected United Nations organizations until stipulated budgetary reforms were adopted. As a result of the amendment, the United States withheld portions of its contributions to WHO from 1986 to 1989 and again in 1996, resulting in considerable financial shortfalls in the organization's income from RBFs. See also Geneva Group; Western European and Other Group.

KO KO, U. (1929–). Dr. U. Ko Ko, of Myanmar (Burma), served as regional director of the South-East Asia Regional Office (qq.v.) from 1981 to 1994. After completing medical training in Myanmar and the United Kingdom, he carried out training, research, and a medical practice as director of disease control in the Department of Health Services; professor in the Department of Social and Preventive Medicine at the Institute of Medicine II; and a member of the policy committee of the Burma Medical Research Institute. He then served as the head of the Burmese delegation to the World Health Assembly and a member of the Executive Board (qq.v.). He joined WHO in 1969, where he was appointed regional advisor in Community Health Services (1969–72), assistant director of Health Services (1972–78), and director of Programme Management (q.v.) (1978–81).

L

LAMBO, THOMAS ADEOYE (1923–   ). Dr. Thomas Lambo, of Nigeria, served as deputy director-general (q.v.) from 1973 to 1988. Trained in medicine and psychiatry in the United Kingdom, he was appointed professor of psychiatry and neurology, dean of the faculty of medicine, and vice chancellor of the University of Ibadan (1968). During this period, he was a member of the Advisory Committee on Medical Research and the Expert Advisory Panel (qq.v.) on Mental Health. He joined WHO in 1971 as assistant director-general (q.v.) for the Divisions of Health, Manpower Development, Noncommunicable Diseases (q.v.), and Prophylactic and Therapeutic Substances. He was also put in charge of the Office of Mental Health before being appointed as deputy director-general to Halfdan Mahler (qq.v.).

LATIN AMERICAN CANCER RESEARCH INFORMATION PROJECT (LACRIP). A project launched in 1974 by the Pan American Health Organization (q.v.), in collaboration with the U.S. National Cancer Institute, the International Union against Cancer, and the International Agency for Research on Cancer (q.v.) to link Latin American and Caribbean countries in a specialized information network. Managed by the Regional Library of Medicine and Health Sciences (BIREME) in Sao Paulo, Brazil, the project maintains a variety of databases (e.g., CANCERLINE, CANCERLIT, CANCERPRO) of articles, protocols, and studies on cancer produced in the Americas region. In 1983, the project created the Selective Cancer Information Dissemination Service, which provides information on diagnosis, epidemiology, and treatment of cancer to subscribers.

LATIN AMERICAN NETWORK OF OFFICIAL DRUG QUALITY CONTROL LABORATORIES. A network created in 1984, with sponsorship from the Pan American Health Organization (q.v.), to promote the domestic manufacture of generic drug products and the use of traditional drugs with proven safety and efficacy. The network's work was extended, following the

Ibero-American Meeting on the Registration, Inspection, and Quality Control of Drugs held in Madrid, Spain, in 1991, to include drug registration and regulation.

LEON BERNARD PRIZE AND MEDAL. An award established in 1937 to commemorate Professor Leon Bernard, one of the founders of the Health Organization of the League of Nations (q.v.) and a pioneer in social medicine. The award is given periodically for outstanding service in social medicine. The recipient is selected by the Leon Bernard Foundation Committee consisting of the chairman, vice chairman, and one to two members of the Executive Board (q.v.). At present, the prize consists of a bronze medal and a sum of 2,500 Swiss francs. *See also* Child Health Foundation Prize and Fellowship; Darling Foundation Medal and Prize; Dr. A. T. Shousha Foundation Prize; Dr. Comlan A. A. Quenum Prize; Sasakawa Foundation; United Arab Emirates Health Foundation Prize.

LEPROSY, ACTION PROGRAMME FOR THE ELIMINATION OF. *See* Action Programme for the Elimination of Leprosy.

LEPROSY AND RELATED DISEASES, PAN AMERICAN CENTER FOR TRAINING AND RESEARCH IN. *See* Pan American Center for Training and Research in Leprosy and Related Diseases.

LEPROSY, SPECIAL ACTION PROJECTS TOWARDS THE ELIMINATION OF. *See* Special Action Projects towards the Elimination of Leprosy.

LIBRARY. A library located at headquarters (q.v.) as the central point of WHO biomedical literature services. The role of the library is to (a) provide services to WHO staff at headquarters; (b) provide a central acquisition and cataloging service for regional office (q.v.) libraries and supplement their resources through loans, photocopies, and assistance in dealing with enquiries; and (c) provide services outside of WHO, including procuring of biomedical literature by governments, advising on library organization and techniques, and assisting in the training of medical librarians. *See also* Division of Publishing, Language, and Library Services.

LIBRARY AND HEALTH LITERATURE SERVICES, OFFICE OF. *See* Division of Publishing, Language, and Library Services.

LJUBLJANA CHARTER. A charter, adopted by member states (q.v.) of the European region at a meeting in Ljubljana, Slovenia, in 1996, on principles that should guide the reform of European health care systems and policy. The charter states that European health care systems should be (a) driven by values of human dignity, equity (q.v.), solidarity, and professional ethics; (b) targeted on protecting and promoting health; (c) centered on people, allowing citizens to influence health services and take responsibility for their own health; (d) focused on quality, including cost-effectiveness; (e) based on sustainable finances to allow universal coverage and equitable access; and (f) oriented toward primary care. The charter is seen as a rejection of an earlier emphasis on cost containment at the expense of improving people's health.

LONDON DECLARATION ON AIDS PREVENTION. See Summit on the Global Impact of AIDS.

LUCAS, ADETOKUNBO, O. (1931–   ). Dr. Adetokunbo Lucas, of Nigeria, served as director of the Special Programme on Research and Training in Tropical Diseases (q.v.) from 1976 to 1986. After training in medicine and public health in the United Kingdom and the United States, he specialized in research on tropical diseases such as schistosomiasis and malaria. He was appointed head of the Department of Preventive and Social Medicine at the University of Ibadan and chairman of the Medical Research Council of Nigeria. His work with WHO began in 1965 when he became a member of the Expert Panel for Parasitic Diseases and consultant and temporary adviser for the regional offices (q.v.). Since leaving WHO, he has served as chair of the Program for Strengthening Human Resources in Developing Countries at the Carnegie Corporation in New York (1986–90), professor and adjunct professor of international health at the Harvard School of Public Health (since 1990), and team leader for a study, sponsored by the Oslo Group (q.v.), of WHO support to programs at the country level (1997).

M

MACKENZIE, MELVILLE D. (1889–1972). Dr. Melville Mackenzie, of the United Kingdom, contributed significantly to the postwar creation of WHO. Prior to this period, he worked in Russia for the Friends' Emergency and War Victims' Relief

Committee and the Epidemic Committee during the 1920s and then became a staff member of the Health Secretariat of the League of Nations in the 1930s. In this capacity, he directed technical assistance (q.v.) in Chile and humanitarian assistance in Liberia and fought epidemic diseases in China. During meetings to create WHO, he served as the alternate British delegate to the Technical Preparatory Committee and the International Health Conference (qq.v.). His proposed plans for a new health organization were widely discussed in these bodies. He later served as chairman of the European Technical Committee of the United Nations Relief and Rehabilitation Administration (q.v.).

MAHLER, HALFDAN (1923–   ). Dr. Halfdan Mahler, of Denmark, served as the third director-general (q.v.) of WHO from 1973 to 1988. After training in medicine and public health, his career in international public health has included planning officer for the tuberculosis campaign in Ecuador (1950–51), almost ten years as a senior WHO officer with the Indian National Tuberculosis Program, chief of the WHO Tuberculosis Unit, secretary of the Expert Advisory Panel (q.v.) on Tuberculosis (1962–69), director (q.v.) of project systems analysis (1969), and assistant director-general (q.v.) in charge of the Division of Strengthening of Health Services and the Division of Family Health (1970–73) (qq.v.). During his tenure as director-general, there was a shift in the nature of WHO activities toward a greater advocacy role and focus on the needs of developing countries. Initiatives during this period include Health for All by the Year 2000, the primary health care (qq.v.) approach, and essential drugs.

MALARIA COMMISSION. *See* Health Organization of the League of Nations.

MALARIA CONTROL (MAL). A strategy launched in 1992 at the International Conference on Malaria held in Amsterdam, the Netherlands, attended by ministers of health and public health experts, to control the incidence of malaria. During the previous decades, malaria had been subject to large-scale eradication and control programs directed at the key vector of the disease, the anopheline mosquito. Despite initial success, the disease underwent a resurgence in many parts of the world, due in part to its increasing resistance to available drugs (e.g., chloroquine). The meeting put forth a World Declaration on the Control of Malaria, which represented a radical change in strategy in that it was directed at people and their treatment and cure. *See also* Intensified Malaria Eradication Programme.

MALARIA ERADICATION, DIVISION OF. *See* Intensified Malaria Eradication Programme.

MALARIA ERADICATION SPECIAL ACCOUNT. A special account set up in 1957 to receive extrabudgetary funds from member states (qq.v.) for the Intensified Malaria Eradication Programme (q.v.). These funds were added to regular budget funds (RBFs) and funds administered by WHO from the United Nations Children's Fund and the Expanded Programme for Technical Assistance (qq.v.). Contributions to the account peaked in 1960 at U.S.$3.9 million but subsequently diminished to an extent that, in 1962, RBFs were transferred to the account to sustain the campaign. *See also* Malaria Control.

MANAGEMENT ADVISORY COMMITTEE. *See* Drug Action Programme/Action Programme on Essential Drugs.

MANAGEMENT COMMITTEE. *See* International Programme on the Health Effects of the Chernobyl Accident.

MANAGEMENT DEVELOPMENT COMMITTEE (MDC). A committee created in 1993, as part of the Executive Board Working Group on the WHO Response to Global Change (q.v.) reform process, composed of selected members of the Executive Board (EB) (q.v.). The purpose of the committee is to contribute to the monitoring of the implementation of recommendations put forth by the reform process. In particular, the committee provides overall supervision on the application of the managerial process at all levels of the organization, including programming, implementation, monitoring, and evaluation; coherence and complementarity of program activities, their technical content and approach, and the proposed program budget in accordance with agreed policies, strategies, and priorities; and follow-up development of the General Programme of Work (q.v.) and related biennial program budgets. It is also intended to ensure that the guidance of the governing bodies, the World Health Assembly (q.v.) and the EB, and the orientation of the General Programme of Work are translated into practical activities through the mechanisms outlined in the procedural guidance issued by the director-general (q.v.). *See also* Global Policy Council.

MANAGEMENT INFORMATION SYSTEM SUPPORT (MIS). *See* Division of Information System Management.

MANAGEMENT REVIEW COMMITTEE (MRC). *See* Division of Diarrhoeal and Acute Respiratory Disease Control.

MANAGERIAL PROCESS FOR WHO'S PROGRAMME DEVELOPMENT. One of three functional components of WHO's management process known as program review (q.v.). This component covers the design and application of methodology, promotion of long-term planning, elaboration of the General Programme of Work (q.v.), program budgeting, monitoring of implementation, and evaluation and information support. The emphasis is on providing mechanisms that ensure a "bottom-up" approach to planning according to the priorities identified by member states (q.v.). To assist this process, links are maintained with technical programs, as well as the Division of Budget and Finance, the Office of Internal Audit and Oversight (qq.v.), and other administrative and managerial offices. At the regional offices, the directors of programme management (qq.v.) are responsible for these functions, with the exception of the Pan American Health Organization (PAHO) (q.v.), where the functions of the PAHO/WHO representative also cover these responsibilities. *See also* Director-General's and Regional Directors' Development Programme; Executive Management.

MANAGERIAL STRATEGY FOR THE OPTIMUM USE OF PAHO/WHO RESOURCES IN DIRECT SUPPORT OF MEMBER COUNTRIES. A strategy adopted in 1983 to improve the Pan American Health Organization's (PAHO) technical cooperation (qq.v.) in carrying out regional strategies and a plan of action for Health for All (q.v.). The strategy is based on five principles: (a) the country constitutes the basic unit for cooperative activities in health; (b) governments are participants in the administration of PAHO's technical cooperation; (c) cooperation should be flexible and capable of adapting to changing conditions in countries and the region; (d) technical cooperation among countries should be promoted and used as much as possible; and (e) linkages between PAHO and other national and international organizations should be intensified.

MANI, CHANDRA (1903–1975). Dr. Chandra Mani, of India, served as the first director of the South-East Asia Regional Office (qq.v.) from 1948 to 1968. After completing medical training in the United Kingdom, he served in the Indian Medical Service, including as a medical officer (1927–36), deputy assistant director of hygiene (1939–43), and deputy director-general of health (1947–48). Dr. Mani became a member of the Technical Preparatory Committee and Interim Commission (qq.v.), where he strongly supported the need for regional decentralization in the proposed international health organization being created. He also represented India at the International Health Conference (q.v.) later the same year.

MANN, JONATHAN. (1947–   ). Dr. Jonathan Mann, of the United States, was the first director of the Global Programme on AIDS (q.v.), from 1987 to 1991. He began as head of the small Control Programme on AIDS (q.v.), created within WHO in 1986 in response to growing international attention to the HIV/AIDS epidemic. He oversaw this small program's transition to the Special Programme, and then the Global Programme, on AIDS (qq.v.), by playing a central role in raising global attention to the impact of the disease and mobilizing staff and resources on a scale and schedule unprecedented in the history of international health. This included a statement to the United Nations General Assembly in October 1987 on the need for a rapid global response. Dr. Mann has taken a strong stance on the human rights aspects of HIV/AIDS, a position that led to conflicts with Director-General Hiroshi Nakajima (qq.v.) in the early 1990s over differences in policy. He resigned from WHO shortly afterward and became professor of health and human rights at the Harvard School of Public Health. He has remained an active campaigner for the rights of people living with HIV/AIDS and currently heads the United States-based Global AIDS Policy Coalition.

MATERNAL AND CHILD HEALTH DEMONSTRATION AND TRAINING CENTERS. A number of centers created by WHO during the 1950s and 1960s in developing countries to help strengthen maternal and child health (MCH) services. While most centers operated as independent units, others were formed as part of existing hospitals or dispensaries. Staffing, often in the form of expatriates, was provided by WHO for the initial years of operation. The United Nations Children's Fund (q.v.) assisted in equipping the facilities. Today, the heavy use of expatriates to staff the centers, many with little or no experience of working in developing countries, and the separation of MCH centers from general health services are generally recognized as unsustainable in the longer term. The emphasis of WHO's support for MCH services shifted during the 1970s to the basic training of traditional birth attendants and integration with primary health care (q.v.). *See also* Mother-Baby Package; Safe Motherhood Initiative.

MATERNAL AND NEWBORN HEALTH/SAFE MOTHERHOOD UNIT. *See* Division of Reproductive Health (Technical Support).

MATERNAL HEALTH AND SAFE MOTHERHOOD PROGRAMME (MSM). *See* Safe Motherhood Initiative.

MEDIA RELATIONS UNIT. *See* Office of Health Communications and Public Relations.

MEDICAL RESEARCH, PAHO ADVISORY COMMITTEE ON. *See* PAHO Advisory Committee on Health Research.

MEETING OF INTERESTED PARTIES (MIP). *See* Division of Diarrhoeal and Acute Respiratory Disease Control; Expanded Programme on Immunization; Global Programme for Vaccines and Immunization; Safe Motherhood Initiative.

MEMBER STATE. A member state is a state that signs or otherwise accepts the constitution (q.v.) of WHO. According to chapter 3 of the constitution, membership in the organization is open to all states. All member states have the right to be represented at the World Health Assembly (q.v.) by three delegates, of whom one is designated as a chief delegate. Delegates should be technically competent in the field of health. Since 1948 membership in WHO has increased from 56 to 189 member states in 1996. The most recent influx (since the early 1990s) has come from the newly independent states of central and eastern Europe.

MEMORANDUM OF UNDERSTANDING FOR THE IMPLEMENTATION OF THE WHO/UNDP ALLIANCE TO COMBAT AIDS. *See* WHO/UNDP Alliance to Combat AIDS.

MENTAL HEALTH AND PREVENTION OF SUBSTANCE ABUSE, DIVISION OF. *See* Division of Mental Health and Prevention of Substance Abuse.

MENTAL HEALTH, PROGRAMME ON. *See* Programme on Mental Health.

MENTAL HEALTH PROMOTION, UNIT OF. *See* Programme on Mental Health.

MENTOR FOUNDATION. A foundation created in 1994 as a global initiative to complement the work of existing organizations engaged in the prevention of youth substance abuse. Based in Geneva, Switzerland, the foundation seeks to combine private sector efficiency and individual involvement with technical expertise provided by WHO and other United Nations organizations. The work of the foundation is funded by private donations. *See also* Rockefeller Foundation; Sasakawa Foundation.

MERSON, MICHAEL (1945–). Dr. Michael Merson, of the United States, served as acting director and director (q.v.) of the Global Programme on AIDS (GPA) (q.v.) from 1990 to 1995. After medical training, his public health career included work in Nepal and Brazil and at the International Center for Diarrhoeal Disease Research, Bangladesh, and the Centers for Disease Control and Prevention (qq.v.). He joined WHO in 1978 as a medical officer in the Programme for the Control of Diarrhoeal Diseases (q.v.), where he became program manager in 1980 and director in 1984. In 1987 he also became head of the Programme for the Control of Acute Respiratory Infections (q.v.) until 1990, when he joined the GPA. In 1995, when the GPA was replaced by the Joint United Nations Programme on HIV/AIDS (q.v.), Dr. Merson left to become dean of the school of public health at Yale University.

MODEL LIST OF ESSENTIAL DRUGS. Also known as the Essential Drugs List. An agreed-on list of selected drugs presented by WHO in 1977 to be used by member states (q.v.), especially developing countries, to guide the acquisition and use of drugs in such a way as to optimize limited financial resources. The development of the model list began when Director-General Halfdan Mahler issued a report to the World Health Assembly (WHA) (qq.v.) in 1975 on the main drug problems facing developing countries and outlined possible new policies. He referred to existing schemes in some countries intended to extend the accessibility and rational use of the most necessary drugs to populations whose basic health needs could not be met by the existing supply system. The report proposed that a model list of essential drugs be drawn up locally, and periodically updated, based on the advice of experts in public health, medicine, pharmacology, pharmacy, and drug management. The listed drugs must be "proven to be therapeutically effective, to have acceptable safety and to satisfy the health needs of the population." Drugs are deemed "essential" if they are "of the utmost importance and are basic, indispensable and necessary for the health needs of the population." In 1976 the WHA required the director-general to implement the proposals of his report and, in particular, to advise member states on the selection and procurement, at reasonable cost, of essential drugs of established quality that correspond to their national health needs. Following wide consultation, the list was included in the first report of the Expert Committee on the Selection of Essential Drugs formed soon thereafter. The adoption of the Model List of Essential Drugs led to the creation of the Essential Drugs Programme (q.v.) in 1977 and the Action Programme on Essential Drugs in 1981. *See also* Drug Action Programme/ Action Programme on Essential Drugs; International Federation of Pharmaceutical Manufacturers Associations; Revised Drug Strategy.

MONEKOSSO, GOTTLIEB LOBE (1928–   ). Dr. Gottlieb Monekosso, of Cameroon, served as regional director of the African Regional Office (AFRO) (qq.v.) from 1985 to 1995. After training in medicine, tropical medicine, and hygiene in the United Kingdom, he became professor of medicine at the University of Lagos, dean of the faculty of medicine at the University of Dar es Salaam, Tanzania, and director of the University Center of Health Sciences and professor of medicine and community medicine at the University of Yaounde, Cameroon. He represented Cameroon at the World Health Assembly (q.v.) and was appointed WHO representative (q.v.) to Jamaica, Bermuda, the Caymans, and the Turks and Caicos Islands. During his tenure as regional director, the regional office experienced difficulties in carrying out its work due to internal conflicts within the Congo. In 1994 AFRO conferred the honorary title of regional director emeritus on Dr. Monekosso in recognition of his contribution to health in Africa.

MONICA PROJECT. A ten-year epidemiological project coordinated by the Cardiovascular Diseases Unit of WHO to monitor trends and determinants in cardiovascular diseases and measure the effectiveness of interventions. The project provides information on mortality, cardiovascular morbidity, and risk factors from 39 different populations in 26 countries. Monitoring is carried out by participating centers, largely in industrialized countries, with plans to extend monitoring to the developing world. *See also* Interhealth Programme.

MOTHER-BABY PACKAGE. A package or minimum set of interventions proposed in the late 1980s to support countries in striving to attain the goals of the Safe Motherhood Initiative (SMI) (q.v.). The goals of the package are to achieve substantial reductions in maternal and neonatal mortality and to improve maternal and infant health care at various levels of the health system. The package provides a detailed, step-by-step description of how the SMI can be implemented in member states (q.v.), including defining national policy and guidelines, assessing needs, preparing national action plans, identifying resources, and monitoring and evaluation. The specific interventions focus on family planning to prevent unwanted and mistimed pregnancies, basic maternity care for all pregnancies, and special care for the prevention and management of complications during pregnancy and delivery and postpartum. The package also presents global goals and targets and outlines the general strategies needed to attain them. *See also* Division of Family Health; Division of Reproductive Health (Technical Support).

MULTIPLE DRUG THERAPY. *See* Action Programme for the Elimination of Leprosy.

N

NAKAJIMA, HIROSHI (1928–). Dr. Hiroshi Nakajima, of Japan, served from 1988 to 1998 as the fourth director-general (q.v.) of WHO. After receiving his medical and postgraduate degrees, he specialized in neuropsychiatry and worked as a postgraduate fellow at Paris University and the Institute of Pharmacology in France. He then worked as a scientist at the National Institute of Health and Medical Research, Paris (1958–67), before returning to Japan to serve as director of research and administration for Nippon Roche Research Centre in Tokyo. Dr. Nakajima joined WHO in 1974 as a scientist in the drug evaluation and monitoring unit. He was appointed director (q.v.) of the Division of Drug Management and Policies (q.v.) in 1976, where he played a key role in developing the concept of essential drugs. He served as regional director of the Western Pacific Regional Office (qq.v.) from 1979 to 1988 and was elected director-general in 1988 and reelected in 1993. During his tenure as director-general, Dr. Nakajima was criticized for his leadership and management style, which led to tensions with prominent senior members of staff. In response to these criticisms and concerns over the need for the reform of WHO, he oversaw the Executive Board Working Group on the WHO Response to Global Change reform process and launched the Renewal of the Health for All Strategy (qq.v.) in 1995. He has also supported a stronger role for WHO in the field of emergency health assistance and emerging diseases.

NATIONAL IMMUNIZATION DAY. A day organized by governments, at WHO's behest, to organize for the purpose of focusing national efforts on promoting and carrying out specific immunization campaigns, such as that for poliomyelitis. See also Children's Vaccine Initiative; Global Programme for Vaccines and Immunization; Interagency Coordinating Committee.

NATIONAL INSTITUTION RECOGNIZED BY WHO. A status conferred on a national institution recognized by WHO as able and willing to participate in collaborative activities with WHO as designated by national authorities. Such activities are of such a scope or nature, however, that they do not warrant designation as a WHO collaborating center (q.v.).

NATIONAL INTEGRATED PROGRAMMES ON ENVIRONMENT AND HEALTH (NIPEH). An initiative of the European Regional Office (q.v.), directed primarily at the countries of central and eastern Europe, to help governments build the systems and skills for national action programs for health.

NEW DELHI STATEMENT. A statement issued at the Global Consultation on Safe Water and Sanitation for the 1990s held in New Delhi, India, in September 1990. The meeting was attended by more than 600 delegates from 115 countries. The statement called on countries to undertake concerted action to enable people to obtain two basic human needs: safe drinking water and environmental sanitation. *See also* Interagency Steering Committee on Water Supply and Sanitation; International Drinking Water and Sanitation Decade.

NONCOMMUNICABLE DISEASES, DIVISION OF. *See* Division of Noncommunicable Diseases.

NONGOVERNMENTAL DEVELOPMENT ORGANIZATIONS COORDINATION GROUP FOR IVERMECTIN DISTRIBUTION. *See* African Programme for Onchocerciasis Control; Onchocerciasis Control Programme.

NONGOVERNMENTAL ORGANIZATION (NGO). An organization defined by WHO as one whose "aims and activities shall be in conformity with the spirit, purposes and principles of the Constitution [q.v.] of WHO, shall center on development work in health or health-related fields, and shall be free from concerns which are primarily of a commercial or profit-making nature." The potential value of cooperative and collaborative relations between WHO and NGOs was first studied by the Interim Commission (q.v.), which set up a special subcommittee to formulate criteria for admitting an NGO into association, devise the mechanisms for approval, and define the privileges of assocation. The recommendations of the commission were adopted by the first World Health Assembly (q.v.) in 1948. As a result, since 1950 NGOs may apply to the Standing Committee on Nongovernmental Organizations (q.v.) for permission to enter into official relations with WHO if it is concerned with matters that fall within the competence of the organization and pursues aims and purposes in conformity with those of the constitution. The NGO must also be of recognized standing and represent a substantial proportion of persons organized for the purpose of participation in the particular field of interest in which it operates.

The objectives for WHO collaboration with NGOs, and the manner in which an NGO may apply for admission into official relations, are set out in the Principles Governing Relations between the World Health Organization and Nongovernmental Organizations. In 1996 there were 181 NGOs in official relations with WHO, from such diverse fields as medicine, science, education, law, labor, industry, professional and occupational societies, women, children, and humanitarian and development organizations. Of particular note is the involvement of

NGOs in the Joint United Nations Programme on HIV/AIDS (q.v.) in consultations leading up to its creation, on its governing body, and in country level activities. *See also* Appendix H.

NONGOVERNMENTAL ORGANIZATIONS, STANDING COMMITTEE ON. *See* Standing Committee on Nongovernmental Organizations.

NORMATIVE ACTIVITIES. A term widely used to describe activities by WHO that are centered on information collection, creation, management, and dissemination. These activities include the production of research, guidelines, and standards and principles for the promotion and protection of health. These activities are generally contrasted with technical cooperation (q.v.) activities, which are defined as more operational and field based. Since 1948, technical cooperation activities have grown in relative terms, leading to frequent debates over the appropriate balance between the two types of activities and, more fundamentally, the most effective role for the organization. In recent years, it has been argued, notably by some governments of the Geneva Group (q.v.), that WHO should focus more strongly on normative activities and reduce its commitments to technical cooperation.

NURSING AND MIDWIFERY. An area of activity promoted by WHO, beginning in the 1950s, in recognition of its contribution to health and health care, including education, policy, planning, management, legislation, health services delivery, emergency response, and research. Nurses and midwives represent over 50 percent of the world's health personnel resources. In 1992 the World Health Assembly (q.v.) adopted a resolution to strengthen nursing and midwifery in support of Health for All (q.v.). This led to the creation of the Nursing Unit, located within the former Programme for Development of Human Resources for Health (HRH) (q.v.), to coordinate the relevant work of all divisions. Activities included the development of information systems for management of health personnel; development and provision of education and training; intercountry workshops on nursing leadership in health development and research; and funding for research projects on various aspects of nursing services.

Regional projects have included developing management skills and national action plans and strengthening primary health care (q.v.) and the safe motherhood initiative (q.v.). This work is supported by six regional nursing advisers and a Global Network of WHO Collaborating Centers (q.v.) for Nursing Development. In addition, the nursing and midwifery unit collaborates with the International Council of Nurses, the International Confederation of Midwives, other nongovernmental organizations (q.v.), and the International Labour Organization and receives advice and support from the Global Advisory Group on Nursing and Midwifery (q.v.). The unit has received particular support for its work through extrabudgetary funds (q.v.) from Denmark and Sweden. The unit was reorganized and renamed Nursing and Midwifery in 1996 as a crosscutting theme within the Health Systems Development Programme (q.v.). In this expanded capacity, it continues to serve as a focal point for nursing and midwifery worldwide. *See also* Coordinating Committee on Nursing and Midwifery.

NURSING AND MIDWIFERY, COORDINATING COMMITTEE ON. *See* Coordinating Committee on Nursing and Midwifery.

NURSING AND MIDWIFERY, GLOBAL ADVISORY GROUP ON. *See* Global Advisory Group on Nursing and Midwifery.

NURSING UNIT. *See* Nursing and Midwifery.

NUTRITION, DIVISION OF FOOD AND. *See* Division of Food and Nutrition.

NUTRITION IN CENTRAL AMERICA AND PANAMA. *See* Institute of Nutrition in Central America and Panama.

NUTRITION, INTERNATIONAL CONFERENCE ON. *See* International Conference on Nutrition.

NUTRITION SUPPORT PROGRAMME, JOINT WHO/UNICEF. *See* JOINT WHO/UNICEF Nutrition Support Programme.

NUTRITION, WORLD DECLARATION AND PLAN OF ACTION FOR. *See* International Conference on Nutrition.

O

OCCUPATIONAL HEALTH UNIT (OCH). A unit created in the 1980s, within the Division of Health Promotion, Education, and

Communication (q.v.), to control occupational health risks and to protect and promote the health of working populations and the humanization of work. The specific objectives of the unit are (a) to promote and protect the health of working populations by developing appropriate programs to meet the occupational health needs of workers; (b) to provide technical guidelines on such topics as occupational health in agriculture and industry, ergonomics, work physiology, and injury prevention; (c) to assist in the establishment of occupational health programs within public health services; (d) to assist in the planning and development of training; (e) to encourage the exchange of experience among member states (q.v.); (f) to develop and review occupational health norms, guides, and criteria; (f) to coordinate and conduct research and epidemiological studies; (g) to assist in the development of occupational health information systems; (h) to cooperate with other organizations, including the International Labour Organization and the International Commission on Occupational Health; and (i) to serve the Expert Advisory Panel (q.v.) on Occupational Health and the Expert Advisory Panel on the Health of Seafarers. *See also* Health Education and Health Promotion Unit; Office of Health Communications and Public Relations; Programme on Aging and Health; Rehabilitation Unit.

OFFICE INTERNATIONAL D'HYGIÈNE PUBLIQUE (OIHP). An organization established by the Rome Agreement of 1907 signed by delegates of 12 countries (Belgium, Brazil, Egypt, France, Italy, the Netherlands, Portugal, Russia, Spain, Switzerland, the United Kingdom, and the United States). The purpose of the organization was to disseminate to member states (q.v.) information of general public health interest, notably on communicable diseases such as cholera, plague, and yellow fever and how to combat them. Based in Paris, its creation was the product of half a century of international health cooperation carried out through the International Sanitary Conferences (q.v.) held between 1851 and 1903. The work of the OIHP was primarily concerned with gathering and disseminating epidemiological intelligence and reporting, and it was financed by contributions from member states.

With the creation of the League of Nations in 1920, it was expected that a new international health organization would be formed, with the OIHP subsumed within it. However, there was resistance by some member states and the organization to this loss of autonomy, not least because of nonmembership in the League of Nations by the United States and the Soviet Union. As a result, the Health Organization of the League of Nations (q.v.) was established to coexist with the OIHP, and at times the two bodies competed in their activities for the next 30 years. During the Second World War, the OIHP moved to near Vichy, France, where it continued to publish epidemiological data and other health statistics, albeit on a more limited range of countries. In 1946 it was agreed by its assembly, and by the International Health Conference (q.v.), to dissolve the organization and have its functions be assumed by the planned health organization of the United Nations, WHO. This did not occur until 1952, when the final three member states of the OIHP agreed to dissolve the Rome Agreement, and the organization formally ceased to exist. In 1948, with the formal establishment of the World Health Organization, the OIHP was officially terminated, and its functions assumed by the new international health organization.

OFFICE OF GLOBAL AND INTEGRATED ENVIRONMENTAL HEALTH (EHG). An office created in 1994, within the Programme for the Promotion of Environmental Health (q.v.), to (a) build and strengthen national capacities for integrated management of environmental health, including health information management, human resources development, and environmental health research; and (b) to deal with health problems related to global environmental change that are of concern to human health, in particular the ozone layer depletion, climate change, and ionizing and nonionizing radiation. These activities are organized into the following units: Environmental Health Information Management (EHI); Environmental Health Planning Methods and Human Resources Development (EHP); and Environmental Health Research, Global Hazards Assessment, and Radiation Protection (EHR). *See also* Global Strategy for Health and Environment.

OFFICE OF HEALTH COMMUNICATIONS AND PUBLIC RELATIONS. An office created in the 1980s, within the Division of Health Promotion, Education, and Communication (q.v.), to carry out the following objectives: (a) to create greater awareness of WHO, foster involvement in its work, and advocate Health for All (q.v.) and an integrated approach to development; (b) to assist in developing an infomed public opinion among all peoples on matters of health and WHO's work and activities; (c) to use modern communications methods to strengthen health promotion and disease prevention actions and programs and to advise on the development of public information policies, programs, and activities; (d) to establish liaison with and support the work of the regional offices and, through them, country offices (qq.v.) on matters relating to public information; (e) to establish liaison with other relevant organizations, including the United Nations and nongovernmental organizations (q.v.); and (f) to implement and evaluate the impact of the WHO communications and public relations policy (q.v.). These responsibilities are carried out by three subunits: the Media Relations Unit, the Public Relations Unit, and the Communications Support Unit. *See also* Programme on Aging and Health; Health Education and Health Promotion Unit; Occupational Health Unit; Rehabilitation Unit.

OFFICE OF HIV/AIDS AND SEXUALLY TRANSMITTED DISEASES (ASD). An office created in 1995, following the disestablishment of the Global Programme on AIDS and the creation of the Joint United Nations Programme on HIV/AIDS (UNAIDS) (qq.v.), to (a) ensure a coordinated global, regional, and country-level WHO response to sexually transmitted diseases (STDs) and HIV/AIDS; (b) facilitate integration of HIV/AIDS-related and STD activities into the work of WHO through provision of technical and normative support to divisions and programs, regional offices, and country offices (qq.v.); (c) ensure liaison between WHO, UNAIDS, and other cosponsoring (q.v.) organizations, as well as with other United Nations organizations, bilateral agencies, and nongovernmental organizations (q.v.); and (d) coordinate within WHO, and jointly with UNAIDS and other cosponsors, the mobilization of resources for HIV/AIDS-related and STD activities. Overall, the ASD serves as the focal point for internal and external communications related to HIV/AIDS and STDs.

OFFICE OF INTERNAL AUDIT AND OVERSIGHT (IAO). An office created in 1948, as the Office of Internal Audit, to examine and appraise, by means of internal audits, investigations, inspections, and other oversight techniques, the way in which activities are carried out in WHO at all organizational levels. The office serves as an internal review, monitoring, and appraisal mechanism for assisting staff of the Secretariat (q.v.) in the effective discharge of their responsibilities. The office examines and evaluates the adequacy and effectiveness of WHO's system of internal control, financial management, compliance with regulations and rules, and the responsible use of resources in order to enhance the achievement of established objectives and goals. It also conducts investigations in cases of alleged misconduct. The office provides the director-general and the programs audited with analyses, recommendations, counsel, and information concerning the activities reviewed.

The objectives of such audits include promoting cost-effective control and identifying means of improving the efficiency and economy of activities and use of resources. To help ensure credibility and independence for such work, the IAO is the sole unit that performs or authorizes others to perform internal audits and oversight investigations. The IAO is headed by a chief who reports directly to the director-general. In 1996 the director-general renamed the office the Office of Internal Audit and Oversight and introduced further measures to strengthen the mandate of the office. These specific measures were: (a) the director-general will consult with the chairman and other officers of the Executive Board (EB) (q.v.) on the appointment and termination of the chief of the IAO; (b) the chief of the IAO may request that any report of the office be submitted to the EB; (c) a summary of IAO activities and follow-up actions on its reports will be presented to the EB and the World Health Assembly (q.v.); and (d) the external auditor (q.v.) will continue to be informed of the work of IAO on a regular basis.

OFFICE OF RESEACH POLICY AND STRATEGY COORDINATION (RPS). An office originally created in 1959 to serve as the secretariat (q.v.) to the Advisory Committee on Medical Research, today known as the Advisory Committee on Health Research (ACHR) (q.v.), to perform analytical, coordinative, and promotional functions in terms of research policy and to play a scientific liaison role within relevant United Nations organizations and nongovernmental organizations (q.v.). The current objectives and functions of the office are (a) to provide secretariat support for the ACHR, the Council for Science and Technology, and the Expert Advisory Panel (q.v.) on Health Science and Technology Policy; (b) to review periodically and provide scientific backing for the policy guidelines set out by the governing bodies and analyze their scientific implications in terms of program implementation; (c) to monitor new and emerging areas in science and technology; (d) to identify impending and evolving global health problems requiring special attention; (e) to provide executive management (q.v.) with appropriate information related to research; (f) to establish liaison, with other

UN organizations and nongovernmental organizations to harmonize science and technology policies; and (g) to coordinate, through regional ties and the ACHR, the work of medical research councils or analogous bodies. For the 1996–97 biennium the office was composed of two professional and two general staff and was allocated regular budget funds (q.v.) of about U.S.$450,000.

OFFICE OF THE DIRECTOR. *See* Division of Personnel.

OFFICE OF THE LEGAL COUNSEL (LEG). An office created in 1948 to handle legal issues arising at headquarters, the regional offices (except the Pan American Health Organization), country offices (qq.v.), and WHO-affiliated centers around the world. In 1996 the office was reorganized into three components by the director-general (q.v.) in response to its increasing workload and to facilitate access to appropriate legal services by users. Governing Bodies and Public International Law is responsible for legal issues arising in connection with the sessions of the Executive Board, the World Health Assembly, regional committees, and governing bodies of cosponsored programs (qq.v.); general management matters; and legal and political issues concerning relations between WHO and member states (q.v.), other intergovernmental organizations, and host states of its headquarters (q.v.), regional offices, and country offices. Personnel and Administrative Matters (PAM) is responsible for legal issues in relation to personnel and general administrative matters, including recruitment, disciplinary measures, use of WHO's name and emblem, and the legal acceptability and appropriateness of proposed activities. Commercial and Contractual Matters (CCM) deals with legal and policy issues relating to relations with industry, including issues of intellectual property, licensing and confidentiality of data, collaboration, donation agreements and fund-raising arrangements with the private sector, and cosponsorship of meetings; and contracts relating to funding and cooperation arrangements with governments, funding agencies, and nongovernmental organizations (q.v.).

ONCHOCERCIASIS CONTROL PROGRAMME (OCP). A program created in 1974, as the Special Programme on Onchocerciasis, by WHO, the United Nations Development Program (UNDP) (q.v.), the Food and Agriculture Organization, and the World Bank (q.v.). The purpose of the program is to control the incidence of the disease onchocerciasis (also known as river blindness). The program initially covered seven West African countries along the Volta River basin and was later extended to the Sene-Gambia basin, involving an additional four countries. The strategy of the program is based on vector control (i.e., worms and snails) activities and the free distribution of the drug ivermectin. Ivermectin was discovered by the pharmaceutical company Merck and Company in the late 1970s, which found that it destroyed Onchocerca worms, and developed in collaboration with the UNDP/World Bank/WHO Special Programme of Research and Training in Tropical Diseases (q.v.). A small dose can be given by mouth, usually once each year, to kill the larvae but not the adult worms. The drug was then registered for human use and has been provided free of charge by the company to disease-endemic countries.

The drug has been applied on an increasing scale in the remaining 16 disease-endemic countries across Africa. This has been initiated by the Nongovernmental Development Organizations Coordination Group for Ivermectin Distribution, with its liaison and coordination office in the Prevention of Blindness (q.v.) program. Since the program began, 25 million hectares of fertile riverine land have been opened up for human settlement and cultivation, and 1.5 million formerly infected people no longer have the disease. Renamed the Onchocerciasis Control Programme (OCP), the program began its final six-year funding cycle (ending in 2002) in 1997, having cost an estimated total of U.S.$550 million (less than U.S.$1 per year for each protected person). *See also* African Programme for Onchocerciasis Control.

OPERATION MECACAR. A campaign launched in 1995 to provide simultaneous poliomyelitis vaccination in 18 countries of the two regions where the disease is endemic. "MECACAR" stands for Mediterranean, Caucasian, and Central Asian republics, and the program is coordinated through the WHO European Regional Office and Eastern Mediterranean Regional Office (qq.v.). It also receives the cooperation of the United Nations Children's Fund (q.v.), the International Federation of Red Cross and Red Crescent Societies, Rotary International, United States Centers for Disease Control and Prevention (q.v.), and the United States Agency for International Development. *See also* Oral Polio Vaccine; Polio Eradication Initiative.

ORAL POLIO VACCINE (OPV). A live attenuated polio vaccine developed by Dr. Albert Sabin and other researchers during the 1950s, licensed in the United States in 1961, and given to WHO free of charge to allow its worldwide use. *See also* Operation MECACAR; Polio Eradication Initiative; Polio Eradication Programme.

ORGANIZATION OF AMERICAN STATES (OAS). An organization created in 1890 as the International Union of American Republics by the first International Conference of American States in Washington, D.C. The second conference of the International Union recommended that a "general convention of representatives of the health organizations of the different American republics" be held to formulate "sanitary agreements and regulations." This led to the first International Sanitary Convention of the American Republics (q.v.) in 1902, which founded the forerunner of the Pan American Health Organization (PAHO) (q.v.), the International Sanitary Bureau. In 1949 PAHO became a specialized body of the OAS, as well as a regional office (q.v.) of WHO.

OSLO GROUP. A group of three governments (Australia, Norway, and the United Kingdom) that initiated a study of the role of extrabudgetary funds (q.v.) in WHO in 1994. The study was followed in 1997 by a second study, of WHO support to programs at the country level, with additional sponsorship from the governments of Canada, Italy, and Sweden and in collaboration with WHO. The findings of the study, undertaken by an international team of consultants, are intended to support the WHO's reform process initiated in 1992. *See also* African Group; Asian Group; Geneva Group; Lucas, Odetokunbo; Western European and Other Group.

OTTAWA CHARTER FOR HEALTH PROMOTION. *See* International Conference on Health Promotion.

P

PAHO ADVISORY COMMITTEE ON HEALTH RESEARCH (ACHR). A committee created in 1962, as the PAHO Advisory Committee on Medical Research, to analyze the proposed research program of the Pan American Health Organization (PAHO) (q.v.) and to make recommendations on long-term research policies. The committee was initiated by the agreement of the Charter of Punta del Este (q.v.), which called for intensified scientific research and its application. Its work also complements that of the global Advisory Committee on Health Research (q.v.). The committee is composed of recognized scientists from the Americas region. The annual meetings of the committee were held at PAHO headquarters in Washington, D.C., during the first 14 years and thereafter has alternated between headquarters and other cities in the Americas region. In 1985 the name of the committee was changed to the PAHO Advisory Committee on Health Research.

PAHO ADVISORY COMMITTEE ON MEDICAL RESEARCH. *See* PAHO Advisory Committee on Health Research.

PAHO-CENDES METHOD. Also known as Latin American and Santiago Method. A method of national health planning developed during the 1960s by the Pan American Health Organization (q.v.) and the Center for Development Studies (CENDES) of the Central University of Venezuela, Caracas. The method was developed in response to PAHO's responsibility to aid Latin American countries in drawing up the health components of national development plans as stipulated under the Charter of Punta del Este (q.v.). The aim of the method is to provide a practical and useful tool for policy makers and planners to tackle the problems of improving health care. Drawing largely on the field of economics, the method prescribes three major steps in the planning process: (a) diagnosis; (b) determination of feasible alternatives in the local area; and (c) preparation of regional and national plans. The method is intended to provide systematic determination of what the significance of a particular health problem will be in some future period, what resources will be available to deal with these problems, and what is the most efficient organization of those resources for solving the specified health problems. *See also* African Regional Office Programme Operations Coordination System; Pan American Center for Health Planning.

PAHO PROCUREMENT OFFICE. An office of the Pan American Health Organization (PAHO) (q.v.) set up in 1948, as the PAHO Supplies Office, to facilitate the acquisition of health and medical supplies and equipment by member states (q.v.).

PAHO REGIONAL PLAN FOR INVESTMENT IN THE ENVIRONMENT AND HEALTH. A plan initiated in 1992 to serve as a framework for investment that would be needed in Latin

America and the Caribbean over a 12-year period to improve living conditions, combat poverty, and provide each person with necessary health care, clean and safe water, and basic sanitation services. The main challenge is to increase the ability of member states (q.v.) to mobilize resources for investment in the environment and health by strengthening institutional capacity to develop and manage sound investment projects. Activities under the plan so far have included analysis of the processes for investment in member states, creation of a central fund to promote investment, and negotiations with bilateral and multilateral donor agencies. *See also* Pan American Network for Normalized Sampling of Air Pollution.

PAHO REGIONAL SYSTEM FOR VACCINES (SIREVA). A system created in 1990 by the Pan American Health Organization (PAHO) (q.v.) to provide essential tools for the implementation of programs aimed at the prevention, control, and eradication of diseases by vaccination. SIREVA's principal objective is to contribute, through the administration and coordination of the region's scientific and technological knowledge, to the development and strengthening of vaccine research and development, production, quality control, and evaluation. To this end, PAHO and WHO promote policies and legislation that commit national resources, mobilize investments, and foster technical (q.v.) and scientific cooperation among member states (q.v.). *See also* Children's Vaccine Initiative; Expanded Programme on Immunization; Global Programme for Vaccines and Immunization.

PAHO SUPPLIES OFFICE. *See* PAHO Procurement Office.

PAMPANA, EMILIO J. (1895–1973). Dr. Emilio Pampana, of Italy, proposed the global eradication of malaria in 1948 based on his long experience as a malariologist. His proposal was put into practice in 1950 by the Pan American Sanitary Conference and adopted by the World Health Assembly (q.v.) in 1955. Dr. Pampana served on the WHO staff from 1947 to 1958, first as chief of the malaria section and later as the first director of the Division of Malaria Eradication.

PANAFRICANS EMERGENCY TRAINING CENTRE (PTC). A center created in the 1980s, currently within the Division of Emergency and Humanitarian Action (q.v.) and based in Addis Ababa, Ethiopia, to carry out three interrelated activities and goals: (a) to promote awareness and build national capacity for health emergency management in Africa (training); (b) to promote Africa's priorities in WHO strategies for emergency and humanitarian action (information clearing); and (c) to promote WHO's technical role in emergencies by providing a center of reference for documentation, information, and services (research). In carrying out these activities, PTC maintains a network of partnerships that includes other WHO programs at headquarters, regional offices (qq.v.), academic institutions, the Organization of African Unity, other United Nations organizations, the International Federation of the Red Cross and other nongovernmental organizations (qq.v.).

PAN AMERICAN AIR POLLUTION SAMPLING NETWORK. *See* Pan American Network for Normalized Sampling of Air Pollution.

PAN AMERICAN CENTER. A group of centers created by the Pan American Health Organization (q.v.) within the Americas region from the mid-1940s for the purpose of organizing regional research and development programs in health. The centers include the Institute of Nutrition in Central America and Panama (INCAP) (q.v.) in Guatemala City, Guatemala; the Pan American Foot-and-Mouth Disease Center (PANAFTOSA) in Rio de Janeiro, Brazil; and the Pan American Zoonoses Center in Buenos Aires, Argentina, known since 1991 as the Pan American Institute for Food Protection and Zoonoses (INPPAZ).

PAN AMERICAN CENTER FOR HEALTH PLANNING. A center set up in 1967 by the Pan American Sanitary Organization in Santiago, Chile, to support health planning in the Americas region. The center was created following recognition of the importance of planning in health development by the Charter of Punta del Este (q.v.). *See also* Pan American Center.

PAN AMERICAN CENTER FOR HUMAN ECOLOGY AND HEALTH (ECO). A center created by the Pan American Health Organization (q.v.) in 1975 in Mexico City as a result of concern about the impact of industrial development on the environment. The center coordinates the evaluation of development projects for their impact on the human environment and health. *See also* Glboal Strategy for Health and Environment; Programme for the Promotion of Environmental Health.

PAN AMERICAN CENTER FOR PERINATOLOGY AND HUMAN DEVELOPMENT (CLAP). A center founded in 1970 by the Pan American Health Organization (q.v.) in Montevideo, Uruguay, to promote education and research aimed at reducing maternal and infant mortality and morbidity, with an emphasis on problems that affect survival during the perinatal period. Its research activities focus on developing and evaluating appropriate technology and conducting epidemiologic studies, including the investigation and application of new methods related to care of expectant mothers during the last months of their pregnancy, during delivery, and during the initial month of a baby's life. *See also* Pan American Center.

PAN AMERICAN CENTER FOR SANITARY ENGINEERING AND ENVIRONMENTAL SCIENCES (CEPIS). A center set up in 1968 in Lima, Peru, to provide centralized advisory services, research, education, and information on sanitary engineering and environmental sciences for the Americas region. *See also* International Drinking Water and Sanitation Decade; Pan American Center.

PAN AMERICAN CENTER FOR TRAINING AND RESEARCH IN LEPROSY AND RELATED DISEASES (CEPIALET). A center (formerly known as the International Center for Training and Research in Leprosy and Related Diseases) created in 1972 in Caracas, Venezuela, and associated with the Pan American Health Organization (q.v.) since 1976, to support research and training on leprosy in the Americas region. *See also* Action Programme for the Elimination of Leprosy; Special Action Projects towards the Elimination of Leprosy.

PAN AMERICAN CHILD CONGRESS. A series of congresses held since 1916 to promote international collaboration in child welfare issues. The purpose of the meetings is to enable pediatricians and other relevant experts to exchange information on medical and social problems afflicting children and on the role of the public sector in resolving them. In 1948, the ninth Pan American Child Congress agreed on a draft declaration, known as the Declaration of Caracas and subsequently adopted by the Pan American Health Organization (q.v.), affirming the right of children to the best possible health protection. *See also* Child Health Phase II; Committee on the Rights of the Child; Division of Child Health and Development.

PAN AMERICAN HEALTH ORGANIZATION (PAHO). An organization created in 1902, as the International Sanitary Bureau, and then the Pan American Sanitary Bureau (PASB) (q.v.), to carry out cooperative international and regional health work in the Americas region. In July 1949, the PASB signed an agreement to become the American Regional Office of WHO as well as the inter-American specialized organization recognized by the Organization of American States (OAS) (q.v.). Because of this multiple role and its long-established history, PAHO is unique among WHO's regional offices (q.v.) in the degree of its independence. It maintains its own governing bodies—the Directing Council (q.v.), the Pan American Sanitary Conference, and the Executive Committee (q.v.), which meet regularly to set the organization's technical and administrative policies. PAHO currently has 38 member states (q.v.), and its secretariat (q.v.) is based in Washington, D.C.

In 1993 the structure of the Secretariat was reorganized to improve the implementation of policies, strategic orientations, and priorities established by the regional committee (q.v.). The new structure introduced four broad functional categories: the Office of the Director; operational coordination of country programs; administrative support; and technical program support (i.e., special programs and technical support divisions). This structural reform was also adopted to encourage improved communication and coordination of regional office units, programming, and evaluation at all levels and to strengthen the capacity to respond to changes in the environment and health situation. PAHO works through 27 country offices (q.v.), atypical within WHO, given their relatively large resources and considerable authority. PAHO is funded from regular budget funds (RFBs) and extrabudgetary funds (EBFs) (qq.v.) from its member states and receives additional funds from the OAS. Notably, unlike other regional offices, PAHO is permitted to receive EBFs directly from other organizations rather than through WHO headquarters (q.v.). *See also* Zone Office.

PAN AMERICAN NETWORK FOR NORMALIZED SAMPLING OF AIR POLLUTION (REDPANAIRE). A network created by the Pan American Health Organization (PAHO) (q.v.) in 1967 to measure the level of certain contaminants in the air of major cities in the Americas region. Coordinated through the Pan American Center for Sanitary Engineering and Environmental Sciences (q.v.), the network comprises sampling stations in 11 cities, which use normalized methods for monitoring and comparing air quality. In 1973 the Pan American Air Pollution Sampling Network (REDPANAIRE) was created by PAHO to collect information on air pollution in the Americas region. The network consists of 85 stations in 25 cities and provides information that can be used to promote legislation for the prevention and control of environmental risks. *See also* PAHO Regional Plan for Investment in the Environment and Health.

PAN AMERICAN SANITARY BUREAU (PASB). An organization established in 1902, as the International Sanitary Bureau (ISB), by the governments of the Americas region to foster cooperation on international and regional health work. The bureau was established almost immediately following the scientific finding of the mode of transmission of yellow fever, a disease having significant impact on the region. Shortly afterwards a campaign to eliminate the disease from the region was commenced by the ISB in cooperation with other organizations such as the Rockefeller Foundation (q.v.). The program has continued over the past 90 years and, while not achieving eradication, has succeeded in developing a yellow fever vaccine and significantly reducing reported cases of the disease. The bureau also collected epidemiological intelligence in member states (q.v.) and exchanged this information with the Office International d'Hygiène Publique, the Health Organization of the League of Nations, and the Egyptian Sanitary, Maritime and Quarantine Board (qq.v.). In 1923, the organization changed its name to the Pan American Sanitary Bureau to distinguish it from the work of other international health organizations operating during this period.

Decisions on overall policies, programs, and budgets were made at annual Pan American Sanitary Conferences attended by PASB member states. It was again restructured in January 1947 and renamed the Pan American Sanitary Organization. This new organization consisted of four organs: the Pan American Sanitary Conference, the Directing Council, the Executive Committee (qq.v.), and the Pan American Sanitary Bureau, with a director (q.v.) and staff. The aim of this restructuring was to emphasize its independence from the soon-to-be-created WHO, which member states strongly wanted to maintain. This was achieved by giving member states greater and more direct control over the organization's policies and programs. In 1949, an agreement was signed by the PASB to become the American Regional Office of WHO, known as the Pan American Health Organization (q.v.).

PAN AMERICAN SANITARY CODE. A code drafted at the seventh Pan American Sanitary Conference held in Havana, Cuba, in 1923 as the first treaty on health ratified by all countries in the Americas. The code gave the Pan American Sanitary Bureau (q.v.) broad functions and duties and a firm juridical basis. It later served as a document that prevented attempts to disestablish the organization. *See also* International Health Regulations.

PAN AMERICAN SANITARY CONFERENCE. *See* Pan American Sanitary Bureau.

PAN AMERICAN SANITARY ORGANIZATION. *See* Pan American Sanitary Bureau.

PAN AMERICAN UNION. *See* Organization of American States.

PAN ARAB PROJECT FOR CHILD DEVELOPMENT (PAP-CHILD). A project initiated in the 1980s consisting of surveys of child health carried out by the Eastern Mediterrannean Regional Office (EMRO) (q.v.), in cooperation with the Arab League and the United Nations Children's Fund (q.v.), as part of its support for the development of health research and appropriate technology. The surveys were conducted in the Arab countries of the Gulf area and then expanded to other member states (q.v.) of the region, including Lebanon, Morocco, Tunisia, and Sudan. The project is governed by a higher steering committee, an expert group, and a technical committee. Since 1983 EMRO has periodically published *The State of Child Health in the Eastern Mediterranean* to describe the status of child health and major approaches to improving conditions in the region.

PAN ARAB REGIONAL HEALTH BUREAU. An organization created in the nineteenth century, which was the forerunner of the Eastern Mediterranean Regional Office (q.v.), to foster health cooperation in Arab countries. In 1949, its functions were integrated into WHO with the adoption of an Executive Board (q.v.) resolution. *See also* Egyptian Sanitary, Maritime, and Quarantine Board.

PARISOT, JACQUES. Professor Jacques Parisot, of France, served as president of the Health Committee of the Health Organization of the League of Nations (1937–40) (q.v.). Prior to this position, he was professor of hygiene and social medicine and director of the Institute of Hygiene at the University of Nancy,

France. In 1934 he was appointed as a member of the Health Committee, where he strongly opposed activities undertaken by Ludwik Rajchman (q.v.) seen to be of a political nature. Following Parisot's death, the Jacques Parisot Foundation Fellowship (q.v.) was initiated by WHO in 1969 to commemorate his contribution to international public health.

PARRAN, THOMAS (1892–1968). Dr. Thomas Parran, of the United States, served as a member of the Technical Preparatory Committee and chair of the International Health Conference (qq.v.) in 1946, where he was a strong supporter of regional decentralization for the proposed international health organization to be created. After completing medical training, he began a long career with the United States Public Health Service, including appointments as surgeon general (1936–48), and dean of the Graduate School of Public Health at the University of Pittsburg (1948–58). During this period, he also served as an American delegate to many international health conferences, including the first conference of the United Nations Relief and Rehabilitation Administration (q.v.) in 1943.

PERSONNEL, DIVISION OF. *See* Division of Personnel.

PESTICIDE EVALUATION SCHEME, WHO. *See* WHO Pesticide Evaluation Scheme.

PHARMACEUTICAL MANUFACTURERS ASSOCIATIONS, INTERNATIONAL FEDERATION OF. *See* International Federation of Pharmaceutical Manufacturers Associations.

PHARMACEUTICAL PRODUCTS MOVING IN INTERNATIONAL COMMERCE, CERTIFICATION SCHEME ON THE QUALITY OF. *See* Certification Scheme on the Quality of Pharmaceutical Products Moving in International Commerce.

PHARMACEUTICALS FOR HUMAN USE, INTERNATIONAL CONFERENCE ON HARMONIZATION OF TECHNICAL REQUIREMENTS FOR REGISTRATION OF. *See* International Conference on Harmonization of Technical Requirements for Registration of Pharmaceuticals for Human Use.

PHARMACEUTICALS, TASK FORCE ON. *See* Task Force on Pharmaceuticals.

PHARMACEUTICALS UNIT (PHA). A unit created in the 1950s to carry out WHO's constitutional responsibilities for defining pharmacopeial standards and other requirements for pharmaceutical and biological products. During the 1950s, the PHA focused on the production of standards, technical guidelines, and nomenclature. This includes publication of the International Pharmacopoeia (q.v.) and annual reports of the Expert Committee on Biological Standardization, which sets norms for in-process control of biological preparations and for the testing of all finished products within national drug control laboratories. In the 1960s its work widened to include concerns for quality control and the safety and efficacy of drugs. The importance of this work was highlighted by the crisis over thalidomide in 1962, which led WHO to set up an international system for providing information on adverse drug reactions. During the 1970s, the rapid growth of the Drug Action Programme (DAP) (q.v.) led to concerns among some Executive Board (q.v.) members over the allocation of responsibilities between the two units. An agreed-strategy for a clearer division of labor eventually emerged between the two units, with DAP focusing on information dissemination and the PHA on normative activities (q.v.).

Hence, between 1978 and 1988 the PHA took over the convening of expert committees (q.v.) concerned with drugs, which met to revise the original Model List of Essential Drugs (q.v.). The PHA also organized the International Conference of Drug Regulatory Authorities (q.v.) in Rome (1982) and Stockholm (1984), produced guidelines on aspects of quality control, revised the certification scheme for drugs, and managed training programs for pharmacists from developing countries. The PHA was located within the Division of Diagnostic, Prophylactic, and Therapeutic Substances until 1984, when it was moved to join DAP in the office of the director-general (q.v.). In 1988, both units were again moved to a newly created Division of Drug Management and Policies (q.v.). In 1992, the PHA was disestablished and replaced by the Quality Assurance Programme (q.v.) and Drug Safety Programme. During its existence, and in contrast to DAP, activities of the PHA were funded by regular budget funds (q.v.).

PIOT, PETER (1949–   ). Dr. Peter Piot, of Belgium, was appointed by the United Nations secretary-general as the first executive director of the Joint United Nations Programme on

HIV/AIDS (UNAIDS) (qq.v.) in 1995 for a period of two years. With medical and doctoral degrees in microbiology, Dr. Piot was professor of microbiology and head of the Department of Infection and Immunity at the Institute of Tropical Medicine in Antwerp, Belgium (1980–92). He was among the first to document a number of important aspects of the HIV/AIDS epidemic and was president of the International AIDS Society (1991–94) and editor of the prominent journal *AIDS*. He then became director of the Division of Research and Intervention Development within the Global Programme on AIDS (GPA) (q.v.), where he was responsible for research and development and advising on policy and technical issues (1992–94). During his period of office as executive director, Dr. Piot oversaw the formal establishment of UNAIDS to cover the transition period until the replacement of the GPA by UNAIDS. He spent much of this time planning and developing the program, including setting up new institutional mechanisms at the global and country level, negotiating with the six cosponsoring (q.v.) organizations on their roles, and raising extrabudgetary funds (q.v.).

PLAN OF ACTION FOR VACCINE SELF-SUFFICIENCY. Also known as Vaccine Independence Initiative. An initiative and plan of action proposed by the Expanded Programme on Immunization (q.v.) to assist the capacity of lower income countries to take responsibility for the provision of adequate quantities of high-quality vaccines. This is to be achieved through appropriate strategies directed toward more sustainable financing and procurement, local production, and quality control practices. *See also* Global Programme for Vaccines and Immunization.

PLENARY MEETING. A meeting of the World Health Assembly (q.v.) that is open to all delegates, alternates, and advisers appointed by member states (q.v.); representatives of associate members (q.v.); and representatives of the Executive Board (q.v.), observers from invited nonmember states and territories, and representatives of the United Nations and other participating intergovernmental and nongovernmental organizations (q.v.) having formal recognition by the organization. *See also* Committee A; Committee B; Committee on Credentials; Committee on Nominations.

POCANTICO RETREAT. *See* Rockefeller Foundation.

POCCHIARI, FRANCESCO. *See* Francesco Pocchiari Fellowship.

POISONINGS PREVENTION AND TREATMENT (PPT). *See* Programme for the Promotion of Chemical Safety.

POLICIES AND RECRUITMENT SERVICE (SPR). *See* Division of Personnel.

POLICY ACTION COORDINATION TEAM. *See* Renewing the Health for All Strategy.

POLICY AND COORDINATION ADVISORY COMMITTEE. *See* Special Programme of Research, Development, and Research Training in Human Reproduction.

POLICY AND COORDINATION COMMITTEE (PCC). *See* Special Programme of Research, Development, and Research Training in Human Reproduction.

POLICY OF ZERO NOMINAL GROWTH. A policy supported by selected member states (q.v.) of the Geneva Group (q.v.) since the mid-1990s that calls for no increase, in nominal or absolute terms, in the regular budget funds (q.v.) of United Nations organizations. In contrast to the policy of zero real growth (q.v.), this policy supports the same U.S. dollars figure for the current and ensuing financial periods, representing a decrease of financing in real terms (i.e., after inflation).

POLICY OF ZERO REAL GROWTH. A policy adopted by member states (q.v.) of the Geneva Group (q.v.) since the early 1980s, during a period of financial austerity, that calls for no increase in real terms (i.e., after inflation) of the regular budget funds (RBFs) (q.v.) of United Nations organizations. The rate of real growth is defined as the rate of increase in the budget, expressed in constant U.S. dollars terms (or other currency of denomination of the budget), from the approved budget for the current financial period to that envisaged for the ensuing financial period. This "zero real growth base" is then adjusted to take account of expected rates of inflation and other anticipated nondiscretionary cost increases (e.g., salaries) during the period covered by the proposed budget. Over the years this principle has become the basis for preparation and presentation of proposed program budgets throughout the UN system. In WHO, the policy was introduced in 1980 in the World Health Assembly (q.v.) and has since been the basis of no increase, in real terms, in RBFs. *See also* Policy of Zero Nominal Growth.

POLIO ERADICATION INITIATIVE. An initiative proposed in 1988 by the Expanded Programme on Immunization (q.v.), and adopted by a resolution of the World Health Assembly (qq.v.) to globally eradicate poliomyelitis by the year 2000. The United Nations Children's Fund (UNICEF) (q.v.) and 130 world leaders adopted the same goal at the World Summit for Children (q.v.) in 1990. The strategy of the initiative centers on the provision of child immunization within the context of primary health care (q.v.), including wider immunization services, the creation of effective surveillance, and other aspects of child care and disease control. Since 1991, the disease has been eradicated from the Western Hemisphere, and worldwide, cases have fallen by 85 percent since the initiative began. There are now 150 countries free of the disease, and an estimated 82 percent of eligible children are immunized with the recommended three doses of oral polio vaccine (q.v.).

Globally, 67 countries remain endemic for poliomyelitis in 1995, including many that experience difficulties in achieving satisfactory immunization coverage due to civil unrest, economic instability, or remote populations. About 90,000 cases are estimated to occur each year, three-quarters in the Indian subcontinent. Polio-endemic countries meet 80 percent of the costs of eradication, with 20 percent (U.S.$100 million annually until the year 2000) dependent on external resources provided by WHO, UNICEF, Rotary International, and other aid agencies. In 1996, 100 million doses of polio vaccine were donated by Chiron Vaccines, Pasteur Merieux Connaught, and Smith-Kline Beecham as the largest single donation of its kind ever made by the vaccine industry. *See also* Operation MECACAR; Polio Eradication Programme.

POLIO ERADICATION PROGRAMME. A program of the Pan American Health Organization (PAHO) (q.v.), approved in 1985, aimed at interrupting poliomyelitis virus transmission within the Americas region by 1990. It was preceded by national vaccination campaigns throughout the Americas region. By 1985 the number of reported cases in the Western Hemisphere had diminished to fewer than 1,000 per year. *See also*

Expanded Programme on Immunization; Operation MECA-CAR; Oral Polio Vaccine; Polio Eradication Initiative.

POLIO VACCINE, ORAL. *See* Oral Polio Vaccine.

POPULATION AND DEVELOPMENT, INTERNATIONAL CONFERENCE ON. *See* International Conference on Population and Development.

POSTERIORITY. A working term describing an activity that has outlived its relevance or usefulness for a number of reasons, such as the disappearance of the problems it was intended to solve as a major public health issue or the solving of a problem through activities by WHO or its member states (q.v.). This concept has been extended to activities suspended or deleted for budgetary reasons. *See also* Priority Setting; Executive Board Working Group on the WHO Response to Global Change.

PREPARATORY COMMITTEE. *See* International Conference on Population and Development.

PREVENTION OF BLINDNESS (PBL). A program created in the 1980s for two purposes: (a) to develop technical guidelines for specific disease control and management and standards of eye care; and (b) technical cooperation with member states (qq.v.) in support of national program development for blindness prevention. The former is based on consultations with members of the WHO Expert Advisory Panel (q.v.) on Trachoma and Prevention of Blindness and with a network of 20 WHO collaborating centers (q.v.). Specific guidelines for control of cataract, trachoma, onchocerciasis, glaucoma, leprosy, and trauma are included. The latter purpose involves working with member states to develop a national plan for the prevention of blindness and to set up a national committee or expert group for technical advisory services, standards, and norms to be applied.

The PBL has developed a model of primary eye care outlining the most essential elements of eye health education and clinical care. This work includes close collaboration with a network of international nongovernmental organizations (NGOs) (q.v.) that provide support to WHO and developing countries for blindness prevention. The joint development of activities, technical strategies, and so on is facilitated by a Programme Advisory Group on the Prevention of Blindness composed of PBL staff, international experts, and NGO representatives. A

Partnership Committee of organizations, including a task force, provides support for specific joint projects on the prevention of blindness and the education and rehabilitation of the blind. A Global Database on Blindness is maintained for the collection of epidemiological information and trends assessment. It is estimated that 160 million people worldwide have a visual disability. The program receives extrabudgetary funds (q.v.) for its work through contributions to the Voluntary Fund for Health Promotion (q.v.). *See also* Onchocerciasis Control Programme; Prevention of Deafness and Hearing Impairment.

PREVENTION OF DEAFNESS AND HEARING IMPAIRMENT (PDH). A program created in the mid-1980s to assist member states (q.v.) in reducing and eventually eliminating avoidable hearing impairment and disability through appropriate preventive measures. Currently more than 120 million people in the world suffer from hearing disability, a condition that can lead to such difficulties as delays in language acquisition, education, and vocational attainment, social isolation, and stigmatization. The main activities of the program at present are to study the global epidemiology and costs of hearing impairment; to prevent hearing impairment from chronic otitis media; to develop primary ear care as part of primary health care (q.v.); to support the planning of national programs; to develop guidelines on prevention, detection, and screening for hearing impairment; and to develop a global data bank on deafness and hearing impairment. In 1991 the program became affiliated with the Prevention of Blindness (q.v.).

PRIMARY HEALTH CARE (PHC). Also known as comprehensive primary health care. An approach to health care adopted in the 1970s based on practical, scientifically sound, and socially acceptable methods and technology made universally accessible to individuals and families in a community and at a cost that a community and country can afford to maintain. Primary health care is intended to be the first level of contact by individuals, families, and communities with the national health system and aims to bring health care as close as possible to where people live and work. The approach is also guided by the principles of community participation, self-reliance, and self-determination.

The primary health care approach was officially adopted by WHO at the International Conference on Primary Health Care (q.v.) in 1977 and has remained the central focus of the Health for All (q.v.) strategy. The approach should include at least the following eight components: education concerning prevailing health problems and methods for prevention and control; promotion of food supply and proper nutrition; an adequate supply of safe water and basic sanitation; maternal and child health care, including family planning; immunization against the major infectious diseases; prevention and control of locally endemic diseases; appropriate treatment of common disease and injuries; and provision of essential drugs. *See also* Selective Primary Health Care.

PRIMARY HEALTH CARE, INTERNATIONAL CONFERENCE ON. *See* International Conference on Primary Health Care.

PRIMARY HEALTH CARE, SELECTIVE. *See* Selective Primary Health Care.

PRIORITY SETTING. The task of identifying and supporting health activities deemed of greatest importance to the member states (q.v.) of WHO. WHO expresses its health priorities in a variety of ways, including policy declarations through the Executive Board, World Health Assembly, or regional committee resolutions (qq.v.); the content of the General Programme of Work (q.v.); budgetary expenditures or reallocations; and advocacy at international, regional, or national forums. The determination of priorities within WHO's policies and strategies is the concern of the director-general (q.v.), supported by the organization's senior management and various internal and external mechanisms and by program managers, who direct the efforts of the organization in discharging its constitutional mandate within its capacities and resources. However, the capacity of WHO to set clear priorities in its activities has been a major source of criticism from member states in recent years.

PROGRAM BUDGETING. *See* Proposed Programme Budget.

PROGRAMME ADVISORY COMMITTEE. *See* International Programme on Chemical Safety.

PROGRAMME ADVISORY GROUP ON THE PREVENTION OF BLINDNESS. *See* Prevention of Blindness.

PROGRAMME COMMITTEE, EXECUTIVE BOARD. *See* Programme Development Committee.

PROGRAMME COORDINATION BOARD. *See* Joint United Nations Programme on HIV/AIDS.

PROGRAMME DEVELOPMENT COMMITTEE (PDC). A committee created in 1994, under the Executive Board (EB) (q.v.), replacing the program committee of nine government representatives, as part of the Executive Board Working Group on the WHO Response to Global Change (q.v.) reform process. The committee was established to streamline the working of the EB. More specifically, its purpose is to follow the reform process and to assist more generally in the process of program development. The seven-member PDC is composed of the chair or vice chair of the EB plus one EB member from each region. The term of office should not exceed two years. The committee selects a chair from among these members and meets annually in January in tandem with the Administration, Budget, and Finance Committee (q.v.).

PROGRAMME FOR DEVELOPMENT OF HUMAN RESOURCES FOR HEALTH (HRH). A program created in the 1970s to promote and cooperate with countries in planning for, training, and deploying the types and numbers of health personnel that they require and can afford and that are socially responsible and equipped with the necessary scientific, technical, and managerial competence; and to help ensure that such personnel are utilized optimally to meet the requirements of national strategies to achieve Health for All (q.v.). Activities have included advising on health personnel policy and planning and providing research training grants and fellowships. The program is also responsible for the staff development program, which is concerned with the provision and maintenance of skills to enable optimal functioning of WHO staff. In the mid-1990s, budgetary constraints in WHO and member states (q.v.) led to efforts to focus activities at headquarters (q.v.) more sharply and to pursue more actively issues of cost effectiveness in the development of human resources for health. The largest contributors of extrabudgetary funds (q.v.) to the program have been Japan and the Kellogg Foundation. *See also* Fellowship Programme.

PROGRAMME FOR THE CONTROL OF ACUTE RESPIRATORY INFECTIONS (ARI). A program created in 1982 when acute respiratory infections (ARIs) were internationally recognized as a leading cause of death. The main objective of the program is to reduce illness severity and mortality, particularly from pneumonia, through improvements in case management, mainly by providing primary health care (q.v.). The program focuses on countries (88 countries in 1987) where infant mortality rates from ARI are 40 per 1,000 or higher. Nearly 60 countries had developed operational national programs by 1994. ARI was initially established within the Tuberculosis and Respiratory Infections Unit, was transferred to the Programme for the Control of Diarrhoeal Diseases (q.v.) in 1987, and then moved to the Division of Diarrhoeal and Acute Respiratory Disease Control (q.v.) when it was formed in 1990.

PROGRAMME FOR THE CONTROL OF DIARRHOEAL DISEASES (CDD). A program established in 1980 to address the high incidence of morbidity and mortality, particularly among young children, due to diarrhoeal diseases in developing countries. The CDD was launched amid growing scientific evidence of the efficacy of interventions, such as oral rehydration salts (ORS) for oral rehydration therapy (ORT), in the prevention and treatment of dehydration. The first objective of the program was to reduce case mortality in infants and young children through emphasis on ORT through health facilities and home-based case management. Thus, the CDD concentrated until the mid-1980s on the development, implementation, and evaluation of national programs for the distribution and wider use of ORS packets. By the late 1980s, activities turned increasingly to prevention through, for example, the promotion of breast-feeding and integrated disease control approaches. The CDD is located within the Division of Diarrhoeal and Acute Respiratory Disease Control (q.v.), and is funded from a combination of regular budget and extrabudgetary funds (qq.v.). Since 1991 the United Nations Children's Fund (q.v.) and WHO, given shared interests in child health, have worked more closely in this field and have adopted a common set of indicators for measuring progress in reducing the incidence and treatment of diarrhoeal diseases. See also Programme for the Control of Acute Respiratory Infections; Sick Child Initiative.

PROGRAMME FOR THE GLOBAL ELIMINATION OF DRACUNCULIASIS. A program set up within the Division of Control of Tropical Diseases (q.v.) in 1980 to eradicate dracunculiasis (guinea-worm infection), a water-borne disease caused by the parasite *Dracunculus medinensis*. This parasite is a nematode worm that lives in the skin of human beings. When the infected part of the body is immersed in water, the female worm emerges in a painful abscess to discharge tiny larvae. Eradication of the disease is thus based on the need to ensure clean drinking water and sanitation in order to interrupt transmission. Because the disease has received less attention by governments than other tropical diseases, WHO has sought to increase political support for eradication in disease-endemic countries during the 1990s. WHO has also intensified monitoring of the status of program interventions within villages, where the disease is endemic, worked to change the behavior of local populations with respect to drinking water use, and mobilized financial and staffing resources. *See also* International Commission for the Certification of Dracunculiasis Eradication.

PROGRAMME FOR THE PROMOTION OF CHEMICAL SAFETY (PCS). A program created in 1980 to carry out coordination functions (e.g., research) and technical work in the field of chemical safety. During the last three decades, the use and number of new man-made chemicals has almost doubled and will reach 100,000 by the year 2000. Since the use of chemicals is increasing, and with it the transport, handling, storage, and disposal of significant quantities and varieties of chemicals, accidents have and will inevitably occur, exposing people and the environment to immediate and long-term deleterious effects. The role of the program is to accelerate the provision of internationally evaluated scientific information on chemicals, to promote the use of such information in national programs, and to enable member states (q.v.) to establish their own chemical safety measures and programs. The program also supports member states in strengthening their capabilities in chemical emergency preparedness and response and in chemical risk reduction.

The program consists of two main units: Assessment of Risk and Methodologies (ARM) and Poisonings Prevention and Treatment (PPT). The program also serves as the central unit of the International Programme on Chemical Safety (q.v.), which works in collaboration with the ILO and UNEP. Activities include the compilation of results from different countries on the effects of chemicals used in industry, agriculture, and the home on health and the environment. These activities are undertaken in close collaboration with the Programme for the Promotion of Environmental Health (q.v.), and since 1994 both programs report directly to the executive director (q.v.) of Health and Environment.

PROGRAMME FOR THE PROMOTION OF ENVIRONMENTAL HEALTH (PEH). A program created in 1994, with the reorganization of the Division of Environmental Health, as part of the WHO Global Strategy for Health and Environment (q.v.). The term environmental health encompasses the health consequences of interactions between human populations and the whole range of factors in their physical (natural and manmade) and social environments. The interdependence of health, development, and environment is manifold and complex, but two aspects predominate: how well the environment can sustain life and health and how free the environment is of hazards to health. The purpose of the program is to address priority issues concerning the interactions between the physical and social environments and health. Its work focuses on WHO's responsibilities for coordinating international work in the area of health and the environment and assisting member states (q.v.) with the development and implementation of national health and environment programs. Through a multidisciplinary staff that includes physicians, epidemiologists, toxicologists, sanitary engineers, economists, and anthropologists, the program carries out work on community water supply and sanitation, environmental health in rural and urban development and housing, and global and integrated environmental health. For this purpose, the program is structured into two components: the Division of Operational Support in Environmental Health and the Office of Global and Integrated Environmental Health (qq.v.).

PROGRAMME FOR VACCINE DEVELOPMENT (PVD). A program created in the 1980s to stimulate and promote research activities at the international level on vaccines for diseases that have so far not been preventable by vaccines. Through its work, the program has encouraged interest in hitherto neglected diseases. The work of the program is overseen by a scientific advisory group of experts (SAGE). In 1994, the program was merged with the Expanded Programme on Immunization and the Children's Vaccine Initiative (qq.v.) and part of the Biologicals Unit to form the Global Programme on Vaccines and Immunization (q.v.).

PROGRAMME MANAGEMENT, DIRECTOR OF. *See* Director of Programme Management.

PROGRAMME OF ACTION. *See* International Conference on Population and Development.

PROGRAMME ON AGING AND HEALTH. A program created in 1995, within the Division of Health Promotion, Education and Communication (q.v.), to promote health and well-being throughout the lifespan, thus seeking the highest possible level of quality of life for the longest possible duration. The program replaced the Global Programme for Health of the Elderly (q.v.), which largely focused on the collection and dissemination of international epidemiological research. As a result of interdivisional and interregional consultations, it was decided that there was a need for increased interaction and collaboration with regional offices (q.v.), other international organizations, bilateral agencies, nongovernmental organizations, and WHO collaborating centers (qq.v.). It was also agreed that WHO should take the lead role within the international community in the field of aging and health.

The scope of the new program was thus broadened to encompass not only diseases associated with aging populations but public health considerations of the whole lifespan; with a view toward healthy aging. This is organized into five integrated program components: information, policy, advocacy, community-based programs, and training and research. For example, by advancing the state of knowledge about geriatrics and gerontology through training and research, the program aims to respond to the health implications of the present shift in the age structure of the world's population, notably in developing countries. Of particular concern is the lack of resources and infrastructure in the developing world to respond to the needs of rapidly aging populations. To begin to address this issue, intersectoral workshops at country level are being held by WHO to support developing countries in formulating health policies for aging populations. The program is also working toward playing a major role in presenting the health component of the International Year of Older Persons (1999).

PROGRAMME ON MENTAL HEALTH. A unit created in 1996, within the Division of Mental Health and Prevention of Substance Abuse (q.v.), to carry out activities related to the promotion of positive mental health and the influence of psychosocial and behavioral factors on overall health. The unit provides support in the field of psychological and sociological expertise to other WHO programs but does not deal with services or research related to mental disorders. Activities include mental health services for particularly vulnerable groups, such as refugees, migrants, and disaster victims, in which broad mental health support forms a component of broader relief aid. For these purposes, the unit is composed of three subunits: Promotion of Mental Health, Psychosocial and Behavioural Science Applications, and Mental Health for Vulnerable Groups.

PROGRAMME ON SUBSTANCE ABUSE (PSA). A program established in 1990 with the mandate of minimizing the health problems associated with the use of alcohol and other drugs. In 1994, the Programme on Tobacco or Health (q.v.) was incorporated into the program, thus expanding its mandate to include tobacco. The PSA is responsible for setting technical and policy norms with regard to the prevention, management, and reduction of the health and social effects of substance abuse. The overall goal of the PSA is to reduce the impact that existing substance abuse has on the health and welfare of populations worldwide and to prevent new substance abuse in all forms. Its activities are organized into (a) prevention, advocacy, and promotion; (b) treatment and care; and (c) regulatory control. *See also* World No Tobacco Day.

PROGRAMME ON TOBACCO OR HEALTH. A program created in 1990 to provide advice and assistance to member states (q.v.) for the adoption of national tobacco control policies and programs. Tobacco use is responsible for an annual global total of three million deaths, a figure expected to rise to ten million by 2020. While there has been a marked decline in tobacco consumption in higher-income countries during the past decade, use has increased in developing countries, largely due to the marketing efforts of the tobacco industry. Between 1970 and 1995 WHO adopted 14 resolutions that call on member states to adopt national control policies and programs. These resolutions, together with a plan of action for 1988–95, have been the framework for the development and implementation of program activities.

The plan of action for 1996–2000 continues the relevant activities from the previous plan, complemented by annual plans and a focus on supporting national and international tobacco control programs, advocacy and public information, and creation of a research and information center. In addition, WHO sponsors regional conferences and publishes a quarterly newsletter, *Tobacco Alert*, for health promotion and public education.

The program also maintains a Tobacco or Health data center for monitoring progress on tobacco control through routine epidemiogical surveillance, and sponsors the annual World No Tobacco Day (q.v.). As part of the Executive Board Working Group on the WHO Response to Global Change (q.v.) reform process, the program was relocated to the Programme on Substance Abuse (q.v.) in 1994 to create a more integrated approach to problems associated with the use of all psychoactive substances. The program is currently exploring the feasibility of developing an international instrument, such as guidelines, convention, or declaration, on tobacco control, to be adopted by the United Nations.

PROGRAM REVIEW. A process of reviewing and evaluating the past performance, outputs, and expected outputs of specific WHO programs begun in 1994 as part of the Executive Board Working Group on the WHO Response to Global Change (q.v.) reform process. In 1993 the Executive Board (EB) (q.v.) recommended the establishment of "subgroups or committees to meet during, and as part of, the EB sessions each year, to review and evaluate a number of specific programmes, giving attention to interrelated elements of programme policy, priority, targets, plans, budgets, and other available resources including technology." The groups were requested to "recommend actions to be taken, including trade-offs within available resources, and report back to the plenary of the EB, which alone can take the final decision." During 1994–96, the EB successively reviewed all WHO programs and requested that the director-general (q.v.) develop a schedule for further reviews to be carried out at a future date.

PROGRAM SUPPORT. One of four broad and interlinked categories of programs of WHO for 1990–95. The aim of this category of program work is to provide information and financial and administrative support to WHO programs. See also Direction, Coordination, and Management; Health Systems Infrastructure; Health Science and Technology.

PROGRAM SUPPORT COST. A standard charge made by WHO since 1982 in partial reimbursement for the cost of technical and nontechnical support and services provided by the organization for activities financed by extrabudgetary funds (EBFs) (q.v.). The precise charge, currently 13 percent of technical project expenditures, has been a subject of contention in recent years because of increased volume of EBFs received by WHO. In 1992 WHO reported that the cost of services in support of EBF activities had risen from 27.4 to 35.5 percent, representing a widened gap between support costs and reimbursement. While the Executive Board Working Group on the WHO Response to Global Change (q.v.) requested that the director-general (q.v.) seek approval from the World Health Assembly (q.v.) to increase program support costs to 35 percent, it was decided in 1994 that the timing for such a revision was not appropriate at the time, given the adverse economic situation faced by many member states (q.v.). Concerns were also expressed not to risk a reduction in EBFs, which have become such an important source of financing for WHO.

PROPOSED PROGRAMME BUDGET. A budgeting cycle for WHO's program of activities carried out by the Division of Budget and Finance (q.v.) under the responsibility of the director-general (q.v.). From 1948 to 1979, budgets were approved on an annual basis. In 1980–81 a biennial program and budget were introduced to reduce time spent by the governing bodies, reduce the Secretariat's (q.v.) workload, promote longer-term planning, facilitate implementation of program budgeting, allow greater flexibility in the management of funds, and facilitate interagency comparability of programs and financial data. The concept of program budgeting in WHO is based on the principle of "programming by objectives and budgeting by programs." A health program budget is one that focuses on priorities for the attainment of health, the health work to be undertaken, and the objectives sought through that work (outputs and outcomes). The objective of program budgeting is to encourage strategic planning and allocation of resources to programs at the country, regional, and global levels to which priority has been given and that respond to the needs of member states (q.v.). The proposed program budget emanates from the General Programme of Work (q.v.) for the period in question and from the overall policies and principles approved by the World Health Assembly (WHA) (q.v.).

In the first year of the budgetary process, policy guidance and instructions on budget preparation are given to senior program staff at headquarters and to regional directors (qq.v.). The instructions also indicate tentative allocations of funds to each region (q.v.). Regional directors must then develop plans for projects of assistance in consultation with requesting national governments in their regions. A proposed Regional Programme Budget is prepared and then examined by the appropriate regional committee (q.v.), which, when approved, is transmitted to the director-general. Until 1995 the six regional program and budget proposals were reviewed by the director-general and consolidated into an annual proposed programme budget (q.v.) known as the Blue Books. These documents were then distributed to each member state and to members of the Executive Board (EB) (q.v.). In the second year, the proposed program and budget estimates are examined by the EB and its Standing Committee on Administration and Finance (q.v.) for comments and recommendations. These documents are then submitted to the WHA for discussion and approval. The budget becomes operational in the third year of the cycle known as the implementation year. Overall, program budgeting is part of a collaborative managerial process whereby WHO and member states jointly determine, implement, control, evaluate, and reprogram the international health work of the organization. As part of the Executive Board Working Group on the WHO Response to Global Change (q.v.) reform process, in 1993 the WHA adopted a resolution (q.v.) on budgetary reform in an effort to ensure that WHO carries out its programs in the most transparent, cost-effective, and productive manner. The resolution served as guidance for the preparation of the 1996–97 program budget, the first strategic program budget for WHO. The most prominent change was the reduction in program headings from 59 to 19. This reduction is the cornerstone of WHO efforts to enable new strategic budgeting by enabling comparisons in real terms of spending priorities. The Proposed Programme Budget is also no longer bound as the Blue Books but left unbound, as the Yellow Books, to allow revisions to its content. Further resolutions on budgetary reform have subsequently been adopted, including requesting the director-general to reorient 2 percent of allocations of the 1998–99 program budget for priority health programs at country level. It was also requested that the program budget be translated into annual operational plans of action, which include income and expenditure from extrabudgetary funds (q.v.). *See also* Priority Setting; Policy of Zero Nominal Growth; Policy of Zero Real Growth; Division of Budget and Finance; Appendix G.

PROVISIONAL HEALTH COMMITTEE. *See* Health Organization of the League of Nations.

PUBLICATIONS COMMITTEE. *See* Division of Publishing, Language, and Library Services.

PUBLIC RELATIONS UNIT. *See* Office of Health Communications and Public Relations.

PUBLISHING, LANGUAGE, AND LIBRARY SERVICES, DIVISION OF. *See* Division of Publishing, Language, and Library Services.

Q

QUALITY ASSURANCE PROGRAMME. A program created in 1992, within the Division of Drug Management and Policies (q.v.), with responsibility for developing guidelines and advising governments on issues related to quality assurance of pharmaceutical preparations in national and international markets, with particular emphasis on generic products. The vast number of guidelines relating to quality assurance have been collated in the publication *Guideline on Good Manufacturing Practices;* others have been issued through the Certification Scheme on the Quality of Pharmaceutical Products Moving in International Commerce (q.v.). The program also publishes the *International Pharmacopoeia* (q.v.) as a means of assuring quality specifications. *See also* Pharmaceuticals Unit.

QUENUM, COMLAN ALFRED AUGUSTE (1926–1984). Dr. Comlan Quenum, of Benin, served as regional director of the African Regional Office (qq.v.) from 1965 to 1984. After training in medicine in France, he specialized in zoology, histology, and embryology; he was later appointed professor in the faculty of medicine and research in Dakar. He represented his country at the World Health Assembly and regional committee (qq.v.) during the early 1960s and became a member of the Expert Committee (q.v.) on Professional and Technical Education of Medical and Auxiliary Personnel (1964). *See also* Dr. Comlan A. A. Quenam Prize.

R

RAFEI, UTON MUCHTAR (1935–   ). Dr. Uton Rafei, of Indonesia, has served as regional director of the South-East Asia Regional Office (qq.v.) since 1994. After completing his training in medicine in 1963, he worked within the Indonesian health system at the municipal, provincial, and regional levels. He also completed postgraduate training in public health in the United States in 1970. He joined WHO in 1981 as regional adviser in primary health care, followed by appointments as senior public health administrator (1982–84), director of health protection and promotion (1984–88), and director of health systems infrastructure (1988–94).

RAJCHMAN, LUDWIK WITOLD (1881–1965). Dr. Ludwik Rajchman, of Poland, served as director of the Health Organization of the League of Nations (q.v.) from 1921 to 1939 and headed the League of Nations mission to China following the Japanese invasion of Manchuria in 1937. He trained in medicine, bacteriology, biomedical research, and public health administration, and early experiences as a member of the Polish Socialist Party reflected a strong personal commitment to social justice. As director, he supported a strong technical approach to international health during the 1920s focused on epidemiological intelligence gathering, disease control campaigns, and training of health professionals. By the late 1920s, he had begun to give greater support to the creation of a program for social medicine aimed at the social (e.g., poverty, malnutrition) causes of ill health. During early negotiations on the creation of WHO, Dr. Rajchman was influential in the agreement to locate the headquarters in Europe rather than the United States. In 1944 he became a member of the Council of the United Nations Relief and Rehabilitation Administration (q.v.) and then served as a key force behind the creation of the United Nations Children's Fund (UNICEF) (q.v.). On becoming chairman of the Executive Board of UNICEF in 1946, one of his aims was to substantially expand the health activities of the organization.

RASKA, KAREL (1909–). Dr. Karel Raska, of the former Czechoslovakia, served as director of the Division of Communicable Diseases (q.v.) from 1963 to 1970. During his career in public health, he was a strong supporter within WHO of global smallpox eradication and played an important role in initiating the Intensified Smallpox Eradication Programme (q.v.) in 1967. Prior to joining WHO, Dr. Raska was director of the Institute of Epidemiology and Microbiology.

REAL ESTATE FUND. A fund of WHO's budget for financing the acquisition and maintenance of WHO office facilities at the international, regional, and national levels. *See also* Working Capital Fund.

REGION. There are no fixed rules relating to the possibility for a country to change its region. There exists only the jurisprudence of the World Health Assembly (q.v.), consisting of a collection of resolutions (q.v.), based on the views of member states (q.v.) as to which region they wish to be assigned. This has led to geographical anomalies such as Israel in the European Regional Office (q.v.), Cyprus in the Eastern Mediterranean Regional Office (q.v.), and Algeria in the African Regional Office (q.v.).

REGIONAL ADVISORY COMMITTEE ON HEALTH RESEARCH. *See* Advisory Committee on Health Research.

REGIONAL COMMITTEE. A governing body of each regional office (q.v.) consisting of the representatives, primarily national ministers of health, of the member states (q.v.) of the region. Each regional committee meets annually to formulate policies with a regional dimension, review the regional program budget proposed by the regional director (q.v.), and monitor WHO's collaborative activities in health development in the region. The committee is also responsible for nominating the regional director, who is formally appointed by the Executive Board (q.v.); overseeing the implementation of collaborative activities; and providing advice to the director-general (q.v.) on international health matters of regional significance. The officers of the regional committee include an elected chair and two vice chairs. In the Pan American Health Organization (q.v.), this body is known as the Pan American Health Conference.

REGIONAL COMMITTEE, STANDING COMMITTEE OF THE. *See* Standing Committee of the Regional Committee.

REGIONAL DIRECTOR. The technical and administrative head of one of the six regional offices (q.v.) of WHO. Because of the decentralized nature of WHO's organizational structure, regional directors play an unusually important role compared with other United Nations specialized agencies. Subject to the overall authority of the director-general (q.v.), a regional director is elected by the member states (q.v.) of the relevant regional committee (q.v.) and then appointed by the Executive Board (EB) (q.v.). Regional directors are responsible for overall planning and management of WHO's regional programs in accordance with the General Programme of Work (q.v.), policies established at the World Health Assembly (WHA) and by regional committees, and regional Health for All (q.v.) strategies. This includes preparation of the biennial regional program budgets, appointment of WHO representatives to country offices (qq.v.), and representation of the region at meetings of the WHA and EB. For technical matters, the regional director is assisted by a director of programme management (q.v.), who, in turn, is supported by directors in charge of individual program groups.

REGIONAL DIRECTORS' DEVELOPMENT FUND (RDDF). A fund of regional directors used for the provision of seed money and specialized support to innovative health development activities in member states (q.v.). The funds may be used to initiate such projects and to raise other forms of external assistance. *See also* Director-General's and Regional Directors' Development Programme.

REGIONAL ENVIRONMENTAL HEALTH INFORMATION NETWORK. *See* Center for Environmental Health Activities.

REGIONAL HEALTH DEVELOPMENT ADVISORY COUNCIL (RHDAC). A council established in 1980, in the aftermath of the International Conference on Primary Health Care (q.v.) held in 1978, to develop a European strategy and action plan for the attainment of the goal of Health for All (q.v.).

REGIONAL INTERAGENCY COORDINATION COMMITTEE. A committee established in 1994 by the Eastern Mediterranean Regional Office (q.v.) to provide an effective mechanism for the participation of interested parties in the Expanded Programme on Immunization (q.v.) in the region. Meetings of the committee are attended by interested donor agencies, recipient countries, nongovernmental organizations (q.v.), and other interested parties. *See also* Children's Vaccine Initiative; Global Programme for Vaccines and Immunization.

REGIONAL OFFICE. An office of one of the six regions of WHO that serves as the administrative organ of the regional committee (q.v.). The offices are "subject to the general authority of the Director-General" and are responsible for carrying out the decisions of the World Health Assembly (WHA) and the Executive Board (EB) (qq.v.) within their region. Decentralization of WHO activities was foreseen in articles 44–54 of the constitution. Six regional offices were established, for Africa (African Regional Office), the Americas (Pan American Health Organization), the Eastern Mediterranean (Eastern Mediterranean Regional Office), Europe (European Regional Office), South-East Asia (South-East Asia Regional Office), and the western Pacific (Western Pacific Regional Office) (qq.v.). The purpose of the regional offices is to provide effective contact between WHO and national governments. The offices are responsible for the execution of WHO programs and for monitoring regional activities. They differ according to the needs of the regions in structural and staffing arrangements and are responsible for formulating policies of a regional character. Each office has its own biennial budget cycle, which is directed to EB meetings at headquarters (q.v.). Since 1980 there has been a major shift in the regional allocation of regular budget funds (RBFs) (q.v.) as a result of Resolution WHA29.48 requesting that by 1980 allocations be at least 60 percent (in real terms) for technical cooperation (q.v.) and provision of services. For the 1994–95 biennium, RBFs were regionally distributed as follows: AFRO 18.7 percent; PAHO, 9.7 percent; SEARO, 12 percent; EURO, 6 percent; EMRO, 10.4 percent; and WPRO, 8.7 percent.

REGIONAL PROGRAMME BUDGET. *See* Proposed Programme Budget.

REGIONAL PROGRAMME OF WORK. *See* General Programme of Work.

REGULAR BUDGET FUNDS (RBFs). Also known as assessed contributions. The financial contribution that each member state (q.v.) is required to pay based on the United Nations formula of ability to pay (i.e., population weighted by gross national product). Contributions are assessed in U.S. dollars and must be paid in either U.S. dollars or Swiss francs unless the director-general, in agreement with the Executive Board (qq.v.), deems otherwise. To ensure that WHO is not overly dependent on a single member state, the World Health Assembly (q.v.) adopted a resolution in 1952 preventing any single country from paying more than one-third of total regular budget funds (RBFs) (q.v.). The United States has historically been the largest contributor of RBFs, providing 25 percent of the regular budget. Other major contributors in 1996–97 include

France, Germany, Japan and the United Kingdom. *See also* Extrabudgetary Funds; Geneva Group; Policy of Zero Nominal Growth; Policy of Zero Real Growth; Western European and Other Group.

REHABILITATION UNIT (RHB). A unit created in the 1980s, within the Division of Health Promotion, Education, and Communication (q.v.), to promote the expansion of rehabilitation services for people with disabilities, particularly in developing countries. The strategy for expanding such services is community-based rehabilitation, which places rehabilitation within a community development context. It includes equalization of opportunities and social integration of people with disabilities. The unit also promotes the strengthening of rehabilitation referral services within the health care system and collaborates with UNESCO and the International Labour Organization in the promotion of special education, vocational training, and employment for disabled people. Its main activities include preparing guidelines and materials, fund-raising to support relevant programs, conducting international meetings on rehabilitation issues, and collaborating with other organizations in promoting the rehabilitation needs of disabled people. *See also* Health Education and Health Promotion Unit; Occupational Health Unit; Office of Health Communications and Public Relations; Programme on Aging and Health.

RENEWING THE HEALTH FOR ALL STRATEGY (RHFA). Also known as the new Global Health Policy. A process of updating the Health for All (q.v.) strategy, begun by the director-general (q.v.) in May 1995, in light of the health effects of fundamental political, economic, environmental, demographic, and social changes that have taken place in the world since the 1980s. As part of the Executive Board Working Group on the WHO Response to Global Change (q.v.) reform process and as recommended by the development team on WHO's policy and mission, the Executive Board (q.v.) requested that the director-general initiate a review of the global and national Health for All strategies that seeks to take into account current realities and trends, adjusts implementation strategies, stimulates renewed political commitment, builds new partnerships across sectoral boundaries, and equips the health sector with the resources to fulfill its responsibilities. In order to renew and reorient the Health for All strategy, a consultation process during 1995–97 was initiated with member states (q.v.) and partners of WHO in health development. A group of WHO staff, known as the Policy Action Coordination Team, were appointed by the director-general to coordinate this review. This consultation process contributes to the elaboration of a new policy that takes into account changes in, and the needs of, member states. The initiative also seeks to improve cooperation within the United Nations system, and among other international and nongovernmental organizations (q.v.), and to support national health development. The new policy will be endorsed and its implementation launched at a special event in 1997, culminating in the adoption of a charter as a pledge of political intent from all member states to implement the new policy. A more sharply defined WHO mission, derived from this policy, is intended to be an integral part of it. *See also* International Conference on Primary Health Care.

REPRODUCTIVE HEALTH. *See* International Conference on Population and Development.

REPRODUCTIVE HEALTH (TECHNICAL SUPPORT), DIVISION OF. *See* Division of Reproductive Health (Technical Support).

REPRODUCTIVE TRACT INFECTIONS, UNIT OF. *See* Division of Reproductive Health (Technical Support).

RESEARCH, ADVISORY COMMITTEE ON HEALTH (ACHR). *See* Advisory Committee on Health Research.

RESEARCH, ADVISORY COMMITTEE ON MEDICAL. *See* Advisory Committee on Health Research.

RESEARCH AND DEVELOPMENT, COMMISSION ON HEALTH. *See* Commission on Health Research and Development.

RESEARCH AND DEVELOPMENT GROUP. *See* Expanded Programme on Immunization.

RESEARCH COORDINATION, OFFICE FOR. *See* Office of Research Policy and Strategy Coordination.

RESEARCH, ESSENTIAL NATIONAL HEALTH. *See* Essential National Health Research.

RESEARCH POLICY AND STRATEGY COORDINATION, OF-FICE OF. *See* Office of Research Policy and Strategy.

RESIDENT COORDINATOR SYSTEM. A system created in 1978 to raise the status of the individual coordinator of United Nations development activities at the country level. From 1970, the United Nations Development Program (UNDP) (q.v.) resident representative held official responsibility to act as the focal point for all such activities. By the mid-1970s, however, a number of changes were adopted to strengthen the coordination capacity of this position. This led to the establishment of the Office of Resident Coordinator (RC), who would be appointed by the United Nations secretary-general rather than the UNDP and would have "over-all responsibility for, and coordination of, operational activities for development carried out at the country level," including that of WHO. While the system is now well established, there remain concerns regarding its capacity to provide effective coordination. Foremost is the perception that the RC remains too closely affiliated with the UNDP. Also, the responsibilities of the RC have expanded to encompass program, administrative, and protocol and humanitarian matters. Finally, many UN organizations such as the World Bank (q.v.) continue to operate outside of the system. *See also* Country Strategy Note.

RESOLUTION. A formal decision of the Executive Board (EB) or World Health Assembly (WHA) (qq.v.) to take action on a specific health matter. For example, the director-general (q.v.) may be asked to take forward an agreed-upon initiative or report on an area of WHO activity. Upon being adopted by the EB or WHA, all resolutions are communicated by the director-general to the members of the EB and all member states (q.v.) of the organization. Resolutions are made available in all working languages.

REVISED DRUG STRATEGY. A revised strategy of the Drug Action Programme (DAP) (q.v.) proposed at the Conference of Experts on the Rational Use of Drugs held in Nairobi, Kenya, in 1985 and endorsed by the World Health Assembly (q.v.) in 1986. The conference was held to enable concerned parties, including governments, the pharmaceutical industry, and patients' and consumers' organizations, to discuss ways of ensuring the rational use of drugs through improved knowledge and flow of information. The conference was also used to discuss the role of marketing practices in this respect, especially in developing countries. The new strategy aims to achieve the target of 85 percent of the world's population having access to essential drugs by the year 2000. This requires a commitment by member states (q.v.) to develop and implement national drug policies to ensure fair access, to intensify efforts promoting the rational use of drugs, to enhance regulatory and quality control mechanisms, to control unethical marketing and inappropriate donations of drugs, and to strengthen support for DAP. *See also* Essential Drugs List.

REVOLVING FUND FOR TEACHING AND LABORATORY EQUIPMENT. A fund created by the World Health Assembly (q.v.) in 1967 for financing the purchase of teaching and laboratory equipment for education and training in medicine and health sciences.

REVOLVING SALES FUND. An account credited with the proceeds from sales of publications, international certificates of vaccination, films and videos, and other information material. Costs of producing additional copies of such items for sale are charged against the fund. *See also* Division of Publishing, Language, and Library Services; Working Capital Fund.

RIGA INITIATIVE. An initiative launched in 1993 at a meeting held in Riga, Latvia, on investment in health jointly organized by WHO and the World Bank (q.v.). Attended by ministers of health and finance from countries of central and eastern Europe (CCEE), the aim of the meeting was to examine the range of policy challenges facing these countries as they reform their health systems. The meeting issued the Riga Statement, which set out principles of action to address the prevention and control of HIV/AIDS, and the Riga Initiative, calling for comprehensive AIDS programs in the region. Follow-up activities by WHO have included practical guidance on legislation, HIV surveillance, economic impact analysis, and training.

ROCKEFELLER FOUNDATION. A charitable foundation set up in the early 20th century by John D. Rockefeller, of the United States, to provide funds for international cooperation. The foundation immediately created an International Health Division, originally known as the Health Commission, to continue the work of the organization's predecessor, the Rockefeller Sanitary Commission for the Eradication of Hookworm Disease.

During the 1920s, it worked with the United States Public Health Service to develop county health units across the United States. After the end of the First World War, the foundation also expanded its work to include malaria and yellow fever, the latter in cooperation with the Pan American Sanitary Bureau (q.v.). The foundation also provided funds during the mid-1920s for the establishment of an Eastern bureau of the Health Organization of the League of Nations (q.v.) to further epidemiological surveillance work in East Asia.

During the Second World War, the scope of the Rockefeller Foundation's work was intended to remain global, but the sphere of operations was limited by conflict (e.g., financing the American Mission to Combat Tuberculosis in France). With the creation of WHO, the foundation, along with W. K. Kellogg, provided interest-free loans in 1951 to purchase interim headquarters in Washington, D.C., for the Pan American Sanitary Organization (PASO). The foundation continued to work closely with PASO, including contributing extrabudgetary funds (q.v.) for malaria eradication.

Since the 1960s, the foundation has also hosted meetings at the Bellagio Conference Center, in Italy, to provide a key forum for discussion of international health and population matters by governments, academic scholars, international organizations, and nongovernmental organizations (q.v.). Other meetings on international health have been held at Pocantico, New York, including Enhancing the Performance of International Health Institutions at the Pocantico Retreat in 1966. In 1990 the Rockefeller Foundation cosponsored the Children's Vaccine Initiative (q.v.). *See also* Mentor Foundation; Sasakawa Foundation.

ROME AGREEMENT. *See* Office International d'Hygiène Publique.

RURAL ENVIRONMENTAL HEALTH. *See* Division of Operational Support in Environmental Health.

S

SAFE MOTHERHOOD INITIATIVE (SMI). An initiative launched at a joint conference sponsored by WHO, the United Nations Population Fund, and the World Bank (qq.v.) held in Nairobi, Kenya, in 1987. With participants from 37 countries, including the heads of the three cosponsoring United Nations organizations, five ministers of health, and representatives of nongovernmental organizations (q.v.) and bilateral aid agencies, the conference reviewed the extent of maternal mortality and morbidity, its causes and contributory factors, and the possible strategies and costs that would be required to ensure safe pregnancy and delivery for all women. The SMI was thus initiated to promote four essential components: family planning, prenatal care, clean and safe delivery, and essential obstetric care. The implementation of these four components has been in the form of the Mother-Baby Package (q.v.) of health care interventions. The initiative was located within the former Division of Family Health (q.v.), yet given its own structure, a meeting of interested parties and a scientific and technical advisory group. It also maintains a link to the interagency Task Force for Child Survival (q.v.). *See also* Baby-Friendly Hospital Initiative; Family and Reproductive Health Programme; International Conference on Population and Development.

SAITAMA PUBLIC HEALTH SUMMIT. A summit held in Saitama, Japan, by WHO and the government of Japan in September 1991 to discuss public health in relation to issues of health transition such as aging populations, new technologies, the changing roles of the public and private sectors, and the impact of environmental factors. Attended by experts in public health and economic development, the meeting issued the Saitama Declaration, which called for a new orientation in public health action based on the link between health and socioeconomic development.

SAMBA, EBRAHIM MALICK (1932–). Dr. Ebrahim Samba of The Gambia, served as regional director of the African Regional Office (AFRO) (qq.v.) from 1984 to 1985 and since 1995. After training in science, medicine, and surgery in Ghana and Ireland, he specialized in surgery in the United Kingdom and became a Fellow of the Royal College of Surgeons. He then worked for several years as a clinician and health officer in The Gambia, where he was appointed director of medical services in 1978. He represented his country at the World Health Assembly (WHA) (q.v.) in 1974 and presided over a WHA commission to examine WHO's structure. In 1980 he was appointed director of the Onchocerciasis Control Programme (OCP) (qq.v.) in West Africa, where he worked until 1995 to extend coverage of OCP activities from seven to 11 countries. The program was recognized as a major success among disease control programs. In 1984, upon the death of Dr. Comlan A. A. Quenum, he was asked by the director-general (q.v.) to serve briefly as regional director of AFRO until another candidate could be elected. Since his election as regional director in 1995, Dr. Samba has been widely recognized for undertaking efforts to reform the management and administration of the AFRO.

SAND, RENE (1877–1953). Dr. Rene Sand, of Belgium, served as chair of the Technical Preparatory Committee (q.v.) in 1946, which was appointed to draft the agenda for the International Health Conference and the constitution (qq.v.) of the soon-to-be-created WHO. Prior to holding this position, he was a technical expert and then secretary-general of the League of Red Cross Societies (1922) and secretary-general for health in the Belgian Ministry of Home Affairs. In 1951 he was awarded the Leon Bernard Prize and Medal (q.v.) for his contributions to international public health.

SASAKAWA FOUNDATION. A charitable foundation created by Ryoichi Sasakawa (1899–1995), a Japanese industrialist and former chairman of the Japan Shipbuilding Industry Foundation, to fund international cooperation. The foundation has contributed to various WHO programs and subsidized the creation of the Sasakawa Health Trust Fund and Sasakawa Health Prize in 1984 with an endowment of U.S.$1 million. The prize, consisting of a bronze statuette and U.S.$100,000, is given to one or more individuals or institutions who have accomplished outstanding innovative work in health development, such as the promotion of given health programs or notable advances in primary health care (q.v.). The recipient of the prize is chosen by the Sasakawa Health Prize Committee, comprised of the chair and vice chair of the Executive Board (q.v.) and a representative of the founder. An international conference, Health in One World, was held in 1989 to mark the fifth anniversary of the founding of the prize. *See also* Rockefeller Foundation.

SCIENTIFIC ADVISORY COMMITTEE. *See* Special Programme of Research, Development and Research Training in Human Reproduction.

SCIENTIFIC ADVISORY GROUP OF EXPERTS (SAGE). *See* Global Programme for Vaccines and Immunization; Programme for Vaccine Developments.

SCIENTIFIC AND TECHNICAL ADVISORY COMMITTEE (STAC). *See* UNDP/World Bank/WHO Special Programme for Research and Training in Tropical Diseases.

SCIENTIFIC AND TECHNICAL ADVISORY GROUP (STAG). *See* Safe Motherhood Initiative; Special Programme of Research, Development, and Research Training in Human Reproduction.

SCIENTIFIC COUNCIL. *See* International Agency for Research on Cancer.

SCIENTIFIC GROUP. A group of experts convened by the director-general (q.v.) to review a given field of medical, health, and health systems research, to assess the current state of knowledge in those fields, and to determine how that knowledge may best be extended. Reports of scientific groups are submitted by the director-general to the global Advisory Committee on Health Research (q.v.) and may be published at his or her discretion. Regional scientific groups may be convened by regional directors (q.v.) to deal with subjects essentially of regional interest. *See also* Expert Advisory Panel; Expert Committee; Study Group.

SCIENTIFIC STEERING COMMITTEE. *See* Global Programme for Health of the Elderly.

SCIENTIFIC WORKING GROUP. *See* UNDP/World Bank/WHO Special Programme for Research and Training in Tropical Diseases.

SECRETARIAT. The organs of WHO, including the director-general (q.v.) and such technical and administrative staff (i.e., professional and general staff) as the organization may require, that are responsible for carrying out day-to-day activities. As a reflection of the decentralized structure of WHO, one-third of the secretariat staff are located at each of the three levels of the organization (i.e., headquarters, regional offices, and country offices [qq.v.]). The director-general formally appoints the staff of the secretariat in accordance with staff regulations established by the World Health Assembly (q.v.). The paramount consideration in the employment of the staff is intended to be efficiency, integrity, and the internationally representative character of the secretariat. Due regard is also given to the importance of recruiting the staff on as wide a geographical basis as possible. Recent efforts have been made to monitor and improve staffing by gender. In the performance of their duties, the director-general and staff are not to seek or receive instructions from any government or from any authority external to the organization.

There has been no detailed analysis of the composition and size of secretariat staff, although WHO, like other United Nations organizations in recent years, has come under greater pressure to rationalize its administrative structure and costs. There has been criticism, for example, of WHO's many hierarchical layers, the increase in the number of senior staff above the director level, and the large proportion of its budget spent on staffing costs. Others cite the need to diversify secretariat staff away from its traditional biomedical emphasis. However, WHO defends its need, as the world's foremost health organization, for high-level professional staff with appropriate technical knowledge and expertise. In 1995 staff totaled approximately 4,500, with about 1,500 located at headquarters. These figures compare favorably with other UN specialized agencies.

SELECTIVE CANCER INFORMATION DISSEMINATION SERVICE. *See* Latin American Cancer Research Information Project.

SELECTIVE PRIMARY HEALTH CARE. An interpretation of primary health care (PHC) (q.v.) proposed by the United Nations Children's Fund (UNICEF) (q.v.) in 1981, which argued that the comprehensive goals of PHC could not be achieved at the same time, given resource constraints in developing countries. For this reason, selective interventions needed to be chosen and prioritized. These "vertical" interventions included vitamin A (q.v.) supplementation and mass immunization against major childhood diseases. This led to debates between WHO and UNICEF, as well as among public health experts, on the relative merits and feasibility of comprehensive versus selective primary health care. *See also* International Conference on Primary Health Care.

SHOUSHA, ALY TEWFIK (1891–1964). Dr. Aly Shousha, of Egypt, served as the first regional director of the Eastern Mediterranean Regional Office (EMRO) (qq.v.) from 1949 to 1957. He was previously an active member of the Technical Preparatory Committee (q.v.), on which he supported the concept of regional decentralization in WHO. At the International Health Conference (q.v.), he continued to argue for the establishment of regional offices (q.v.) akin to the Pan American Sanitary Bureau (q.v.). In 1948–49 he served as the first chairman of the Executive Board (q.v.). During his tenure as regional director, he worked to build the Egyptian Quarantine Board into a fully active regional office. The Dr. A. T. Shousha Foundation Prize (q.v.) was created by EMRO following his death to commemorate his contribution to international public health.

SICK CHILD INITIATIVE (SCI). *See* Integrated Management of the Sick Child.

SINGLE CONVENTION ON NARCOTIC DRUGS. A convention adopted by governments in 1961, and amended by the Protocol and Convention on Psychotropic Substances of 1972, to control the production and use of narcotic drugs. The responsibilities of WHO under the convention are to evaluate data on the benefit:risk ratio of substances that may produce addiction in order to make recommendations to the United Nations Commission on Narcotic Drugs. *See also* United Nations Fund for Drug Abuse Control.

SMALLPOX ERADICATION, GLOBAL COMMISSION FOR THE CERTIFICATION OF. *See* Global Commission for the Certification of Smallpox Eradication.

SMALLPOX ERADICATION PROGRAMME, INTENSIFIED. *See* Intensified Smallpox Eradication Programme.

SMALLPOX ERADICATION UNIT. A small unit at headquarters (q.v.) created in the mid-1960s to provide limited support to national campaigns of mass vaccination against smallpox. With the initiation of the Intensified Smallpox Eradication Programme (q.v.), these efforts were expanded to a broader range of activities, including surveillance, testing of vaccines, and fund-raising. However, these greater demands on the unit were not met with an increase in staffing, due to the desire by member states (q.v.) to limit the size of WHO staff at headquarters. The growing problems of the Intensified Malaria Eradication Programme (q.v.) by the middle to late 1960s also diverted resources from other disease control programs. Despite these constraints, the Smallpox Eradication Unit managed to provide worldwide support for the eradication of smallpox through the strong leadership of Donald Ainslie Henderson (q.v.), of the United States, and the recruitment of highly skilled consultants largely financed by extrabudgetary funds (q.v.).

SMALLPOX VACCINE, WHO INTERNATIONAL/REGIONAL REFERENCE CENTERS FOR. *See* WHO International/Regional Reference Centers for Smallpox Vaccine.

SOCIAL DEVELOPMENT, WORLD SUMMIT ON. *See* World Summit on Social Development.

SOPER, FRED LOWE (1893–1977). Dr. Fred Soper, of the United States, served as director of the Pan American Sanitary Bureau (PASB) (q.v.), forerunner of the Pan American Health Organization (q.v.), from 1947 to 1958. During his medical training, he developed an early interest in research in histology and embryology. He then used this experience as a staff member of the Rockefeller Foundation (q.v.), where he directed the yellow fever eradication program in Brazil during the 1930s. He also worked with Marcelino Candau (q.v.) during this period on malaria control, and made substantial contributions to the control and treatment of yaws, yellow fever, and typhus. During his tenure as director, the PASB was substantially reorganized and became a regional office (q.v.) of WHO in 1949, receiving increased extrabudgetary funding (q.v.) and initiating regional programs for the eradication of Aedes aegypti, smallpox, yaws, and malaria. During his career, Dr. Soper was awarded numerous prizes, including the Leon Bernard Prize and Medal (q.v.) in 1967.

SOUTH-EAST ASIAN CHARTER FOR HEALTH DEVELOPMENT. A charter endorsed by the South-East Asia Regional Committee (q.v.) in 1978 for the purpose of improving health in the region through agreed-upon priorities for primary health care (q.v.), appropriate personnel development, provision of safe water and sanitation, promotion of maternal and child health, control of communicable diseases, and improvement of nutrition. The charter recognized health as a fundamental human right and set in motion a series of activities in the region aimed at improving the health and quality of life of its inhabitants.

SOUTH-EAST ASIA REGIONAL OFFICE (SEARO). One of six regional offices (q.v.) of WHO, this office was established in

1948 in New Delhi, India. It currently has ten member states (q.v.) representing almost one-quarter (1.3 billion) of the world's population: Bangladesh, Bhutan, the Democratic People's Republic of Korea, India, Indonesia, the Maldives, Myanmar, Nepal, Sri Lanka, and Thailand. Mongolia transferred to the Western Pacific Regional Office (q.v.) in 1994. Over the past four decades, there have been steady gains in health development within the region, with notable declines in infant mortality and increases in life expectancy. However, health needs and capacities are diverse in a region where GNP per capita ranges from U.S.$180 (Nepal) to U.S.$2,000 (Thailand) and 80 percent of the region's population fall below the poverty line. Many states continue to face serious problems with malaria, tuberculosis, leprosy, diarrhoeal diseases, and malnutrition, while others in addition are experiencing the emergence of lifestyle-related health problems such as substance abuse and noncommunicable diseases (e.g., cardiovascular disease, cancer). This double burden of disease poses the main challenge to member states of the region. For 1996–97 the priority areas identified by the regional committee (q.v.) were new, emerging, and reemerging diseases (e.g., malaria, tuberculosis); strengthening epidemiological surveillance and preparedness; and acute respiratory infections and diarroheal diseases.

SPECIAL ACTION PROJECTS TOWARDS THE ELIMINATION OF LEPROSY (SAPEL). An initiative introduced in 1994 to identify special situations and areas requiring rapid action for leprosy elimination and to develop and implement special operational and technical solutions for leprosy-endemic countries. *See also* Action Programme for the Elimination of Leprosy; Pan American Center for Training and Research in Leprosy and Related Diseases.

SPECIAL COMMUNITY WATER SUPPLY FUND. A fund set up in 1959 by the governments of the United States and Venezuela to provide assistance to governments in the Americas region in planning, preparing for, and obtaining other technical assistance in the development of community water supply. The fund was created following the increased emphasis given to sanitation by the Charter of Punta del Este (q.v.). The funds have been used by the Pan American Health Organization (q.v.) to support water and sewerage projects through, for example, financing the assignment of sanitary engineers to community water supply programs and supporting the training of engineers. *See also* Interagency Steering Committee on Water Supply and Sanitation; International Drinking Water and Sanitation Decade; Programme for the Global Elimination of Dracunculiasis.

SPECIAL MIXED COMMITTEE. *See* Health Organization of the League of Nations.

SPECIAL OFFICE FOR EUROPE. *See* European Regional Office.

SPECIAL PROGRAMME OF RESEARCH, DEVELOPMENT, AND RESEARCH TRAINING IN HUMAN REPRODUCTION (HRP). Formerly known as the Expanded Programme of Research, Development, and Research Training in Human Reproduction (q.v.), this program was renamed as a special program in 1977 and moved from the Division of Family Health to the director-general's (qq.v.) office. Its main emphasis of work continued to be research for the development and assessment of contraceptive technology and treatment of infertility, as well as the introduction of new and improved methods in family planning services. In 1988, the program became cosponsored (q.v.) by WHO, the United Nations Development Program, the United Nations Population Fund, and the World Bank (qq.v.) (with WHO as executing agency [q.v.]). This has led, in more recent years, to increased research on the gender, socioeconomic, and cultural aspects of fertility regulation within the context of reproductive health. In 1996, the program was moved to the newly created Family and Reproductive Health Programme (q.v.).

The HRP is governed by a Policy and Coordination Committee (PCC) established in 1985 as the Policy and Coordination Advisory Committee to exercise overall authority for policy and management. The PCC holds decision-making authority for policies and priorities, overall resource allocation, and organization and management of the HRP program. There are 32 members of the PCC: representatives of the 11 largest financial contributors, 14 member states (q.v.) elected by the regional committees (q.v.) for three-year terms according to population distribution and regional needs, two other interested cooperating parties, and the four cosponsoring United Nations organizations. Observers from other cooperating parties may also attend meetings of the PCC. The PCC also has authority to appoint scientists to the Scientific and Technical Advisory Group (STAG), which is responsible for providing the technical and scientific direction for the HRP program, including recommendations on priorities and continuous evaluation. STAG members serve in a personal capacity.

Almost all of the total budget for the program comes from extrabudgetary funds (q.v.). Income for the program has declined in recent years, from U.S.$46.5 million in 1992–93 to U.S.$41.2 million in 1994–95. Currently, the HRP has a staff of about 63. The program collaborates with 108 institutions in 56 countries, including 33 WHO collaborating centers (q.v.) for research in human reproduction. In 1996 the program was relocated, along with other related sections of WHO, into the Family and Reproductive Health Programme (q.v.). *See also* Adolescent Health and Development Programme; Division of Reproductive Health (Technical Support); International Conference on Population and Development; Women's Health.

SPECIAL PROGRAMME ON ONCHOCERCIASIS. *See* Onchocerciasis Control Programme.

STAMPAR, ANDRIJA (1888–1958). Dr. Andrija Stampar, of Croatia, one of the founders of WHO, served as chairman of the Interim Commission and president of the first World Health Assembly (qq.v.) in 1948. After receiving his medical degree in 1911, he worked as a physician until the end of the First World War. His career in international public health began with his appointment as a medical adviser to the provisional Croatian government in 1918, followed by appointments as the Croatian inspector-general of public health (1919–31), member of the Health Committee of the League of Nations (1930–32), and member of the Technical Preparatory Committee (q.v.) for the International Health Conference (q.v.) of 1946. In 1931 he was also appointed professor of hygiene and social medicine at the University of Zagreb. Dr. Stampar was awarded the Leon Bernard Prize and Medal (q.v.) in 1955 for his contributions to international public health. During his work with WHO, Dr. Stampar frequently stressed the importance of seeing health in terms of its socioeconomic, political, and cultural dimensions and not solely as a technical matter.

STANDING COMMITTEE. A committee of organizations cosponsoring (q.v.) a program that meets periodically to review activities, advise staff, and prepare for annual meetings of the main government body. In the Special Programme of Research, Development, and Research Training in Human Reproduction (q.v.), this is the Policy and Coordination Committee. In the UNDP/World Bank/WHO Special Programme for Research and Training in Tropical Diseases (q.v.), it is the Joint Coordinating Board.

STANDING COMMITTEE OF THE REGIONAL COMMITTEE (SCRC). An ad hoc committee formed in 1991 by the European Regional Office (EURO) (q.v.) to discuss the future orientation of the regional office (q.v.) and WHO. The committee was institutionalized in 1993 to serve as a kind of regional Executive Board (q.v.). The aim of the committee is to create a closer link between EURO and its member states (q.v.), provide an impetus for change, and prioritize health care development within the region. *See also* Executive Board Working Group on the WHO Response to Global Change.

STANDING COMMITTEE ON ADMINISTRATION AND FINANCE. A former committee of the Executive Board (q.v.) responsible for overseeing the organization's biennial budgeting process. It was replaced by the Administration, Budget, and Finance Committee (q.v.) in 1995 as part of reforms under the WHO Response to Global Change. *See also* Executive Board Working Group on the WHO Response to Global Change.

STANDING COMMITTEE ON AIDS. *See* Steering Committee on AIDS.

STANDING COMMITTEE ON NONGOVERNMENTAL ORGANIZATIONS. A committee created in 1950 to review and make recommendations to the Executive Board (EB) on applications by nongovernmental organizations (NGOs) (qq.v.) for admission into official relations with WHO. The committee also periodically reviews the status of all NGOs having official relations with WHO and, depending on their conformity to agreed-on principles, they may or may not be granted continued relations. In 1996 the EB agreed to maintain official relations with 42 NGOs.

STEERING COMMITTEE. *See* Global Tuberculosis Programme.

STEERING COMMITTEE ON AIDS. A committee organized by the United Nations Department of International Economic and Social Affairs in 1987 to facilitate the exchange of information on AIDS among UN organizations. Initially limited to major

UN departments and relevant funds under United Nations General Assembly authority—namely, the United Nations Children's Fund, the United Nations Development Program, and the United Nations Population Fund (qq.v.)—meetings of the committee were later attended by a WHO representative (q.v.). The committee, in turn, set up a Standing Committee on AIDS as a working-level body.

STRATEGIC SUPPORT TO COUNTRIES IN GREATEST NEED, DIVISION OF. *See* Division of Strategic Support to Countries in Greatest Need.

STRENGTHENING OF HEALTH SERVICES, DIVISION OF. *See* Division of Strengthening of Health Services.

STUDY GROUP. A group convened by the director-general, instead of an expert committee (qq.v.), when one or more of the following conditions apply: (a) knowledge on the subject to be studied is still too uncertain and the opinions of competent specialists too diverse for there to be reasonable expectation of authoritative conclusions; (b) the study envisaged concerns too limited an aspect of a general problem, which may or may not come within the purview of an expert committee; (c) the study envisaged implies the collaboration of narrowly specialized participants who may belong to very different disciplines and on whom the organization occasionally calls; (d) certain nontechnical facts render unsuitable an expert committee meeting because it would appear to be too official in character; or (e) urgent or exceptional circumstances call for some other administrative procedure that would be simpler and more rapidly applicable than that involved in meetings of expert committees. In appointing a study group, the director-general is guided by the rules governing an expert committee, including technical and geographical balance in membership. Meetings of study groups may be held at the regional level to deal with subjects essentially of regional interest. *See also* Expert Advisory Panel; Scientific Group.

SUBCOMMITTEES A AND B. *See* Eastern Mediterranean Regional Office.

SUBSTANCE ABUSE, PROGRAMME ON. *See* Programme on Substance Abuse.

SUMMIT ON THE GLOBAL IMPACT OF AIDS. A summit held in London in 1988, organized by WHO and the United Kingdom, to support the development of national AIDS programs worldwide. The meeting was attended by 117 ministers of health and participants from 148 countries. Participants put forth the London Declaration on AIDS Prevention, which stated that human rights and dignity must be protected, that discrimination undermines public health goals, and that a spirit of social tolerance should be forged in the prevention and control of HIV/AIDS.

SUNDSVALL DECLARATION ON HEALTH PROMOTION. *See* International Conference on Health Promotion.

SZE, SZEMING (1908–). Dr. Szeming Sze, of China, played an active role between 1945 and 1948 in the initiation and creation of WHO, including serving as a member of the Technical Preparatory Committee (q.v.). He is noted for taking joint action with Dr. Karl Evang, of Norway (q.v.), and Dr. Geraldo de Paula Souza of Brazil to rectify the omission of health from the Charter of the United Nations. In 1945 Dr. Sze served as the private secretary of the head of the Chinese delegation to the San Francisco conference. In this capacity, he presented the adopted proposal to set up a single international health organization. Prior to 1945, Dr. Sze was general secretary of the Chinese Medical Association (1937–41) and founded the Chinese Health League in 1937. In 1938 he was appointed senior technical expert of the National Health Administration, where he served until he was promoted to the Ministry of Foreign Affairs (1941–45). In 1948 he joined the United Nations Secretariat, where he became medical director in 1954. After his retirement in 1968, Dr. Sze created the LISZ Foundation, whose work includes support for WHO in health education.

T

TABA, ABDOL HOSSEIN (1912–1982). Dr. Abdol Taba, of Iran, served as regional director of the Eastern Mediterranean Regional Office (EMRO) (qq.v.) from 1957 until his death in 1982. After training in medicine in the United Kingdom and France, he served as director-general of health in Iran, honorary chairman of the International Health Relations Department, and a member of the Supreme Health Council. He was a member of parliament (1946–51) and president of its health commission. Dr. Taba represented his country at the World Health Assembly (q.v.) and as a member of the Executive Board (q.v.) during the 1950s. He joined WHO in 1952 as deputy regional director of EMRO and was later elected for five consecutive terms as regional director.

TASK FORCE FOR CHILD SURVIVAL. A nonpartisan body created at a meeting (known as Bellagio I) held at the Rockefeller Foundation's (q.v.) Conference Center, in Bellagio, Italy, in 1984 to discuss shared concerns over child morbidity and mortality in developing countries from six diseases preventable through immunization. The meeting was also intended to provide a forum for WHO and the United Nations Children's Fund (UNICEF) (q.v.) to meet and discuss their respective approaches and activities during a period of conflict and competition between the two organizations. The meeting led to the formation of the Task Force for Child Survival (q.v.) cosponsored by WHO, UNICEF, the United Nations Development Program, the World Bank (q.v.), and the Rockefeller Foundation and chaired by Dr. William Foege, of the United States. Bellagio I, which agreed on the goal of immunizing all the world's children, was followed by a series of further meetings including Bellagio II (Colombia, 1985), on progress in accelerating and expanding childhood immunization programs and strategies for using these programs to build primary health care (q.v.) systems, and Bellagio III (France, 1988), to ensure continued commitment to the goal of universal childhood immunization by 1990 and the provision of support to this end. One of the main activities of the task force has been to propose specific targets for the improvement of child health, which national and international bodies are requested to consider. *See also* Children's Vaccine Initiative; World Summit for Children.

TASK FORCE ON EMERGENCY AND HUMANITARIAN ACTION. A task force set up in 1993 by the director-general, and chaired by an assistant director-general (qq.v.), to consider how WHO could respond best to the need for emergency and humanitarian health activities. The 1994 report of the task force made recommendations for restructuring in this area, including revising and updating WHO's mandate for such actions; clarifying guidelines for the roles of headquarters, regional offices, and country offices (qq.v.) for emergency preparedness and response; reorganizing to strengthen core staff, support services, and training; harmonizing field emergency procedures with other United Nations organizations; and mobilizing resources for effective emergency management. In response to the recommendations of the task force, the director-general issued a new WHO strategy and mandate for emergency and humanitarian action centered on normative (q.v.) and technical guidance activities. The Division of Emergency and Humanitarian Action (q.v.) was created and given responsibility for fulfilling this mandate. *See also* Division of Emergency Relief Operations.

TASK FORCE ON ENVIRONMENT AND HEALTH. *See* United Nations Conference on Environment and Development.

TASK FORCE ON HEALTH AT THE MINISTERIAL LEVEL. A task force convened by the Pan American Health Organization (q.v.) in 1963 to define the existing health situation, forecast future needs, and examine areas where efforts should be directed to achieve the Ten-Year Public Health Program adopted with the Charter of Punta del Este (q.v.) in 1961. The task force recommended, among other things, study of existing health programs, incorporation of all levels of health service within a general framework, rational distribution and utilization of resources, integration of preventive and curative services, and regionalization of services. The meeting was the first of four special meetings of ministers of health in the region over a 15-year period that addressed the region's health needs.

TASK FORCE ON HEALTH ECONOMICS. A task force created in 1993 by the director-general (q.v.) to further the use of health economics in the formulation and implementation of national health policies, particularly in countries in greatest need. Working across programs and disciplines, the task force comprises 20 staff members from headquarters and WHO regional offices (qq.v.). The main component of country support by the task force is the provision of up-to-date information on current topics in health economics, geared to health policy making and developing countries, to help meet the needs of those involved in the organization, planning, and financing of the health sector and to health professionals whose expertise may lie elsewhere. The task force distributes a series of documents free of charge to ministries of health, schools of public health, international organizations, donors, WHO representatives (q.v.) and other staff, and other interested institutions and individuals.

TASK FORCE ON HEALTH IN DEVELOPMENT. A task force set up in 1992 by the World Health Assembly (q.v.) as an advisory body to address critical issues concerning health in development and to act as an advocacy body on behalf of WHO to uphold the cause of health within the framework of the development process. For the task force's first meeting in 1994, a background paper entitled "Health in Development: Prospects for the 21st Century" was published, which presented a rationale for health in development and a framework for the work of the task force. The action plan adopted at this meeting included providing input to major international events such as the World Summit on Social Development (q.v.). Membership of the multidisciplinary task force included world leaders, politicians, senior WHO staff, senior aid officials, and experts in health, economics, and development. Based in the WHO Office of Health and Development Policies, the task force identified four strategic areas of concern: (a) equity in health and market forces; (b) quality of life and health security of specific population groups; (c) accountability for health; and (d) health as a bridge for peace. An Office of Health and Development Policies was created in 1994 to organize the work of the Task Force on Health in Development. The office also contains the Secretariat of the Global Commission on Women's Health (q.v.).

TASK FORCE ON HIV/AIDS COORDINATION. A task force created by the GPA Management Committee of the Global Programme on AIDS (q.v.) in November 1992 to improve interagency coordination of HIV/AIDS activities within the United Nations. Its ad hoc working group recognized the need for (a) a forum to function as a consultative mechanism for the United Nations system, other intergovernmental organizations, bilateral donors, developing countries and nongovernmental organizations (q.v.) working in the AIDS field; and (b) coordination of support to national AIDS programs at the country level. The task force comprises three representatives of governments financially contributing to international AIDS activities; three representatives of the Interagency Advisory Group on AIDS, namely, WHO, the United Nations Development Program, and the World Bank (qq.v.); and three representatives of nongovernmental organizations.

TASK FORCE ON PHARMACEUTICALS. A task force set up jointly in 1976 by WHO, the United Nations Conference on Trade and Development (UNCTAD), the United Nations Industrial Development Organization (UNIDO), the United Nations Department of Technical Cooperation for Development, and the United Nations Action Programme for Economic Cooperation among Non-Aligned and Other Developing Countries. The task force published a report in 1979 entitled *Pharmaceuticals in the Developing World: Policies on Drugs, Trade, and Production,* which provided the first major review of problems faced by governments in developing countries in obtaining safe, effective, and affordable drugs. The report formed the basis of new national and international policies to address these problems. *See also* Drug Action Programme; Essential Drugs Programme; International Conference on Harmonization of Technical Requirements for Registration of Pharmaceuticals for Human Use.

TAX EQUALIZATION FUND. A fund created by the World Health Assembly (q.v.) in 1969 to be credited with the revenue for staff assessments (i.e., the deduction made from the gross salary of a staff member of an amount in lieu of income tax), the credits being recorded in the name of individual member states (q.v.) in proportion to their contribution of regular budget funds (q.v.) for the financial period involved. In establishing the contributions to be made to the regular budget, the assessments of member states are reduced by the amount standing to the credit of each. However, the credits of those member states that require WHO staff to pay income taxes on their emoluments are reduced by the estimated amounts of the tax to be reimbursed by the organization.

TECHNICAL AND RESEARCH ADVISORY COMMITTEE. *See* Global Tuberculosis Programme.

TECHNICAL ASSISTANCE. A function of WHO, as stated in the constitution (q.v.), requiring the organization "to furnish appropriate technical assistance and, in emergencies, necessary aid upon the request or acceptance of Governments." The approach implied by the term technical assistance, as defined until the 1970s, suggested a donor-recipient relationship between WHO and member states (q.v.) in health development. During the late 1970s, this term was replaced by the concept of technical cooperation (q.v.), which seeks a more equal partnership relationship.

TECHNICAL ASSISTANCE, EXPANDED PROGRAMME FOR. *See* Expanded Programme for Technical Assistance.

TECHNICAL CONSULTATIVE GROUP. *See* Expanded Programme on Immunization.

TECHNICAL COOPERATION. An approach to health development used by WHO since the late 1970s that implies a partnership relationship between WHO and member states (q.v.) for the purpose of attaining national health goals defined in and by countries themselves. In contrast with technical assistance (q.v.), technical cooperation activities are characterized by an emphasis on equal partnership among cooperating parties and respect for the sovereign right of every country to develop its national health system and services in the way that it finds most rational and appropriate to its needs. In 1976 the World Health Assembly (q.v.) adopted Resolution WHA29.48, calling for a reorientation of the organization's program budget to provide greater support to member states. By 1987 technical cooperation activities accounted for 70 percent of the expenditure of regular budget funds (q.v.).

TECHNICAL COOPERATION AMONG DEVELOPING COUNTRIES (TCDC). A concept advocated by the countries of the nonaligned movement (NAM) since the 1970s, defined as collaboration between two or more developing countries for social and economic development. Following the United Nations Conference on Technical Cooperation among Developing Countries held in Buenos Aires, Brazil, in 1978, the United Nations has supported TCDC as a vital force in promoting solidarity and collaboration among developing countries in their efforts to achieve sustainable development through individual and collective self-reliance. In 1993 WHO and the United Nations Development Program (q.v.) held an interregional consultation on TCDC in health in Jakarta, Indonesia, which proposed the full integration of TCDC into the Health for All (q.v.) strategy. WHO has supported TCDC at the country level through training in aid negotiation and regional meetings to exchange expertise among developing countries. WHO has also provided support to the health secretariat of the NAM and meetings of health ministers. *See also* Technical Cooperation.

TECHNICAL DISCUSSION. A discussion that takes place during, but is separate from, either the World Health Assembly (WHA) or the regional committee (qq.v.) on a topic of priority concern to world health. Participation is open to delegates of member states (q.v.). The specific topic of discussion is selected by the Executive Board (q.v.) and regional committee, respectively. Discussions may be supported by working documents and set objectives and may result in recommendations being proposed to guide future activities. Technical discussions were held annually at the global level until the mid-1990s, when, in order to improve the effective working of the WHA, it was agreed that they would be held in alternate years to biennial discussion of the proposed programme budget (q.v.). At the regional level, regional technical discussions provide an opportunity for a regional director (q.v.) to seek the opinion of experts on a topic known to be of general interest. In the Western Pacific Regional Office (q.v.), technical discussions were replaced by technical briefings in 1996 on an experimental basis, by which a report on an issue of concern to public health in the region is presented to participants.

TECHNICAL DOCUMENT. A document that conveys information that is relatively short-lived, intended for a less wide readership, or less fully validated (i.e., not subject to scrutiny by an interdepartmental committee, lightly edited, or unedited) than information in publications. These include premeeting documents, working papers and reports of meetings and consultations, reports of or for special programs, other program and project documents, papers on technical subjects, policy documents, draft guidelines, manuals and other learning material circulated for field trial or for comment, and assignment and consultant reports. Most but not all technical documents in languages other than English are translations of original English texts. *See also* Administrative Document; Governing Body Document.

TECHNICAL PREPARATORY COMMITTEE (TPC). A committee established by ECOSOC in 1946 to prepare for the International Health Conference (q.v.) on the creation of a health organization of the United Nations. The committee consisted of 16 experts from 16 countries and was chaired by Dr. Rene Sand (q.v.). In addition, representatives from existing health organizations (i.e., the Pan American Sanitary Organization, the Office International d'Hygiène Publique [q.v.], the Health Organization of the League of Nations, and the United Nations Relief and Rehabilitation Administration [qq.v.]) attended meetings in a consultative capacity. During its 22 meetings in Paris from 18 March–5 April 1946, the committee prepared an agenda for the World Health Conference and a draft constitution for the proposed World Health Organization. Among its recommendations were that all countries, not only member states (q.v.) of the United Nations, be invited to the conference, along with the Control Commissions of the Occupied Territories, and that all existing health organizations be subsumed under the new WHO.

TECHNICAL REPORT SERIES. A series of reports published by WHO beginning in 1950 that provides concise summary information on state-of-the-art technical and scientific advances in health. The reports are the result of WHO's responsibilities, under the terms of its constitution (q.v.), to act as the directing and coordinating authority on international health work and to provide information and counsel on questions of health. The data for the reports are gathered through meetings of top experts representing all major lines of health research, with the aim of achieving international consensus.

TECHNOLOGICAL SERVICES (TES). *See* Division of Information System Management.

TELEMEDICINE. A form of medical care that uses interactive audio, visual, and data communications, including medical care delivery, consultation, diagnosis and treatment, education, and the transfer of medical data. WHO is currently cooperating with countries in studies on the feasibility and cost-effectiveness of TeleMedicine services and participating in scientific forums to identify the needs and problems associated with its wider use within and between countries. Responsibility for promoting TeleMedicine and other health information capacity building in developing countries is carried out by an adviser on informatics.

TEN-YEAR PUBLIC HEALTH PROGRAM. *See* Charter of Punta del Este.

TOBACCO DAY, WORLD NO. *See* World No Tobacco Day.

TOBACCO OR HEALTH, PROGRAMME ON. *See* Programme on Tobacco or Health.

TRANSITION TEAM. *See* Joint United Nations Programme on HIV/AIDS.

TROPICAL DISEASES, DIVISION OF CONTROL OF. *See* Division of Control of Tropical Diseases.

TRUST FUND. A fund established by the director-general (q.v.) for a specified purpose such as technical cooperation (q.v.) or disease prevention and control. At present there are 18 trust funds for technical cooperation and seven for supply services. *See also* Real Estate Fund; Voluntary Fund for Health Promotion; Working Capital Fund.

TUBERCULOSIS DAY, WORLD. *See* World Tuberculosis Day.

TUBERCULOSIS PROGRAMME. A program established in the early 1950s, encompassing the Tuberculosis Research Office (q.v.), to coordinate the campaign to control the spread of tuberculosis worldwide. The strategy of the campaign centered on the use of the BCG (Bacille Calmert Guerrian) vaccine. While the campaign proved successful at dramatically reducing the number of tuberculosis cases in Europe, tens of millions of cases continued to occur in the developing world. In 1951 WHO took on the responsibility of coordinating a worldwide tuberculosis campaign, with the United Nations Children's Fund (q.v.) providing much of the funding. Until the late 1950s, the program concentrated on mass campaigns to vaccinate children and adolescents. By 1957, however, doubts began to be raised as to the efficacy of this mass campaign approach. In 1964, WHO announced a new approach, which used direct BCG vaccination and an improved version of the drug isoniazid, as well as the integration of disease prevention, diagnosis, and treatment activities into existing national health systems. In 1995 the program was replaced by the Global Tuberculosis Programme (q.v.). *See also* Antituberculosis Drug Resistance Surveillance; Directly Observed Treatment, Short-Course.

TUBERCULOSIS PROGRAMME, GLOBAL. *See* Global Tuberculosis Programme.

TUBERCULOSIS RESEARCH OFFICE. An office set up by WHO in Copenhagen, Denmark, in 1949 to conduct research on the prevention, control, spread, and treatment of tuberculosis. This research was initiated to support a tuberculosis control campaign, initially in the war-affected countries of Europe. The campaign was funded by the United Nations Children's Fund (q.v.), carried out by the Danish Red Cross and nongovernmental organizations (q.v.) from Norway and Sweden, and coordinated by WHO from 1951. The office was replaced by the Tuberculosis Programme in the early 1950s, when the control campaign was expanded worldwide. *See also* Global Tuberculosis Programme.

20/20 INITIATIVE. An initiative presented at the World Summit for Social Development (q.v.) held in Copenhagen, Denmark, in 1994. The initiative calls on governments to spend 20 percent of public funds, and aid agencies to give 20 percent of official development assistance, for the social sectors (e.g., health, education). The initiative was cosponsored (q.v.) by WHO, the United Nations Children's Fund, the United Nations Population Fund, and the United Nations Development Program (qq.v.). *See also* Task Force on Health in Development.

U

UNDP/FAO/WHO FOOD CONTAMINATION MONITORING AND ASSESSMENT PROGRAMME. *See* Codex Alimentarius Commission; Division of Food and Nutrition; International Conference on Nutrition.

UNDP/WORLD BANK/WHO SPECIAL PROGRAMME FOR RESEARCH AND TRAINING IN TROPICAL DISEASES (TDR). A special program set up in 1974, and formally launched in 1976, by WHO, the United Nations Development Program, and the World Bank (qq.v.) to intensify and promote research and research training on the fundamental public health problems of tropical countries. Among the TDR's scientific achievements have been collaboration on the development of disease-controlling drugs: ivermectin for onchocerciasis control, mefloquine for malaria treatment, and multiple drug therapy for leprosy. WHO serves as the executing agency (q.v.). Despite significant advances in biomedical research during this period, there was a need to develop new methods (e.g., new drugs, vaccines, diagnostics, vector control methods) of preventing, diagnosing, and treating selected tropical diseases. The diseases targeted include malaria, schistosomiasis (bilharzia), lymphatic filariasis (leading to elephantiasis), onchocerciasis (river blindness and onchocercal skin disease), leprosy, African trypanosomiasis (sleeping sickness), Chagas disease (American trypanosomiasis), and leishmaniasis (including kala-azar). The program's mandate also includes strengthening the national capacity of developing countries through training in biomedical and social sciences and support to institutions to undertake the research required to develop new disease control technologies. The TDR is a special and cosponsored program (q.v.), with WHO as the executing agency.

The overall management body is the Joint Coordinating Board (JCB), which consists of 30 members including 12 representatives of financial contributors, 12 governments of disease-endemic countries selected by the regional committee (q.v.), and the three cosponsoring United Nations organizations. The JCB meets annually to review activities, decide on the budget, evaluate progress, and consider long-term plans and financing. A standing committee (q.v.) of representatives of the three cosponsoring organizations monitors the management of the TDR, its financial status, and fund-raising. The TDR is also regularly reviewed by the Executive Board and the World Health Assembly (qq.v.). The scientific work of the program, carried out by a number of scientific steering committees, is reviewed by a scientific and technical advisory committee (STAC) composed of 15–18 scientific experts, with additional periodic review by the Executive Board and the World Health Assembly. Various steering committees provide specialist advice on specific aspects of work (e.g., malarial mosquitoes, leishmaniasis). In 1990 a product development unit was set up to draw on expertise for different stages of the drug product development process, including testing, production, and packaging, and on intellectual property rights. In addition, a special steering committee, the Research Strengthening Group, was set up to oversee the TDR's commitment to developing country research and to manage the TDR's research capability-strengthening activities.

For 1995–98, the TDR's goals include continued research on specific disease control strategies; investigation of the relation of tropical diseases, particularly malaria, to environmental change; and increased emphasis on practical training in research capabilities. The program is primarily financed by extra-budgetary funds (q.v.) from governments, international organizations, and charitable foundations. *See also* Division of Control of Tropical Diseases; Field Links for Intervention and Control Studies; Intensified Malaria Eradication Programme; Onchocerciasis Control Programme.

UNICEF PACKING AND ASSEMBLY CENTRE (UNIPAC). A center of the United Nations Children's Fund (UNICEF) (q.v.)

based in Copenhagen, Denmark, which purchases large quantities of drugs on the world market and ships them to developing countries in support of the Drug Action Programme (q.v.). Through international competitive tendering and ordering in large quantities, UNIPAC is able to purchase drugs for the developing world at a reduced cost.

UNITED ARAB EMIRATES HEALTH FOUNDATION PRIZE. A prize awarded to an individual, group of individuals, or institution not more than once each year. The prize consists of a certificate of award, a plaque from the founder, and a sum of money derived from the interest earned on the foundation's capital. See also Child Health Foundation Prize and Fellowship; Darling Foundation Medal and Prize; Dr. A. T. Shousha Foundation Prize; Dr. Comlan A. A. Quenum Prize; Jacques Parisot Foundation Fellowship; Leon Bernard Prize and Medal.

UNITED NATIONS CHILDREN'S FUND (UNICEF). A fund of the United Nations created in 1946, as the International Children's Emergency Fund, "to be utilized for the benefit of children and adolescents of countries which were the victims of aggression." The fund is located under ECOSOC, headed by an executive director (q.v.), and wholly funded by extrabudgetary funds (q.v.). Initially intended to operate temporarily after the Second World War, UNICEF was made a permanent organization in 1953 because of the continued needs of children worldwide in the midst of war, poverty, and other causes of deprivation. Upon the creation of WHO in 1948, the Joint Committee on Health Policy (q.v.) was immediately established to encourage the two organizations to work together in the health field. Collaborative activities have included the International Conference on Primary Health Care, the Children's Vaccine Initiative, Integrated Management of the Sick Child, the Task Force for Child Survival, the Joint United Nations Programme on HIV/AIDS (qq.v.), the Joint Programme on Data Management and Mapping for Public Health, and the Tuberculosis Research Offices. Despite much collaborative work, WHO and UNICEF have also disagreed on health policies. Notably, from the late 1970s UNICEF has favored a vertical or selective (q.v.) approach to primary health care (q.v.), that contrasts with WHO's comprehensive approach. More recently, UNICEF's support of the Bamako Initiative (q.v.) has been questioned in WHO. See also Committee on the Rights of the Child; World Summit for Children.

UNITED NATIONS CONFERENCE ON ENVIRONMENT AND DEVELOPMENT (UNCED). Also known as Earth Summit; Rio Conference. A conference held in Rio de Janiero, Brazil, in 1992 to discuss and achieve international agreement on a wide range of issues concerning the relation between the environment and development. The conference was attended by 120 heads of state and over 15,000 delegates. The conference put forth Agenda 21, which serves as a plan of action for the environment and sustainable development into the 21st century. The contribution of WHO to the conference was to carry out a series of high-level meetings on health and the environment, including the creation of a Commission on Health and Environment in 1990. In 1991 the commission issued its report, "Our Planet, Our Health," on the adverse health and social consequences of environment deterioration due to unsustainable development practices. To follow up UNCED, the United Nations Economic and Social Council created the Commission on Sustainable Development in 1993 to ensure the implementation of the agreements reached, including Agenda 21. In the follow-up process, WHO has been given the responsibility of task manager for health-related goals. For this purpose, the director-general (q.v.) established the Council on the implementation of the Earth Summit's Action Programme for Health and the Environment (q.v.) and the Task Force on Environment and Health comprising representatives of appropriate WHO programs.

UNITED NATIONS DEVELOPMENT PROGRAM (UNDP). A special United Nations fund originally established in 1949 as the Expanded Program for Technical Assistance (EPTA) (q.v.), in response to the Point 4 Program put forth by United States President Harry Truman to provide technical assistance (q.v.) to the developing world. With the rapidly growing needs of developing countries from the 1950s, an expanded organization was formed with the 1965 consolidation of EPTA and the United Nations special fund in 1965 known as the UNDP. The fund was formally located under the authority of the secretary general. Today, the UNDP is headed by a director, usually an American citizen, and governed by a 48-member council. It is financed almost entirely from extrabudgetary funds (q.v.), with the United States being its largest contributor. Its role is to channel resources to developing countries, either directly or through executing agencies (q.v.), and to coordinate with the development work of the United Nations at the country level through the resident coordinator system (q.v.).

About 6 percent of UNDP resources are directed toward the health sector (approximately U.S.$55 million in 1993). This makes it the largest single source of multilateral grant funding for health development. An important part of the UNDP's health work is carried out in cooperation with WHO, with the latter receiving funds (approximately U.S.$40 million in 1992–93) to serve as an executing agency (q.v.) of the UNDP, while WHO in turn provides technical knowledge and expertise. In the field of HIV/AIDS, the Global Programme on AIDS formed the WHO/UNDP Alliance to Combat AIDS (qq.v.) in 1988 to improve the implementation of activities at the country level. The UNDP is also a cosponsoring (q.v.) organization of a number of WHO-based programs, including the Joint United Nations Programme on HIV/AIDS, the Special Programme of Research, Development, and Research Training in Human Reproduction, and the UNDP/World Bank/WHO Special Programme for Research and Training in Tropical Diseases (qq.v.). Finally, the UNDP served on the Management Review Committee of the former Division of Diarrhoeal and Acute Respiratory Disease Control; the Coordination, Advisory, and Review Group of the Global Tuberculosis Programme; and the meeting of interested parties of the Global Programme for Vaccines and Immunization (qq.v.).

UNITED NATIONS FUND FOR DRUG ABUSE CONTROL (UNFDAC). A fund created by the UN General Assembly in 1971 to support efforts to control the abuse of drugs. As a separate fund of the UN, the UNFDAC has provided assistance to WHO, for example, for the creation of a program of research on the epidemiology of drug dependence, studies on maintenance methods for the management of drug addiction, and the preparation of information on drug abuse by the health professions.

UNITED NATIONS INTER-AGENCY STANDING COMMITTEE (IASC). *See* Division of Emergency and Humanitarian Action.

UNITED NATIONS INTERNATIONAL CHILDREN'S EMERGENCY FUND. *See* United Nations Children's Fund.

UNITED NATIONS JOINT PROGRAMME ON HIV/AIDS. *See* Joint United Nations Programme on HIV/AIDS.

UNITED NATIONS POPULATION FUND (UNFPA). A fund of the United Nations created by ECOSOC in 1969 to "play a leading role in the United Nations system in promoting population programs." Funded wholly from extrabudgetary funds (q.v.), the main activities of the UNFPA have included support for the development of national population programs and policies, channeling of funding to governments, nongovernmental organizations (q.v.), and other United Nations organizations for population activities, and monitoring and evaluating the achievement of national and international population goals. Since the early 1970s, UNFPA has cosponsored (q.v.) three decennial conferences on population and has been the leading multilateral donor in the field of population.

UNFPA has collaborated with WHO in a variety of ways. WHO is an executing agency (q.v.) for the UNFPA through its work in research on human reproduction. The UNFPA is a partner in the cosponsored Special Programme of Research, Development, and Research Training in Human Reproduction and the Joint United Nations Programme on HIV/AIDS (qq.v.). Since the 1994 International Conference on Population and Development (ICPD) (q.v.), WHO has been an active member of the Inter-Agency Task Force on the Follow-up to the ICPD Plan of Action. *See also* Division of Family Health; Division of Reproductive Health (Technical Support); Family and Reproductive Health Programme.

UNITED NATIONS RELIEF AND REHABILITATION ADMINISTRATION (UNRRA). An organization created in 1943 to provide short-term emergency assistance for relief and rehabilitation to the war-affected countries of Europe and the Far East. Health-related activities, which were seen as primary and fundamental to the organization's work, were carried out by a health division. This work included provision of essential medical supplies; administration of the International Sanitary Conventions (q.v.) from 1945, when the Office International d'Hygiène Publique (q.v.) could no longer carry out this task; epidemiological surveillance and notification; aiding governments to rebuild their health services; and awarding fellowships and other educational activities. In order to bridge the gap between the cessation of UNRRA's work and the creation of WHO, the Interim Commission (q.v.) agreed in December 1946 to take responsibility for UNRRA's health activities. A notable exception was the medical care of displaced persons, which remained the remit of the International Refugee Organization (later known as the United Nations High Commissioner for Refugees).

UNITED NATIONS SPECIAL INITIATIVE ON AFRICA. An initiative of the United Nations launched in 1996 as a set of concrete and coordinated strategic actions aimed at maximizing international support for development efforts in Africa within priority sectors (e.g., health). The initiative has 14 components for action, for each of which one or more lead UN organizations have been designated as responsible for resource mobilization and coordination of implementation. The role of WHO in the initiative is to lead and coordinate international efforts in the field of basic health in 54 African member states (q.v.), including 47 lowest-income countries. In these efforts, WHO works in collaboration with the World Bank, the United Nations Children's Fund, and the United Nations Development Program (qq.v.).

UNITED NATIONS TECHNICAL ASSISTANCE BOARD (UNTAB). *See* Expanded Programme for Technical Assistance.

URBAN ENVIRONMENTAL HEALTH. *See* Division of Operational Support in Environmental Health.

USER SUPPORT AND TRAINING (USP). *See* Division of Information System Management.

V

VACCINE DEVELOPMENT, PROGRAMME FOR. *See* Programme for Vaccine Development.

VACCINE INDEPENDENCE INITIATIVE. *See* Plan of Action for Vaccine Self-Sufficiency.

VACCINE INITIATIVE, CHILDREN'S. *See* Children's Vaccine Initiative.

VACCINE INSTITUTE, INTERNATIONAL. *See* International Vaccine Institute.

VACCINES AND IMMUNIZATION, GLOBAL PROGRAMME FOR. *See* Global Programme for Vaccines and Immunization.

VACCINE SELF-SUFFICIENCY, PLAN OF ACTION FOR. *See* Plan of Action for Vaccine Self-Sufficiency.

VACCINES, PAHO REGIONAL SYSTEM FOR. *See* PAHO Regional System for Vaccines.

VAN DE CALSEYDE, PAUL J. J. (1903–1971). Dr. Paul van de Calseyde, of Belgium, served as regional director of the European Regional Office (qq.v.) from 1957 to 1967.

VETERINARY PUBLIC HEALTH PROGRAMME (VHP). A program that addresses the transmission of diseases from animals to human beings (i.e., zoonoses). Zoonoses continues to represent an important health hazard in most member states (q.v.) and are the cause of considerable expense and loss for the health and agricultural sectors. For example, the incidence of diseases from the consumption of food of animal origin, such as salmonellosis, Escherichia coli, and Campylobacter, has been increasing in many developing and industrialized countries. In addition, a significant proportion of recently emerging human infectious diseases have been due to an infectious agent transmission cycle that involves an animal host (e.g., nonhuman primates, rodents, domestic animals). The program conducts a wide range of activities aimed at surveillance and control of such diseases, including epidemiological monitoring, promotion of research; advocacy (e.g., immunization of foxes); and development of training modules for veterinary epidemiology and population medicine. Many of these activities are conducted with the assistance of a worldwide network of WHO collaborating centers (q.v.). *See also* Division of Emerging and Other Communicable Diseases.

VICTORIA DECLARATION ON HEART HEALTH. A declaration adopted in 1992 at the International Heart Health Conference held in Victoria, Canada, to give a greater sense of urgency to the prevention and control of cardiovascular disease as a major cause of death in most countries. Recognizing that scientific knowledge and widely tested methods exist to prevent most cardiovascular diseases, the declaration calls on health, media, education, and social science professionals, the scientific research community, government agencies and international organizations concerned with health, and nongovernmental organizations (q.v.) to join forces in eliminating the epidemic of such diseases through new policies, regulatory changes, and implementation of health promotion and disease prevention programs directed at entire populations. *See also* Division of Health Promotion, Education and Communication.

VITAMIN A. The focus of an initiative adopted by the World Health Assembly (q.v.) in 1984 to intensify efforts to prevent and control the impact of vitamin A deficiency and xerophthalmia on child health, blindness, and survival. This was followed by a ten-year plan of action begun in 1985, which presented an overall strategy, measures to increase the availability and consumption of vitamin A, and administration of high-dose supplementation. Programs for the distribution of vitamin A supplements expanded steadily over the next few years, leading WHO, together with the International Vitamin A Consultative Group and the United Nations Children's Fund (q.v.), to prepare guidelines for health administrators and program managers for national and regional programs. The guidelines were introduced in 1988, and the goal of preventing and controlling vitamin A deficiency has since been supported in the World Declaration on the Survival, Protection, and Development of Children and the World Declaration and Plan of Action for Nutrition of 1992. *See also* International Conference on Nutrition.

VOLUNTARY CONTRIBUTION. *See* Extrabudgetary Funds.

VOLUNTARY FUND FOR HEALTH PROMOTION (VFHP). A fund created in 1960 to receive extrabudgetary funds (EBFs) for technical cooperation (qq.v.) activities. The fund consists of a number of special accounts to which donations can be made in support of specific activities (e.g., community water supply, cholera, leprosy, mental health) or for undesignated purposes. Most of the funds contributed (99 percent) have been earmarked for specific activities. The fund accounts for about 38 percent of all EBFs. *See also* Real Estate Fund; Trust Fund; Working Capital Fund.

W

WATER AND SANITATION DECADE, INTERNATIONAL DRINKING. *See* International Drinking Water and Sanitation Decade.

WATER PROGRAMME, GLOBAL ENVIRONMENT MONITORING SYSTEM *See* Global Environment Monitoring System Water Programme.

WATER SUPPLY AND SANITATION, INTERAGENCY STEERING COMMITTEE ON. *See* Interagency Steering Committee on Water Supply and Sanitation.

WATER SUPPLY AND SANITATION MONITORING PROGRAMME, WHO/UNICEF JOINT. *See* WHO/UNICEF Joint Water Supply and Sanitation Monitoring Programme.

WATER SUPPLY FUND, SPECIAL COMMUNITY. *See* Special Community Water Supply Fund.

WEEKLY EPIDEMIOLOGICAL RECORD (WER). A mechanism set up in 1948 for the rapid and accurate dissemination of epidemiological information on cases and outbreaks of diseases listed within the International Health Regulations (q.v.), other communicable diseases of public health importance including newly emerging and reemerging infections, noncommunicable diseases, and other health problems. A bilingual (English/French) edition of WER is distributed each Friday in paper and electronic forms. *See also* Division of Emerging and Other Communicable Diseases; *World Health Situation Report; World Health Statistics Annual and Quarterly.*

WESTERN EUROPEAN AND OTHER GROUP (WEOG). A group of 26 WHO member states (q.v.) from Western Europe, North America, and other industrialized areas (Japan, New Zealand, and Australia) whose representatives to the United Nations meet to discuss and plan official positions on specific health issues with relevance to WHO. The meetings were begun by Australia, which served as chair of the group from 1993 to 1955. The United Kingdom has served as chair since 1995. Representatives initially met quarterly with the director-general (q.v.) and his senior officials to discuss major issues such as the Executive Board Working Group on the WHO Response to Global Change (q.v.) reform process. Since 1985 meetings on policy issues have continued at the subambassadorial level. *See also* African Group; Asian Group; Geneva Group; Oslo Group.

WESTERN PACIFIC REGIONAL OFFICE (WPRO). One of six WHO regional offices (q.v.), the WPRO was created in 1951 with headquarters in Manila, the Philippines. The regional committee (q.v.) is composed of representatives from member states (q.v.) as well as France, Portugal, the United Kingdom, and the United States, which maintain territories in the region. In 1995 there were 27 member states and one associate member (q.v.). The region is diverse, with 1.6 billion people, including some of the world's least industrialized countries, emerging economies, and industrialized countries such as Australia and New Zealand. Thirty-five percent of the region's population is under the age of 15. Priority areas for 1996–97 include the eradication and control of selected diseases (e.g., leprosy, poliomyelitis), child immunization and nutrition, reproductive health, noncommunicable diseases, and addressing the health impact of rapid urbanization and increased affluence. *See also* Regional Director.

WHO COLLABORATING CENTER. An institution designated by the director-general (q.v.) as one carrying out activities in support of WHO's program of work. A department or laboratory within an institution or a group of facilities for reference, research, or training belonging to different institutions may be designated as a center, with one institution acting in relations with WHO. The functions of a collaborating center may include: (a) collection, collation, and dissemination of information; (b) standardization terminology and nomenclature, technology, diagnostic, therapeutic, and prophylactic substances, and methods and procedures; (c) development and application of appropriate technology; (d) provision of reference materials and other services; (e) participation in collaborative research developed under WHO's leadership; (f) training, including research training; and (g) coordination of activities carried out by several institutions on a given subject. There are currently some 1,220 WHO collaborating centers worldwide. WHO collaborating centers are recognized as one of the unique strengths of the organization, giving it the capacity to draw on the knowledge and expertise of individuals and institutions in both industrialized and developing countries.

WHO COMMISSION ON HEALTH AND THE ENVIRONMENT. *See* United Nations Conference on Environment and Development.

WHO GLOBAL DATABASE ON CHILD GROWTH. A database created in 1986 by the Nutrition Unit of the Division of Family Health (q.v.) to compile, systematize, and disseminate the results of anthropometric surveys performed in industrialized and developing countries. The database covers 87 percent of the total population of under-five-year-olds in developing countries, and its objectives are to describe the worldwide distribution of child growth failure, permit intercountry and interregional comparisons, and facilitate the monitoring of global, regional, and national trends. The existence of the database, and its continual updating, stimulates new anthropometric surveys, particularly in countries and regions thus far scarcely investigated.

WHO INTERNATIONAL/REGIONAL REFERENCE CENTERS FOR SMALLPOX VACCINE. A mechanism for periodic testing of the quality of vaccines for use in smallpox-endemic countries. In 1966 an agreement was signed between the Pan American Health Organization (q.v.) and the Connaught Medical Research Laboratories, University of Toronto, Canada, for the provision of technical services to improve the quality of smallpox vaccine being produced in the region. A similar agreement was signed by WHO with the National Institute of Public Health, Bilthoven, the Netherlands, in 1967. In 1969 the Connaught Laboratories were officially designated as the WHO Regional Reference Center for Smallpox Vaccine for the Americas, and the National Institute of Public Health became the WHO International Reference Center for Smallpox Vaccine.

WHONET. An information and communication system developed by WHO to support the global surveillance of bacterial resistance to antimicrobial agents. The system draws on the tens of thousands of tests carried out by laboratories worldwide each year on the susceptibility of patients to antimicrobial agents. The results of these tests are put into universal file format by WHONET and made available, in the form of computer software, to health workers to monitor and manage the quality of tests and the spread of resistance. WHONET also enables aggregate databases to be formed for collaborative national, regional, and global surveillance. In 1995 the network consisted of 177 laboratories located in 31 countries or areas. Information is used to detect and monitor resistance and to support research and development on new antibiotics to replace those no longer effective. *See also* Antituberculosis Drug Resistance Surveillance; Division of Emerging and Other Communicable Diseases.

WHO PESTICIDE EVALUATION SCHEME (WHOPES). A program, within the Division of Control of Tropical Diseases (q.v.), created in response to the need for a variety of alternative pesticide products with different formulations, as well as packaging and application technologies, for the control of tropical disease vectors, animal reservoirs, and intermediate hosts. The program evaluates the active ingredients and formulations of pesticides and promotes the efficacy, safe use, cost-effective application, and quality control of pesticides for public health use. WHOPES has two main components: (a) evaluation and assessment of alternative and existing pesticides for their impact and risks to human health and the environment; and (b) standardization, development of specifications, and analytical methods for assuring product quality. The strategy of the program is intensified collaboration with member states (q.v.), the pesticide industry, and nongovernmental organizations (q.v.); coordination of relevant activities and technical support to disease-endemic countries; harmonization of activities with international or regional agencies concerned with pesticide management, legislation, and manufacture; and implementation and promotion of the International Code of Conduct for the Distribution and Use of Pesticides. Operational costs at the country level are covered by the pesticide industry through bilateral agreements, whereas coordination and technical support activities are paid by regular budget funds and extrabudgetary funds (qq.v.).

WHOQOL. A measure of quality of life developed by WHO, in collaboration with 15 centers in 14 countries, to complement established methods of assessing health status in terms of disease through positive measurements of health (e.g., mobility).

WHO REPRESENTATIVE (WR). The chief representative of WHO in member states (q.v.) where a country office (q.v.) is located. The specific responsibilities of the WR varies among the six WHO regions. In general, the WR supports the formulation, implementation, and evaluation of national Health for All (q.v.) strategies; develops and manages at the country level the organization's program of technical cooperation (q.v.); and coordinates the organization's activities with the national health program and those of other relevant health agencies. In addition, WRs are responsible for keeping the regional director (q.v.) informed of any special health problems in the country. WRs are appointed by and answerable to the relevant regional office (q.v.) and conduct their work through the national ministry of health. In recent years, there has been criticism of the variable quality of WRs and their capacity to carry out the above tasks. Under the Executive Board Working Group on the WHO Response to Global Change (q.v.) reform process, there have been efforts to strengthen procedures for recruiting and appointing WRs. A study sponsored by the Oslo Group (q.v.) on WHO's support to programs at the country level also seeks to strengthen the role of the WR and the country office.

WHO RESPONSE TO GLOBAL CHANGE, EXECUTIVE BOARD WORKING GROUP ON THE. *See* Executive Board Working Group on the WHO Response to Global Change.

WHO/UNDP ALLIANCE TO COMBAT AIDS. An alliance between WHO and the United Nations Development Program (UNDP) (q.v.) formed in 1988 for the purpose of combining WHO's coordinating role in international health policy and scientific and technical matters with the UNDP's leadership role in socioeconomic development in a combined effort to combat HIV/AIDS. By joining forces with the UNDP and its network of resident representatives, the Global Programme on AIDS (q.v.) sought to carry its activities through national ministries of health to other ministries such as education, planning, and finance. More specifically, the alliance was intended to (a) ensure that AIDS is treated as more than a health problem by involving a wide spectrum of government ministries; (b) help to include AIDS activites in governments' overall development plans, priorities, and resource allocations; (c) coordinate support from United Nations organizations to national AIDS programs and help governments to coordinate all external support for their national AIDS programs; and (d) strengthen support for teams from the WHO Global Programme on AIDS based at the country level. Under the agreement, the UNDP was compensated by WHO for administrative expenses, while WHO joined in UNDP-financed projects at the country level. In July 1992, a Memorandum of Understanding for the Implementation of the WHO/UNDP Alliance to Combat AIDS was signed, which amended the original agreement. However, differences between the two organizations' approaches to the most appropriate strategy for the prevention and control of HIV/AIDS led to tensions and the eventual ineffectiveness of the alliance.

WHO/UNICEF JOINT PROGRAMME ON DATA MANAGEMENT AND MAPPING FOR PUBLIC HEALTH. A program established in 1993 by WHO and the United Nations Children's

Fund (UNICEF) (q.v.) to facilitate effective targeting of interventions for the eradication of selected diseases through improved mapping of affected areas. The program followed a collaborative effort to map guinea-worm-endemic villages in remote areas in Africa that did not appear on available maps and were thus underserved by the public health system. UNICEF field staff mapped the location of disease-endemic areas, and the information was then combined with WHO information on health facilities and epidemiological data. This led to the creation of the joint program, which, using a similar geographical information system, monitors results of epidemiological surveillance for dracunculiasis and other diseases. Information from the program enables district-level coordinators and national policymakers to more effectively target activities, monitor the situation, and plan future operations. *See also* Division of Health Situation and Trend Assessment.

WHO/UNICEF JOINT WATER SUPPLY AND SANITATION MONITORING PROGRAMME. A program jointly created by WHO and the United Nations Children's Fund (q.v.) to monitor access to safe water supply and sanitation by people in developing countries. The program reported that, at the end of 1990, 1.6 billion people were without access to adequate and safe water supply, and 2.8 billion to appropriate means of sanitation. This information is used to encourage increased efforts by the international community to improve basic infrastructure. *See also* Interagency Steering Committee on Water Supply and Sanitation; International Drinking Water and Sanitation Decade; Special Community Water Supply Fund.

WOMEN'S HEALTH (WHD). An area of work formed in 1996, within the Family and Reproductive Health Programme (q.v.), to contribute to the promotion of women's health and well-being. Women provide 70–80 percent of the health care in developing countries and, in some countries, up to 60 percent of household incomes. Yet women also carry a disproportionate burden of ill health. The work of the division focuses on the inclusion of gender and women's perspectives in health policies and programs and on women's participation in such programs. The division is also developing advocacy and training materials on gender and reproductive health, violence against women, and female genital mutilation. *See also* Adolescent Health and Development Programme; Division of Child Health and Development; Global Commission on Women's Health; International Conference on Population and Development; Mother-Baby Package; Special Programme for Research, Development, and Research Training in Human Reproduction.

WOMEN'S HEALTH, GLOBAL COMMISSION ON. *See* Global Commission on Women's Health.

WORKING CAPITAL FUND. A fund created by the World Health Assembly (WHA) (q.v.) in 1948 for the primary purpose of providing funds as may be required to finance the regular budget pending receipt of contributions from member states (q.v.), with sums advanced being subject to reimbursement to the fund as contributions become available. Initially, the fund received only advances of regular budget funds (q.v.) contributed by member states in accordance with their scale of assessments. By the mid-1960s, however, the ratio of the fund to the overall budget had declined substantially, and the WHA decided it was necessary to increase the level of the fund to 20 percent of WHO's annual budget. It was not felt appropriate to assess additional advances on member states to finance this increase. Thus, it was agreed that the fund would be divided into two parts: part 1 consisted of advances from member states made in accordance with the scale of assessments; part 2 consisted of casual income transferred into the fund from time to time. All subsequent increases to the fund have been financed from this latter source. In 1994, a review of the need to maintain the fund's division into two parts led to an agreement to consolidate them once again. *See also* Real Estate Fund; Trust Fund; Voluntary Fund for Health Promotion.

WORKING GROUP ON CONTINENTAL AFRICA. A working group established in 1994 to facilitate WHO's contribution to the implementation of the United Nations New Agenda for the Development of Africa in the 1990s. WHO's policy orientation in Africa is to support the specific and collective health plans of African member states (q.v.) in collaboration with other organizations. *See also* Cairo Agenda.

WORLD AIDS DAY. A day set aside each year since 1988 on 1 December to raise public awareness about HIV/AIDS, spread prevention messages into communities, improve care for those infected by HIV, and combat discrimination. Sponsored by the Global Programme on AIDS and, since 1996, the Joint United Nations Programme on HIV/AIDS (qq.v.), activities include exhibitions, educational programs, and media campaigns. Each year, a theme is chosen by WHO to focus on a particular aspect of the disease. Recent themes include "AIDS and the Family" (1994), "Shared Rights, Shared Responsibilities" (1995), and "One World, One Hope" (1996).

WORLD BANK. A specialized agency of the United Nations consisting of five separate institutions: the International Bank for Reconstruction and Development (IBRD), the International Development Assocation (IDA), the International Finance Corporation, the Multilateral Investment Guarantee Agency, and the International Center for Settlement of Investment Disputes. In relation to the health sector, the IBRD and the IDA are the most relevant institutions and are often referred to colloquially as the World Bank.

The World Bank did not lend specifically for health projects until the 1980s, although it has financed population projects since the late 1960s and nutrition and health as a component of other projects since the 1970s. In 1980 the Population, Health, and Nutrition department was created within the Bank, and lending for such projects increased rapidly as part of the Bank's support for "basic needs" and investment in "human capital." Between 1981 and 1990, annual loan disbursements for health (excluding population and nutrition) rose from U.S.$33 million to U.S.$263 million. To provide such loans and credits, the Bank has increased health expertise among its staff. This has been accompanied by a more vocal role in the development of health policy, marked by the publication of the "World Development Report: Investing in Health in 1993." With social sector lending expected to account for 15 percent of all World Bank lending by the late 1990s, the World Bank has become the largest single source of health financing.

WHO and the World Bank participate in a number of joint activities. These include partnership in cosponsored programs (q.v.) such as the Special Programme on Research, Development, and Research Training in Human Reproduction, the UNDP/World Bank/WHO Special Programme for Research and Training in Tropical Diseases, and the Joint United Nations Programme on HIV/AIDS (qq.v.). The rapid expansion of the World Bank's role in the health sector has led to concerns that it has taken a lead role in setting international health policy based on economic criteria at the expense of equity (q.v.) considerations. In an effort to address these concerns and to initiate greater cooperation between WHO and the World Bank, a

WHO/World Bank review meeting was held in 1994 in Geneva to improve the collaborative framework between WHO and the World Bank for supporting health and health-related development sectors in developing countries. The meeting was attended by senior government officials from four selected countries, senior representatives from the headquarters and regional offices of the World Bank, and staff of WHO from headquarters, regional offices, and country offices (qq.v.). Participants reviewed collaboration between the two organizations and agreed on a joint memorandum of World Bank/World Health Organization health activities containing recommendations for strengthening relations between the two organizations. *See also* Equity; Global Burden of Disease.

WORLD CONFERENCE ON WOMEN. *See* Global Commission on Women's Health.

WORLD DECLARATION AND PLAN OF ACTION FOR NUTRITION. *See* International Conference on Nutrition.

WORLD DECLARATION ON THE CONTROL OF MALARIA. *See* Malaria Control.

WORLD HEALTH ASSEMBLY (WHA). The highest legislative and policy organ of WHO, which determines the organization's overall policies, gives directives to the Executive Board and the director-general (qq.v.), adopts international health regulations, approves the biennial budget, and monitors and evaluates the implementation of policies. The WHA is composed of representatives of all member states (q.v.), which can express their views, make collective commitments, and advocate compliance with agreed policies. Since 1948 the WHA has met annually (usually in May) for two to three weeks. Each member state is represented by three delegates, generally from its national ministry of health. While decisions are governed by the principles of "One state, one vote" and a two-thirds majority, most decisions are taken by consensus. Representatives of other international institutions and nongovernmental organizations (q.v.) also attend as observers. As WHO's membership and the scope of its work have grown over time, efforts have been made to improve the method of work of the WHA. For example, technical discussions (q.v.) are no longer held annually but in alternate years when the biennial budget is not being discussed.

WORLD HEALTH ASSEMBLY PRESIDENT. An official elected, upon the recommendation of the Committee on Nominations (q.v.), to chair the proceedings of a regular session of the World Health Assembly (q.v.). Among the president's responsibilities are to open and close plenary meetings, ensure observance of rules, accord the right to speak, put questions and announce decisions, and rule on points of order. The president may call on any of five vice presidents to assist in these functions.

WORLD HEALTH DAY. A day celebrated annually, on 7 April, to commemorate the ratification of the constitution (q.v.) of WHO. While the constitution was formally approved on 22 July 1946, it was not until 7 April 1948 that the required 26 signatures were finally received from among the 51 governments participating in the International Health Conference (q.v.) of 1946. The day is also used to draw world attention to a particular aspect of health, such as "Oral Health for a Healthy Life" (1994), polio eradication (1995) and "Emerging Infectious Diseases" (1997).

WORLD HEALTH REPORT. An annual report launched in 1995 on the state of human health worldwide. The report presents up-to-date statistical data on major health issues and the health status of specific populations. Each year the report centers on a specific theme in health. The titles of reports so far have been *Bridging the Gaps* (1995) and *Fighting Disease, Fostering Development* (1996), with the control of noncommunicable diseases planned as the theme for 1997.

WORLD HEALTH SITUATION REPORT. A report published periodically by the Division of Health Situation and Trend Assessment (q.v.) to provide global analysis and individual country reviews of health status in member states (q.v.). The purpose of the report is to provide analyses of health problems in different countries within a global framework and comparative analysis across member states. *See also* World Health Statistics Annual and Quarterly.

WORLD HEALTH STATISTICS ANNUAL AND QUARTERLY. An annual and quarterly publication of the Division of Health Situation and Trend Assessment (q.v.) to provide comparative data on vital statistics; national death registration statistics by country, age, and sex according to the International Classification of Diseases and Related Health Problems (q.v.); causes of mortality and morbidity; and health personnel and hospital infrastructure. The publication is used as an international standard reference by member states (q.v.). Each issue of the *World Health Statistics Quarterly* focuses on a selected topic of current public health interest.

WORLD NO TOBACCO DAY. A day set aside each year since 1988 to raise public awareness of the health hazards of tobacco use and to reaffirm WHO's and member states' (q.v.) commitment to work toward a tobacco-free world. Events are organized around an annual theme; past themes have included "Tobacco Costs More than You Think" (1995), on the economic aspects of tobacco use, and "Sport and the Arts without Tobacco" (1996). The campaign is supported by the quarterly newsletter, *Tobacco Alert*, which publishes information on the adverse health effects of tobacco use.

WORLD SUMMIT FOR CHILDREN. A meeting convened by the United Nations Children's Fund (UNICEF) (q.v.) in New York in 1990 attended by 71 heads of state and representatives from 146 countries. The meeting was the culmination of UNICEF's direct efforts to promote child health beginning in the early 1980s, when it declared the "Children's Revolution." The participants of the meeting signed the World Declaration on the Survival, Protection, and Development of Children and the Plan of Action for Governments. Twenty-one of the goals set by the declaration concerned the health sector, including reductions in child and maternal mortality and morbidity, improvements in sanitation and access to safe drinking water, programs for malnutrition and illiteracy, and the global eradication of poliomyelitis. Following the summit, WHO agreed on regional plans of action for the achievement of these health goals. *See also* Children's Vaccine Initiative; Integrated Management of the Sick Child; Task Force for Child Survival.

WORLD SUMMIT ON SOCIAL DEVELOPMENT. A summit of world leaders held in Copenhagen, Denmark, in 1995 to promote public policies and sectoral activities, at the national and international level, to achieve objectives of social development. The three themes of the meeting were social integration, reduction of poverty, and expansion of productive employment. Participants, including 118 world leaders, agreed to a declaration and program of action toward these ends. WHO's participation in the summit focused on promotion of health as an indispensi-

252 • WORLD TUBERCULOSIS DAY

ble component of development policies, strengthening of partnerships for health development, mobilization of political commitment to health in the context of economic and social development, and support of the 20/20 Initiative (q.v.). In addition, the annual monitoring of the world health situation by WHO and member states (q.v.) was expected to contribute to the ongoing monitoring of progress in social development. *See also* Task Force on Health in Development.

WORLD TUBERCULOSIS DAY. A day reserved each year since 1996 for the purpose of drawing attention to the current and unprecedented spread of tuberculosis. The event commemorates the day, 24 March 1882, when Dr. Robert Koch officially informed the scientific community of his discovery of the tuberculosis bacillus. World Tuberculosis Day is marked by the release of a WHO report entitled "Report on the TB Epidemic," which discusses the extent of the disease's incidence and how it affects women, children, workers, and other risk groups. *See also* Antituberculosis Drug Resistance Surveillance; Directly Observed Treatment, Short-Course; Tuberculosis Programme; Global Tuberculosis Programme.

WYMAN, WALTER. (1848–1911). Dr. Walter Wyman, of the United States, served as the first chairman of the Pan American Sanitary Bureau (q.v.), forerunner of the Pan American Health Organization (q.v.), from 1902 to 1911.

Y

YELLOW BOOKS. *See* Proposed Programme Budget.

Z

ZERO NOMINAL GROWTH, POLICY OF. *See* Policy of Zero Nominal Growth.

ZERO REAL GROWTH, POLICY OF. *See* Policy of Zero Real Growth.

ZHDANOV, VIKTOR M. (1914–   ). Dr. Viktor Zhdanov, then deputy minister of health for the former Soviet Union, successfully proposed to the World Health Assembly (q.v.) in 1958 that

WHO should undertake the global eradication of smallpox. Director-General Brock Chisholm (q.v.) had proposed eradication in 1953, but at the time it was considered too vast and complicated an endeavor. Dr. Zhdanov's interest in disease eradication began in 1951, when he was appointed chief of the Department of Sanitary and Epidemiological Services. He initiated a study of infectious diseases in the Soviet Union shortly thereafter for the purpose of identifying those diseases that might be successfully eradicated. With the withdrawal of the Soviet Union from WHO between 1948 and 1957, Dr. Zhdanov was unable to present his findings until the country resumed its membership. Finally, in 1958, he presented a formal and lengthy report arguing that smallpox was an important problem for all countries, that eradication was theoretically feasible, and that national programs had demonstrated it to be a practicable possibility. The report was accompanied by a contribution of 25 million doses of vaccine and a draft resolution, which led to the adoption of Resolution WHA12.54 in 1959 for WHO to undertake the eradication of smallpox. *See also* Intensified Smallpox Eradication Programme.

ZONE OFFICE. A former administrative division of the Pan American Health Organization (PAHO) (q.v.) created during the 1950s for the purpose of moving resources closer to their sphere of action. Six zones were established, following an evaluation of PAHO's structure in light of its functions, to enable decentralization of authority, each with an office, one or more medical officers, a sanitary engineer, a public health nurse, and other staff as required. During the early 1970s the zone office was replaced by the area office (q.v.), with responsibility for program delivery at the country level, and then by the country office (q.v.) as part of a further delegation of authority and administration.

Bibliography

This bibliography is a selected collection of the main primary and secondary literature on the World Health Organization. The bibliography is organized into two main sections: Selected Publications by the World Health Organization (primary) and General Bibliography (secondary). It is recognized that the two types of publications cannot be wholly separated, given that many individuals have published works related to the organization as current or former WHO staff members. The first section is a list of selected major publications produced by WHO divided into Official Proceedings, Periodic Reports and Documents, Books, Booklets, Report Series, Periodicals, and Newsletters. WHO produces a wide range of publications on all aspects of public health. The publications cited represent key aspects of the organization's work in the form of fundamental decisions taken by governing bodies, major policy statements, or major sources of reporting on WHO's work. For an early listing of selected publications, see WHO, *Publications of the World Health Organization 1968–1972: A Bibliography* (Geneva, 1974). For a comprehensive list of new publications each year, see WHO, *Publications Catalogue: New Books* (Geneva, annual). All past and present official proceedings are available from the WHO Library, located at WHO Headquarters in Geneva, Switzerland, which is open for use by the public, and from most national departments of health who act as depository libraries for WHO. The WHO Library has also recently established an archival section for historical material on the Health Organization of the League of Nations and other predecessor health organizations. Selected publications, such as news releases and brief descriptions of the work of specific divisions and programs, are available from the Internet (http://www.who.ch).

The second section is a list of the main secondary literature on WHO, published mainly in English but with some French language literature. This section has been organized to help the reader to locate key publications on specific aspects of WHO and its work. The following subsections have been used: History of Medicine and the Founding of WHO; WHO's Structure and

Functions; WHO Regional Offices; Finances of WHO; Reform of WHO; Primary Health Care/Health for All Strategy; Technical Cooperation for Health Development; WHO/UNICEF Code on the Marketing of Breastmilk Substitutes; Drug Policies; Disease Prevention, Control, Treatment, and Eradication Programs; Vaccines and Immunization; Health Legislation, Standards, and Guidelines; Reproductive Health; Environmental Health; Human Resources Development, Education, and Training; Health Research; Nutrition; and Miscellaneous. Works have been selected for inclusion for a number of reasons. On the early history of WHO, there are relatively few publications. Effort has been made to provide a comprehensive list, including the memoirs of key individuals who have contributed to the creation and development of WHO. The seminal works remain N. Goodman, *International Health Organizations and Their Work*, 2nd ed. (Edinburgh: Churchill Livingstone, 1971), and the series of articles by N. Howard-Jones published during the 1970s. More recent publications, which provide an overview of the organization's historical evolution, are J. Siddiqi, *World Health and World Politics* (London: Hurst and Company, 1995), and Y. Beigbeder, *L'Organisation Mondiale de la Santé* (Geneva: Publications de l'Institut Universitaire de Hautes Etudes Internationales, 1995). In other subsections, major publications frequently cited by other authors have been included as useful sources of description of key aspects of WHO's work.

Selected Publications by the World Health Organization

Official Proceedings

AFRO. *Handbook of Resolutions and Decisions of the Regional Committee for Africa. 2 vol. (1951–1988)*. Brazzaville, 1989.

EMRO. *Handbook of Resolutions and Decisions of the Regional Committee for the Eastern Mediterranean (1949–1980)*. Alexandria, 1985.

EURO. *Handbook of Resolutions and Decisions of the Regional Committee for Europe Covering the Period 1951–1987. 12th ed.* Copenhagen, 1989.

Executive Board. *Official Documents*. Geneva (semi-annual).

———. IARC. *Handbook of Resolutions of the Governing Council of the International Agency for Research on Cancer (1965–1988)*. Geneva, 1988.

PAHO. *Basic Documents of the Pan American Health Organization. 15th ed.* Official Document No. 240. Washington, D.C., 1991.

———. *Basic Principles for Action of the Pan American Health Organization, 1987–1990*. Washington, D.C., 1987.

——. *Handbook of Resolutions of the Governing Bodies of the Pan American Health Organization. Vol. 1, 1942–1970.* Washington, D.C., 1971.

——. *Handbook of Resolutions of the Governing Bodies of the Pan American Health Organization. Vol. 2, 1971–1982.* Washington, D.C., 1983.

——. *Handbook of Resolutions of the Governing Bodies of the Pan American Health Organization. Vol 3, 1983–1986.* Washington, D.C., 1987.

SEARO. *Handbook of Resolutions and Decisions of the Regional Committee for South-East Asia (1948–1994).* 2 vols. New Delhi, 1994.

UN General Assembly. "Prevention and Control of Acquired Immune Deficiency Syndrome (AIDS)." Resolution 42/8, 42d Session, New York, October 26, 1987.

WHA. *Official Documents.* Geneva (annual).

WHO. *Basic Documents.* 41st ed. Geneva, 1966.

——. *Handbook of Resolutions and Decisions of the World Health Assembly and the Executive Board. Vol. 1, 1948–1972.* Geneva, 1973.

——. *Handbook of Resolutions and Decisions of the World Health Assembly and the Executive Board. Vol. 2, 1973–1984.* Geneva, 1985.

——. *Handbook of Resolutions and Decisions of the World Health Assembly and the Executive Board, Vol. 3, 1985–1992.* Geneva, 1993.

WPRO. *Handbook of Resolutions and Decisions of the Regional Committee for the Western Pacific (1957–1987).* 3 vols. Manila, 1988.

Periodic Reports and Documents

AFRO. *The Work of WHO in the African Region: Biennial Report of the Regional Director.* Brazzaville (biennial).

EMRO. *The Work of WHO in the Eastern Mediterranean Region: Annual Report of the Regional Director.* Alexandria (annual).

IARC. *International Agency for Research on Cancer: Biennial Report.* Geneva (biennial).

PAHO. *Report of the Director.* Washington, D.C. (annual).

——. *Strategic Orientations and Program Priorities.* Washington, D.C. (every five years).

SEARO. *Bulletin of Regional Health Information.* New Delhi (biennial).

——. *The Health Situation in South-East Asia Region.* New Delhi (biennial).

——. *The Work of WHO in the South-East Asia Region.* New Delhi (biennial).

WHO. *General Programme of Work.* Geneva (every five years).

——. *International Classification of Impairment, Disability, and Handicap.* Geneva (periodic).

——. *Manual of the International Statistical Classification of Diseases, Injuries, and Causes of Death.* Geneva (periodic).

——. *Proposed Programme Budget.* Geneva (biennial).

————. *The Work of the World Health Organization*. Geneva (annual).
————. *The World Health Report*. Geneva (annual).

Books

Acuña, H. R. *Toward 2000: The Quest for Universal Health in the Americas*. Washington, D.C.: PAHO, 1983.

Basu, R., Z. Jezek, and N. Ward. *The Eradication of Smallpox in India*. New Delhi: SEARO, 1979.

Bustamante, M. E. *The Pan American Sanitary Bureau: Half a Century of Health Activities, 1902–1954*. Washington, D.C.: PAHO, 1955.

Cummings, H. S. *The Pan American Sanitary Bureau and Its Cooperative Work in the Improvement of Milk Supplies*. Publication No. 148. Washington, D.C.: PASB, 1940.

————. *The Work of the Pan American Sanitary Bureau in Relation to Child Welfare*. Publication No. 167. Washington, D.C.: PASB, 1941.

Djukanovic, V., and E. Mach. *Alternative Approaches to Meeting Basic Health Needs in Developing Countries*. Geneva: WHO, 1975.

Duffy, J., ed. *Ventures in World Health: The Memoirs of Fred Lowe Soper*. Washington, D.C.: PAHO, 1977.

Fenner, F., D. A. Henderson, I. Arita, Z. Jezek, and I. D. Ladnyi. *Smallpox and Its Eradication*. Geneva: WHO, 1975.

Gonzalez, C. L. *Mass Campaigns and General Health Services*. Geneva: WHO, 1965.

Hilleboe, H. E., A. Barkhuus, and W. C. Thomas. *Approaches to National Health Planning*. Geneva: WHO, 1972.

Howard, L. *A New Look at Development Cooperation for Health*. Geneva: WHO, 1981.

Howard-Jones, N. *The Scientific Background of the International Sanitary Conference, 1851–1938*. History of International Public Health Series, No. 1. Geneva: WHO, 1975.

Joarder, A. K., D. Taratola, and J. Tullock. *The Eradication of Smallpox from Bangladesh*. New Delhi: SEARO, 1980.

Kaprio, L. A. *Forty Years of WHO in Europe: The Development of a Common Policy*. European Series, No. 40. Copenhagen: WHO, 1991.

Ko Ko, U. *Ideas and Action for Health*. New Delhi: SEARO, 1995.

Mach, E. P., and B. Abel-Smith. *Planning the Finances of the Health Sector: A Manual for Developing Countries*. Geneva: WHO, 1983.

Manuila, A., ed. *Partner in Health in the Eastern Mediterranean: 1949–1989*. Alexandria: EMRO, 1991.

Molineaux, L., and G. Gramiccia. *The Garki Project*. Geneva: WHO, 1980.

Moll, A. *The Pan American Sanitary Bureau: 1902–1944*. Publication No. 240. Washington, D.C.: PASB, 1948.

Murray, C. J. L., and A. D. Lopez, eds. *Global Comparative Assessments in the Health Sector: Disease Burden, Expenditures, and Intervention Packages.* Geneva: WHO, 1994.

PAHO. *Caribbean Cooperation in Health: What It Is, How It Works.* Washington, D.C., 1989.

———. *Policies for the Production and Marketing of Essential Drugs.* Washington, D.C., 1984.

———. *Pro Salute Novi Mundi: A History of the Pan American Health Organization.* Washington, D.C., 1992.

Quenum, A. A. *Twenty Years of Political Struggle for Health.* Brazzaville: AFRO, 1985.

SEARO. *Contraceptive Research and Development, 1984–1994: The Road from Mexico City to Cairo.* New Delhi: Oxford University Press, 1994.

———. *WHO Representatives in the South-East Asian Region: Early Concept and Development of Functions.* New Delhi, 1964.

———. *The World Health Organization: Collaboration in Health Development in South-East Asia, 1948–1988.* New Delhi, 1988–92.

———. *The World Health Organization: A Decade of Health Development in South-East Asia, 1968–1977.* New Delhi, 1978.

———. *The World Health Organization: Twenty Years in South-East Asia, 1948–1967.* New Delhi, 1967.

Tabibzadeh, I., A. Rossi-Espagnet, and R. Maxwell. *Spotlight on the Cities: Improving Urban Health in Developing Countries.* Geneva: WHO, 1989.

Tarimo, E., and A. Creese. *Achieving Health for All by the Year 2000.* Geneva: WHO, 1990.

Tulloch, J., ed. *Smallpox Eradication in Somalia.* Alexandria: EMRO, 1981.

Weil, D. E. C., A. P. Alicbusan, J. F. Wilson, M. R. Reich, and D. J. Bradley. *The Impact of Development Policies on Health, A Review of the Literature.* Geneva: WHO, 1990.

WHO. *Achieving Reproductive Health for All: The Role of WHO.* Geneva, 1995.

———. *From Alma Ata to the Year 2000: Reflections at the Midpoint.* Geneva, 1988.

———. *Effects of Nuclear War on Health and Health Services.* Geneva, 1984.

———. *Essential Drugs: Action for Equity.* Geneva: Action Programme on Essential Drugs, 1995.

———. *The First Ten Years of the World Health Organization, 1948–1957.* Geneva, 1958.

———. *Guidelines on National Drug Policies.* Geneva, 1988.

———. *Health Aspects of Chemical and Biological Weapons.* Geneva, 1970.

———. *Health Programme Evaluation.* Geneva, 1981.

———. *Introducing WHO.* Geneva, 1976.

———. *Malaria Eradication: A Plea for Health.* Geneva, 1958.

———. *Perspectives for Health Development in the South-East Asia Region.* New Delhi: SEARO, 1981.

————. *The Primary Health Worker: Working Guide—Guidelines for Training, Guidelines for Adaptation.* Geneva, 1976.

————. *Publications of the World Health Organization, 1947–1957: A Bibliography.* Geneva, 1958.

————. *The Rational Use of Drugs: Report of the Conference of Experts, Nairobi, 25–29 November 1985.* Geneva, 1987.

————. *The Second Ten Years of the World Health Organization, 1958–1967.* Geneva, 1968.

————. *The Selection of Essential Drugs.* Geneva, 1977.

————. *Terminology of Malaria and Malaria Eradication.* Geneva, 1963.

————. *Women's Health: Across Age and Frontier.* Geneva, 1992.

————. *The World Drug Situation.* Geneva, 1988.

Wickett, J., and G. Meiklejohn, eds. *Smallpox Eradication in Ethiopia.* Brazzaville: AFRO, 1984.

Booklets

EMRO. *Hand in Hand towards Health for All.* Rev. ed. Alexandria, 1987.

EURO. *European Charter on Environment and Health.* Copenhagen, 1989.

————. *Health Promotion: A Discussion Document on the Concepts and Principles.* Copenhagen, 1985.

————. *WHO in a New Europe.* Copenhagen, 1993.

SEARO. *World Health Organization in the South-East Asia Region: Fostering the Spirit of Partnership.* New Delhi, 1994.

UNDP/UNESCO/UNFPA/UNICEF/WHO. *The 20/20 initiative.* New York: UNICEF, 1994.

WHO. *Development of Indicators for Monitoring Progress towards Health for All by the Year 2000.* Geneva, 1981.

————. *Evaluation of the Global Strategy for Health for All by the Year 2000.* Vol. 1, Global Review. Geneva, 1987.

————. *Facts about WHO.* Geneva, 1990.

————. *Four Decades of Achievement: Highlights of the Work of WHO.* Geneva, 1988.

————. *Global Strategy for Health for All by the Year 2000.* Geneva, 1981.

————. *Global Strategy for Health for All by the Year 2000: Political Dimensions.* Geneva, 1986.

————. *Glossary of Terms in the Health for All Series, nos. 1–8.* Geneva, 1984.

————. *Health in Development, Prospects for the 21st Century: Background Paper for the Task Force on Health and Development Policies.* Geneva, 1994.

————. *Implementation of the Global Strategy for Health for All by the Year 2000.* Vol. 1, Global Review. Geneva, 1993.

————. *International Code of Marketing of Breast-Milk Substitutes.* Geneva, 1981.

————. *Introducing WHO.* Geneva, 1976.

————. *IWC: Health Development in Countries in Greatest Need: Recent Experience, Current Trends, and Future Direction*. Geneva, 1993.

————. *IWC: Recent Experiences, Current Trends, and Future Directions*. Geneva, 1993.

————. *Our Planet, Our Health: A Report of the WHO Commission on Health and Environment*. Geneva, 1992.

————. *Renewing the Health-For-All Strategy: Guiding Principles and Essential Issues for the Elaboration of a Policy for Equity, Solidarity, and Health*. Geneva, 1995.

————. *Stop TB at the Source: WHO Report on the Tuberculosis Epidemic, 1995*. Geneva, 1995.

————. *Targets in Support of the European Strategy for Health for All*. Geneva: WHO/EURO, 1985.

————. *TB, A Global Emergency: WHO Report on the TB Epidemic*. Geneva, 1993.

————. *WHO: What It Is, What It Does*. Geneva, 1988.

————. *World Health Organization/World Bank Partnership: Recommendations for Action for Health Development*. Geneva, 1995.

WHO/Health and Welfare Canada/Canadian Public Health Association. *Ottawa Charter for Health Promotion*. Copenhagen: EURO, 1986.

WHO/UNICEF. *Alma-Ata: Primary Health Care*. Geneva, 1983.

WHO/UNICEF. *Primary Health Care*. Geneva, 1978.

Report Series

CIOMS (Council for International Organizations of Medical Sciences) Series

EMRO Technical Publications

Environmental Health Criteria

European Health for All Series (EURO)

Health and Safety Guides

Health for All Series

History of International Public Health

IARC Monographs on the Evaluation of Carcinogenic Risks to Humans

IARC Technical Reports

International Nomenclature of Diseases

PAHO Scientific Publications

PEEM Guidelines Series

Public Health in Action

Public Health in Europe (EURO)

Public Health Papers

SEARO Regional Health Papers

Technical Report Series

Western Pacific Education in Action Series

WHO AIDS Series
WHO Food Additives Series
WHO Offset Publications
WHO Public Health Papers
WHO Regional Publications, Eastern Mediterranean Series
WHO Regional Publications, European Series
WHO Regional Publications, South-East Asia Series
WHO Regional Publications, Western Pacific Series

Periodicals

Bulletin of the Pan American Health Organization
Bulletin of the World Health Organization
Essential Drugs Monitor
International Digest of Health Legislation
Weekly Epidemiological Record
WHO Chronicle
WHO Drug Information
WHO Features
World Health
World Health Forum
World Health Statistics Annual
World Health Statistics Quarterly

Newsletters

Action Contre le SIDA
African Community Health Newsletter (AFRO)
AIDS Action (Global Programme on AIDS)
AIDS/STD Health Promotion Exchange (Global Programme on AIDS)
Alerte PEV (Global Programme for Vaccines and Immunization)
Border Epidemiological Bulletin (PAHO)
Bridge (WHO Health Systems Research and Development Unit)
Bulletin: PanAfrican Centre for Emergency Preparedness and Response
Bulletin du Groupé Africain d'Action en Santé Mentale (Division of Mental
    Health)
Cancer Care (WHO National Cancer Control Programmes)
Changing Medical Education and Medical Practice (Division of Development
    of Human Resources for Health)
Child Survival–World Development (WHO/UNICEF/World Bank/
    UNDP/Rockefeller Foundation)
CIDA-SCAN-IPDE Newsletter (Division of Mental Health)
CINDI Connection (EURO)

CVI Forum: News from the Children's Vaccine Initiative (Global Programme for Vaccines and Immunization)

Diabcare, St. Vincent Declaration Newsletter (EURO)

Disasters: Preparedness and Mitigation in the Americas (PAHO)

Entre Nous (EURO)

EPI Alert (Global Programme for Vaccines and Immunization)

EPI Newsletter (Special Programme for Vaccines and Immunization)

Epidemiological Bulletin (PAHO)

Essential Drugs Monitor (Action Programme on Essential Drugs)

European Bulletin on Environment and Health (EURO)

Europharm Forum Newsletter (EURO)

GEENET Update (Office of Global and Integrated Environmental Health)

GETNET Update (Office of Global and Integrated Environmental Health)

Global AIDSNEWS (Global Programme on AIDS)

HBI News (Health and Biomedical Information Programme)

Health and Development (WPRO)

Healthy Aging (EURO)

HEDIP Forum (Division of Emergency and Humanitarian Action)

HELLIS Newsletter (SEARO)

HFA 2000 (SEARO)

Human Ecology and Health (PAHO)

INPPAZ (Pan American Institute for Food Protection and Zoonoses)

IPCS (International Programme on Chemical Safety)

LEP News (Action Programme for the Elimination of Leprosy)

Liaison (Office of Library and Health Literature Services)

Mental Health News (Division of Mental Health)

ONCHO Information (Onchocerciasis Control Programme)

Oratel Newsletter (EURO)

PAHO Today

Progress in Human Reproduction Research (Special Programme of Research, Development and Research Training in Human Reproduction)

Quality of Care and Technologies Newsletter (EURO)

Safe Motherhood (Division of Family Health)

SEARO News

Skills for Life (Division of Mental Health)

TDR News (UNDP/World Bank/WHO Special Programme for Research and Training in Tropical Diseases)

Technet News: Logistics for Health (Global Programme for Vaccines and Immunization)

Tobacco Alert (Tobacco or Health Programme)

Update (Division of Diarrhoeal and Acute Respiratory Disease Control)

Update: Global Programme for Vaccines (Global Programme for Vaccines and Immunization)

WHO *Environmental Health Newsletter* (Division of Environmental Health)

WHO *Library Digest for Africa* (Office of Library and Health Literature Services)

WHO *Pharmaceuticals Newsletter* (Division of Drug Management and Policies)

WHO *Surveillance Programme for Control of Foodborne Infections and Intoxications in Europe Newsletter* (EURO)

General Bibliography

History of Medicine and the Founding of WHO

Alexandrowijz, C. "The World Health Organization." In *World Economic Agencies: Law and Practice,* ed. C. Alexandrowijz, 125–32. London: Stevens and Sons, 1962.

Allen, C. "World Health and World Politics." *International Organization* 4, no. 1 (1950): 27–43.

Balinska, M. "Ludwik Rajchman, International Health Leader." *World Health Forum* 12 (1991): 456–65.

———. *Une Vie pour l'Humanitaire: Ludwik Rajchman, 1881–1965.* Paris: La Découverte, 1995.

Berridge, V. "Health and Medicine in the Twentieth Century: Contemporary History and Health Policy." *Social History of Medicine* (1992): 307–16.

"Bibliography of the Technical Work of the Health Organization of the League of Nations, 1920–1945." *Bulletin of the Health Organization* 11 (1945): 1–235.

Boudreau, F. "International Health: Our stake in World Health." *American Journal of Public Health* 41 (1951): 1477–82.

Brockington, F. "The World Health Organization (W.H.O.)." In *The United Nations: The First Ten Years,* ed. B. Wortley, 130–49. Manchester: Manchester University Press, 1957.

Calderwood, H. "The Founding of a Single International Health Organization." *WHO Chronicle* 29 (1975): 435–37.

Candau, M. "W.H.O.—Prospects and Opportunities: The Road Ahead." *American Journal of Public Health* 44 (1954): 1499–1504.

———. "World Health Catalysts." *American Journal of Public Health* 47 (1957): 675–81.

Chisholm, B. "Barriers to World Health." *International Conciliation* 491 (1953): 260–66.

———. "International Health: The Role of W.H.O., Past, Present, and Future." *American Journal of Public Health* 41 (1951): 1460–63.

———. "Is the World Health Organization Succeeding in Its Work?" In *Uphill,* ed. S. W. Pollak. London: United Nations Association, pp. 25–32.

———. "The World Health Organization." *British Medical Journal* 1 (May 6, 1950): 1021–27.

———. "World Health Organization." *External Affairs* 2: 135–38.

Clark, R. "The Work of W.H.O." *Sanitarian* 64 (1955): 53–55.

Dorolle, P. "L'Organisation Mondiale de la Santé." In *Somme de Médicine contemporaine, vol. 4,* 241–52. Paris: Editions médicales, 1955.

Doull, J. "The World Health Organization." *International Journal of Leprosy* 14 (1946): 110–115.

Dubin, M. "The League of Nations Health Organisation." In *International Health Organisations and Movements 1918–1939,* ed. P. Weindling, 56–80. Cambridge: Cambridge University Press, 1995.

Farley, J."The International Health Division of the Rockefeller Foundation: The Russell Years, 1920–1934. In *International Health Organisations and Movements 1918–1939,* ed. P. Weindling, 203–21. Cambridge: Cambridge University Press, 1995.

Ferreira, M. J. "The Structure, Functions and Aims of the World Health Organization." *International Nursing Review* 1, (1954): 27–34.

Gear, H. "Developments in the World Health Organization." *South African Medical Journal* 23 (1949): 608–12.

———. "Some Principles and Methods of International Health Work." *British Medical Journal* 2 (August 25, 1956): 471–75.

———. "The World Health Organization: New York Conference, 1946." *South African Medical Journal* 20, (1946): 515–17.

———. "World Health Organization and the Palais des Nations, Geneva." *Nursing Times* 51 (1955): 377–78, 383–84.

Goodman N. *International Health Organizations and Their Work,* 2nd ed. Edinburgh: Churchill Livingstone, 1971.

———. "The World Health Organization and Its Interim Commission." *Lancet* 2 (1946): 358–59.

Grmek, M. D., ed. *Serving the Cause of Public Health: Selected Papers of Andrija Stampar.* Zagreb: University of Zagreb, 1966.

Hobson, W. *World Health and History.* Bristol: John Wright, 1963.

Howard-Jones, N. "International Public Health: The Organizational Problems between the Two World Wars, Epilogue." *WHO Chronicle* 32 (1978): 156–66.

———. *International Public Health between the Two World Wars: The Organizational Problems.* Geneva: WHO History of International Public Health Series, 1978.

———. *The Scientific Background of the International Sanitary Conferences, 1851–1938.* Geneva: WHO History of International Public Health Series, 1975.

Hutchinson, J. "'Custodians of the Sacred Fire': The ICRC and the Postwar Reorganisation of the International Red Cross." In *International Health Organisations and Movements, 1918–1939*, ed. P. Weindling, 17–35. Cambridge: Cambridge University Press, 1995.

———. "Rethinking the Origins of the Red Cross." *Bulletin of the History of Medicine* 63 (1989): 557–78.

Kerr, J., ed. *Building the Health Bridge: Selections from the Works of Fred L. Soper*. Bloomington: Indiana University Press, 1970.

Lacaisse, R. *L'Hygiène internationale et la Société des Nations*. Paris: Editions du 'Mouvement Sanitaire', 1926.

Levy, D. "L'Organisation mondiale de la Santé." *Revue International Histoire Politique Constitutional* 4 (January–March 1954): 64–79.

MacKenzie, M. "International Collaboration in Health." *International Affairs* 26 (1950): 515–21.

———. "The World Health Organization." *British Medical Journal* 2 (September 21, 1946): 428–30.

Maclean, F. "The World Health Organization and Its Work." *New Zealand Medical Journal* 52 (1953): 469–74.

Mani, C. "The Early Days of WHO." Parts 1 and 2. *WHO Dialogue* 14 (October 1973); 15 (November 1973).

———. "The Interim Commission, 1946–1948." *WHO Dialogue* 22 (July/August 1974):

Martikainen, A. "The Work for World Health." *Health Education Journal* 13 (1955): 239–45.

Masters, R. *International Organization in the Field of Public Health*. Washington, D.C.: Carnegie Endowment for International Peace, 1947.

Osborne A. S. (1954), "W.H.O.: Report from the United States." *American Journal of Public Health* 44 (1954): 1505–08.

Parran, T. "Charter for World Health." *Public Health Reports* 61 (1946): 1265.

———. "World Health Organization." *Yale Journal of Biological Medicine* 19 (1947): 401–10.

Parran, T., and F. Boudreau. "The World Health Organization: Cornerstone of Peace." *American Journal of Public Health* 36 (1946): 1267–72.

Penrose, A., and J. Seaman. "The Save the Children Fund and Nutrition for Refugees." In *"The Conscience of the World": The Influence of Non-Governmental Organisations in the U.S. System*, ed. P. Willets, 214–40. London: C. Hurst and Co., 1996.

Perkins, J. "The World Health Organization." *Journal of Dental Medicine* 10 (1953): 107–15.

Roemer, M. "Internationalism and Public Health." In *Companion Encyclopaedia of the History of Medicine*. London: Routledge, 1991.

Sand, R. "The World Health Organization." *Survey Graphic* 35 (1946): 352–53.

Sharp, W. "The New World Health Organization." *American Journal of International Law* 41, no. 3 (1947): 509–30.

Shimkin, M. "World Health Organization." *Science* 104 (1946): 281–83.

Soper, F. "The Pioneer International Health Organization." *Boletin de la OSP* 27, no. 10 (1948): 912–16.

———. *Ventures in World Health: The Memoirs of Fred Lowe Soper.* Washington, D.C.: PAHO, 1977.

Sutton, S. "G. Brock Chisholm: Canadian and World Citizen." *Canadian Mental Health* (November/December 1971):

Sze, S. "The Birth of WHO: Interview with Szeming Sze." *World Health* (May 1989): 28–29.

———. *The Origin of the World Health Organization: A personal Memoire, 1945–1948.* Boca Raton, Fla.: LISZ Publications, 1982.

———. "WHO: From Small Beginnings." *WHO Health Forum* 9 no. 1 (1988): 29–34.

United Nations Relief and Rehabilitation Administration. *The Story of UNRRA.* Washington, D.C.: UNRRA, 1948.

van Hyde, H. Z. "Challenges and Opportunities in World Health." *Department of State Bulletin* 19 (1948): 391–98.

———. "The International Health Conference." *Department of State Bulletin* 16 (1946): 453.

———. "The Nature of the World Health Organization." *Public Health Report* 68 (1953): 601–5.

———. "W.H.O.: The Catalyst in International Health." *Public Health Report* 70 (1955): 887–92.

———. "World Health Organization: Progress and Plans." *Department of State Bulletin* 18 (1948): 431–40.

Watson, J. "Ten Years of Progress: The Record of the World Health Organization." *Quarterly Review* (January 1959): 14–27.

Weindling, P. "The League of Nations and Medical Communication between the First and Second World Wars." In *Sciences et langues en Europe,* ed. P. Corsi and R. Chartier, 209–20. Paris: Centre Alexandre Koyre, 1996.

———, ed. *International Health Organisations and Movements, 1918–1939.* Cambridge: Cambridge University Press, 1995.

Williams, L. "The World Health Organization." *Southern Medical Journal* 40 (1947): 66–72.

Wilson, C. M. *One Half the People: Doctors and the Crisis of World Health.* New York: Sloane Associates, 1949.

Winslow, C. "International Co-operation in the Service of Health." *Annals of the American Academy of Political and Social Sciences* 273 (1951): 192–200.

———. "World Health Organization: Program and Accomplishments." *International Conciliation* 437 (1948): 109–52.

Wood, C., ed. *Tropical Medicine: From Romance to Reality*. London: Academic Press, 1978.

Woodbridge, G., ed. *UNRRA: The History of the United Nations Relief and Rehabilitation Administration*. New York: Columbia University Press, 1950.

"World Health Organization: Aims and Functions" *World Today* 6 (1950): 386–94.

WHO's Structure and Functions

Basch, P. *International Health*. Oxford: Oxford University Press, 1978.

———. *Textbook of International Health*. Oxford: Oxford University Press, 1990.

Beigbeder, Y. *L'Organisation Mondiale de la Santé*. Geneva: Publications de l'Institut Universitaire de Hautes Etudes Internationales, 1995.

Berkov, R. *The World Health Organization: A Study in Decentralized International Administration*. Geneva: Librairie E. Droz, 1957.

Brockington, F. *World Health*. London: Churchill Livingstone, 1975.

Buse, K. "Coordination of UN Health Activities at the Country Level: What Are the Formal Mechanisms?" *UN and Health Briefing Note* 4 (July 1996): 1–6.

Collinson, S. "Global Coordination of UN Health Activities: What Are the Formal Mechanisms?" *UN and Health Briefing Note* 2 (October, 1995): 1–6.

Corrigan, P. *The World Health Organization: People, Politics, and Powers*. Hove, East Sussex: Wayland, 1979.

Daes, E., and A. Daoudy. *Decentralization of Organisations within the United Nations System*. Part 3, *The World Health Organization*. Geneva: UN Joint Inspection Unit, 1993.

Fluss, S. S., and F. Gutteridge. *World Health Organization*. Boston: Kluwer Law and Taxation Publishers, 1993.

Foster, G. "Bureaucratic Aspects of International Health Agencies." *Social Science and Medicine* 25, no. 9 (1987): 1039–48.

Freeman, H. *The Politics of Global Health*. Washington, D.C.: U.S. House of Representatives Committee on Foreign Affairs, Committee Print in Science, Technology, and American Diplomacy Series, 1971.

Jacobson, H. K. "WHO: Medicine, Regionalism, and Managed Politics." In *The Anatomy of Influence: Decision Making in International Organization*, ed. R. W. Cox and H. K. Jaconson, 175–215. New Haven: Yale University Press, 1974.

Koivusalo, M., and E. Ollila. *International Organizations and Health Policies*. Helsinki: National Research and Development Centre for Welfare and Health, 1996.

Lee, K. "Who Does What in Health? Mandates within the United Nations System." *UN and Health Briefing Note* 1 (September, 1995): 1–6.

Lee, K., S. Collinson, G. Walt, and L. Gilson. "Who Should Be Doing What in International Health: A Confusion of Mandates in the United Nations?" *British Medical Journal* 312 (February 3, 1996): 302–7.

Leive, D. *International Regulatory Regimes: Case Studies in Health, Meterology, and Food. Vol. 1.* Lexington, Mass.: Lexington Books, 1976.

Lucas, A., S. Mogedal, G. Walt, S. Hodne Steen, S. E. Kruse, K. Lee, L. Hawken. *A Study of WHO's Support to Countries.* London: London School of Hygiene and Tropical Medicine, 1997.

Mahler, H. "An International Health Conscience." *WHO Chronicle* 28 (1974): 207–11.

Peabody, J. "An Organizational Analysis of the World Health Organization: Narrowing the Gap between Promise and Performance." *Social Science and Medicine* 40, no. 6 (1995): 731–42.

Siddiqi, J. *World Health and World Politics: The World Health Organization and the UN System.* London: Hurst and Company, 1995.

WHO Regional Offices

Begg, N. "W.H.O. in Europe, with Particular Reference to Work in Public Health Fields." *Public Health* 68 (1954): 43–47.

Calderwood, H. "The World Health Organization and Its Regional Organizations." *Temple Law Quarterly* 37, no. 1 (1963): 15–27.

Chagas, A. "The Work of W.H.O. in Latin America." *American Journal of Nursing* 53 (1953): 410–11.

Clements, F. "The W.H.O. in Southern Asia and the Western Pacific." *Pacific Affairs* 25, no. 2 (1952): 334–48.

Csillag, C. "Europe: Aid for WHO's New Members." *Lancet* 342 (September 26, 1992): 781.

Fang, I. "W.H.O. in the Western Pacific Region." *Journal of the American Medical Women's Association* 39 (1954): 31–36.

Godlee, F. "The Regions: Too Much Power, Too Little Effect (Part 3)." *British Medical Journal* 39 (December 10, 1994): 1566–70.

Goel, S. *International Administration: WHO South-East Asia Regional Office.* New Delhi: Sterling Publications, 1977.

Haralson, M. "The Organization and Aims of the Pan American Sanitary Bureau in the Americas and along the U.S.–Mexico Border." *Boletin de la OSP* 27, no. 10 (1948): 917–25.

Hasselmann, C. "Aims and Activities of the World Health Organization, Especially in South-East Asia," *O.S.R. News* 3 (1951): 222–24.

Horine, F. "Public Health in Asia: The Personal Impressions of a Public Information Officer." *Journal of Tropical Medicine and Hygiene* 59 (1956): 175–79.

Howard-Jones, N. "The Pan American Health Organization: Origins and Evolution." *WHO Chronicle* 34 (1980): 367–75, 419–26; also available as WHO History of International Public Health Series, No. 5, Geneva.

Mani, C. "International Health 4: Application of W.H.O. Programs and Policies in a Region." *American Journal of Public Health* 41 (1951): 1469–72.

Prost, A. "WHO and the European Union: A Partnership for Health." *Eurohealth* 2, no. 1 (1996): 4–5.

Samson, K. "The Record of WHO and PAHO." *UN Special* 1 (1995): 18–20.

Shousha, A. "Activities of the World Health Organization in the Eastern Mediterranean Region." *American Journal of Public Health* 44 (1954): 18–25.

Soper, F. "International Health 3: Some Aspects of the W.H.O.'s Programs in the Americas." *American Journal of Public Health* 41 (1951): 1464–68.

———. "The Pan American Sanitary Bureau." *Courier of the George Washington University Medical Center* 7, no. 1 (1955): 20–24.

Strong, P. "A New-Modelled Medicine? Comments on the WHO's Regional Strategy for Europe." *Social Science and Medicine* 22, no. 2 (1986): 193–99.

United States Senate. *Health in the Americas and the Pan American Health Organization.* Washington, D.C.: Committee on Government Operations of the United States Senate, 1980.

Wegman, M. "A Salute to the Pan American Health Organization." *American Journal of Public Health* 67, no. 12 (1977): 1198–1204.

"WHO's Six Regions." *World Health* (October 1980).

Finances of WHO

Boudreau, F. "Meeting World Health Problems: The Need for Money Resources." *Public Health Report* 67 (1952): 329–32.

Hoole, F. *Politics and Budgeting in the World Health Organization.* Bloomington: Indiana University Press, 1976.

Howard, L. "Where is the money to come from?" *World Health* (1986): 9–10.

Michaud, C., and C. J. L. Murray. "External Assistance to the Health Sector in Developing Countries: A Detailed Analysis, 1972–1990." *Bulletin of the World Health Organization* 72, no. 4 (1994): 639–51. Also in *Global Comparative Assessments in the Health Sector: Disease Burden, Expenditures, and Intervention Packages,* ed. C. J. L. Murray and A. D. Lopez, 157–70. Geneva: WHO, 1994.

Revzin, P. "Money Squeeze: UN's Health Agency Finds Funds Shrinking." *Wall Street Journal* April 7, 1988.

Roemer, J. E. "Distributing Health: The Allocation of Resources by an International Agency." In *The Quality of Life*, ed. A. Sen and M. Nussbaum. Oxford: Oxford University Press, 1993.

Taylor, P. "The United Nations System under Stress: Financial Pressures and Their Consequences." *Review of International Studies*, 17, no. 4 (1991): 365–82.

Vaughan, J. P., S. Mogedal, S. E. Kruse, K. Lee, G. Walt, and K. de Wilde. *Cooperation for Health Development: Extrabudgetary Funds in the World Health Organisation*, Oslo: Governments of Australia, Norway and the United Kingdom, 1995.

———. "Financing the World Health Organisation: Global Importance of Extrabudgetary Funds." *Health Policy* 35 (1996): 229–45.

Vaughan, J. P., S. Mogedal, G. Walt, S. E. Kruse, K. Lee, and K. de Wilde. "WHO and the Effects of Extrabudgetary funds: Is the Organization Being Donor Driven?" *Health Policy and Planning* 11, no. 3 (1996): 253–64.

Reform of WHO

Ascher, C. "Current Problems in the World Health Organization's Program." *International Organization* 6, no. 1 (1952): 27–50.

Brooks, R. "Saving the World Health Organization from a Poison Pill." *Heritage Foundation Backgrounder* no. 471 (November 19, 1985).

Chen, L., D. Bell, and L. Bates. "World Health and Institutional Change." In *Enhancing the Performance of International Health Institutions*, by Pocantico Retreat, 9–21. New York: Rockefeller Foundation, Social Science Research Council, Harvard School of Public Health, February 1996.

Dag Hammarskjold Foundation. "Global Health Cooperation in the Twenty-first Century and the Role of the UN System: Report from a Consultation in Uppsala, Sweden." April 1996.

Edgren, G., and B. Moller. "The Agencies at a Crossroads: The Role of the United Nations Specialized Agencies." In *The United Nations Issues and Options: Five Studies on the Role of the UN in the Economic and Social Fields, Report of the Nordic UN Project*, 115–78. Stockholm: Almqvist and Wiksell, 1991.

Ermakov, V. "Reform of the World Health Organization." *Lancet* 347 (1996): 1536–37.

Forss, K., B. Stenson, and G. Sterky. "The Future of Global Health Cooperation: Designing a New World Health Organization." *Current Issues in Public Health* 2 (1996): 138–42.

Frenk, J., C. Gwin, and J. Nelson. "The Multilateral Development Banks and Health." In *Enhancing the Performance of International Health Institutions*, by Pocantico Retreat, 40–48. New York: Rockefeller Foundation,

Social Science Research Council, Harvard School of Public Health, February 1996.

Godlee, F. "Interview with the Director General." *British Medical Journal* 310 (March 4, 1995): 583–86.

———. "WHO at Country Level: A Little Impact, No Strategy." *British Medical Journal* 309 (December 17, 1994): 1636–39.

———. "WHO in Crisis." *British Medical Journal* 309 (November 26, 1994): 1424–29.

———. "WHO in Europe: Does It Have a Role?" *British Medical Journal* 310 (February 11, 1995): 389–93.

———. "WHO in Retreat: Is It Losing Its Influence?" *British Medical Journal* 309 (December 3, 1994): 1491–95.

———. "Who's Special Programmes: Undermining from Above." *British Medical Journal* 310 (January 21, 1995): 178–82.

———. "The World Health Organisation in Africa: Too Much Politics, Too Little Effect." *British Medical Journal* 309 (September 3, 1994): 553–54.

Kickbusch, I. "World Health Organization: Change and Progress." *British Medical Journal* 310 (June 10, 1995): 1518–20.

Lee, K., and G. Walt. "What Role for WHO in the 1990s?" *Health Policy and Planning* 7, no. 4 (1992): 387–90.

Pilon, J. "For the World Health Organization, the Moment of Truth: A United Nations Assessment Project." *Heritage Foundation Backgrounder* (April 1986).

Sapirie, S. "What Does 'Health Futures' Mean to WHO and the World?" *World Health Statistics Quarterly* 47 no. 3/4 (1994): 98–100.

Smith, R. "The WHO: Change or Die." *British Medical Journal* 310 (March 4, 1995): 543–44.

Stenson, B., and G. Sterky. "What Future WHO?" *Health Policy* 28 (1994): 235–56.

Sterky, G., K. Forss, and B. Stenson. *Tomorrow's Global Health Organization: Ideas and Options.* Stockholm: Swedish Ministry for Foreign Affairs, 1997.

Tollison, R. D., and R. E. Wagner. *Who Benefits from WHO? The Decline of the World Health Organization.* London: Social Affairs Unit, 1993.

Walt, G. "International Organizations in Health: The Problem of Leadership." In *Enhancing the Performance of International Health Institutions,* by Pocantico Retreat, 23–37. New York: Rockefeller Foundation, Social Science Research Council, Harvard School of Public Health, February 1996.

———. "WHO under Stress: Implications for Health Policy." *Health Policy* 24 (1993): 125–44.

Wildavsky, A. "Doing Better and Feeling Worse: The Political Pathology of Healthy Policy." *Daedalus* 106 (1989): 105–24.

Primary Health Care/Health for All Strategy

Baum, F., and D. Sanders. "Can Health Promotion and Primary Health Care Achieve Health for All without a Return to Their More Radical Agenda?" *Health Promotion International* 10 (1995): 149–60.

Bossert, T., and D. Parker. "The Political and Administrative Context of Primary Health Care in the Third World." *Social Science and Medicine* 18, no. 8 (1984): 693–702.

Bryant, J. "Health for All: The Dream and the Reality." *World Health Forum* 9, no. 3 (1988): 291–302.

Christiansen, J. "WHO and UNICEF Conference in the Soviet Union: Development of Primary Health Care Is Major Concern Everywhere." *Sairaanhoitaja* 54, no. 22 (1978): 16–18.

Gunning-Schepers, L. "Health for All by the Year 2000: A Mere Slogan or a Workable Formula?" *Health Policy* 6 (1986): 227–34.

Ko Ko, U. "MCH in the Context of Primary Health Care: The WHO Perspective." In *Health Care of Women and Children in Developing Countries*, ed. H. Wallace and K. Giri. Oakland: Third Party, 1990.

Mahler, H. "The Meaning of 'Health for All by the Year 2000.' " *World Health Forum* 2, no. 1 (1981): 5–22.

———. "Springboard for Action for Health for All." *WHO Chronicle* 40, no. 3 (1986): 109–15.

Navarro, V. "A Critique of the Ideological and Political Positions of the Willy Brandt Report and the WHO Alma Ata Declaration." *Social Science and Medicine* 18, no. 6 (1984): 467–74.

Patel, M. "An Economic Evaluation of 'Health for All,' " *Health Policy and Planning* 1, no. 1 (1986): 37–47.

Rathwell, T. "Realities of Health for All by the year 2000." *Social Science and Medicine* 35, no. 4 (1992): 541–47.

Rifkin, S., and G. Walt. "Why Health Improves: Defining the Issues Concerning Comprehensive Primary Health Care and Selective Primary Health Care." *Social Science and Medicine* 23 (1986): 559–66.

Segall, M. "The Politics of Primary Health Care." *IDS Bulletin* 14 (1983): 27–37.

Unger, J., and J. Killingsworth. "Selective Primary Health Care: A Critical Review of Methods and Results." *Social Science and Medicine* 22 (1986): 1001–13.

Walsh, J. "Selectivity within Primary Health Care." *Social Science and Medicine* 26, no. 9 (1988): 899–902.

Walsh, J. and K. Warren, "Selective Primary Health Care: An Interim Strategy for Disease Control in Developing Countries." *New England Journal of Medicine* 301 (1979): 967–74.

———, eds. *Strategies for Primary Health Care*. Chicago: Chicago University Press, 1986.

Walt, G., and S. Rifkin. *The PHC Approach in Developing Countries*. London: London School of Hygiene and Tropical Medicine, 1981.

Warren, K. "The Alma-Ata Declaration: Health for All by the Year 2000." *Encyclopaedia Britannica Year Book*. Chicago: Encyclopaedia Britannica, 1990.

Werner, D. "The Life and Death of Primary Health Care." *Third World Resurgence* 42/43 (1994): 10–14.

Wisner, B. "GOBI versus PHC? Some Dangers of Selective Primary Health Care." *Social Science and Medicine* 26, no. 9 (1988): 963–69.

Technical Cooperation for Health Development

Alleyne, G. "Towards a Taxonomy of Technical Cooperation in Health." *Bulletin of the PAHO* 25, no. 4 (1991): 356–65.

Antezana, F. "A View from the World Health Organization: Cooperation between WHO and Industry on Projects in the Third World." In *Pharmaceutical Industry Projects in the Third World: Proceedings of the IFPMA International Seminar, Geneva, 13–14 December 1989*. Geneva: International Federation of Pharmaceutical Manufacturers Association, 1990.

COWIConsult. "Evaluation of WHO's Development Cooperation, WHO's Position and Role in the United Nations: Trends and Reform Requirements." Discussion Paper for the Governments of Australia, Netherlands, Norway, and the United Kingdom, Copenhagen, September 1993.

DANIDA. *Effectiveness of Multilateral Agencies at Country Level: WHO in Kenya, Nepal, Sudan, and Thailand*. Copenhagen: CowiConsult/Ministry of Foreign Affairs, 1991.

Forbes, J. "International Cooperation in Public Health and the World Health Organization." In *The Theory and Structures of International Political Economy*, ed. T. Sandler, 115–31. Boulder, Co.: Westview, 1980.

Forrest, W. "Health Aspects of International Approaches to Problems of Undeveloped Areas." *Milbank Memorial Fund Quarterly* 26 (1948): 280–91.

Howard, L. "The Evolution of Bilateral and Multilateral Cooperation for Health in Developing Countries. In *International Cooperation for health: problems, prospects and priorities*, ed. M. Reich and E. Mariu, 332–57. Dover, Mass.: Auburn House, 1989.

"International Technical Assistance in Public Health." *Public Health Report* 67 (19521): 333–57.

"The Rise of International Cooperation in Health." *World Health Forum* 16, no. 4 (1995): 388–93.

Severyns, P., I. Buxell, J. Martin, and L. Friero. *Evaluation of UNFPA/WHO Inter-Country Project in Family Health*. New York: UNFPA, 1982.

Stenson, B., and G. Sterky. *SAREC/SIDA and WHO: A New Approach*.

Stockholm: Department of International Health Care Research, Karolinska Institutet, 1993.

Turshen, M., and A. Thebaud. "International Medical Aid." *Monthly Review* (December 7, 1981): 39–50.

WHO/UNICEF Code on the Marketing of Breast Milk Substitutes

Adelman, C. "The Case against the Case against Infant Formula." *Policy Review* (Winger 1983): 107–26.

Allain, A. "Breastfeeding Is Politics: A Personal View of the International Baby Milk Campaign." *Ecologist* 21 (1991): 206–13.

Chetley, A. *The Baby Killer Scandal.* London: War on Want, 1979.

———. *The Politics of Babyfood.* London: Frances Pinter, 1986.

Fatouros, A. "On the Implementation of International Codes of Conduct: An Analysis of Future Experience." *American University Law Review* 30 (1980):

Feld, W. *Multinational Corporations and U.N. Politics: The Quest for Codes of Conduct.* New York: Pergamon, 1980.

Fikentscher, W. "United Nations Codes of Conduct: New Paths in International Law." *American Journal of Comparative Law* 30 (1982): 590–93.

Lemaresquier, T. "Beyond Infant Feeding: The Case for Another Relationship between NGOs and the United Nations System." *Development Dialogue* 1 (1980): 120–25.

Leonard, S. "International Health and Transnational Business: Conflict or Cooperation?" *Review Internationale des Sciences Administratives* 49, no. 3 (1986): 259–68.

Mingst, K. "The United States and the World Health Organization." In *The United States and Multilateral Institutions,* ed. M. Karns and K. Mingst, 205–30. Boston: Unwin Myman, 1990.

"The Rational Use of Drugs and WHO." *Development Dialogue* 2 (1985): 1–4.

Reid, S. "Pressure and Policy in the Specialized Agencies of the United Nations: The Role of Interest Groups in the Creation and Implementation of the WHO/UNICEF International Code of Marketing of Breast-Milk Substitutes, 1979–1992." Master's thesis, Cambridge University, 1992.

Sethi, P. *The Righteous and the Powerful: Corporations, Religious Institutions, and International Social Activism—The Case of the Infant Formula Controversy and the Nestle Boycott.* Marshfield, Mass.: Pitman, 1985.

Shubber, S. "The International Code of Marketing of Breast-Milk Substitutes." *International Digest of Health Legislation* 36 (1985): 877–908.

Sikkink, K. "Codes of Conduct for Transnational Corporations: The Case of the WHO/UNICEF Code." *International Organization* 40, no. 4 (1986): 815–40.

Starrels, J. *The World Health Organization: Resisting Third World Ideological Pressures.* Washington, D.C.: Heritage Foundation, 1985.

Drug Policies

Bennet, F. "The Dilemma of Essential Drugs in Primary Health Care." *Social Science and Medicine* 28, no. 28 (1989): 1085–90.

Berridge, V. *The Society for the Study of Addiction: Alcohol and Drug Treatment and Control, 1884–1988.* London: Society for the Study of Addiction, 1990.

Chetley, A. *A Healthy Business? World Health and the Pharmaceutical Industry.* London: Zed Books, 1990.

Chowdhury, Z. *The Politics of Essential Drugs, The Makings of a Successful Health Strategy: Lessons from Bangladesh.* London: Zed Books, 1996.

Chowdhury, Z., and S. Chowdhury. "Essential Drugs for the Poor: Myth and Reality in Bangladesh." *Ecodevelopment News (Paris)* (December 23, 1982).

Collier, J., and R. Fox. "WHO Seeks Ways to Improve Control of Drug Promotion." *Lancet* 343 (April 17, 1993): 1017.

Cone, E. "International Regulation of Pharmaceuticals: The Role of the World Health Organization." *Virginia Journal of International Law* 23 (1982–83).

Howard, N., and R. Laing. "Changes in the World Health Organisation Essential Drug List." *Lancet* 338 (September 21, 1991): 743–45.

Kanji, N., A., Hardon, J. W. Harmeijer, M. Mamdani, and G. Walt. *Drugs Policy in Developing Countries.* London: Zed Books, 1992.

Lauridsen, E. "The World Health Organization Action Programme on Essential Drugs." *Danish Medical Bulletin* 31, no. 1 (1984):

London School of Hygiene and Tropical Medicine/Royal Tropical Institute. *An Evaluation of WHO's Action Programme on Essential Drugs.* London: Management Advisory Committee, 1989.

Lunde, P. "WHO's Programme on Essential Drugs: Background, Implementation, Present State, and Prospectives." *Danish Medical Bulletin* 31, no. 1 (1982):

Mamdami, M., and G. Walker. *Essential Drugs and Developing Countries.* London: London School of Hygiene and Tropical Medicine, 1985.

Medewar, C. *Drugs and World Health.* The Hague: International Organization of Consumers Unions, 1984.

———. "International Regulation of the Supply and Use of Pharmaceuticals." *Development Dialogue* 2 (1985): 15–37.

Melrose, D. *Bitter Pills: Medicines and the Third World.* Oxford: Oxfam, 1982.

Mills, A., and G. Walker. "Drugs for the Poor of the Third World: Consumption and Distribution." *Journal of Tropical Medicine and Hygiene* 86 (1983): 139–45.

Nakajima, H. "How Essential is an Essential Drugs Policy?" *World Health* (March/April 1992): 3.

Reich, M. "Essential Drugs: Economics and Politics in International Health." *Health Policy* 8 (1987): 39–57.

Wolff, P. O. "The Activities of the World Health Organization in Drug Addiction." *British Journal of Addiction* 50 (1953): 12–28.

Disease Prevention, Control, Treatment, and Eradication Programs

HIV/AIDS

"AIDS and the World Health Organization." *Bulletin of the World Health Organization* 63 (1985): 667–72.

Berridge, V. "The History of AIDS." *AIDS 92/93: A Year in Review* 7, no. 1 (1993): S243–48.

Berridge, V., and P. Strong, eds. *AIDS and Contemporary History*. Cambridge: Cambridge Monographs in the History of Medicine, 1993.

Bhatt, R. "Building Cooperation: The Formation of an International AIDS Regime, 1981–1988." Master's thesis, Oxford University, 1994.

Collinson, S., and K. Lee. "What the United Nations Does on HIV/AIDS: From the WHO Global Programme on AIDS to UNAIDS." *UN and Health Briefing Note* 5 (September 1996): 1–6.

Ewing, T. "AIDS Programme Faces Donor Fatigue." *Nature* 346 (1990): 595.

Gordenker, L., R. Coate, C. Jonsson, and P. Soderholm. *International Cooperation in Response to AIDS*. London: Frances Pinter, 1995.

Johnstone, B. "World Health Organization Plans Better AIDS Management." *Nature* 325 (1987): 473.

Lee, K., and A. Zwi. "A Global Political Economy Approach to AIDS: Ideology, Interests, and Implications." *New Political Economy* 1, no. 3 (1996): 355–73.

Leeson, J. "Health for All: Lessons from HIV/AIDS Reflections of a Jobbing Public Health Doctor." *Public Health* 105, no. 1 (1991): 51–54.

MacGregor, A. "Renewed UN Drive against AIDS." *Lancet* 334 (December 17, 1994): 1693–94.

———. "WHO: Combined Forces against AIDS." *Lancet* 343 (May 22, 1993): 1336.

MacKenzie, M. "AIDS Director's Resignation Deepens Crisis in WHO." *New Scientist* (March 24, 1990).

Mann, J. "Global AIDS: Critical Issues for Prevention in the 1990s." *International Journal of Health Services* 21, no. 3 (1991): 553–59.

Mann, J., and J. Chin. "AIDS: A Global Perspective." *New England Journal of Medicine* 319 (1988): 302–3.

Mann, J., and K. Kay. "Confronting the pandemic: the World Health Organization's Global Programme on AIDS, 1986–1989." *AIDS* 5, supplement 2 (1991): S221–29.

Place, J. "WHO AIDS Program: Moving on a New Track." *Science* 254, no. 10 (1991): 511–12.

"Switzerland (WHO): Resignation of Dr. Jonathan Mann." *Lancet* 340, (March 24, 1990): 716.

Weindling, P. "The Politics of International Co-ordination to Combat Sexually Transmiotted Diseases, 1900–1980s." In *AIDS and contemporary History*, ed. V. Berridge and P. Strong, 93–107. Cambridge: Cambridge Monographs in the History of Medicine, 1993.

Malaria

Brown, J. Haworth, and A. Zahar. "Malaria Eradication and Control from a Global Standpoint." *Journal of Medical Entimology* 13, no. 1 (1976): 1–25.

Cleaver, H. "Malaria and the Political Economy of Public Health." *International Journal of Health Services* 7, no. 4 (1977): 557–79.

Farid, M. "The Malaria Programme: From Euphoria to Anarchy." *World Health Forum* 1, no. 1/2 (1980): 8–33.

Jackson, J. "Cognition, Power, and Interest in WHO Decision Making: Malaria, Leprosy, and the Creation of the World Health Organization." Ph.D. diss., University of Wales, Aberystwyth, 1997.

Jeffery, G. "Malaria Control in the Twentieth Century." *American Journal of Tropical Medicine and Hygiene* 25 (1976): 361–71.

Litsio, S. *The Tomorrow of Malaria*. London: Pluto Press/Pacific Press, 1996.

Manevy, J. "Il est quatre heures, docteur Malaria." *Realites* 122 (1956): 48–55.

Pampana, E. "The Eradication of Malaria." *Journal of the American Medical Women's Association* 7 (1952): 248–50.

———. "Malaria as a Problem for the World Health Organization." In *Proceedings of the Fourth International Congress of Tropical Medicine and Malaria*, 940–46. Washington, D.C.: U.S. Department of State, 1948.

Scholtens, R., R. Kaiser, and A. Langmuir. "An Epidemiologic Examination of the Strategy of Malaria Eradication." *International Journal of Epidemiology* 1 (1972): 15–24.

Siddiqi, J. *World Health and World Politics: The World Health Organization and the UN System*. London: Hurst and Company, 1995.

Polio

de Quadros, C., J. Andrus, J. Olive, C. de Macedo, and D. A. Henderson. "Polio Eradication from the Western Hemisphere." *Annual Review of Public Health* 113 (1992): 239–52.

de Quadros, C., J. Andrus, J. Olive, C. da Silveira, R. Eikhof, P. Carrasco, J. Fitzsimmons, and F. Pinheiro. "Eradication of Poliomyelitis: Progress in the Americas." *Pediatric Infectious Disease Journal* 10, no. 3 (1991): 222–29.

Melnick, J. "The Polio Virus and the Vaccines." *World Health* (December 1989): 13–15.

Smallpox

Bowers, J. "The Odyssey of Smallpox Vaccination." *Bulletin of the History of Medicine* 55 (1981): 17–33.

Brown, D. "Last Sufferer, Where Smallpox Hit End of the Road." *Washington Post,* January 28, 1993.

Deria, A., Z. Jezek, K. Markvart, P. Carrasco, and J. Weisfeld. "The World's Last Endemic Case of Smallpox: Surveillance and Containment Measures." *Bulletin of the World Health Organization* 58 (1980): 279–83.

Fenner, F. "Smallpox, 'The Most Dreadful Scourge of the Human Species': Its Global Spread and Recent Eradication." *Medical Journal of Australia* 2 (1985): 728–35, 841–46.

Foege, W. H., J. D. Millar, and D. A. Henderson. "Smallpox Eradication in West and Central Africa." *Bulletin of the World Health Organization* 52 (1975): 209–22.

Foster, S. "Smallpox Eradication: Lessons Learned in Bangladesh." *WHO Chronicle* 31 (1977): 245–47.

Henderson, D. A. "Smallpox-Eradication and Measles-Control Programs in West and Central Africa: Theoretical and Practical Approaches and Problems." In *Industry and Tropical Health.* Cambridge: Harvard School of Public Health, 1967.

Hopkins, D. "Lessons Learned beyond Smallpox Eradication." *Assignment Children* 69/72 (1985): 235–42.

———. "After Smallpox Eradication: Yaws?" *American Journal of Tropical Medicine and Hygiene* 25 (1976): 860–65.

Razzell, P. *The Conquest of Smallpox.* Firle: Caliban, 1977.

———. "Smallpox Extinction: A Note of Caution." *New Scientist* 71 (1976): 35.

Rodrigues, B. A. "Smallpox Eradication in the Americas." *Bulletin of the Pan American Health Organization* 9 (1975): 53–68.

Soper, F. L. "Smallpox: World Changes and Implications for Eradication." *American Journal of Public Health* 56 (1966): 1652–56.

Tulloch, J. "The Last 50 Years of Smallpox in Africa." *WHO Chronicle* 34 (1980): 407–12.

Tuberculosis

Berthet, E. "The Campaign against Tuberculosis and the World Health Organization." *Bulletin of the International Union against Tuberculosis* 20 (1950): 476–515.

Holm, J. "The Work of the W.H.O. in the Field of Tuberculosis." *Berita Kementerian Kesehatan Republik Indonesia* 6 (1957): 12–23.

Kochi, A. "The Global Tuberculosis Situation and the New Control Strategy of the World Health Organization." *Tubercle* 72 (1991): 1–6.

McDougall, J. "The World Health Organization and Tuberculosis." *British Medical Journal* 2 (August 13, 1949): 379–80.

———. "The World Health Organization and Tuberculosis: Aims, Objects, and Accomplishments." *American Review of Tuberculosis* 64 (1951): 218–22.

McWeeney, E. "The World Health Organization and Tuberculosis in India." *Journal of the American Medical Women's Association* 10 (1955): 231–33.

Soper, F. "Problems to Be Solved If the Eradication of Tuberculosis Is to Be Realized." *American Journal of Public Health* 52 (1962): 734–45.

Yuan, I., and C. Palmer. "The W.H.O. Tuberculosis Research Office: A Review of the First Four Years." *Public Health Report* 68 (1953): 678–86.

Other Diseases

Andrewes, C. "Work of World Influenza Centre." *Journal of the Royal Institute of Public Health* 15 (1952): 309–18.

Bauer, T. "Half Century of International Control of Venereal Diseases." *Public Health Report* 68 (1953): 779–87.

Chaussinand, R. "W.H.O. and Leprosy." *International Journal of Leprosy* 20 (1952): 115–16.

Culbertson, J. T. "Plans for United States Co-operation with the World Health Organization in the International Influenza Study Program." *American Journal of Public Health* 39 (1949): 37–43.

Cutler, J. C. "The Venereal Disease Programme of the World Health Organization: The Simla Training Centre and Demonstration Area." *Indian Medical Gazette* 85 (1950): 22–24.

Deutsch, A. *The World Health Organization: Its Global Battle against Disease.* New York: Public Affairs Committee, 1958.

Giaquinto, M. "Onchocerciasis: A New Field of Activities." *Journal of the American Medical Women's Association* 10 (1955): 226–30.

Hemming, J. *Mankind against the Killers,* London: Longman, 1956.

Henderson, D. A. "Round Table discussion: Lessons from the Big Eradication Campaigns." *World Health Forum* 2 (1981): 482–84.

Hinman, E. *World Eradication of Infectious Diseases*. Springfield, Ill.: Thomas, 1966.

Hopkins, D., A. Hinman, J. Koplan, and J. Lane. "The Case for Global Measles Eradication." *Lancet* 1 (1982): 1396–98.

Kaplan, M. "W.H.O. Progress in Brucellosis." *C.D.C. Bulletin* 10, no. 8 (1951): 8–11.

Meslin, F. K. Stohr, and D. Heymann. "BSE and Variant CJD: The Response of the World Health Organization." *Eurohealth* 2 (1996): 8–9.

Soper, F. "Rehabilitation of the Eradication Concept in Prevention of Communicable Diseases." *Public Health Reports* 80 (1965): 855–69.

Tsalikis, G. "The Onchocerciasis Control Programme in West Africa: A Review of Progress." *Health Policy and Planning* 8 (1993): 349–59.

Wade, H. "The I.L.A. and the W.H.O." *International Journal of Leprosy* 18 (1950): 525–29.

———. "The World Health Organization and Leprosy." *International Journal of Leprosy* 21 (1953): 78–82.

Williams, G. "WHO: The Days of the Mass Campaigns." *World Health Forum* 9, no. 1 (1988): 7–23.

World Bank. *Roger Chaufournier and the Onchocerciasis Program: A Tribute to One of its Founding Fathers*. Washington, D.C.: Africa Region, 1994.

Yekutiel, P. "Lessons from the Big Eradication Campaigns." *World Health Forum* 2, no. 4 (1981): 465–81.

Vaccines and Immunization

Goodfield, J. *A Chance to Live: The Heroic Story of the Global Campaign to Immunize the World's Children*. New York: Macmillan, 1991.

Goodman, H. "Immunodiplomacy: The story of WHO's Immunology Research Program, 1961–1975." In *Essays on the History of Immunology*, ed. P. Mazumdar. Toronto: Wall and Thompson, 1989.

Muraskin, W. "Origins of the Children's Vaccine Initiative: The Intellectual Foundations." *Social Science and Medicine* 42, no. 12 (1996): 1703–19.

———. "Origins of the Children's Vaccine Initiative: The Political Foundations." *Social Science and Medicine* 42, no. 12 (1996): 1721–34.

Weindling, P. "Victory with Vaccines: The Problem of Typhus Vaccines during the Second World War." In *Vaccina, Vaccination, Vaccinology: Jenner, Pasteur, and Their Successors*, ed. S. Plotkin and B. Fantini, 341–47. Paris: Elsevier, 1996.

Wright, P. "Global Immunization: A Medical Perspective." *Social Science and Medicine* 41, no. 5 (1995): 609–16.

Health Legislation, Standards, and Guidelines

Biraud, Y. "Epidemiological Aspects of the Work of the World Health Organization." *Proceedings of the Royal Society of Medicine* 44 (1951): 905–9.

Black, R., and D. Spencer. "The Long-Term Future of the International Health Regulations." *WHO Chronicle* 32 (1978): 439–47.

Cockburn, W. "The International Contribution to the Standardization of Biological Substances. Part 1: Biological Standards and the League of Nations, 1921–1946." *Biologicals* 19 (1991): 161–69.

Dobbert, J. "Le Codex Alimentarius: Vers une nouvelle methode de reglementation internationale." *Annuaire Française de Droit International* 15 (1969): 677–717.

Fluss, S., and F. Gutteridge. "Some Contributions of the World Health Organization to Legislation." In *Issues in Contemporary International Health*, ed. T. Lambo and S. Day, 35–54. New York: Plenum Medical, 1990.

Gutteridge, F. "Notes on Decisions of the World Health Organization." In *The Effectiveness of International Decisions*, ed. S. Schwebel, 227–84. Dobbs Ferry, NY: Oceana, 1971.

Howard-Jones, N. "International Medical Documentation and the World Health Organization." *Bulletin of the Medical Librarians Association* 41 (1953): 191–97.

Izant, H. "The World Health Organization Library Service." *Library Trends* 1 (1952): 240–43.

Outschoorn, A. "The Biological Standardization Programme of the World Health Organization." *Journal of Biological Standardization* 1 (1973): 203–13.

Sizaret, P. "Evolution of Activities in International Biological Standardization since the Early Days of the Health Organization and the League of Nations." *Bulletin of the World Health Organization* 66, no. 1 (1988): 1–6.

Skrabanek, P., M. Gibney, and J. Le Fanu. *Who Needs WHO? Three Views on the World Health Organization's Dietary Guidelines.* London: Social Affairs Unit, 1992.

Taylor, A. "Making the World Health Organization Work: A Legal Framework for Universal Access to the Conditions for Health." *American Journal of Law and Medicine* 18 (1992): 301–10.

Vignes, C. H. "Le Reglement sanitaire international: Aspects juridiques." *Annuaire Français de Droit International* 11 (1965): 665–67.

"The Work of the World Health Organization's Expert Committees." *Public Health Report* 67 (1952): 358–69.

Reproductive Health

Conly, S. *Taking the Lead: The United Nations and Population Assistance.* Washington, D.C.: Population Action International, 1996.

Finkle, J., and B. Crane. "The World Health Organization and the Population Issue: Organizational Values in the United Nations." *Population and Development Review* 2, no. 3 (1976): 367–93.

Green, C. *Profiles of UN Organizations Working in Population.* Washington, D.C.: Population Action International, 1996.

"International Conference on Better Health for Women and Children through Family Planning: Recommendations for Action." *Studies in Family Planning* 19, no. 1 (1988): 58–60.

Johnson, S. "The Role of the Agencies." In *World Population and the United Nations,* 34–47. Cambridge: Cambridge University Press, 1987.

Kessler, A. "Family Planning and the Role of WHO." *World Health* 3 (1994): 4–6.

Lane, S. "From Population Control to Reproductive Health: An Emerging Policy Agenda." *Social Science and Medicine* 39, no. 9 (1996): 1303–14.

Lee, K. "What the United Nations Does on Population: Towards a Coordinated Approach to Reproductive Health." *UN and Health Briefing Note* 3 (February 1996): 1–6.

Lee, K., and G. Walt. "Linking National and Global Population Agendas: Case Studies from Eight Developing Countries." *Third World Quarterly* 16, no. 2 (1995): 257–72.

Mahler, H. "The Safe Motherhood Initiative." *Lancet* (March 21, 1987): 668–70.

Symonds, R., and M. Carder. *The United Nations and the Population Question, 1945–1970.* New York: McGraw-Hill, 1973.

Verhoestraete, L. "L'Organisation mondiale de l'hygiène de la maternité et de l'enfance." In *Somme de médecine contemporaine,* vol. 4, 43–56. Paris: Editions Medicales, 1955.

Wolfson, M. *Profiles in Population Assistance, A Comparative Review of the Principal Donor Agencies.* Paris: OECD Development Centre Studies, 1983.

Zahra, A., and R. Strudwick. "The Role of the World Health Organization in Health-Related Aspects of Family Planning." *International Journal of Health Services* 3, no. 4 (1973): 701–7.

Environmental Health

Ashton, J., ed. *Healthy Cities.* Milton Keynes: Open University Press, 1992.

Ashton, J., P. Grey, and K. Barnard. "Healthy Cities: WHO's New Public Health Initiative." *Health Promotion* 1, no. 3 (1986): 319–24.

Bosch, H. "W.H.O. and Environmental Health." *Public Health Report* 67 (1952): 370–75.

Chellappah, S. "The World Health Organization and Environmental Sanitation." *People's Health* 4 (1950): 359–61, 366.

Kickbusch, I. "Healthy Cities: A Working Project and a Growing Movement." *Health Promotion International* 4 (1989): 77–85.

MacGregor, A. "WHO: Global Strategy on Agenda 21." *Lancet* 343 (May 1, 1993): 1142–43.

Tsouros, A. "The WHO Healthy Cities Project: State of the Art and Future Plans." *Health Promotion International* 10 (1995): 133–41.

Human Resources Development, Education, and Training

Baggallay, O. "Nursing in the World Health Organization." *International Nursing Bulletin* 6, no. 1 (1950): 9–10.

———. "W.H.O. Nurses in Peru and El Salvador." *American Journal of Nursing* 54 (1954): 1234–35.

Burton, J. "The WHO Fellowships and Training Programme." *WHO Chronicle* 29, no. 9 (1975): 350–53.

Creelman, L. "Developments in Nursing in the World Health Organization." In *Yearbook of Modern Nursing, 1956*, 381–82. New York: Putnam, 1956.

Fang, I. "The W.H.O. and Nursing in the Western Pacific." *Philippines Journal of Nursing* 25 (1956): 105–7.

Godlee, F. "WHO Fellowships: What Do They Achieve? *British Medical Journal* 310 (January 14, 1995): 110–12.

Hill, E. "The World Health Organization Nursing Programme in the Western Pacific Region." *International Nursing Buletin* 9, no. 1 (1953): 11–14.

Leahy, K. "Nursing and the World Health Organization." *Public Health Nursing* 44 (1952): 185–86.

Levine, S. "Some Impressions of Teaching Medical Missions of the World Health Organization." *New England Journal of Medicine* 251 (1954): 813–16.

Majia, A., and B. Amaru. "A New Look at Fellowships." *World Health* (December 1983):

Martikainen, A. "Education for Health: Work of World Health Organization in Many Lands." *Nursing Mirror* 102, no. 1 (1955): 44.

———. "The Role of W.H.O. in Health Education." *Health Education Journal* 10 (1952): 167–72.

———. "World Goals in Health Education of the Public." *American Journal of Public Health* 47 (1957): 852–55.

Messinezy, D. "Fellowships, a Part of the Education and Training Programme of W.H.O." *Journal of the American Medical Women's Association* 12 (1957): 216–18.

Rafferty, A. M. "Internationalising Nursing Education during the Interwar Period." In *International Health Organisations and Movements, 1918–1939*, ed. P. Weindling, 266–82. Cambridge: Cambridge University Press, 1995.

Williams, C. "The World Health Organization and the Training of Personnel in Maternal and Child Health." *International Child Welfare Review* 3 (1949): 195–200.

Health Research

Caldwell, M. "The UN and Science: Past and Future Implications for World Health." *American Society of International Law Proceedings* 64, no. 4 (1970).

Foster, G. "World Health Organization Behavioural Science Research: Problems and Prospects." *Social Science and Medicine* 24, no. 9 (1987): 709–17.

Goodman, H., and T. Lambo. "The World Health Organization: Its Influence on Worldwise Research Policies." In *Biomedical Institutions, Biomedical Funding, and Public Policy*, ed. H. Fudenberg. New York: Plenum Publishing, 1983.

Kaplan, M. "Science's Role in the World Health Organization." *Science* 180 (1973): 1028.

Rose, H. "A Rejection of the WHO Research Centre: A Case Study of Decision-Making in International Scientific Collaboration." *Minerva* 5 (1967): 340–56.

Rosenfield, P., C. Widstrand, and A. Ruderman. "Social and Economic Research in the UNDP/World Bank/WHO Special Programme for Research and Training in Tropical Diseases." *Social Science and Medicine* 16, no. 5 (1981): 529–38.

Nutrition

Burgess, R. "W.H.O. and Nutrition." *Proceedings of the Nutrition Society* 15 (1956): 13–21.

O'Brien, H. "The World Health Organization and Global Nutrition." *Journal of the American Dietary Association* 23 (1947): 85–89.

Weindling, P. "The Role of International Organisations in Setting Nutritional Standards in the 1920s and 30s." In *The Science and Culture of Nutrition*, ed. A. Kamminga and A. Cunningham, 319–32. Amsterdam: Rodopi, 1995.

Miscellaneous

"Articles and Studies on the World Health Organization, 1946–1957." *Chronicle of the World Health Organization* 12 (1958): 427–38.

Aujaleu, E. "WHO and the Developed World." *World Health Forum* 7, no. 2 (1986): 131–43.

Breslow, L. "A Quantitative Approach to the World Health Organization

Definition of Health: Physical, Mental, and Social Well-Being." *International Journal of Epidemiology* 4 (1972): 347–55.

Calder, R. *Men against the Jungle*. London: Allen and Unwin, 1954.

Ferguson, J. "The Health of Adolescents and Youth: WHO's Expanded Programme for the 1990s." *Health Promotion International* 5 (1990): 173–76.

Forrest, W. "The World Health Organization and Social Welfare." In *Proceedings of the National Conference of Social Work: Atlantic City, 1948*, 40–47. New York: Columbia University Press, 1949.

Forssman, S. "World Health Organization and Occupational Health." *British Journal of Industrial Medicine* 45, no. 538 (1979): 211–12.

Key, D. "World Security and the World Health Organization." *Department of State Bulletin* 31 (1954): 616–19.

Krapf, E. "The Promotion of Mental Health by International Organizations." In *Mental Health and the World Community*, ed. F. Brockington, 106–10. London: World Federation for Mental Health, 1957.

Lambo, T., and S. Day. *Issues in Contemporary International Health*. London: Plenum Medical, 1990.

Larkin, T. "The Great Ghat at Hardwar." *Bulletin of the Atomic Scientists* 18, no. 1 (1962): 6–11.

Mahler, H. "Health Strategies in a Changing World." *WHO Chronicle* 29 (1975): 209–18.

———. "Of mud and alligators." *Health Policy and Planning* 1, no. 4 (1986): 345–52.

Mudalair, A. "World Health Problems." *International Conciliation* 491 (1953): 229–59.

Muller, M. *The Health of Nations: A North-South Investigation*. London: Faber and Faber, 1982.

Nakajima, H. "Through Health to World Peace." *World Health* (August/September, 1988): 8–9.

Riggs, R. "The Bank, the IMF, and the WHO." *Journal of Conflict Resolution* 24, no. 2 (1980): 329–57.

Sapirie, S., and S. Orzeszyna. "WHO's Health Futures Consultation." *Futures* 27, no. 9/10 (1995): 1077–85.

Scheele, L. "Public Health and Foreign Policy." *Annals of the American Academy of Political and Social Science* 278 (1951): 64–72.

Selvaggio, K. "World Health Organization Bottles Up Alcohol Study." *International Journal of Health Services* 14 (1984): 303–9.

Weller, T. "World Health in a Changing World." *American Journal of Tropical Medicine and Hygiene* 77, supplement (1974).

Wells, R. *Peace by Pieces—United Nations Agencies and Their Roles: A Reader and Selective Bibliography*. Metuchen, N.J.: Scarecrow Press, 1991.

Appendix A

Constitution of the World Health Organization

THE STATES to this Constitution declare, in conformity with the Charter of the United Nations, that the following principles are basic to the happiness, harmonious relations and security of all peoples:

Health is a state of complete physical, mental and social well-being and not merely the absence of disease or infirmity.

The enjoyment of the highest attainable standard of health is one of the fundamental rights of every human being without distinction of race, religion, political belief, economic or social condition.

The health of all peoples is fundamental to the attainment of peace and security and is dependent upon the fullest co-operation of individuals and States.

The achievement of any State in the promotion and protection of health is of value to all.

Unequal development in different countries in the promotion of health and control of disease, especially communicable disease, is a common danger.

Health development of the child is of basic importance; the ability to live harmoniously in a changing total environment is essential to development.

The extension to all peoples of the benefits of medical, psychological and related knowledge is essential to the fullest attainment of health.

The constitution was adopted by the International Health Conference held in New York from 19 June to 22 July 1946, signed on 22 July 1946 by the representatives of 61 states (Off. Rec. Wld Hlth Org., 2, 100), and entered into force on 7 April 1948. Amendments adopted by the 26th, 29th, and 39th World Health Assemblies (Resolutions WHA26.37, WHA29.38, and WHA39.6) came into force on 3 February 1977, 20 January 1984, and 11 July 1994, respectively, and are incorporated in the present text.

Informed opinion and active co-operation on the part of the public are of the utmost importance in the improvement of the health of the people.

Governments have a responsibility for the health of their peoples which can be fulfilled only by the provision of adequate health and social measures.

ACCEPTING THESE PRINCIPLES, and for the purpose of co-operation among themselves and with others to promote and protect the health of all peoples, the Contracting Parties agree to the present Constitution and hereby establish the World Health Organization as a specialized agency within the terms of Article 57 of the Charter of the United Nations.

CHAPTER I — OBJECTIVE
Article 1

The objective of the World Health Organization (hereinafter called the Organization) shall be the attainment by all peoples of the highest possible level of health.

CHAPTER II — FUNCTIONS
Article 2

In order to achieve its objective, the functions of the Organization shall be:

a) to act as the directing and co-ordinating authority on international health work;

b) to establish and maintain effective collaboration with the United Nations, specialized agencies, governmental health administrations, professional groups and such other organizations as may be deemed appropriate;

c) to assist Governments, upon request, in strengthening health services;

d) to furnish appropriate technical assistance and, in emergencies, necessary aid upon the request or acceptance of Governments;

e) to provide or assist in providing; upon the request of the United Nations, health services and facilities to special groups, such as the peoples of trust territories;

f) to establish and maintain such administrative and technical services as may be required, including epidemiological and statistical services;

g) to stimulate and advance work to eradicate epidemic, endemic, and other diseases;

h) to promote, in co-operation with other specialized agencies where necessary, the prevention of accidental injuries;

i) to promote, in co-operation with other specialized agencies where necessary, the improvement of nutrition, housing, sanitation, recreation, economic or working conditions and other aspects of environmental hygiene;

j) to promote co-operation among scientific and professional groups which contribute to the advancement of health;

k) to propose conventions, agreements and regulations, and make recommendations with respect to international health matters and to perform such duties as may be assigned thereby to the Organization and are consistent with its objective;

l) to promote maternal and child health and welfare and to foster the ability to live harmoniously in a changing total environment;

m) to foster activities in the field of mental health, especially those affecting the harmony of human relations;

n) to promote and conduct research in the field of health;

o) to promote improved standards of teaching and training in the health, medical and related professions;

p) to study and report on, in co-operation with other specialized agencies where necessary, administrative and social techniques affecting public health and medical care from preventive and curative points of view, including hospital services and social security;

q) to provide information, counsel and assistance in the field of health;

r) to assist in developing an informed public opinion among all peoples on matters of health;

s) to establish and revise as necessary international nomenclatures of diseases, of causes of death and of public health practices;

t) to standardize diagnostic procedures as necessary;

u) to develop, establish and promote international standards with respect to food, biological, pharmaceutical and similar products;

v) generally to take all necessary action to attain the objective of the Organization.

CHAPTER III — MEMBERSHIP AND ASSOCIATE MEMBERSHIP

Article 3

Membership in the Organization shall be open to all States.

Article 4

Members of the United Nations may become Members of the Organization by signing or otherwise accepting this Constitution in accordance with the provisions of Chapter XIX and in accordance with their constitutional processes.

Article 5

The States whose Governments have been invited to send observers to the International Health Conference held in New York, 1946, may become Members by signing or otherwise accepting this Constitution in accordance with the provisions of Chapter XIX and in accordance with their constitutional processes provided that such signature or acceptance shall be completed before the first session of the Health Assembly.

Article 6

Subject to the conditions of any agreement between the United Nations and the Organization, approved pursuant to Chapter XVI, States which do not become Members in accordance with Articles 4 and 5 may apply to become members and shall be admitted as Members when their application has been approved by a simple majority vote of the Health Assembly.

Article 7

If a member fails to meet its financial obligations to the Organization or in other exceptional circumstances, the Health Assembly may, on such conditions as it thinks proper, suspend the voting privileges and services to which a Member is entitled. The Health Assembly shall have the authority to restore such voting privileges and services.[1]

---

1. The amendment to this article adopted by the 18th World Health Assembly (Resolution WHA18.48) has not yet come into force.

Article 8

Territories or groups of territories which are not responsible for the conduct of their international relations may be admitted as Associate Members by the Health Assembly upon application made on behalf of such territory or group of territories by the Member or other authority having responsibility for their international relations. Representatives of Associate Members to the Health Assembly should be qualified by their technical competence in the field of health and should be chosen from the native population. The nature and extent of health should be chosen from the native population. The nature and extent of the rights and obligations of Associate Members shall be determined by the Health Assembly.

CHAPTER IV — ORGANS
Article 9

The work of the Organization shall be carried out by:
a) The World Health Assembly (herein called the Health Assembly);
b) The Executive Board (herein called the Board);
c) The Secretariat

CHAPTER V — THE WORLD HEALTH ASSEMBLY
Article 10

The Health Assembly shall be composed of delegates representing Members.

Article 11

Each member shall be represented by not more than three delegates, one of whom shall be designated by the Member as chief delegate. These delegates should be chosen from among persons most qualified by their technical competence in the field of health, preferably representing the national health administration of the Member.

Article 12

Alternates and advisers may accompany delegates.

Article 13

The Health Assembly shall meet in regular annual session and in such special sessions as may be necessary. Special sessions shall be convened at the request of the Board or of a majority of the Members.

Article 14

The Health Assembly, at each annual session, shall select the country or region in which the next annual session shall be held, the Board subsequently fixing the place. The Board shall determine the place where a special session shall be held.

Article 15

The Board, after consultation with the Secretary-General of the United Nations, shall determine the date of each annual and special session.

Article 16

The Health Assembly shall elect its President and other officers at the beginning of each annual session. They shall hold office until their successors are elected.

Article 17

The Health Assembly shall adopt its own rules of procedure.

Article 18

The functions of the Health Assembly shall be:

a) to determine the policies of the Organization;
b) to name the Members entitled to designate a person to serve on the Board;
c) to appoint the Director-General;
d) to review and approve reports and activities of the Board and of the Director-General and to instruct the Board in regard to matters upon which action, study, investigation or report may be considered desirable;
e) to establish such committees as may be considered necessary for the work of the Organizations;
f) to supervise the financial policies of the Organization and to review and approve the budget;
g) to instruct the Board and the Director-General to bring to the attention of Members and of international organizations, governmental or non-governmental, any matter with regard to health which the Health Assembly may consider appropriate;

h) to invite any organization, international or national, governmental or non-governmental, which has responsibilities related to those of the Organization, to appoint representatives to participate, without right of vote, in its meetings or in those of the committees and conferences convened under its authority, on conditions prescribed by the Health Assembly; but in the case of national organizations, invitations shall be issued only with the consent of the Government concerned;

i) to consider recommendations bearing on health made by the General Assembly, the Economic and Social Council, the Security Council or Trusteeship Council of the United Nations, and to report to them on the steps taken by the Organization and the United Nations;

j) to report to the Economic and Social Council in accordance with any agreement between the Organization and the United Nations;

k) to promote and conduct research in the field of health by the personnel of the Organization, by the establishment of its own institutions or by co-operation with official or non-official institutions of any Member with the consent of its Government;

l) to establish such other institutions as it may consider desirable;

m) to take any other appropriate action to further the objective of the Organization.

Article 19

The Health Assembly shall have authority to adopt conventions or agreements with respect to any matter within the competence of the Organization. A two-thirds vote of the Health Assembly shall be required for the adoption of such conventions or agreements, which shall come into force for each Member when accepted by it in accordance with its constitutional processes.

Article 20

Each Member undertakes that it will, within eighteen months after the adoption by the Health Assembly of a convention or agreement, take action relative to the acceptance of such convention or agreement. Each member shall notify the Director-General of the action taken, and if it does not accept such convention or agreement within the time limit, it will furnish a statement of the reasons for non-acceptance. In case of acceptance, each Member agrees to make an annual report to the Director-General in accordance with Chapter XIV.

Article 21

The Health Assembly shall have authority to adopt regulations concerning:
a) sanitary and quarantine requirements and other procedures designed to prevent the international spread of disease;
b) nomenclatures with respect to diseases, causes of death and public health practices;
c) standards with respect to diagnostic procedures for international use;
d) standards with respect to the safety, purity and potency of biological, pharmaceutical and similar products moving in international commerce;
e) advertising and labelling of biological, pharmaceutical and similar products moving in international commerce.

Article 22

Regulations adopted pursuant to Article 21 shall come into force for all Members after due notice has been given of their adoption by the Health Assembly except for such Members as may notify the Director-General of rejection or reservations within the period stated in the notice.

Article 23

The Health Assembly shall have authority to make recommendations to Members with respect to any matter within the competence of the Organization.

CHAPTER VI — THE EXECUTIVE BOARD
Article 24

The Board shall consist of thirty-two persons designated by as many Members. The Health Assembly, taking into account an equitable geographical distribution, shall elect the Members entitled to designate a person to serve on the Board, provided that, of such Members, not less than three shall be elected from each of the regional organizations established pursuant to Article 44. Each of these Members should appoint to the Board a person technically qualified in the field of health, who may be accompanied by alternates and advisers.

Article 25

These Members shall be elected for three years and may be re-elected, provided that of the Members elected at the first session of the Health Assembly held after the coming into force of the amendment to this Constitution increasing the membership of the Board from thirty-one to thirty-two the term of office of the additional Member elected shall, insofar as may be necessary, be of such lesser duration as shall facilitate the election of at least one Member from each regional organization in each year.

Article 26

The Board shall meet its Chairman from among its members and shall adopt its own rules of procedure.

Article 27

The Board shall elect its chairman from among its members and shall adopt its own rules of procedure.

Article 28

The functions of the Board shall be:
a) to give effect to the decisions and policies of the Health Assembly
b) to act as the executive organ of the Health Assembly;
c) to perform any other functions entrusted to it by the Health Assembly;
d) to advise the Health Assembly on questions referred to it by that body and on matters assigned to the Organization by conventions, agreements and regulations;
e) to submit advice or proposals to the Health Assembly on its own initiative;
f) to prepare the agenda of meetings to the Health Assembly;
g) to submit to the Health Assembly for consideration and approval a general programme of work covering a specific period;
h) to study all questions within its competence;
i) to take emergency measures within the functions and financial resources of the Organization to deal with events requiring immediate action. In particular it may authorize the Director-General to take the necessary steps to combat epidemics, to participate in the organization of health relief vic-

tims of a calamity and to undertake studies and research the urgency of which has been drawn to the attention of the Board by any Member or by the Director-General.

Article 29

The Board shall exercise on behalf of the whole Health Assembly the powers delegated to it by that body.

CHAPTER VII — THE SECRETARIAT
Article 30

The Board shall comprise the Director-General and such technical and administrative staff as the Organization may require.

Article 31

The Director-General shall be appointed by the Health Assembly on the nomination of the Board on such terms as the Health Assembly may determine. The Director-General, subject to the authority of the Board, shall be the chief technical and administrative officer of the Organization.

Article 32

The Director-General shall be *ex-officio* Secretary of the Health Assembly, of the Board, of all commissions and committees of the Organization and of conferences convened by it. He may delegate these functions.

Article 33

The Director-General or his representative may establish a procedure by agreement with Members, permitting him, for the purpose of discharging his duties, to have direct access to their various departments, especially to their health administrators and to national health organizations, governmental or non-governmental. He may also establish direct relations with international organizations whose activities come within the competence of the Organization. He shall keep regional offices informed on all matters involving their respective areas.

Article 34

The Director-General shall prepare and submit to the Board the financial statements and budget estimates of the Organization.

Article 35

The Director-General shall appoint the staff of the Secretariat in accordance with staff regulations established by the Health Assembly. The paramount consideration in the employment of the staff shall be to assure that the efficiency, integrity and internationally representative character of the Secretariat shall be maintained at the highest level. Due regard shall be paid also to the importance of recruiting the staff on as wide a geographical basis as possible.

Article 36

The conditions of services of the staff of the Organization shall conform as far as possible with those of other United Nations organizations.

Article 37

In the performance of their duties the Director-General and the staff shall not seek or receive instructions from any government or from any authority external to the organization. They shall refrain from any action which might reflect on their position as international officers. Each Member of the Organization on its part undertakes to respect the exclusively international character of the Director-General and the staff and not to seek to influence them.

CHAPTER VIII — COMMITTEES
Article 38

The Board shall establish such committees as the Health Assembly may direct and, on its own initiative or on the proposal of the Director-General, may establish any other committees considered desirable to serve any purpose within the competence of the Organization.

Article 39

The Board, from time to time and in any event annually, shall review the necessity for continuing such a committee.

Article 40

The Board may provide for the creation of or the participation by the Organization in joint or mixed committees with other organizations and for the representation of the Organization in committees established by such other organizations.

CHAPTER IX — CONFERENCES
Article 41

The Health Assembly or the Board may convene local, general, technical or other special conferences to consider any matter within the competence of the Organization and may provide for the representation at such conferences of international organizations and, with the consent of the Government concerned, of national organizations, governmental or non-governmental. The manner of such representation shall be determined by the Health Assembly or the Board.

Article 42

The Board may provide for representation of the Organization at conferences in which the Board considers that the Organization has an interest.

CHAPTER X — HEADQUARTERS
Article 43

The location of the headquarters of the Organization shall be determined by the Health Assembly after consultation with the United Nations.

CHAPTER XI — REGIONAL ARRANGEMENTS
Article 44

a) The Health Assembly shall from time to time define the geographical areas in which it is desirable to establish a regional organization.

b) The Health Assembly may, with the consent of a majority of the Members situated within each area so defined, establish a regional organization to meet the special needs of such area. There shall not be more than one regional organization in each area.

Article 45

Each regional organization shall be an integral part of the Organization in accordance with this Constitution.

Article 46

Each regional organization shall consist of a regional committee and a regional office.

Article 47

Regional committees shall be composed of representatives of the Member States and Associate Members in the region concerned. Territories or groups of territories within the region, which are not responsible for the conduct of their international relations and which are not Associate Members, shall have the right to be represented and to participate in regional committees. The nature and the extent of the rights and obligations of these territories or groups of territories in regional committees shall be determined by the Health Assembly in consultation with the Member or other authority having responsibility for the international relations of these territories and with the Member States in the region.

Article 48

Regional committees shall meet as often as necessary and shall determine the place of each meeting.

Article 49

Regional committees shall adopt their own rules of procedure.

Article 50

The functions of the regional committee shall be:
a) to formulate policies governing matters of an exclusively regional character;
b) to supervise the activities of the regional office;
c) to suggest to the regional office the calling of technical conferences and such additional work or investigation in health matters as in the opinion of the regional committee would promote the objective of the Organization within the region;
d) to co-operate with the respective regional committees of the United Nations and with those of other specialized agencies and with other regional international organizations having interests in common with the Organization;
e) to tender advice, through the Director-General, to the Organization on international health matters which have wider than regional significance;

f) to recommend additional regional appropriations by the Governments of the respective regions if the proportion of the central budget of the Organization allotted to that region is insufficient for the carrying-out of the regional functions;

g) such other functions as may be delegated to the regional committee by the Health Assembly, the Board or the Director-General.

Article 51

Subject to the general authority of the Director-General of the Organization, the regional office shall be the administrative organ of the regional committee. It shall, in addition, carry out within the region the decisions of the Health Assembly and of the Board.

Article 52

The head of the regional office shall be the Regional Director appointed by the Board in agreement with the regional committee.

Article 53

The staff of the regional office shall be appointed in a manner to be determined by agreement between the Director-General and the Regional Director.

Article 54

The Pan American Sanitary Organization[2] represented by the Pan American Sanitary Bureau and the Pan American Sanitary Conferences, and all other inter-governmental regional health organizations in existence prior to the date of signature of this Constitution, shall in due course be integrated with the Organization. This integration shall be effected as soon as practicable through common action based on mutual consent of the competent authorities expressed through the organizations concerned.

CHAPTER XII—BUDGET AND EXPENSES
Article 55

The Director-General shall prepare and submit to the Board the budget estimates of the Organization. The Board shall consider and submit to the Health Assembly such budget estimates, to-

---

2. Renamed Pan American Health Organization by decision of the 15th Pan American Sanitary Conference, September–October 1958.

gether with any recommendations the Board may deem advisable.

Article 56

Subject to any agreement between the Organization and the United Nations, the Health Assembly shall review and approve the budget estimates and shall apportion the expenses among the Members in accordance with a scale to be fixed by the Health Assembly.

Article 57

The Health Assembly or the Board acting on behalf of the Health Assembly may accept and administer gifts and bequests made to the Organization provided that the conditions attached to such gifts or bequests are acceptable to the Health Assembly or the Board and are consistent with the objective and policies of the Organization.

CHAPTER XIII
Article 58

A special fund to be used at the discretion of the Board shall be established to meet emergencies and unforseen contingencies.

Article 59

Each member shall have one vote in the Health Assembly.

Article 60

a) Decisions of the Health Assembly on important questions shall be made by a two-thirds majority of the Members present and voting. These questions shall include: the adoption of conventions or agreements; the approval of agreements bringing the Organization into relation with the United Nations and inter-governmental organizations and agencies in accordance with Articles 69, 70 and 72; amendments to this Constitution.

b) Decisions on other questions, including the determination of additional categories of questions to be decided by a two-thirds majority, shall be made by a majority of the Members present and voting.

c) Voting on analogous matters in the Board and in committees of the Organization shall be made in accordance with paragraphs a) and b) of this Article.

CHAPTER XIV — REPORTS SUBMITTED BY STATES
Article 61

Each Member shall report annually to the Organization on the action taken and progress achieved in improving the health of its people.

Article 62

Each Member shall report annually on the action taken with respect to recommendations made to it by the Organization and with respect to conventions, agreements and regulations.

Article 63

Each Member shall communicate promptly to the Organization important laws, regulations, official reports and statistics pertaining to health which have been published in the State concerned.

Article 64

Each Member shall provide statistical and epidemiological reports in a manner to be determined by the Health Assembly.

Article 65

Each Member shall transmit upon the request of the Board such additional information pertaining to health as may be practicable.

CHAPTER XV — LEGAL CAPACITY, PRIVILEGES AND IMMUNITIES
Article 66

The Organization shall enjoy in the territory of each Member such legal capacity as may be necessary for the fulfilment of its objective and for the exercise of its functions.

Article 67

a) The Organization shall enjoy in the territory of each Member such privileges and immunities as may be necessary for the fulfilment of its objective and for the exercise of its functions.
b) Representatives of Members, persons designated to serve on

the Board and technical and administrative personnel of the Organization shall similarly enjoy such privileges and immunities as are necessary for the independent exercise of their functions in connexion with the Organization.

Article 68

Such legal capacity, privileges and immunities shall be defined in a separate agreement to be prepared by the Organization in consultation with the Secretary-General of the United Nations and concluded between the Members.

CHAPTER XVI — RELATIONS WITH OTHER ORGANIZATIONS
Article 69

The Organization shall be brought into relation with the United Nations as one of the specialized agencies referred to in Article 57 of the Charter of the United Nations. The agreement or agreements bringing the Organization into relation with the United Nations shall be subject to approval by a two-thirds vote of the Health Assembly.

Article 70

The Organization shall establish effective relations and co-operate closely with such other inter-governmental organizations as may be desirable. Any formal agreement entered into with such organizations shall be subject to approval by a two-thirds vote of the Health Assembly.

Article 71

The Organization may, on matters within its competence, make suitable arrangements for consultation and co-operation with non-governmental international organizations and, with the consent of the Government concerned, with national organizations, governmental or non-governmental.

Article 72

Subject to the approval by a two-thirds vote of the Health Assembly, the Organization may take over from any other international organization or agency whose purpose and activities lie within the field of competence of the Organization such functions, resources and obligations as may be conferred upon the Organization by international agreement or by mutually acceptable arrangements entered into between the competent authorities of the respective organizations.

CHAPTER XVII — AMENDMENTS
Article 73

Texts of proposed amendments to this Constitution shall be communicated by the Director-General to Members at least six months in advance of their consideration by the Health Assembly. Amendments shall come into force for all Members when adopted by a two-thirds vote of the Health Assembly and accepted by two-thirds of the Members in accordance with their respective constitutional processes.

CHAPTER XVIII — INTERPRETATION
Article 74

The Chinese, English, French, Russian and Spanish texts of this Constitution shall be regarded as equally authentic.[3]

Article 75

Any question or dispute concerning the interpretation or application of this Constitution which is not settled by negotiation or by the Health Assembly shall be referred to the International Court of Justice in conformity with the Statute of the Court, unless the parties concerned agree on another mode of settlement.

Article 76

Upon authorization by the General Assembly of the United Nations or upon authorization in accordance with any agreement between the Organization and the United Nations, the Organization may request the International Court of Justice for an advisory opinion on any legal question arising within the competence of the Organization.

Article 77

The Director-General may appear before the Court on behalf of the Organization in connexion with any proceedings arising out of any such request for an advisory opinion. He shall make ar-

---

3. The amendment to this article adopted by the 31st World Health Assembly (Resolution WHA31.18) has not yet come into force.

rangements for the presentation of the case before the Court, including arrangements for the argument of different views to the question.

CHAPTER XIX — ENTRY-INTO-FORCE
Article 78

Subject to the provisions of Chapter III, this Constitution shall remain open to all States for signature or acceptance.

Article 79

a) States may become parties to this Constitution by

   i) signature without reservation as to approval;
   ii) signature subject to approval followed by acceptance; or
   iii) acceptance.
b) Acceptance shall be effected by the deposit of a formal instrument with the Secretary-General of the United Nations.

Article 80

This Constitution shall come into force when twenty-six Members of the United Nations have become parties to it in accordance with the provisions of Article 79.

Article 81

In accordance with Article 102 of the Charter of the United Nations, the Secretary-General of the United Nations will register this Constitution when it has been signed without reservation as to approval on behalf of one State or upon deposit of the first instrument of acceptance.

Article 82

The Secretary-General of the United Nations will inform States parties to this Constitution of the date when it has come into force. He will also inform them of the dates when other States have become parties to this Constitution.

IN FAITH WHEREOF the undersigned representatives, having been duly authorized for that purpose, sign this Constitution.

DONE in the City of New York this twenty-second day of July 1946, in a single copy in the Chinese, English, French, Russian and Spanish languages, each text being equally authentic. The and Spanish languages, each text being equally authentic. The original texts shall be deposited in the archives of the United Nations. The Secretary-General of the United Nations will send certified copies to each of the Governments represented at the Conference.

Source: WHO (1994), Basic Documents, 40th ed. (Geneva: WHO).

Appendix B
Member States by Year of Membership

Canada	1946	Czechoslovakia	1948
China	1946	Denmark	1948
Iran	1946	Dominican Republic	1948
New Zealand	1946	El Salvador	1948
Syrian Arab Republic	1946	France	1948
United Kingdom	1946	Greece	1948
Albania	1947	Hungary	1948
Austria	1947	Iceland	1948
Egypt	1947	India	1948
Ethiopia	1947	Mexico	1948
Finland	1947	Monaco	1948
Haiti	1947	Burma (Myanmar)	1948
Iraq	1947	Pakistan	1948
Ireland	1947	Philippines	1948
Italy	1947	Poland	1948
Jordan	1947	Portugal	1948
Liberia	1947	Romania	1948
Netherlands	1947	Russian Federation	1948
Norway	1947	Sri Lanka	1948
Saudi Arabia	1947	Turkey	1948
South Africa	1947	Ukraine	1948
Sweden	1947	United States of America	1948
Switzerland	1947	Venezuela	1948
Thailand	1947	Bolivia	1949
Yugoslavia	1947	Costa Rica	1949
Afghanistan	1948	Ecuador	1949
Argentina	1948	Guatemala	1949
Australia	1948	Honduras	1949
Belarus	1948	Israel	1949
Belgium	1948	Lebanon	1949
Brazil	1948	Luxembourg	1949
Bulgaria	1948	Paraguay	1949
Chile	1948	Peru	1949

Republic of Korea	1949	Mongolia	1962
Uruguay	1949	Rwanda	1962
Cambodia	1950	Samoa	1962
Cuba	1950	United Republic of Tanzania	1962
Indonesia	1950	Jamaica	1963
Laos	1950	Kenya	1963
Nicaragua	1950	Trinidad and Tobago	1963
Vietnam	1950	Uganda	1963
Germany	1951	Malawi	1964
Japan	1951	Guyana	1965
Panama	1951	Maldives	1965
Spain	1951	Malta	1965
Libyan Arab Jamahiriya	1952	Zambia	1965
Nepal	1953	Singapore	1966
Yemen	1953	Barbados	1967
Morocco	1956	Lesotho	1967
Sudan	1956	Mauritius	1968
Tunisia	1956	Bahrain	1971
Ghana	1957	Gambia	1971
Malaysia	1958	Oman	1971
Colombia	1959	Bangladesh	1972
Guinea	1959	Fiji	1972
Benin	1960	Qatar	1972
Burkino Faso	1960	United Arab Emirates	1972
Cameroon	1960	Swaziland	1973
Central Africa Republic	1960	Bahamas	1974
Congo	1960	Grenada	1974
Côte d'Ivoire	1960	Guinea-Bissau	1974
Gabon	1960	Botswana	1975
Kuwait	1960	Comoros	1975
Mali	1960	Mozambique	1975
Niger	1960	Tonga	1975
Nigeria	1960	Angola	1976
Senegal	1960	Cape Verde	1976
Togo	1960	Papua New Guinea	1976
Chad	1961	Sao Tome and Principe	1976
Cyprus	1961	Suriname	1976
Madagascar	1961	Djibouti	1978
Mauritania	1961	Seychelles	1979
Sierra Leone	1961	Equatorial Guinea	1980
Somalia	1961	Saint Lucia	1980
Zaire	1961	San Marino	1980
Algeria	1962	Zimbabwe	1980
Burundi	1962	Dominica	1981

Bhutan	1982	Bosnia and Herzegovinia	1992
Saint Vincent and the		Croatia	1992
Grenadines	1983	Georgia	1992
Solomon Islands	1983	Kazakhstan	1992
Vanuatu	1983	Kyrgystan	1992
Antiqua and Barbuda	1984	Republic of Moldova	1992
Cook Islands	1984	Slovenia	1992
Kiribati	1984	Tajikstan	1992
Saint Kitts and Nevis	1984	Turkmenistan	1992
Brunei Darussalam	1985	Uzbekistan	1992
Belize	1990	Eritrea	1993
Namibia	1990	The former Yugoslav	
Latvia	1991	Republic of Macedonia	1993
Lithuania	1991	Tuvalu	1993
Marshall Islands	1991	Slovakia	1993
Micronesia	1991	Estonia	1994
Armenia	1992	Nauru	1994
Azerbaijan	1992	Niue	1994

Appendix C

Addresses of WHO Headquarters and Regional Offices

World Health Organization
20 Avenue Appia
CH-1211 Geneva 27
SWITZERLAND

African Regional Office (AFRO)
P.O. Box No. 6
Brazzaville
CONGO

Pan American Health Organization (PAHO)/American Regional
Office (AMRO)
525 23d Street, NW
Washington, DC 20037
UNITED STATES OF AMERICA

Eastern Mediterranean Regional Office (EMRO)
P.O. Box 1517
Alexandria 21511
EGYPT

European Regional Office (EURO)
8 Scherfigsvej
DK 2100 Copenhagen
DENMARK

South-East Asia Regional Office (SEARO)
World Health House
Indraprastha Estate
Mahatma Gandhi Road
New Delhi 110002
INDIA

Western Pacific Regional Office
P.O. Box 2932
1099 Manila
PHILIPPINES

Appendix D
Organizational Structure of WHO, Various Years

Structure of Headquarters
(at 31 December 1957)

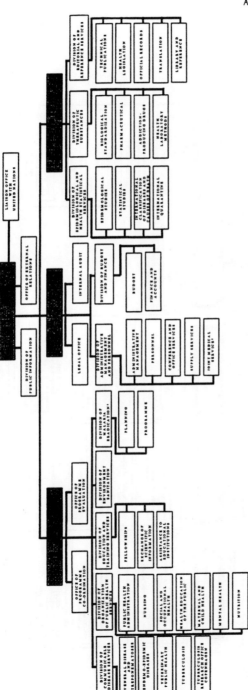

1. This division, which is not subdivided into sections, deals with municipal and regional sanitation, rural and community sanitation, housing and town planning, vector control and insecticides, milk and food sanitation, environmental aspects of occupational health, and transportation sanitation.

2. As from 1 January 1958.

Source: Adapted from WHO, The First Ten Years of the World Health Organization (Geneva: WHO 1957).

Structure of the Secretariat at Headquarters
(at 15 October 1988)

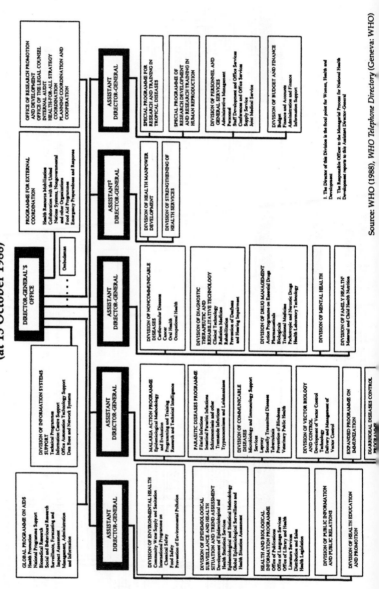

Source: WHO (1988), *WHO Telephone Directory* (Geneva: WHO)

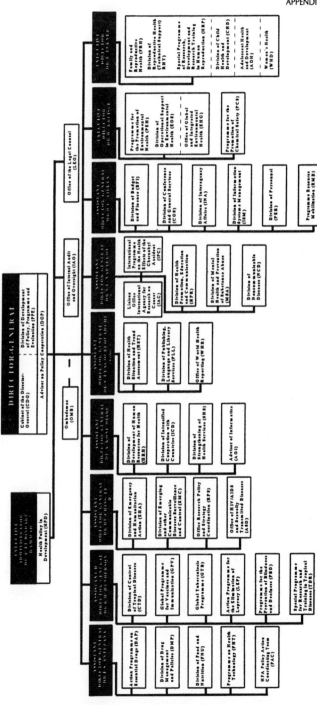

Source: WHO (1996), WHO Telephone Directory (Geneva: WHO).

Appendix E

WHO Directors-General
and Regional Directors

WHO Directors-General
- Dr. George Brock Chisholm, Canada (1948–53)
- Dr. Marcelino Gomez Candau, Brazil (1953–73)
- Dr. Halfdan Mahler, Denmark (1973–88)
- Dr. Hiroshi Nakajima, Japan (1988–1998)
- Dr. Gro Harlem Brundtland (1998–   )

WHO Regional Directors

African Regional Office (AFRO)
- Dr. François Daubenton, South Africa (1952–54)
- Dr. Francisco Jose Cambournac, Portugal (1954–64)
- Dr. Comlan Alfred Auguste Quenum, Benin (1965–84)
- Dr. Ebrahim Malick Samba, Gambia (1984–85)
- Dr. Gottlieb Lobe Monekosso, Cameroon (1985–95)
- Dr. Ebrahim Malick Samba, Gambia (1995–   )

Eastern Mediterranean Regional Office (EMRO)
- Dr. Aly Tewfik Shousha, Egypt (1949–57)
- Dr. Abdol Hossein Taba, Iran (1957–82)
- Dr. Hussein Abdul Razzak Gezairy, Saudi Arabia (1982–   )

European Regional Office (EURO)
- Dr. Norman D. Begg, United Kingdom (1952–56)
- Dr. Paul J. J. van de Calseyde, Belgium (1957–67)
- Dr. Leo A. Kaprio, Finland (1967–85)
- Dr. Jo Eirik Asvall, Norway (1985–   )

South-East Asia Regional Office (SEARO)
- Dr. Chandra Mani, India (1948–68)
- Dr. V. T. Herat Gunaratne, Sri Lanka (1968–81)
- Dr. U Ko Ko, Myanmar (1981–94)
- Dr. Uton Muchtar Rafei, Indonesia (1994–   )

Pan American Health Organization (PAHO)/American Regional Office (AMRO)

Dr. Walter Wyman, United States (1902–11)
Dr. Rupert Blue, United States (1911–20)
Dr. Hugh Smith Cumming, United States (1920–46)
Dr. Fred Lowe Soper, United States (1947–58)
Dr. Abraham Horwitz, Chile (1958–75)
Dr. Héctor R. Acuña, Mexico (1975–83)
Dr. Carlyle Guerra de Macedo, Brazil (1983–94)
Sir George A. O. Alleyne, Barbados (1995–   )

Western Pacific Regional Office (WPRO)

Dr. I. C. Fang, China (1951–66)
Dr. Francisco J. Dy, Philippines (1966–79)
Dr. Hiroshi Nakajima, Japan (1979–88)
Dr. Sang Tae Han, Republic of Korea (1989–   )

Appendix F

Declaration on Primary Health Care, Alma-Ata (1978)

Declaration adopted at the WHO/UNICEF International Conference on Primary Health Care, Alma-Ata, Russia, 6–12 September 1978.

The International Conference on Primary Health Care, meeting in Alma-Ata this twelfth day of September in the year Nineteen hundred and seventy-eight, expressing the need for urgent action by all governments, all health and development workers, and the world community to protect and promote the health of all the people of the world, hereby makes the following Declaration:

I

The Conference strongly reaffirms that health, which is a state of complete physical, mental and social wellbeing, and not merely the absence of disease or infirmity, is a fundamental human right and that the attainment of the highest possible level of health is a most important world-wide social goal whose realization requires the action of many other social and economic sectors in addition to the health sector.

II

The existing gross inequality in the health status of the people particularly between developed and developing countries as well as within countries is politically, socially and economically unacceptable and is, therefore, of common concern to all countries.

III

Economic and social development, based on a New International Economic Order, is of basic importance to the fullest attainment of health for all and to the reduction of the gap between the health status of the developed and developing countries. The promotion and protection of the health of the people is essential to sustained economic and social development and contributes to a better quality of life and to world peace.

IV

The people have the right and duty to participate individually and collectively in the planning and implementation of their health care.

V

Governments have a responsibility for the health of their people which can be fulfilled only by the provision of adequate health and social measures. A main social target of governments, international organizations and the whole world community in the coming decades should be the attainment by all peoples of the world by the year 2000 of a level of health that will permit them to lead a socially and economically productive life. Primary health care is the key to attaining this target as part of development in the spirit of social justice.

VI

Primary health care is essential health care based on practical, scientifically sound and socially acceptable methods and technology made universally accessible to individuals and families in the community through their full participation and at a cost that the community and country can afford to maintain at every stage of their development in the spirit of self-reliance and self-determination. It forms an integral part both of the country's health system, of which it is the central function and main focus, and of the overall social and economic development of the community. It is the first level of contact of individuals, the family and community with the national health system bringing health care as close as possible to where people live and work, and constitutes the first element of a continuing health care process.

VII

Primary health care:

1. reflects and evolves from the economic conditions and socio-cultural and political characteristics of the country and its communities and is based on the application of the relevant

results of social, biomedical and health services research and public health experience;

2. addresses the main health problems in the community, providing promotive, preventive, curative and rehabilitative services accordingly;

3. includes at least: education concerning prevailing health problems and the methods of preventing and controlling them; promotion of food supply and proper nutrition; an adequate supply of safe water and basic sanitation; maternal and child health care, including family planning; immunization against the major infectious diseases; prevention and control of locally endemic diseases; appropriate treatment of common diseases and injuries; and provision of essential drugs;

4. involves, in addition to the health sector, all related sectors and aspects of national and community development, in particular agriculture, animal husbandry, food, industry, education, housing, public works, communications and other sectors; and demands the coordinated efforts of all those sectors;

5. requires and promotes maximum community and individual self-reliance and participation in the planning, organization, operation and control of primary health care, making fullest use of local, national and other available resources; and to this end develops through appropriate education the ability of communities to participate;

6. Should be sustained by integrated, functional and mutually-supportive referral systems, leading to the progressive improvement of comprehensive health care for all, and giving priority to those most in need;

7. relies, at local and referral levels, on health workers, including physicians, nurses, midwives, auxiliaries and community workers as applicable, as well as traditional practitioners as needed, suitably trained socially and technically to work as a health team and to respond to the expressed health needs of the community.

VIII

All governments should formulate national policies, strategies and plans of action to launch and sustain primary health care as part of a comprehensive national health system and in coordination with other sectors. To this end, it will be necessary to exercise political will, to mobilize the country's resources and to use available external resources rationally.

IX

All countries should cooperate in a spirit of partnership and service to ensure primary health care for all people since the attainment of health by people in any one country directly concerns and benefits every other country. In this context the joint WHO/ UNICEF report on primary health care constitutes a solid base for the further development and operation of primary health care throughout the world.

X

An acceptable level of health for all the people of the world by the year 2000 can be attained through a fuller and better use of the world's resources, a considerable part of which is now spent on armaments and military conflicts. A genuine policy of independence, peace, détente and disarmament could and should release additional resources that could well be devoted to peaceful aims and in particular to the acceleration of social and economic development of which primary health care, as an essential part, should be allotted its proper share.

The International Conference on Primary Health Care calls for urgent and effective national and international action to develop and implement primary health care throughout the world and particularly in developing countries in a spirit of technical cooperation and in keeping with a New International Economic Order. It urges governments, WHO and UNICEF, and other international organizations, as well as multilateral and bilateral agencies, non-governmental organizations, funding agencies, all health workers and the whole world community to support national and international commitment to primary health care and to channel increased technical and financial support to it, particularly in developing countries. The Conference calls on all the aforementioned to collaborate in introducing, developing and maintaining primary health care in accordance with the spirit and content of this Declaration.

Source: WHO–UNICEF (1978), Alma-Ata: Primary Health Care (Geneva–New York).

Appendix G
WHO Financial Budget, 1976–1995

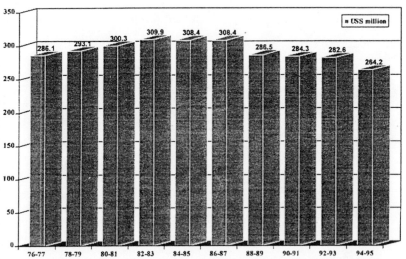

Figures and definition of working budgets in real terms as defined by WHO.
Source: WHO (1996), Financial report and audited financial statements,
Geneva.

Appendix H

Nongovernmental Organizations in Official Relations with WHO (1994)

African Medical and Research Foundation International
Aga Khan Foundation
Association of the Institutes and Schools of Tropical Medicine in
    Europe
Christoffel-Blindenmission
CMC–Churches' Action for Health
Collegium Internationale Neuro-Psychopharmacolgicum
Commonwealth Association for Mental Handicaps and
    Developmental Disabilities
Commonwealth Medical Association
Commonwealth Pharmaceutical Association
Council for International Organizations of Medical Sciences
Helen Keller International Incorporated
Industry Council for Development
Inter-American Association of Sanitary and Environmental
    Engineering
Inter-Parliamentary Union
International Academy of Legal Medicine
International Agency of Pathology
International Agency for the Prevention of Blindness
International Air Transport Association
International Alliance of Women
International Association for Accident and Traffic Medicine
International Association for Adolescent Health
International Association for Child and Adolescent Psychiatry
    and Allied Professions
International Association for Suicide Prevention
International Association for the Study of Pain
International Association for the Study of the Liver
International Association of Agricultural Medicine and Rural
    Health

International Association of Cancer Registries
International Association of Hydatid Disease
International Association of Lions Clubs
International Association of Logopedics and Phoniatrics
International Association of Medical Laboratory Technologists
International Association on Water Quality
International Astronautical Federation
International Bureau for Epilepsy
International Catholic Committee of Nurses and Medico-Social
    Assistants
International Clearinghouse for Birth Defects Monitoring
    Systems
International College of Surgeons
International Commission on Nonionizing Radiation
International Commission on Occupational Health
International Commission on Radiation Units and Measurements
International Commission on Radiological Protection
International Committee of the Red Cross
International Confederation of Midwives
International Conference of Deans of French Language Faculties
    of Medicine
International Consultation on Urological Diseases
International Council for Control of Iodine Deficiency Disorders
International Council for Laboratory Animal Science
International Council for Standardization in Haematology
International Council of Nurses
International Council of Scientific Unions
International Council of Societies of Pathology
International Council of Women
International Council on Jewish Social and Welfare Services
International Council on Social Welfare Services
International Cystic Fibrosis (Mucoviscidosis) Association
International Dental Federation
International Diabetes Federation
International Electrotechnical Commission
International Epidemiological Association
International Ergonomics Association
International Eye Foundation
International Federation for Family Life Promotion
International Federation for Housing and Planning
International Federation for Information Processing
International Federation for Medical and Biological Engineering
International Federation for Preventive and Social Medicine
International Federation of Business and Professional Women

International Federation of Chemical, Energy, and General
   Workers' Unions
International Federation of Clinical Chemistry
International Federation of Fertility Societies
International Federation of Gynaecology and Obstetrics
International Federation of Health Records Organizations
International Federation of Hospital Engineering
International Federation of Hydrotherapy and Climatotherapy
International Federation of Medical Students Associations
International Federation of Multiple Sclerosis Societies
International Federation of Ophthalmological Societies
International Federation of Oto-Rhino-Laryngological Societies
International Federation of Pharmaceutical Manufacturers
   Associations
International Federation of Physical Medicine and Rehabilitation
International Federation of Red Cross and Red Crescent Societies
International Federation of Sports Medicine
International Federation of Surgical Colleges
International Federation on Aging
International Group of National Associations of Manufacturers
   of Agrochemical Products
International Hospital Federation
International Lactation Consultant Association
International League against Epilepsy
International League of Associations for Rheumatology
International League of Dermatological Societies
International Leprosy Association
International Leprosy Union
International Life Sciences Institute
International Medical Informatics Association
International Medical Society of Paraplegia
International Occupational Hygiene Association
International Organization against Trachoma
International Organization for Standardization
International Organization of Consumers Unions
International Pediatric Association
International Pharmaceutical Federation
International Physicians for the Prevention of Nuclear War
International Planned Parenthood Federation
International Radiation Protection Association
International Society and Federation of Cardiology
International Society for Biomedical Research on Alcoholism
International Society for Burn Injuries
International Society for Human and Animal Mycology

International Society for Preventive Oncology
International Society for Prosthetics and Orthotics
International Society for the Study of Behavioural Development
International Society of Biometeorology
International Society of Blood Transfusion
International Society of Chemotherapy
International Society of Hematology
International Society of Nurses in Cancer Care
International Society of Orthopaedic Surgery and Traumatology
International Society of Radiographers and Radiological
    Technologists
International Society of Radiology
International Society of Surgery
International Sociological Association
International Solid Wastes and Public Cleansing Association
International Special Dietary Food Industries
International Union against Cancer
International Union against Tuberculosis and Lung Disease
International Union against the Venereal Diseases and the
    Treponematoses
International Union for Conservation of Nature and Natural
    Resources
International Union for Health Promotion and Education
International Union of Architects
International Union of Biological Sciences
International Union of Family Organizations
International Organization of Immunological Societies
International Union of Local Authorities
International Union of Microbiological Societies
International Union of Nutritional Sciences
International Union of Pharmacology
International Union of Pure and Applied Chemistry
International Union of Toxicology
International Water Supply Association
Joint Commission on International Aspects of Mental Retardation
La Leche League International
Medical Women's International Association
Medicus Mundi Internationalis (International Organization for
    Cooperation in Health Care)
Mother and Child International
National Council for International Health
Network of Community-Oriented Educational Institutions for
    Health Sciences
OXFAM

Rehabilitation International
Rotary International
Save the Children Fund (UK)
Soroptimist International
The Population Council
The Royal Commonwealth Society for the Blind (Sight Savers)
World Assembly of Youth
World Association for Psychosocial Rehabilitation
World Association of Girl Guides and Girl Scouts
World Association of Societies of (Anatomic and Clinical)
    Pathology
World Association of the Major Metropolises
World Blind Union
World Confederation for Physical Therapy
World Federation for Medical Education
World Federation for Mental Health
World Federation of the Association of Poisons Centres and
    Clinical Toxicology Centres
World Federation of Hemophilia
World Federation of Neurology
World Federation of Neurosurgical Societies
World Federation of Nuclear Medicine and Biology
World Federation of Occupational Therapists
World Federation of Parasitologists
World Federation of Proprietary Medicine Manufacturers
World Federation of Public Health Associations
World Federation of Societies of Anaesthesiologists
World Federation of the Deaf
World Federation of United Nations Associations
World Hypertension League
World Medical Association
World Organization of Family Doctors
World Organization of the Scout Movement
World Psychiatric Association
World Rehabilitation Fund
World Veterans Federation
World Veterinary Association
World Vision International

About the Author

KELLEY LEE (B.A., University of British Columbia; M.P.A., University of Victoria; M.A., University of Sussex; D.Phil., University of Sussex) is a lecturer in international health policy at the London School of Hygiene and Tropical Medicine, University of London. Her main interests are the United Nations, international organization, and the global political economy of health. She is a member of the Academic Council on the United Nations System, the British International Studies Association, and the International Studies Association. Her recent publications include "Linking National and Global Population Agendas: Case Studies from Eight Developing Countries," *Third World Quarterly* (1995), with Gill Walt; *Global Telecommunications Regulation: A Political Economy Perspective* (1995); "A Global Political Economy Approach to AIDS: Ideology, Interests, and Implications," *New Political Economy* (1996), with Anthony Zwi; and "Who Should Be Doing What in International Health: A Confusion of Mandates in the United Nations?" *British Medical Journal* (1996), with Susan Collinson, Gill Walt, and Lucy Gilson. She is also editor of a series of *UN and Health Briefing Notes.* She was a team member on the study, *Cooperation for Health Development: Extrabudgetary Funds in the World Health Organisation* (1995), and the follow-up study, *WHO Support to Programmes at Country Level* (1997), sponsored by six governments and in cooperation with WHO.